Formal Methods for Real-Time Computing

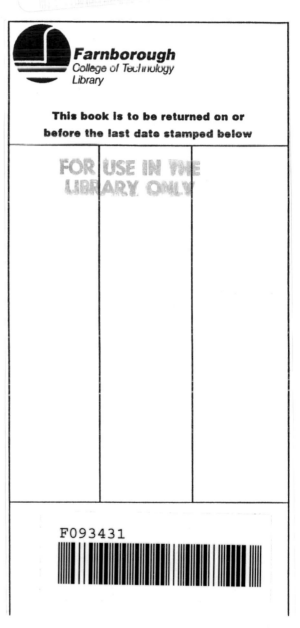

Farnborough
College of Technology
Library

**This book is to be returned on or
before the last date stamped below**

FOR USE IN THE
LIBRARY ONLY

F093431

TRENDS IN SOFTWARE

User Interface Software
ed. Len Bass and Prasun Dewan

Configuration Management
ed. Walter Tichy

Software Fault Tolerance
ed. Michael Lyu

Software Process
ed. Alfonso Fuggetta and Alexander Wolf

Formal Methods for Real-Time Computing
ed. Constance Heitmeyer and Dino Mandrioli

Formal Methods for Real-Time Computing

Edited by
Constance Heitmeyer
Naval Research Laboratory, Washington DC., USA
and
Dino Mandrioli
Politecnico di Milano, Italy

JOHN WILEY & SONS
Chichester · New York · Brisbane · Toronto · Singapore

FARNBOROUGH COLLEGE OF
TECHNOLOGY LIBRARY

Copyright © 1996 by John Wiley & Sons Ltd,
Baffins Lane, Chichester,
West Sussex, PO19 1UD, England
National Chichester (01243) 779777
International (+44)1243 779777

Reprinted August 1996

All rights reserved.

No part of this book may be reproduced by any means, or transmitted, or translated
into a machine language without the written permission of the publisher.

Other Wiley Editorial Offices

John Wiley & Sons, Inc., 605 Third Avenue,
New York, NY 10158-0012, USA

Jacaranda Wiley Ltd, 33 Park Road, Milton,
Queensland 4064, Australia

John Wiley & Sons (Canada) Ltd, 22 Worcester Road,
Rexdale, Ontario M9W 1L1, Canada

John Wiley & Sons (SEA) Pte Ltd, 2 Clementi Loop #02-01,
Jin Xing Distripark, Singapore 0512

LIBRARY

Acc. No. 093431

17 AUG 1998

Class 004 · 33

FOR

British Library Cataloguing in Publication Data

A catalogue record for this book is available from the British Library

ISBN 0 471 95835 2

Produced by camera-ready copy supplied by the editor
Printed and bound in Great Britain by Bookcraft (Bath) Ltd.
This book is printed on acid-free paper responsibly manufactured from sustainable forestation,
for which at least two trees are planted for each one used for paper production.

Contents

Series Editor's Preface

During 1990, the twentieth anniversary of *Software Practice and Experience*, two special issues (one on UNIX Tools and the other on the X Window System) were published. Each issue contained a set of refereed papers related to a single topic; the issues appeared a short time (roughly nine months) after the authors were invited to submit them. The positive experience with the special issues resulted in *Trends in Software*, a fast turn-around serial that devotes each issue to a specific topic in the software field. As with the special issues of SPE, each *Trend* will be edited by an authority in that area.

By collecting together a comprehensive set of papers on a single topic, *Trends* makes it easy for readers to find a definitive overview of a given topic. By ensuring timely publication, *Trends* guarantees readers that the information presented captures the state of the art. The collect of papers will be of practical value to software designers, researchers, practitioners and users in that field.

Papers in each *Trend* are solicited by a guest editor who is responsible for soliciting them and ensuring that the selected papers span the topic. The guest editor then subjects each paper to the rigorous peer review expected in any archival journal. As much as possible, electronic communication (e.g. electronic mail) is used as the primary means of communication between the series editor, members of the editorial board, guest editor, authors, and referees. A style document and macro package is available to reduce the turn-around time by enabling authors to submit papers in camera-ready form. During the editorial process, papers are exchanged electronically in an immediately printable format

We aim to produce three *Trends* each year. Topics to be covered in forthcoming issues include Data Visualization.

The editorial board encourages readers to submit suggestions and comments. You may send them via electronic mail to bala@research.att.com or by postal mail to the address given below. Please clarify if a communication is intended for publication or not.

I would like to thank the editorial advisory board as well as the staff at John Wiley for their help in making *Trends* a reality.

Balachander Krishnamurthy
Room 2B-140
AT&T Research
600 Mountain Avenue
Murray Hill, NJ 07974
USA

Preface

Real-time computer systems are computer systems which must produce their results within specified time intervals. Common examples of real-time systems include flight control programs, air traffic control systems, control systems for nuclear power plants, patient monitoring systems, weapons systems, and military command and control systems. Real-time systems are having an ever increasing impact on the quality of human life. In many cases, human safety depends on their correct performance.

Despite the importance of real-time systems, the state of the art for developing them remains quite primitive. It is universally acknowledged that many operational real-time systems lack the necessary reliability. Although still somewhat controversial in the computing community, there is a growing consensus that the use of *formal methods*, development methods based on some formalism, could have significant benefits in developing real-time systems due to the enhanced rigor these methods bring.

The objective of this book, which is addressed to the developers of real-time systems, is to introduce a number of formal approaches that should prove useful in building industrial strength real-time systems. The book should also be helpful to graduate students and others who seek a comprehensive understanding of how real-time systems can be developed using formal specification notations and formal analysis techiques. However, the book is not a general textbook on real-time systems: It stresses formal approaches, omitting other important topics in the real-time computing literature, such as scheduling and resource management.

The book presents some of the most promising and relevant ideas in formal methods for real-time computing. In inviting and selecting prospective contributors, our goal was to provide a fairly complete and balanced view of the state of the art. However, such a goal is impossible to achieve in full. In fact, the selection process has been necessarily affected by our personal acquaintances and by the different responses of the prospective contributors that we contacted. Nonetheless, we are very satisfied with the quality and thoroughness of the topics that the book offers its readers.

The ten chapters are organized as follows.

- Chapter 1 introduces the topic of formal methods for real-time computing and provides an overview of all of the major approaches (graphical notations, state-machine and logic languages, process algebras, model-theoretic and proof-theoretic techniques). The book contains contributions representing each of the major approaches.
- Chapters 2 through 4 describe approaches based on state machines. In some cases, these are strictly finite state machines, whereas, in other cases, the approach handles infinite state spaces as well. In all cases, the focus is on how one can use formal analysis to rigorously analyze a real-time system's properties, a major motivation for using formal approaches.

- Chapter 5 introduces the Duration Calculus, a logic-based approach aimed at describing real-time sytems and their properties with logic formulas. In this approach, the focus is on the duration of given conditions (e.g., system states).
- Chapter 6 introduces a "dual language approach": A timed version of Petri nets is used to describe the operational behavior of a given real-time system, and a logic language is used to specify and to reason about the system properties.
- Chapters 7 and 8 introduce two approaches based on process algebra, an algebraic formalism inspired by Milner's Calculus of Communicating Systems (CCS) and Hoare's Communicating Sequential Processes (CSP).
- Chapter 9 introduces symbolic model checking, a practical technique for analyzing state machine models, which checks all possible states of the model for violations of a property of interest.
- Finally, Chapter 10 presents a methodology for designing a real-time system as a collection of tasks, which together guarantee some given constraints.

Some of the approaches presented are promising intellectual work, whereas others have already been applied in industry, although mostly in an experimental way. In all cases, however, the presentation is tutorial in style and avoids excessive technical detail. Our objective is to provide a general, easy to understand introduction to each approach in the hope of generating the reader's interest. For each approach, many additional references are provided so that interested readers can delve further into the subject matter.

To help the reader understand and compare the various approaches, we suggested (but did not require) that the authors use their approaches to specify and solve a particular benchmark problem, the Generalized Railroad Crossing (GRC) problem. This problem is stated as follows:

> The system to be developed operates a gate at a railroad crossing. The railroad crossing I lies in a region of interest R, i.e., $I \subseteq R$. A set of trains travel through R on multiple tracks in both directions. A sensor system determines when each train enters and exits region R. To describe the system formally, we define a gate function $g(t) \in [0, 90]$, where $g(t) = 0$ means the gate is down and $g(t) = 90$ means the gate is up. We define a set $\{\lambda_i\}$ of *occupancy intervals*, where each occupancy interval is a time interval during which one or more trains are in I. The ith occupancy interval is represented as $\lambda_i = [\tau_i, \nu_i]$, where τ_i is the time of the ith entry of a train into the crossing when no other train is in the crossing and ν_i is the first time since τ_i that no train is in the crossing (i.e., the train that entered at τ_i has exited as have any trains that entered the crossing after τ_i).
>
> Given two constants ξ_1 and ξ_2, $\xi_1 > 0$, $\xi_2 > 0$, the problem is to develop a system to operate the crossing gate that satisfies the following two properties:
>
> **Safety Property:** $t \in \cup_i \lambda_i \Rightarrow g(t) = 0$ (The gate is down during all occupancy intervals.)
> **Utility Property:** $t \notin \cup_i [\tau_i - \xi_1, \nu_i + \xi_2] \Rightarrow g(t) = 90$ (The gate is up when no train is in the crossing.)

Although it is a "toy" problem, the different specifications and solutions of the GRC benchmark provide many insights into the strengths and weaknesses of different formal approaches for representing and reasoning about real-time systems. The above formulation, though fairly precise, still permits many different interpretations. This is done on purpose, so that the real-life process of moving from informal to formal notations is better represented. Further, this gives authors more freedom to emphasize the special features of their own approaches. The GRC problem, or small variations thereof, is used as an example in most chapters of the book, including Chapter 1.

Acknowledgments. At least two referees reviewed each chapter. We gratefully acknowledge the significant time and effort each referee devoted to the review process. The book's quality would have been substantially lower without their thoughtful and constructive comments. Besides the authors, who also acted as reviewers, we thank the following external reviewers: Myla Archer, Josef Baeten, Jan Bergstra, Gerard Berry, Ramesh Bharadwaj, Luca Breveglieri, Monica Brockmeyer, Emanuele Ciapessoni, Alberto Coen, Stuart Faulk, David Jackson, Ralph Jeffords, Bruce Labaw, Manlio Migliorati, Sandro Morasca, Fabio Schreiber, and some anonymous reviewers. Connie Heitmeyer also acknowledges the encouragement and support of her husband, Richard, her daughters, Carolyn and Dana, and her parents, Albert and Ursula Pontello. She also thanks her sponsors at NRL and ONR, who include Gary Koob and Elizabeth Wald. Dino Mandrioli thanks his wife, Cristina, and his children, Leonardo, Laura, and Claudio, who were supportive and helped relieve the difficult hours of joint work with Connie with many pleasurable moments.

Constance Heitmeyer
Code 5546
Naval Research Laboratory
Washington, DC 20375
USA
heitmeyer@itd.nrl.navy.mil

Dino Mandrioli
Dipartimento di Elettronica e Informazione
Politecnico di Milano
Piazza Leonardo Da Vinci 32
20133 Milano
Italy
mandriol@elct.polimi.it

List of Authors

Rajeev Alur
Room 2D-144
AT&T Laboratories
600 Mountain Avenue
Murray Hill
New Jersey 07974
USA
alur@research.att.com

Hanêne Ben-Abdallah
Department of Computer & Information
Science
University of Pennsylvania
200 South 33rd Street
Philadelphia
Pennsylvania 19104-6389
USA
hanene@saul.cis.upenn.edu

Tommaso Bolognesi
C.N.R. Istituto CNUCE
36, Via. S. Maria
56100 Pisa
Italy
t.bolognesi@cnuce.cnr.it

Sergio Campos
School of Computer Science
Carnegie Mellon University
5000 Forbes Avenue
Pittsburgh
Pennsylvania 15213-3891
USA
Sergio.Campos@cs.cmu.edu

Jin-Young Choi
Department of Computer & Information
Science
University of Pennsylvania
200 South 33rd Street
Philadelphia
Pennsylvania 19104-6389
USA
choi@saul.cis.upenn.edu

Edmund Clarke
School of Computer Science
Carnegie Mellon University
5000 Forbes Avenue
Pittsburgh
Pennsylvania 15213-3891
USA
emc@cs.cmu.edu

David L Dill
Department of Computer Science
Stanford University
Stanford
California 94305
USA
dill@breeze.stanford.edu

Richard Gerber
Department of Computer Science
University of Maryland
College Park
Maryland 20742
USA
gerber@cs.umd.edu

Constance Heitmeyer
Code 5546
Naval Research Laboratory
Washington, DC 20375
USA
heitmeyer@itd.nrl.navy.mil

Seongsoo Hong
Department of Computer Science
Seoul National University
Sinlim-dong, Kwanak-gu
Seoul 151
South Korea
sshong@redwood.snu.ac.kr

Farnam Jahanian
Department of Electrical Engineering and
Computer Science
University of Michigan
Ann Arbor
Michigan 48109
USA
farnam@eecs.umich.edu

Dong-In Kang
Department of Computer Science
University of Maryland
College Park
Maryland 20742
USA
dikang@cs.umd.edu

Insup Lee
Department of Computer & Information
Science
University of Pennsylvania
200 South 33rd Street
Philadelphia
Pennsylvania 19104-6389
USA
lee@cis.upenn.edu

Nancy Lynch
Department of Computer Science &
Engineering
M.I.T., Cambridge
Massachusetts 02139
USA

Dino Mandrioli
Dipartimento di Elettronica e
Informazione
Politecnico di Milano
Piazza Leonardo Da Vinci 32
20133 Milano
Italy
mandriol@elet.polimi.it

Marius Minea
School of Computer Science
Carnegie Mellon University
5000 Forbes Avenue
Pittsburgh
Pennsylvania 15213-3891
USA
marius@cs.cmu.edu

Aloysius K Mok
Department of Computer Sciences
University of Texas at Austin
Austin
Texas 78712
USA
mok@cs.utexas.edu

Angelo Morzenti
Dipartimento di Elettronica e
Informazione
Politecnico di Milano
Piazza Leonardo Da Vinci 32
20133 Milano
Italy
morzenti@elet.polimi.it

Ernst-Rüdiger Olderog
FB Informatik
Universität Oldenburg
Postfach 2503
D-26111 Oldenburg
Germany
olderog@informatik.uni-oldenburg.de

Mauro Pezzè
Dipartimento di Elettronica e
Informazione
Politecnico di Milano
Piazza Leonardo Da Vinci 32
20133 Milano
Italy
pezze@elet.polimi.it

Anders P Ravn
Department of Information Technology
Technical University of Denmark
Building 344
DK-2800 Lyngby
Denmark
apr@it.dtu.dk

Manas Saksena
Concordia University
1455 de Maisonneuve Bld West
Montréal
Québec
Canada
H3G 1M8
manas@cs.concordia.ca

Pierluigi San Pietro
Dipartimento di Elettronica e
Informazione
Politecnico di Milano
Piazza Leonardo Da Vinci 32
20133 Milano
Italy
sanpietr@elet.polimi.it

Sergio Silva
Dipartimento di Elettronica e
Informazione
Politecnico di Milano
Piazza Leonardo Da Vinci 32
20133 Milano
Italy
silva@elet.polimi.it

Jens U Skakkebæk
CRI A/S
Bregnerødvej 144
DK-3460 Birkerød
Denmark
jus@spd.crl.dk

Douglas A Stuart
Department of Computer Sciences
University of Texas at Austin
Texas 78712
USA
dastuart@cs.utexas.edu

1

Formal Methods for Real-Time Computing: An Overview

CONSTANCE HEITMEYER
Naval Research Laboratory, Washington DC

DINO MANDRIOLI
Politecnico di Milano

ABSTRACT

This chapter defines real-time systems and illustrates them with a number of small examples. It also discusses issues central to applying formal methods in the development of real-time systems: the trade-offs between operational and descriptive specifications, different levels of formality that can be applied, and the requirements of formal methods for building industrial-strength systems. To put the newer formal methods into perspective, two methods widely used in practice to design and analyze real-time systems, namely, structured analysis and Statecharts, are reviewed. Several promising new techniques for specifying and analyzing real-time systems are then summarized and illustrated with examples. These include graphical notations, state machine and logic-based models, process algebras, and analysis techniques, such as model checking and deductive reasoning.

1.1 INTRODUCTION

A *real-time computer system* is a computer system which must produce its results within specified time intervals. Common examples of real-time systems include flight control programs, air traffic control systems, control systems for power plants, patient monitoring systems, weapons systems, and military command and control systems. To be acceptable, such systems must not only be functionally correct—produce correct results—but must also be temporally correct—act within specified time intervals.

Many real-time systems are control systems which monitor quantities of interest in the environment and perform externally visible actions in response to changes in the monitored quantities. Consider, for example, a control system for safety injection in a nuclear power

---

Formal Methods For Real-Time Computing, Edited by Heitmeyer and Mandrioli
© 1996 John Wiley & Sons Ltd

plant. This system monitors water pressure and must inject coolant into the reactor core within 30 seconds of when water pressure drops below some threshold V. Such a system is a real-time system because it must act within a specified time interval: if water pressure falls below V at time t, then the system is required to start safety injection at some time in the interval $[t, t + 30s]$.

The above timing requirement can be contrasted with other timing requirements. First, it is a *hard* timing requirement, that is, one that must be satisfied without exception. Other system timing requirements, called *soft* timing requirements, can be missed occasionally. Suppose that the safety injection system must update an operator display of the water pressure level within some given time interval. If the system can occasionally be late in updating the display, then this timing requirement is soft. Most real-time systems have both hard and soft timing requirements. Second, although in most cases, a real time system (such as the safety injection system above) must act before a deadline, in some situations, a system must not act *too soon*. For example, a missile launched from an aircraft must not activate its tracking system too early: if it does, the missile may attack the launching aircraft rather than enemy targets.

Many timing requirements are derived from other requirements. In the missile launching system, the requirement is to fire the missile so that a target is hit with a given precision. To achieve the needed precision, the aircraft must launch the missile within some time interval. This time interval is derived from the estimated target location, the required precision, and other parameters, such as the aircraft velocity and the wind speed.

The correct behavior of a real-time system may depend not only on the timing of its outputs but also on time-varying functions of its inputs. Given some function of time, the system takes one action if the function has one set of values and a different action (possibly the null action) otherwise. Consider a slight modification of the safety injection system, which injects coolant only if water pressure falls below V at some time t and remains below V for at least 10 seconds. If within the interval $[t, t + 10s]$, water pressure rises above V, the system simply updates a display (or alternatively does nothing). Clearly, this system's behavior depends on a time-varying function of the monitored quantity, water pressure.

Related to real-time systems are *safety-critical systems*, systems which must prevent unintended events that could result in death, injury, illness, or damage to or loss of property. To avoid entering an unsafe state, a safety-critical system must often perform a given action by a specified deadline. Most (if not all) safety-critical systems are also real-time systems.

Consider an air traffic control system, a real-time system with many stringent timing requirements. The failure of such a system to act in time can have disastrous consequences. If, for example, the system fails to warn an approaching aircraft that a second aircraft is flying nearby, the two aircraft may collide, killing or seriously injuring the people aboard and severely damaging both aircraft and possibly objects on the ground below. Thus, air traffic control may be classified as both real-time and safety-critical. The safety injection system introduced above is also both real-time (because it must act by a specified deadline) and safety-critical (because it must take some action to avoid a serious accident).

Although systems, such as telephone networks and financial systems, are not normally classified as safety-critical, the consequences of such systems missing their timing requirements can also be very serious. If someone is critically ill and the telephone network fails to establish a connection to medical personnel in time, the person may die. Similarly, the failure of a bank to receive a large electronic funds transfer on time may result in huge financial losses.

Because the failure of systems, such as those described above, to satisfy their timing requirements can have such catastrophic consequences, customers and developers need compelling evidence that these systems deliver their results on time. To gather such evidence, people are willing to invest considerable time, effort, and money. A promising means of producing such evidence is to apply "formal methods" in the development of safety-critical systems. These methods may use formal specification languages and formal modeling techniques to describe the required system behavior and formal analysis techniques to demonstrate that system behavior (or a specification of the required system behavior) satisfies critical properties.

In recent years, many new formal models, specification languages, and analysis techniques have been proposed for developing real-time systems. A large number of these are timed versions of formalisms originally designed to specify and to analyze untimed system behavior. Some of the new formalisms are already being used to specify and to analyze practical real-time systems, while others, though not yet used in practice, are quite promising.

Although the cost-effectiveness of applying formal methods based on these new languages and techniques is most obvious for safety-critical systems [BS93], formal methods should also prove useful in representing and reasoning about non-safety-critical systems, such as multimedia systems which have especially demanding timing requirements due to the many varied tasks they must synchronize. Although the current cost of applying formal methods can be high, in the future these costs are expected to decrease. Hence, using formal methods in the development of non-safety-critical systems, such as multimedia systems (and even office systems), should become more cost-effective in the years to come.

The purpose of this book is to introduce the major formalisms for developing real-time systems. We have limited the book's scope in two ways. First, although a few of the new real-time approaches (for example, the synchronous approaches such as Esterel [BG92]) are most useful during the implementation phase of software development, most of the included formalisms are designed to be used early in system development, namely, during the requirements and early software design phases. Second, the book's focus is on hard real-time systems because most of the existing formalisms are designed to specify and to reason about hard timing requirements. Because most reasoning about hard timing requirements is based on logic, this book introduces a number of logics useful in analyzing real-time systems. Statistical methods useful in reasoning about the stochastic properties of soft timing requirements (see, e.g., [AMBC86]) are outside the book's scope.

The study of real-time formalisms is complementary to the study of scheduling and resource management, the problem of managing system resources so that the system's timing behavior is predictable. While the formal methods described herein are usually used to represent and to reason about the requirements and high-level design of a real-time system, scheduling and resource management focus on detailed software design issues, such as finding optimal and suboptimal algorithms for job scheduling and resource allocation. In systems where most jobs have hard deadlines, an optimum scheduling algorithm always finds a feasible schedule if one exists. Other major areas of study in real-time scheduling are performance prediction, which derives worst-case performance bounds, and schedulability analysis, which seeks efficient algorithms that determine whether all system timing constraints are met despite scheduling anomalies. Recently, a few researchers have begun to attack problems that span both 1) formal methods for specifying and analyzing real-time systems and 2) scheduling algorithms for synthesizing real-time systems. Chapter 10 describes such a problem and its solution.

This chapter is organized as follows. Section 1.2 describes different classes of formal methods and the special requirements of formal methods useful in developing practical systems. Section 1.3 briefly summarizes two widely used approaches for developing real-time systems: SA/RT, a form of structured analysis designed for real-time applications, and Statecharts, a graphical notation that models systems in terms of finite state machines. Section 1.4 presents a framework for describing real-time formalisms, organizing them into three broad categories: notations, formal models, and analysis techniques. Each category is illustrated with a small number of formalisms selected from those with which the authors are most familiar. Sections 1.5–1.8 introduce several graphical notations and three classes of formal models (logic-based models, state machine models, and process algebras) for specifying real-time systems. Section 1.9 summarizes two classes of techniques (model-theoretic and proof-theoretic) for formally reasoning about real-time systems. The goal of Sections 1.5–1.9 is to be comprehensive. Thus, the length of a section describing a technique depends, not on the technique's importance, but on the amount of text that is needed to introduce the technique. Finally, Section 1.10 contains some concluding remarks.

1.2   FORMAL METHODS: BACKGROUND

To help put formal methods into perspective, this section describes the phases of the software life-cycle when formal methods are usually applied, discusses different levels of formality, contrasts operational specifications with descriptive specifications, and discusses verification based on formal methods. The section concludes by describing the characteristics formal methods require to be useful in practice.

1.2.1   What Are Formal Methods?

Generally, the term *formal method* refers to a "development method based on some formalism." Some methods are intrinsically bound to a given formalism. Thus a proof method for proving mathematical correctness cannot be formulated independently of the algebraic or logic formalism that supports it. Other formalisms are not bound to a single method but can be coupled with several methods. For example, a finite state machine is a formalism that is not a formal method per se but one that supports many formal specification and verification methods. In other cases, a method—but not necessarily a formal method—can be combined with an existing formalism to produce a new formal method. Thus an object-oriented method can be combined with a logic language to produce a formal specification method. Not surprisingly, an introduction to formal *methods* cannot ignore the formal *models* which provide their foundation.

1.2.2   Development Methods and the Software Life-Cycle

Any development method must be placed in the appropriate context within the software life-cycle. Some methods are associated with only a single life-cycle phase. For example, methods for requirements specification are most useful during the analysis phase, whereas code testing and debugging strategies are most useful during the implementation phase. In contrast, other methods, such as structured analysis and the more recent object-oriented approach, can be applied throughout the life-cycle. In developing real-time systems, formal methods can have an impact, in principle, on any single phase as well as on the whole life cycle. This book focuses on the earlier phases of the software life-cycle—specification and analysis—for two major reasons:

- The early phases in any system development are by far the most critical. For example, a study by Lutz of errors detected in two space systems built by the U.S. agency NASA found that a very high percentage of the most serious errors were requirements errors [Lut93].
- Despite their importance, the early phases are not well supported by high quality methods and tools. Unlike the later phases, where one can rely on good programming languages and environments, in the early phases, much is left to the designers' intuition and common sense.

1.2.3 Different Levels of Formality

Traditionally, a distinction is made between formal methods, methods with a precise, often mathematical definition, and more informal methods (for example, natural language prose). Because many methods have both formal and informal components, it is quite common to talk about *semiformal* methods, that is, methods that are only partially defined in a precise, mathematical way. Some aspects of the method are left undefined; understanding these aspects requires intuition and common sense. In many cases, semiformal methods define the syntax of a given notation rigorously but leave the notation's semantics (i.e., meaning) undefined. Often, formality can be achieved incrementally by starting with a purely informal notation (say prose and unstructured figures) and moving towards a precise mathematical formulation. Such a process does not necessarily lead to complete formality: for instance, in some cases, one could alternate prose with formulas, reserving the latter for the critical cases only.

1.2.4 Operational and Descriptive Specification Styles

An approach widely used in system and computer science to describe and analyze a system is to develop an abstract machine, a mathematical formalism in which the concepts of state and transition between states are precisely defined. An abstract machine is a model of the real system to be built. Its main features can be rigorously analyzed without building the real system. Many types of abstract machines have been defined for both real-time and non-real-time systems.

The most common example of an abstract machine in computer science and one of the most popular models in real-time computing is the finite state machine. A *finite state machine* is a four-tuple (S, s_0, E, T), where S is a set of states, s_0 is the initial state, E is a set of inputs, and T, called the *transition relation*, describes how the machine makes transitions from one state to the next.

To illustrate a finite state machine, we consider the railroad crossing system introduced in the preface. To keep the example simple, we consider a single train that travels through the region R. Region R is split into subregions P and I, where I is the crossing through which automobiles can travel. First, the train enters a region P within R but outside the crossing, then it travels through the crossing, and finally it exits. Figure 1.1 illustrates the regions P and R and the crossing I. Figure 1.2 contains a diagram (called a *finite state diagram*) of a finite state machine model of the train. The train model is defined by $S = \{\texttt{Out}, \texttt{P}, \texttt{I}\}$, $s_0 = \texttt{Out}$, $E = \{\texttt{EnterR}, \texttt{EnterI}, \texttt{ExitI}\}$, and $T = \{(\texttt{Out}, \texttt{EnterR}, \texttt{P}), (\texttt{P}, \texttt{EnterI}, \texttt{I}), (\texttt{I}, \texttt{ExitI}, \texttt{Out})\}$.

The train model is an example of a *deterministic* finite state machine, because T maps each input and starting state to a unique new state. If an input and a state can be mapped to more than one new state, then the finite state machine is called *nondeterministic*. Consider a

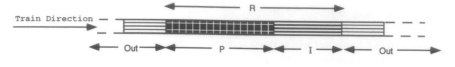

Figure 1.1   The region R consists of P and the railroad crossing I

second train model in which the train is in the crossing I and receives the input ExitI. If the train can make a transition to either Out or P, i.e., T contains both (I, ExitI, Out) and (I, ExitI, P), then the model is nondeterministic.

   A specification based on abstract machines, such as the finite state machine shown in Figure 1.2, is often called *operational* (or *model-based*) because it describes the system's operating rules. An operational specification may be contrasted with a *descriptive* (also called *property-based*) specification, which describes the required system properties. A descriptive approach is especially important during the early phases of software development when the objective is to describe precisely *what* the system must do rather than *how* the system is to be implemented.

   To contrast the two specification styles, consider the above railroad crossing example. To prevent automobiles from traveling through the crossing I when a train is present, suppose a gate moves down when a train is near I. Figure 1.3 contains a finite state machine model of the gate with two states, Up and Down. To prevent trains and automobiles from colliding, an operational specification might state that "Whenever a train enters region R, the command MoveDown must be sent to the gate." In contrast, a descriptive specification might include the following Safety Property: "At any time t, if a train is in the crossing I, then the gate must be in the state Down." Unlike an operational specification, a descriptive specification does not state how the gate should be controlled; it only states the essential property the gate must satisfy.

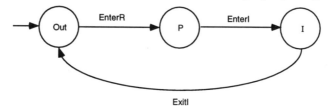

Figure 1.2   Finite state diagram of a train

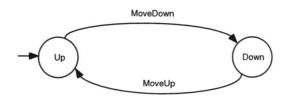

Figure 1.3   Finite state diagram of a crossing gate

   Although most formal specifications cannot be classified as purely operational or descriptive, the contrast between the two styles does suggest their relative merits. Typically, operational specifications are easier to develop, because they are closer to the designer's intuition. However, they can bias designers toward particular solutions. In contrast, descriptive specifications usually have less implementation bias, but because they are more abstract, generating them often requires more mathematical training.

Experience has shown both styles to be useful. For this reason, some researchers advocate a *dual language approach* [Ost89]. With this approach, the system to be built is modeled using a suitable abstract machine, say a finite state machine, while the system properties are expressed in a descriptive notation, such as a logic-based language. For example, in describing the railroad crossing system, operational specifications of a train and the gate, such as the finite state machines in Figures 1.2 and 1.3, can be combined with descriptive specifications of the required properties, such as the Safety Property given above. Additional examples of the dual language approach to real-time computing are given in this and later chapters. Although not yet common in practice, the approach appears quite promising.

1.2.5   Verification

After a system has been specified and an implementation built, verification of the implementation is required. The goal of verification is to ensure that the right implementation has been built, i.e., that the behavior of the implementation is what was intended.[1] Verification not only applies to implementations, which must be checked against the specifications, but also to specifications themselves: the specifications must be complete and consistent (not contradictory), capture the user's needs, and satisfy critical application properties.

Verification, a critical aspect of any engineering activity, can be performed with different levels of confidence and in different ways. In principle, formal methods support verification based on formal proofs: once the system and its properties have been stated in a suitable mathematical notation, that the system satisfies the properties may be proved as a mathematical theorem. The consequence is that the same increased level of confidence typical of mathematical reasoning can be obtained for engineering systems.

Often, verification, mainly performed through testing, is associated with informal design methods and correctness proofs (sometimes called *formal verification*) with formal methods. In practice, the situation is more complex. Below, we argue that during verification as well as during requirements specification and design, one may adopt several strategies for checking correctness, each with its pros and cons. Which strategies are selected can depend on many factors, including the characteristics of the application and the designer's experience and taste.

- Informal reasoning can be applied even to a formal specification or design. For example, traditional walkthroughs and inspections can be applied to any informal design notation as well as to code written in some programming language.
- Formal specifications may be used to derive sample executions of the system. Users can experiment with these "system models" to determine whether the specifications capture the intended system behavior. This is called *simulation* [CHLR93] or *specification testing* [Kem85].

---

[1] This chapter's use of the term "verification" is very general. Elsewhere, *verification* of an artifact (that is, an implementation or a specification) is distinguished from *validation* of the artifact: The goal of verification is to ensure that the artifact satisfies properties of interest, whereas the goal of validation is to ensure that the artifact captures the user's intent. When the terms are used in this narrower sense, proving a property about a specification is a form of verification, whereas simulation is a form of validation.

- Formal methods can increase the reliability of more traditional techniques, such as testing. For example, test cases can be derived from formal specifications either automatically or semiautomatically.
- The most common formal verification technique is mathematical deduction: basic system features are stated as axioms and related properties are then proven as theorems. However, mathematical deduction is not the only formal verification technique. For more discussion of formal verification, see Section 1.9.
- Generally, applying formal verification requires more mathematical skill and training than simply writing formal specifications. One approach to introducing formal methods in industry is for industrial personnel themselves to formalize the required system properties and for others, inside or outside the company, with mathematical expertise to formally verify the properties.

1.2.6   Using Formal Methods to Develop Practical Systems

To date, industry has been reluctant to adopt formal methods. One barrier to industrial use of formal methods is that many developers lack the mathematical sophistication needed to apply the methods. Another barrier is that many industrial systems which are candidates for formal methods are much more complex than the toy examples that appear in technical papers. Finally, the method associated with a given formalism is often quite weak; although much attention has been focused on the *formal* aspects of formal methods, too little effort to date has been devoted to the supporting method.

To be useful in developing practical systems, formal methods must not only provide rigor and lead to increased system reliability, they must also have some additional features, including:

1. **Readability.** Formal documents have often been criticized as hard to understand. To improve their readability, the formal descriptions can be supplemented with more intuitive notations, such as graphical ones, or annotated with explanatory comments. With the addition of graphical notations and explanatory comments, a formal document can be understood even by those with little technical background.
2. **Scalability.** The method should scale up from small examples to large, complex real-world systems. Like design documents and source code, large and complex formal specifications should be maintainable and reusable. Moreover, when teaching a method, tutorial examples, whose main goal is illustrating the method's features, should be clearly distinguished from practical case studies, whose purpose is to demonstrate scalability.
3. **Tool support.** The method should be supported by well-engineered tools. In many practical cases, a large amount of detail is required to apply a formal method; for example, a fully formal proof is usually much longer than an informal one. This detail is unmanageable without some automation. In principle, the user should be in charge of the creative part of the task, and clerical details should be managed by the tool. While informal and semiformal methods can at most be supported by good documentation tools (such as editors and data dictionaries), formal methods can be supported by many classes of tools, including tools for automatic property verification (e.g., model checkers), mechanical proof systems, test case generators, and simulators.

1.3 STATE OF THE PRACTICE

This section describes two methods currently used in practice to model real-time systems. These are Ward and Mellor's SA/RT [WM85], a method based on structured analysis, and Statecharts [Har87]. Both have been widely applied to practical systems and are supported by well-engineered commercial tools. This, coupled with the fact that they are semiformal, suggests that they are a first step toward achieving the practical application of formal methods.

1.3.1 Structured Analysis

Structured analysis is a general term used for more than 30 years to describe systematic methods for the analysis and design of complex software systems. Such methods can be contrasted with more ad hoc approaches, which are based largely on designers' experience and intuition. Since the 1970's, many types of structured analysis have been proposed (see, e.g., [DeM78]). Most are semiformal, operational notations closely related to data flow diagrams (DFDs), a graphical notation used to describe the structure of an information system. SA/RT (Structured Analysis/Real Time) is an enhancement of structured analysis designed to model real-time systems. Major constructs of SA/RT are *Transformation Schemata* (TS), an extension of traditional DFDs.

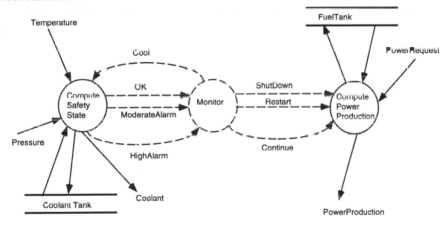

Figure 1.4   Transformation schemata for a power plant

Figure 1.4 describes a control system for a power plant using the SA/RT method. This control system checks the amount of power to be produced by the plant, and, using this information, manages the amount of fuel or coolant to be injected into the plant. In an emergency, the system may even shut down the plant. The TS of Figure 1.4 contains the following components:

- Information flows, denoted by arrows;
- Functions, denoted by circles, which elaborate information flows.

Both information flows and functions can be of two types:

- Information can consist of either data or signals: data flows are denoted by continuous arrows, whereas signal flows are denoted by dashed arrows.
- Similarly, functions can be either *data transformers* (DT), denoted by continuous circles, or *control transformations* (CT), denoted by dashed circles.

In Figure 1.4, the arrows labeled `Temperature` and `Pressure` denote the values of quantities that come from the system's environment. The arrow labeled `PowerRequest` also denotes information from the environment, specifically, how much power is requested by the plant. The arrows labeled `Coolant` and `PowerProduction`, which represent the amount of coolant to be injected into the plant under some circumstances and the amount of power that the plant should produce, represent outputs from the system to the environment. Figure 1.4 also shows two *data repositories* (DR), `CoolantTank` and `FuelTank`, which represent the amount of coolant and fuel available in the tanks.

From Figure 1.4, it is clear that the system performs two kinds of functions:

- **Service Functions.** The system either increases or decreases the amount of power produced based on the amount of available power, the safety state of the plant, and whether an external request for power has been received. It also updates the amount of available fuel based on the amount produced.
- **Safety Function.** Based on the temperature and pressure, the system may determine that the plant is in a hazardous state. In response, the sytem may either inject further coolant into the coolant tank, reduce the amount of available power below some safety threshold, or, in an emergency, shut down the plant.

These functions are implemented by two DTs and one supervising CT. The specification in Figure 1.4 explicitly separates the system's data computation from its control functions. Whereas the DTs, `Compute Safety State` and `Compute Power Production`, perform numerical computations on their input data, control functions are allocated to the CT `Monitor`, which receives signals from `Compute Safety State` and decides which commands should be sent both to `Compute Safety State` and to `Compute Power Production`. For example, `Compute Power Production` defines the amount of power to be generated as a function of the power requests and the available fuel. Its operation, however, also depends on the commands coming from the `Monitor`.

To make control aspects explicit, each CT in SA/RT is associated with a finite state machine. In the power plant example, the CT `Monitor` is associated with the finite state machine shown in Figure 1.5. The inputs of the finite state machine are the signals entering the CT, whereas the machine's outputs correspond to the CT's outputs. Unlike the finite state machines in Figures 1.2 and 1.3 which can only change state, the finite state machine in Figure 1.5 may respond to input by changing state *and* producing output. In Figure 1.5, a transition from state s_1 to state s_2 with the label $\frac{x}{y}$ means that if the machine in state s_1 receives input x, then it moves to state s_2 and outputs the signal y. This model of a finite state machine is known as a *Mealy machine*. Although states in finite state diagrams are usually represented by circles, in Figure 1.5, states are represented by squares to distinguish them from the circles in the DFD.

Initially, `Monitor` is in the state `Normal`. It remains there as long as it receives the signal `OK` from the DT `Compute Safety State`. In `Normal`, the CT does not produce any output. When it receives the signal `ModerateAlarm`, the CT switches to the state `Alert` and outputs the signal `Cool` to the DT `Compute Safety State`. This DT then sends a command to inject coolant into the plant. It computes the amount of coolant that is injected from the current values of temperature and pressure and the amount of coolant available in the coolant tank. The CT `Monitor` remains in the `Alert` state and continues to send the `Cool` signal until it receives either an `OK` signal or a `HighAlarm` signal from the DT `Compute Safety State`. In the former case, it stops sending the `Cool` signal and returns to `Normal`; in the latter case, it switches to the state `Off` and sends a `Shutdown`

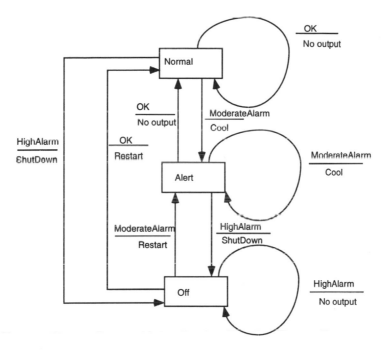

Figure 1.5   A Finite State Diagram of the Monitor

signal to the DT Compute Power Production. The CT remains in the Off state until it receives either a ModerateAlarm signal or an OK signal. In the former case, the DT sends a Restart to the DT, Computer Power Production, and enters Alert; in the latter case, the DT also sends a Restart but enters Normal.

A detailed set of rules (mostly inspired by Petri Nets, which are introduced in Section 1.4) are used to define the actions associated with DTs and CTs. Many of these rules can be inferred from the above example. For example, the computation associated with a DT starts whenever an enabling signal is present.

To model time in SA/RT, a deadline is associated with each DT. Once the computation of a DT is triggered, the output produced by the DT must be available to the external world by the deadline. The transitions that involve CTs require zero time, since it is assumed that CTs can react immediately to external stimuli.

The above description, while highly simplified, suggests why we classify TSs as an "operational semiformalism" and SA/RT as an operational semiformal method. As illustrated above, some aspects of TSs are precisely defined. For example, Mealy machines, an operational formalism, are an important component of TSs. However, other aspects of TSs, such as the semantics of data transformations, are not defined at all. Neglecting the semantics of data is useful when one wishes to focus attention on control and abstract away purely functional behavior. However, in many cases, the specification of a system's control structure depends on the specification of its functional behavior. Assume in the power plant example that Restart can be issued only if the fuel level is above a specified amount. In this situation, a control decision depends on a data value that cannot be specified within a classical state machine formalism. Even more critical is the case in which the signals and the computed data depend on time. For instance, the requirement, "Issue the Shutdown signal whenever HighAlarm has been continuously present for 10 seconds," cannot be described in SA/RT.

Like other similar approaches, SA/RT provides refinement mechanisms useful in building large, well-structured specifications. Moreover, many commercial tools, such as Teamwork and Software Through Pictures, are compatible with SA/RT. In most cases, such tools suffer from the limitations of other semiformal approaches: they are essentially documentation tools and cannot support semantic analysis. Despite these limitations, they have proven useful in many industrial projects.

Recently, object-oriented methods have been heralded as an improvement over structured analysis for both general software development and real-time computing. In some cases, object-oriented versions of structured analysis methods have been proposed. Three of these methods, Shlaer and Mellor [SM88], HOORA [ESA93], and ROOM [SGW94], are designed for developing real-time systems. Since they maintain part of the original philosophy of SA/RT, they are in some sense the "object-oriented heirs" of SA/RT.

1.3.2   Statecharts

Statecharts [Har87], a graphical language for specifying real-time systems, exploits the naturalness and simplicity of the classical finite state machine. The Statecharts notation also overcomes, to a large extent, the state machine's major shortcomings. The most important is the combinatorial explosion in the number of states. Given two machines with h and k states each, a system combining the two has a state space that is the Cartesian product of the original ones, i.e., $h \times k$ states. Statecharts uses two constructs to overcome the state explosion problem: AND and OR composition. Described below is AND composition.

The AND of two component machines formalizes the composition of two concurrent subsystems into a single aggregate machine. To illustrate AND composition, we consider the railroad crossing example introduced above. Figures 1.2 and 1.3 describe the two individual components of this system, a train and the crossing gate, as two independent finite state machines.

The set of states in the composition of the two machines contains all possible combinations of the individual states, i.e., <Out, Down>, <Out, Up>, <P, Down>, <P, Up>, <I, Down>, and <I, Up>. The transitions between states are combined similarly: the set of possible transitions is the union of the original sets. In Statecharts, the concurrent composition of the component machines is left implicit but formally defined through the AND construct, which composes the two components into a single, larger machine as shown in Figure 1.6.

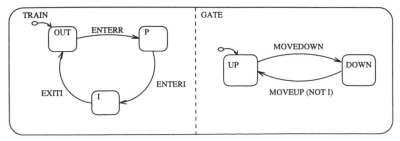

Figure 1.6   Statecharts specification showing AND-composition of train and gate

In the larger state machine, some state transitions may not be possible because when the system is in a state in one of the smaller machines, it cannot enter a specified state in the second machine. One way to model the coordination of the two smaller machines is to label a transition with a formula. The transition can only be taken if the formula is true. For example, in Figure 1.6, attaching the formula "not in I" to the transition MoveUp specifies that the gate cannot be raised if a train remains in I.

The example in Figure 1.6 illustrates some important limitations of the classical state machine model for describing real-time systems:

- Time-dependent behavior, e.g., "The gate must be down within 10 seconds after a train enters P", cannot be expressed.
- Figure 1.6 captures only a small fraction of the required system behavior. For example, labeling MoveUp as described above prevents this transition when a train is in I but does not guarantee that the gate will be down whenever a train is in I (the gate could move up and remain there). More information is needed to describe the system in detail, such as when the gate must start moving down once a train has entered R.
- Consider a generalization of the system in which several trains can be in R simultaneously. In the classical model, each train must be described separately. Unfortunately, the model not only becomes unwieldly as the number of trains grows; in addition, the model cannot handle an unbounded number of trains.

Statecharts has addressed each of the above problems, at least in part [i-L91]. First, two simple classes of time-dependent behavior can be expressed in Statecharts: a *timeout event*, an event scheduled to occur a fixed number of time units after another event, and a *scheduled action*, an operation (e.g., fire the missile) scheduled to occur a fixed number of time units after the current time. In addition, Statecharts allows parameterized states (e.g., "the ith train enters R") and the attachment of generalized logic formulas to transitions.

The commercial version of Statecharts, called STATEMATE [HLN+90, i-L93], offers these features as well as others. STATEMATE has had considerable success in industry because it has a a user-friendly interface that complements the intuitive appeal of the classical state machine formalism. Moreover, STATEMATE offers two forms of analysis:

- The user can run STATEMATE's simulator to analyze the behavior of a "system model" in scenarios of interest.
- STATEMATE's Dynamic Tests tool can do some reachability analysis. From the Statecharts specification, the tool builds a reachability graph containing possible states the system can be in. Using this graph, the tool can check for deadlock, nondeterminism, and race conditions. It can also search for a reachable state in which a certain condition is true. For example, a violation of the Safety Property in Section 1.2.4 can be detected by checking the specification in Figure 1.6 for the condition in(UP) and in(I).

Statecharts' capabilities lie somewhere between the capabilities of semiformal approaches and more advanced, fully formal approaches, such as those introduced in Section 1.4-1.9. Like semiformal approaches, Statecharts provides documentation support but, unlike them, Statecharts also supports some semantic analysis. However, compared to some of the newer formal methods (e.g., model checking techniques), Statecharts' analysis capability, which is confined to using reachability analysis to check a small set of properties, is quite limited. Moreover, the ability to specify and reason about a system's timing behavior using Statecharts is also quite limited.

Statecharts has been applied to several industrial projects. For example, Israel Aircraft Industries has used Statecharts to develop avionics systems. Especially useful in these applications was the availability of a common and clear specification "language" to people (such as electrical engineers, software engineers, and pilots) with diverse backgrounds.

1.4   NEW FORMALISMS FOR DEVELOPING REAL-TIME SYSTEMS

Over the last decade, real-time researchers have proposed many new techniques for specifying and analyzing real-time systems. These include new notations and new formal models for describing real-time systems and new techniques for analyzing their behavior. Many real-time techniques are not completely new but adaptations of techniques originally designed to describe and reason about non-real-time systems.

1.4.1   Notations and Formal Models

Formal notations for specifying real-time systems fall into two classes: textual and graphical. Like SA/RT and Statecharts, the newer graphical notations, such as Modechart, produce specifications that practitioners often find more readable and intuitive than specifications expressed in a textual (e.g., logic-based) notation. Because the newer graphical notations have an explicit formal semantics, specifications in these notations are more amenable to formal analysis than specifications based on semiformal approaches, such as SA/RT.

Both textual and graphical notations have been proposed to represent the various formal models introduced to describe and reason about real-time systems. These formal models fall into three major classes—models based on logic, state machine models, and models that extend process algebra. Usually, models expressed in a graphical notation, such as Modechart and Timed Transition Models, are based on the state machine formalism. Logic-based models and models based on process algebra are expressed most often in a textual notation.

Most logics designed to reason about real-time systems are either first-order logics or special temporal logics. In contrast to classical first-order logic, temporal logics include special operators such as "always", "eventually", and "until" to allow certain classes of properties to be expressed concisely [Kro87, Koy90]. Just as first-order and temporal logics have been adapted to describe timing properties, the classical state machine model has been adapted in a number of ways to reason about time. The same is true of process algebras. Although the original process algebras, Hoare's CSP [Hoa69] and Milner's CCS [Mil89], abstract away time, many timed versions of these models have been proposed.

1.4.2   Analysis Techniques

Techniques for verifying properties of real-time systems, many of which are adaptations of techniques originally designed to reason about non-real-time properties, fall into two classes: model-theoretic (also called *model-based*) reasoning and proof-theoretic reasoning. In model-theoretic reasoning, the user invokes a software tool (often called a "verifier") that examines a state machine model of a system for a specified property. Because models that enumerate all possible states can become very large, a number of approaches have been developed to handle the "state explosion" problem—e.g., unreachable states and impossible states are pruned, large sets of states are described symbolically, and special decision procedures called *binary decision diagrams* are used to evaluate large boolean formulas efficiently (see, e.g., [BCM+90, McM92]). An important feature of model-theoretic techniques is that they are automatic and can therefore be applied by users with little mathematical training.

In proof-theoretic reasoning, the logical rules of deduction are used to prove formally that a specification satisfies a property of interest or that one system specification is equivalent to, or a special case of, another system specification. Unlike model-theoretic techniques, which produce results automatically, most proofs based on logical deduction are done by hand and require mathematical skill and training. For example, reasoning about the timed automaton model [LV91] produces hand proofs of invariants and simulation mappings [LV91] and is based on standard proof techniques, such as mathematical induction. Similarly, showing equivalence between two system descriptions expressed in process algebra is achieved manually using algebraic manipulation. To date, some hand proofs of timing properties have been checked using automated proof systems.

Simulation, another technique for analyzing the behavior of real-time systems, is a form of testing applied to a formal specification. To initiate simulation, the user provides a sequence of input events, generated either manually or automatically, to the simulator. The simulator then executes the system symbolically, using the system specification to determine the system's response to each input. By means of simulation, the user can investigate many different system executions, each derived from the formal specifications, to check that the specifications capture the intended behavior.

1.4.3 Combining Techniques

A single formal method may combine several of the above techniques. For example, the formal method described in Chapter 6 applies the dual language approach: the system model is described using an operational specification language, Timed Petri Nets, whereas system properties are described in a logic-based language, TRIO. Given specifications of a system model and some property of interest, two different verification techniques may be applied. First, the user may use a model-theoretic technique to determine automatically whether a state-machine model of the system satisfies the property. Alternatively, the user may develop a hand proof that derives the given property from the system specification.

1.5 MODELS BASED ON LOGIC

Mathematical logic has been used for many years to specify and to prove properties about computer programs (see, e.g., [McC62, Hoa69, Flo67]. Using logic, one can describe and reason about the behavior of a system without building the system first. Such reasoning is based on correctness proofs rather than on experimental testing.

The most widely known logic is first-order logic. As in other logics, formulas in first-order logic are constructed by combining variables, functions, predicates, and logical connectives according to certain rules. Consider, for example, the power production plant introduced in Section 3. In a first-order theory, the plant and its properties can be described as follows. First, variables, such as `Temp` for temperature, `Pres` for pressure, and `PowerRequested` for the amount of power requested, are used to represent all relevant system quantities. Because time is also a critical system component, a variable t is used to represent time.

Next, predicates are used to specify system properties and constraints. For example, a predicate stating that the produced power cannot exceed the requested power is defined by

$$\texttt{PowerProduced} \leq \texttt{PowerRequested}.$$

For a more precise description, P can be rewritten to show the time dependence of the variables:

$$\forall t: \texttt{PowerProduced}(t) \leq \texttt{PowerRequested}(t),$$

The universal quantifier "$\forall t$" means that "for every value of the quantified variable t the following formula is true." Similarly, the existential quantifier "$\exists t$" means "there exists a value of the quantified variable t such that the following formula is true."

Finally, logical connections, such as $\wedge$ for AND, $\vee$ for OR, $\neg$ for NOT, and $\rightarrow$ for IMPLIES, are used to construct more complex formulas.

In the power production plant, suppose that if temperature and pressure have been continuously above the limits T_{max} and P_{max} for D time units, then the signal ModerateDanger must be raised. This can be expressed formally as

$$\forall t \, [\forall t', \, t - D \leq t' < t: \texttt{Pres}(t') > P_{max} \wedge \texttt{Temp}(t') > T_{max} \rightarrow \texttt{ModerateDanger}(t)].$$

In other words, if for every instant t' in the interval $[t - D, t)$, Pres is greater than P_{max} and Temp is greater than T_{max}, then at time t, signal ModerateDanger must occur.

Using such formulas, we can completely describe the required behavior of the power plant. For example, requirements such as the following can be specified:

- The system must be shut down within h time units after the HighDanger alarm sounds.
- The amount of coolant injected in the plant is proportional to the product of the difference between the actual temperature and the ideal temperature times the difference between the actual pressure and the ideal pressure. However, if there is no more coolant in the tank, then the HighDanger alarm sounds immediately.

Unlike the SA/RT notation, logic notation can describe the above requirements and similar functional, control, or timing requirements completely and precisely.

The logical approach can be used to formalize basic system properties as *axioms*, i.e., fundamental facts that by assumption are guaranteed, and to derive additional properties as *theorems*, consequences that follow from the basic assumptions. As an example, suppose the following two axioms are assumed:

1. Once the plant is turned off, temperature and pressure decrease with time according to some given mathematical function.
2. As soon as temperature and pressure are again within safety limits, the plant is immediately restarted.

Using these axioms, we can prove as a theorem that the plant will never be off for more than some maximum time.

Because first-order theories are a basic mathematical formalism, they are not well suited for describing real-world complexities. Thus, in practical systems, logic is most useful for proving properties about critical system components rather than the whole system. Another complication in practical application of first-order theories is that sufficiently general theories are undecidable; that is, no algorithm exists that can determine whether a given property can be proven as a theorem.

Although time, in principle, can be incorporated into a logic in the same way as other system variables, many researchers advocate a special role for time (e.g., special axioms and syntax) and have introduced new logics for reasoning about time. Some are first-order logics, whereas others are special temporal logics.

In temporal logics, special symbols, such as $\Diamond$ for "eventually" and $\square$ for "always", are used to describe desired properties. The original temporal logics could only describe temporal ordering. For example, the formula,

$$\square(\text{Train} = \text{InP} \rightarrow \Diamond\text{Gate} - \text{Down}), \tag{1.1}$$

means that "if a train enters P, then eventually the gate is in the down position." The formula simply describes the order in which two events must occur. Temporal logics designed for reasoning about real-time systems, such as Real-Time Temporal Logic (RTTL) [Ost89], can also describe temporal distance. For example, the formula

$$\square(\text{Train} = \text{InP} \rightarrow \Diamond_{\leq 5}\text{Gate} = \text{Down}), \tag{1.2}$$

means that "if a train enters P, then within 5 time units the gate is in the down position." This formula sets an upper bound on the time between two events: they are at most 5 time units apart. Finally, the formula,

$$\square(\text{Train} - \text{InI} \rightarrow \text{Gate} - \text{Down}), \tag{1.3}$$

means "if a train is in the crossing, then (it is always true that) the gate is down." Formula 1.3 is a formulation in temporal logic of the Safety Property introduced in Section 1.2.4.

Three examples of first-order logics designed for reasoning about real-time are Real-Time Logic or RTL [JM86], TRIO [GMM90], and ASTRAL [CPKM94]. RTL, which is described briefly in Section 1.6.1 and more fully in Chapter 2, was one of the first real-time logics. A special feature of TRIO, which is described in detail in Chapter 6, is that specifications expressed in TRIO are executable. This executability is achieved through a special interpreter.

ASTRAL [CPKM94], another logic-based language, combines the timing features of TRIO with the structuring mechanisms of ASLAN [AK86], an earlier language for describing non-real-time systems. ASTRAL specifications describe a system in a fairly operational style by defining its states and its transitions. Proof obligations are built to drive the formal analysis of the specification in a deductive style. The system specifications are treated as a set of axioms, from which the system properties are derived as theorems. Though presently no tools are available to support ASTRAL proofs, in principle, semiautomatic tools that generate proof obligations from a given specification could support formal analysis in a manner similar to that previously demonstrated for ASLAN.

Most real-time logics describe systems in terms of events, points in time when something significant occurs. In contrast, a few other real-time logics, called *interval logics*, focus on conditions (e.g., states) that hold for some nonzero time interval. Allen [All83] describes a classical example of an interval logic. The Duration Calculus, a real-time formalism described in Chapter 5, is a special case of interval logic. For more information on real-time logics, see [Ost92].

1.6   GRAPHICAL NOTATIONS

Modechart [JM94] and Timed Transition Models (TTM) [Ost89, Ost94], two examples of graphical notations designed for specifying real-time systems, borrow heavily from Statecharts but are more expressive than Statecharts for describing and reasoning about timing properties. Another important class of graphical notations for real-time computing are timed versions of Petri nets, a graphical formalism developed originally by Petri to describe concurrent processes [Pet62]. This section briefly describes Modechart and TTMs as well as timed Petri nets.

1.6.1   Statecharts-like Notations

Modechart. Important constructs in Modechart [JM94] include *modes*, which correspond to states in Statecharts, and *actions*, which assign values to data variables. A third Modechart construct is the *event*. Different types of events are *external* events, which represent changes in the system environment (e.g., the operator pushed the START button); *mode entry* and *mode exit* events, which mark entry into or exit from a mode; and *start* and *stop* events, which mark the start and stop of an action. To specify the time that the system can remain in a mode, Modechart provides *deadlines* and *delays*, upper and lower bounds on the time interval from mode entry to mode exit. Modechart uses a discrete time model: its delays and deadlines are represented as non-negative integers. In Modechart, events are instantaneous, whereas actions require at least one time unit to complete.

In Modechart, modes may be serial or parallel. Modechart's notion of serial and parallel modes corresponds to OR and AND composition in Statecharts. If M is a *serial* mode with child modes M_1 and M_2, then at any given time the system is in exactly one of M_1 and M_2. If M is a *parallel* mode with child modes M_1 and M_2, then when the system is in M, it is simultaneously in both modes M_1 and M_2. Modechart's semantics is defined in terms of the real-time logic RTL [JM86, JM94].

Modechart may be applied as part of a dual language approach. The system model can be expressed operationally in Modechart, whereas properties of interest may be expressed in RTL. In RTL, the expression "$@(e, i)$" represents the time of the ith occurrence of event e.

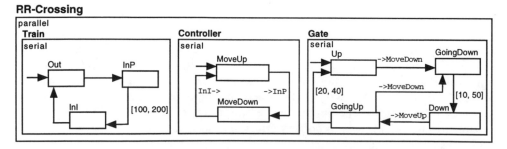

Figure 1.7   Modechart specification of simple railroad crossing

Figure 1.7 contains a Modechart specification of a simple single-train version of the railroad crossing problem.[2] The mode RR-Crossing is a parallel mode with three serial children,

---

[2] To keep Figure 1.7 simple, we have slightly modified the Modechart notation. Unlike the Modechart toolset (see Chapter 2), we denote the initial model using an arrow without a source and omit the label "deadline infinity" from transitions that can occur at any time (e.g., the transition from Out to InP in Train).

Train, Controller, and Gate. The mode Controller is the system model, whereas the modes Train and Gate are models of the system environment. In Figure 1.7, the timing constraint [100, 200] indicates that a train spends a minimum of 100 time units and a maximum of 200 time units in mode InP before it moves to mode InI. The expression "->InP" marks a train's entry into the region P, whereas the expression "InI->" marks a train's exit from the crossing I.

Suppose the user wants to check the Modechart specification in Figure 1.7 for the Safety Property described in Section 1.2.4, that is, "If at any time t a train is in the crossing I, then the gate is down." This property is expressed by the RTL formula

$$\forall i, \exists j: @(-> \text{Down}, j) \le @(-> \text{InI}, i) \wedge @(\text{InI->}, i) \le @(\text{Down->}, j). \tag{1.4}$$

This statement says that "for all i there exists j such that the time of the gate's jth entry into Down is less than or equal to the time of the ith train entry into InI and the time of the ith train exit out of InI is less than or equal the time of the gate's jth exit out of Down." That is, each interval during which a train is in the crossing is contained in an interval during which the crossing gate is down.

Modechart is supported by a set of software tools [CHLR93], which include an editor for creating the formal specifications, a consistency checker for testing the specifications for application-independent properties (such as nondeterministic behavior), a simulator for symbolic execution of the system, and a verifier which checks the specifications for application properties using model-theoretic reasoning. Thus to check the specification in Figure 1.7 for the formula in (1.4), the user would invoke Modechart's verifier and the verifier would determine automatically the validity of the formula for the given specification. It does so by building a graph of all possible system states and checking that the property holds in each.

As with Statecharts, Modechart's graphical notation and its support for hierarchy produce specifications that are relatively easy to understand and to develop. The use of a dual language approach—the operational language Modechart and the descriptive language RTL—provides more expressiveness than a single language would.

Timed Transition Models. The activity variables (or activities) in a Timed Transition Models (TTM) specification [Ost89, Ost94] correspond to states in Statecharts. A group of sub-activities may be composed into an activity using the Statecharts notions of AND and OR composition. Other major components of a TTM specification are events and integer variables. In contrast to Modechart which does not support arithmetic, TTM supports both the usual relational operations *and* integer arithmetic. As in Modechart, time in the TTM framework is discrete, and timing constraints are represented as lower and upper bounds on transitions between activities. Also like Modechart, this method supports the dual language approach. To specify properties of Timed Transition Models, Real Time Temporal Logic (RTTL) can be used. This approach is also supported by a suite of tools, that includes a verifier based on model-theoretic reasoning. To check a system model for a given property, the user expresses the model as a TTM specification and the property in RTTL and then executes the verifier.

1.6.2 Petri Nets

A Petri net consists of a set of *places*, usually denoted as circles, and a set of *transitions*, usually denoted as bars. Arrows connect places to transitions and transitions to places. A place is called an *input* of a transition (a transition is called an *input* of a place) if there is an arrow

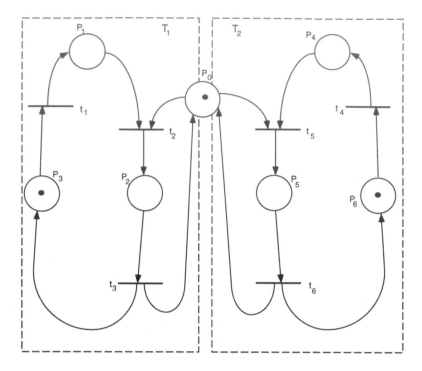

Figure 1.8   Example Petri net

going from the place to the transition (from the transition to the place). A similar definition holds for *output* places and transitions. Figure 1.8 illustrates a simple Petri net.

Petri nets are an operational formalism; they support the notion of a state and its evolution. The state of a Petri net is represented graphically as a *marking* of its places, an assignment of a nonnegative number of tokens to each place. The evolution of a Petri net occurs according to the following rules:

- A transition is *enabled* in a given marking if all of its input places are marked, i.e., each has at least one token.
- An enabled transition may *fire*. This means that one token is removed from each input place of the transition and one token is put into each output place thereof. Thus the firing of a transition produces a new marking.

A natural interpretation of Petri nets is as follows: The presence of a token in a place means that a condition is satisfied, for example, that a resource is available. This condition is needed for an action to be executed; the firing of an output transition describes the execution of an action. For example, the net in Figure 1.8 can be interpreted as a pair of independent tasks, say T_1 and T_2, that evolve through transitions t_1, t_2, and t_3 and transitions t_4, t_5, and t_6, respectively. The two tasks share a resource, say a CPU, modeled by place P_0. Each task requires this resource to perform some critical action and then releases the resource when it is no longer needed. Transitions t_1 and t_4 describe independent activities of T_1 and T_2, whereas t_2 and t_5 model the acquisition of the shared resource by T_1 and T_2, respectively, and t_3 and t_6 model release of the resource. The resource can be granted arbitrarily to only one at a time. The presence initially of two tokens in place P_0 models the availability of two instances of the resource. One can be granted independently to a task without any synchronization.

Petri nets can describe both asynchronous and nondeterministic behavior. In fact, the token flow through places and transitions may happen in parallel in several parts of the net without synchronizing the firing of independently enabled transitions (e.g. transitions t_1 and t_4 in the net of Figure 1.8.) Only when the different tasks compete for a shared resource do they need to synchronize. The model is also nondeterministic, because, in general, several transitions may be enabled. This is the case for transitions t_1 and t_4 in the marking of Figure 1.8. In such situations, which transition actually fires is nondeterministic.

The Petri net model cleanly separates concurrency and conflict. For example, when the net is in the marking shown in Figure 1.8, transitions t_1 and t_4 may fire nondeterministically (both are enabled and both can fire) and concurrently. However, once both have fired and there is one token in each of P_1, P_0, and P_4 while both t_2 and t_5 are enabled, only one can fire nondeterministically (the firing of one disables the firing of the other). In this case, we say the two transitions are in conflict. Petri nets allow a natural modeling of many common properties of concurrent systems, such as deadlock, starvation, and fairness.

Given their naturalness for describing asynchronous processes and their properties, Petri nets have been the topic of considerable research and have been used successfully in some industrial applications. For more information on Petri nets, see Peterson's text [Pet81].

Before Petri nets can be effectively used in designing real-time systems, some problems need to be addressed, e.g.,

- Because Petri nets are designed to describe concurrency rather than the passage of time, they cannot express timeouts and durations.
- Petri nets lack abstraction mechanisms and thus become large and unmanageable when one moves from toy examples to practical applications.
- Petri nets only model a system's control features, not its data dependencies. Because tokens are "anonymous", dependencies between control and data cannot be modeled. For example, a rule, such as "uncorrupted messages must be forwarded through channel 1, whereas damaged ones must be sent back through channel 2," cannot be described formally.

A number of approaches, some with tool support, have been proposed to solve these problems. In particular:

- Time has been added to Petri nets in many different ways. One of the most general extensions associates a minimum and a maximum firing time with each transition [MF76]. Once enabled, a transition cannot fire before the minimum time and must fire by the maximum time, unless previously disabled by the firing of a conflicting transition. For example, suppose in Figure 1.8, transition t_2 has a minimum and maximum firing time of 0 and t_3 has a minimum firing time of 1 and a maximum firing time of 2. Then, as soon as it is ready, task T_1 is immediately granted the resource P_0 (unless T_2 gets it first) and requires between 1 and 2 time units to complete its work before releasing P_0.
- Several abstraction and modularization mechanisms, essential in modeling real-world systems, have been proposed to support the construction of hierarchical, well-structured Petri nets. Recently, such mechanisms have exploited the object-oriented paradigm [Bru95].
- Tokens may have associated values: the firing of transitions can depend on these values (see, e.g., [Gen87]).

All of the above features are described in more detail in Chapter 6.

Many tools are available to support the development of real-time systems using Petri nets, including editors, tools for analyzing system properties, and, often, tools that help drive the system implementation through the lower level phases of the life cycle. While some tools are prototypes, others are production-quality and available to the public. Among the available tools are Artifex [Bru95], Cabernet (described in Chapter 6), and Design/CPN. Some have already been applied successfully in industrial projects. For instance, Artifex has been used for about a decade by several Italian and other European companies, largely in automobile manufacturing.

An unfortunate complication in modeling with Petri nets is that most significant properties of Petri nets are either intractable or undecidable [Pet81]. Thus, in most cases, analyzing properties of interest is done using simulation, which can be time-consuming and somewhat unreliable. An important exception is the Berthomieu-Diaz algorithm for analyzing a timed Petri net for reachability [BD91] . The reachablity problem for Petri nets is to determine whether a marking m' can be reached from another marking m through a suitable firing sequence. In some sense, this is the fundamental problem for Petri nets, since many other problems can be reduced to it. Under some reasonably general conditions, this analysis can be completed in polynomial time.

1.7   STATE MACHINE MODELS

The finite state machine introduced in Section 1.2 is ubiquitous in computer science because it is an intuitive, natural model for describing computer systems. This section briefly describes two methods that extend the state machine model to describe real-time systems. Chapter 3 presents a third method that uses a special class of finite state machines, called Buchi automata, which have infinite length input strings.

1.7.1   Timed Automaton Model

The timed automaton model, which is formally defined in [LV91, MMT91], is based on dense time. Unlike the classical state machine model which has a finite number of states, the timed automaton model allows infinitely many states. The model describes a system as a collection of automata (i.e., state machines) interacting by means of common actions. Important actions in the model are input and output actions, both of which are visible outside the system. Time is added to the model through a special time passage action.

To describe the simple railroad crossing problem in the timed automaton model [HL94a], the trains, the crossing gate, and a simple gate controller are initially represented as untimed state machines. The common actions are sensors reporting the arrival of trains and actuators controlling the raising and lowering of the gate. For example, the *Trains* component is described with no inputs and three types of outputs, *enterR(r)*, *enterI(r)*, and *exit(r)*, for each train r. The state consists of a *status* component for each train, indicating where the train is relative to the crossing.

State:
    for each train r:
        $r.status \in \{out, P, I\}$, initially *out*

The state transitions are described by specifying the "preconditions" under which each action can occur and the "effect" of each action. The symbol s denotes the state before the event occurs and s' the state afterwards.

Transitions:

enterR(r)
    Precondition:
        $s.r.status = out$
    Effect:
        $s'.r.status = P$

enterI(r)
    Precondition:
        $s.r.status = P$
    Effect:
        $s'.r.status = I$

exit(r)
    Precondition:
        $s.r.status = I$
    Effect:
        $s'.r.status = out$

To add time to the model, time bounds are associated with each action. In this example, trivial bounds (that is, $[0, \infty]$) are associated with the enterR(r) and exit(r) actions. The bounds $[\epsilon_1, \epsilon_2]$, where $\epsilon_1 \leq \epsilon_2$, are associated with each enterI(r) action. This means that from the time when any train r has reached R, it is at least time ϵ_1 and at most time ϵ_2 until the train reaches I. With this technique, variables as well as constants may be used to represent timing information. Representing time with variables allows constraints on variables to be derived later on from other information in the specifications.

To convert the *Trains* automaton to a timed automaton, some components are added to the state—a current time component *now*, and *first* and *last* components for each action. The *first* and *last* components give the earliest and latest times at which an action can occur once enabled. The transition relation is augmented with the *time passage action* ν, the only action that allows time to pass, and which enforces the bound assumptions. An action is not allowed to start before its *first* time, and time cannot pass beyond any *last* time. In this example, only the state components *now* and *first*(enterI(r)) and *last*(enterI(r)) for each r contain nontrivial information, so the other cases are ignored. Adding the timing information yields a timed automaton with the following states and transitions.

State:
    now, a nonnegative real, initially 0
    for each train r:
        $r.status \in \{out, I', I\}$, initially *out*
        first(enterI(r)), a nonnegative real, initially 0
        last(enterI(r)), a nonnegative real or ∞, initially ∞

Transitions:

enterR(r)
    Precondition:
        $s.r.status = out$
    Effect:
        $s'.r.status = P$
        $s'.first(enterI(r)) = now + \epsilon_1$
        $s'.last(enterI(r)) = now + \epsilon_2$

enterI(r)
    Precondition:
        $s.r.status = P$
        $now \geq s.first(enterI(r))$
    Effect:
        $s'.r.status = I$
        $s'.first(enterI(r)) = 0$
        $s'.last(enterI(r)) = \infty$

exit(r)
    Precondition:
        $s.r.status = I$
    Effect:
        $s'.r.status = out$

$\nu(t)$
    Precondition:
        for all r, $s.now + t \leq s.last(enterI(r))$
    Effect:
        $s'.now = s.now + t$

The above specification illustrates how the timed automaton model overcomes the limitations of the classical state machine: time is built into the state, and any number of trains, even an unbounded number, can be modeled easily and concisely. Further, general logic formulas may be used to specify transitions.

To solve a problem using the timed automaton model, one develops two system descriptions, one specifying the problem, the other the solution. In the railroad crossing example, the problem description is the composition of the individual state machines—in this case, timed automaton models of the train, the gate, and the system—and the required system properties, for example, the Safety Property described in Section 1.2.4. The system model is a trivial specification of the computer system; it receives inputs from the trains and sends outputs to the gate. The properties constrain the system model to allow only certain behavior in the environment. The problem solution is the composition of the same train and gate models in the problem description with a computer system implementation that raises and lowers the gate in a manner that satisfies the required properties.

Given two system descriptions, one the problem description and the other the problem solution, proofs must show a "simulation mapping" between the two descriptions. A simulation mapping between two descriptions holds if every behavior of one description is a behavior of the other description. Two specifications are equivalent if the two sets of behaviors are equal. In this method, many of the proofs are done by mathematical induction. To demonstrate such a proof, we state and prove a lemma (a small theorem) about the train model using induction [HL94b]:

Lemma: In any reachable state of *Trains*: For any r such that $r.status = P$, $first(enterI(r)) + \epsilon_2 - \epsilon_1 = last(enterI(r))$.

Proof: By induction on the length, i.e., the total number of non-time-passage and time-passage steps, of an execution. Because $\epsilon_2 - \epsilon_1$ is a constant, the only actions that need be considered are those that change $first(enterI(r))$ or $last(enterI(r))$ or make $r.status = P$. These are $enterR(r)$ and $enterI(r)$. The actions $exit(r)$ and the time passage action do not affect the statement.

After 0 steps, the claim is vacuously satisfied. Assume the claim is true after m steps. We must prove it is true after $m + 1$ steps. For $enterI(r)$, the claim is vacuously satisfied. For $enterR(r)$, the effect is $s'.r.status = P$. Then, $s'.first(enterI(r)) = now + \epsilon_1$ and $s'.last(enterI(r)) = now + \epsilon_2$, which implies that $s'.first(enterI(r)) + \epsilon_2 - \epsilon_1 = s'.last(enterI(r))$ as required. ∎

For a complete solution of the railroad crossing problem using the timed automaton model, see Chapter 4.

1.7.2   Esterel Family

Esterel [BG92] is the most widely known member of a family of languages that use the state machine model to describe real-time systems. The Esterel family is based on the *synchrony hypothesis*, which states that each system response to a set of inputs is instantaneous. At the practical level, this means that the system must complete all computations before the next input from the environment arrives. Esterel, the imperative member of the family, provides typical programming language constructs, such as assignments, loops, and parallel statements. Lustre, a declarative member of the family, is based on the data flow formalism, but, unlike traditional DFDs, has a precise semantics. ARGOS is a graphical notation, patterned after Statecharts, that provides a front-end for specifications in the Esterel family.

What distinguishes the Esterel family of languages from many other real-time formalisms is their emphasis on the later phases of the software life cycle. Compilers are available which automatically produce running code from specifications written in the language of some family member. A comprehensive description of the synchronous approach and the Esterel family of languages is given in [Hal93, Ber91]. Esterel and other members of the family have been applied to many industrial projects, mainly in the fields of nuclear plant safety and avionics (see, e.g., [LRD95]).

1.8 PROCESS ALGEBRAS

Process algebras, such as CCS [Mil89], CSP [Hoa85], and ACP [BK85], were developed originally to specify and to analyze concurrent systems without the notion of time. A process algebra has four components: a concise language, a precisely defined semantics, a notion of equivalence or preorder, and a set of algebraic laws allowing syntactic manipulation. The language is based on a small set of operators and a few syntactic rules for constructing a complex process from simpler processes. The semantics describes the possible execution steps a process can take. Two processes are *equivalent* when they have the same behavior (that is, when every execution step of one process is also an execution step of the other process and vice versa). A *preorder* between two processes exists when the behavior of one process is a subset of the behavior of another. To verify a system using a process algebra, one writes a specification as an *abstract* process and an implementation as a *detailed* process. To prove correctness, the two processes are shown to be equivalent or a preorder between the two processes is shown. This proof of correctness is accomplished by syntactically manipulating the algebraic laws.

Recently, a number of *timed* process algebras have been proposed. These include ACSR, which adds time to CCS [BGCL93, LBGG94]; Timed CSP, a timed version of CSP [RR87]; Timed LOTOS, a timed version of the ISO standard LOTOS [BB87], which is also based on CSP and has already been applied to several industrial projects; and a timed version of ACP [BB91]. Below, we briefly summarize ACSR, which is described in detail in Chapter 7. Chapter 8 provides a detailed description of Timed LOTOS.

1.8.1 ACSR

The Algebra of Communicating Shared Resources (ACSR) uses the notion of priorities to arbitrate between processes competing for shared resources and events ready for synchronization. Important constructs in ACSR are timed actions, which compete for shared resources, and events, which allow synchronization between processes. In ACSR, each timed action consumes one unit of time, whereas events are instantaneous and do not consume time.

ACSR's semantics is defined in two steps. First, transitions are defined without priority. Second, the definitions are refined to include priority. To illustrate this, we consider the definition of the choice operator, denoted '+', which in ACSR represents nondeterminism. First, the choice operator is defined without priorities. Let P and Q be processes, and let α be an action. Then, the semantics of the execution step $P + Q$ is defined by

$$\frac{P \xrightarrow{\alpha} P'}{P + Q \xrightarrow{\alpha} P'}$$

and

$$\frac{Q \xrightarrow{\alpha} Q'}{P + Q \xrightarrow{\alpha} Q'}.$$

This means that either P or Q may execute the action α. If P is chosen, then P executes α and proceeds to P'. If Q is chosen, then Q executes α and proceeds to Q'.

When priorities are considered, the process selected to execute the action depends on the priorities of P and Q relative to the resources they request. Suppose P requests resource r_1 with priority 1 and Q requests resource r_1 with (higher) priority 2. Then, given $P + Q$ and action α, Q is selected to execute α, since Q's priority for resource r_1 is greater than P's priority for the same resource.

Example. To illustrate resource arbitration based on priorities, we consider an example in which a process *System* can allocate a buffer resource to either P or Q. The notation $\{(\text{buffer}, n)\}$ represents a request for the resource, buffer, with priority n.

$$P \stackrel{\text{def}}{=} \{(\text{buffer}, 1)\} : P$$
$$Q \stackrel{\text{def}}{=} \{(\text{buffer}, 2)\} : Q$$
$$System \stackrel{\text{def}}{=} P + Q$$

Without priorities, the choice between the two processes is nondeterministic. Thus, *System* has two possible execution steps:

$$System \xrightarrow{\{(\text{buffer}, 1)\}} P$$

or

$$System \xrightarrow{\{(\text{buffer}, 2)\}} Q$$

With priorities, *System* allocates the buffer to process Q, since Q needs the resource with a higher priority. Thus, *System* will execute the second execution step only. Normally, the consumption of a resource by a process takes one time unit. However, ACSR models can also be formulated so that resource consumption takes more than one time unit.

A number of tools have been developed to support ACSR. These include a tool that, under user direction, applies rewriting rules to an ACSR specification to deduce system properties; a verifier that constructs a state machine model from the specifications and analyzes the state space to verify properties and to test equivalence of alternative process specifications; and a simulator that can symbolically execute the system based on the specifications.

Similar tools have been developed to support other process algebras. Examples include the FDR (Failure Divergence Refinement) tool [For92], a verifier for CSP specifications, and the Concurrency Work Bench [CPS93], a verifier for CCS specifications.

1.9   ANALYSIS TECHNIQUES

This section summarizes model-theoretic reasoning and proof-theoretic reasoning, the two major classes of techniques developed for formally reasoning about real-time systems.

1.9.1   Model-Theoretic Reasoning

In recent years, a number of algorithms have been developed to verify properties of systems modeled as state machines. One class of algorithms, called *model checkers* [CES86], were invented by Clarke and Emerson in 1981 to verify properties of untimed specifications [CE81]. These algorithms take a finite state machine model of a system and a temporal logic formula and determine if the formula is true of the model. They have been especially effective in verifying models with binary variables, such as hardware and protocol specifications. In 1992, for example, a model checker, called the Symbolic Model Verifier (SMV) [McM92], was used to detect several errors in the Futurebus+ Cache Coherency Protocol, an IEEE standard. Like other techniques based on model-theoretic reasoning, SMV uses binary decision diagrams to perform the analysis efficiently. Some models with more than 10^{20} states have been verified using these techniques [BCM$^+$90].

While model checkers have detected design errors in practical systems, the errors were in untimed specifications. The application of model-theoretic techniques to timed specifications remains largely a research area. The problem in verifying specifications of real-time systems is one of scale: adding time to the system specification produces a model that is, in most cases, much too large to analyze.

For example, the Modechart verifier [JS88], part of the real time toolset described in Section 1.6.1, is designed to analyze properties of real-time specifications using model-based techniques. This tool builds a "computation graph" to represent all possible states that a system can enter. Various approaches are used to prune unreachable nodes in the graph and to combine duplicate nodes. Although this tool (and similar ones) can verify small real-time models, the computation graph becomes too large to build and to analyze as the number of states and the timing constants in the model become large. A related approach can handle larger models. This approach extends SMV to real-time models by incorporating an efficient technique for timing and event counting. According to its authors, in comparison with SMV, this enhanced model checker achieves one to two orders of magnitude in speedup and space saving in timing and event counting [YMW93]. For a detailed description of a model checker that analyzes discrete time models, see Chapter 9.

The techniques described above are designed to handle discrete time. Techniques have also been developed for dense time models. One promising approach [AIKY93, BSV93, DWT95] uses approximations to avoid dealing with the timing information in a specification until it is needed. Successive approximations are made until conclusive results are obtained. For example, one technique [AIKY93] begins by ignoring all timing constraints. If the verifier detects an error, the error is checked to determine whether it is real or an artifact of the approximation. In the latter case, timing constraints that exclude the error are added to the specification, and the verification is repeated. Recently, approximation techniques were used to verify a CSMA (Carrier Sense Multiple Access) protocol [DWT95].

1.9.2   Proof-Theoretic Reasoning

In proof-theoretic reasoning, the user develops a theory about the system of interest based on some logic, such as first-order logic. System properties are then represented as formulas in the logic. Unlike model-theoretic techniques, applying logical deduction requires mathematical maturity and theorem proving skills. Moreover, in comparison to the effort required to use a tool, such as a model checker, to verify a property, the effort needed to develop a proof of a property using deductive reasoning can be significant.

Although developing proofs can be arduous and requires significant time, the deductive approach has some advantages over model-based reasoning. First, in developing the proofs, the user gains a deep understanding of the specification and its properties—what the dependencies are, where the boundary conditions are, etc. [RvH91]. Second, proof-theoretic techniques can handle more abstract models and thus produce more general results. In the case of the state machine model, one can reason about an infinite (rather than a finite) number of states and variable (rather than constant) timing parameters. Further, unlike model checking and other similar techniques, deductive reasoning can be applied to any mathematical model; there is no restriction to state machine models.

A number of mechanical proof systems have been developed in recent years to support deductive reasoning. These include the Boyer-Moore theorem prover [BM88], EVES [KPS+93], and the Larch Prover (LP) [GH93], all based on first-order logic, as well as HOL [Gor88] and PVS [OSR93], which are based on Higher Order Logic. Such systems can do some proofs automatically. For example, decision procedures exist for theories such as Presburger arithmetic for doing simple integer addition and multiplication. Most nontrivial proofs, however, require user guidance; the user must develop the overall proof strategy. Mechanical proof systems can be very useful in checking such hand proofs. Of special interest for safety-critical systems is that the proof system validates each step in the formal reasoning. As a result, one has more confidence in the proof's validity than one would have in a more informal proof which was not checked mechanically.

As with other formal techniques, techniques designed to reason about untimed systems have been extended to reason about real-time systems. Chapter 4 describes a hand proof of a solution to the railroad crossing problem based on the timed automaton model. Both references [Sha93] and [Jef95] present proofs of the railroad crossing problem that were checked mechanically using the proof system PVS. The first is based on a state machine model; the second uses a model expressed in the TRIO logic.

Reference [LSGL94] describes the use of LP to verify hand proofs based on the timed automata model. First, the concepts in the proof (simulations, timed automata, etc.) were formalized in the Larch Shared Language. Then, instructions to LP were encoded as scripts. The general strategy was to mimic the hand proof as closely as possible. Thus, if the proof began by considering each action separately, the script did so too. If the proof required consideration of several cases, the script also did this. However, some scripts explicitly considered cases omitted from the hand proof, usually because in the hand proof some general observation indicated a particular variable could be ignored. The main difficulties were 1) determining exactly what facts were used to establish other facts (the hand proof omits mention of some "obvious" facts which LP may not find easily) and 2) deciding how LP "knows" those facts, either by finding the name that LP knows them by or by filling in the gaps LP needs to derive these facts from what it knows. Such facts are sometimes omitted in hand proofs, either unintentionally or because they are obvious. It is not too surprising that LP's notion of obvious does not always coincide with the human notion.

An approach that goes beyond proof checking encodes a real-time formalism within the logic of a proof system. Reference [SS94] describes a "proof assistant" for the Duration Calculus (see Chapter 5), which was developed within the framework of PVS. This proof assistant, which consists of a specification front-end and a proof checker, allows the user to develop specifications using the Duration Calculus syntax and to construct proofs using the proof rules of the Duration Calculus. The Duration Calculus proof rules are encoded in the logic of PVS but this is transparent to the user. To the user, proofs constructed with the proof assistant appear very similar to the corresponding hand proofs. The advantage of using such a tool is that a significant subset of PVS' underlying base logic and proof checking capabilities can be exploited to support reasoning in the Duration Calculus. Arithmetic and logical decision procedures in PVS relieve the user of trivial proofs. Moreover, the user can reason about a problem in the logic that is natural for the problem rather than the raw PVS logic.

1.10   SUMMARY AND CONCLUSIONS

Above, we have presented an overview of formal methods for the development of real-time systems. Our main purpose in doing so is to help the reader evaluate the advantages and disadvantages of adopting such innovative methods. We believe that several of the surveyed methods are ready to be used in developing practical systems. It is important to stress, however, that conceptual maturity does not guarantee practical success. Little can be achieved by a development method without two kinds of support: well-engineered and user-friendly tools and sufficient investment in the training of the people who are to use the new methods.

Effective tools and adequate training are essential for any innovative design method. Unfortunately, some attempts by industry to use a new design method have failed because an organization invested in a state-of-the-art CASE tool but failed to train its staff to use the tool. Training is especially critical if the innovation is based on some formal method, because formal methods often require more insight and training than less formal ones. But herein lies a dilemma. On the one hand, one needs well engineered tools to make a formal method practical. (We note that tools that exploit formal methods are much more than simple editors and therefore usually require considerably more investment.) On the other hand, one needs a large user population to justify the expense of constructing such tools. Resolving this dilemma will be difficult. One promising approach is to introduce the tools and the method incrementally. However, achieving the benefits of formal methods will require a significant commitment and investment in both tool development and staff training.

ACKNOWLEDGMENTS

Thanks to G. Berry, R. Bharadwaj, S. Faulk, R. Jeffords, F. Schreiber, and two anonymous reviewers for their very helpful comments on earlier drafts and to M. Brockmeyer for comments and help with Figure 1.6. We also received useful input from R. Alur, H. Ben Abdallah, E. Clarke, D. Dill, R. Gerber, I. Lee, V. Luchangco, J. McLean, A. Mok, and J. Rushby.

REFERENCES

[AIKY93]   R. Alur, A. Itai, R. Kurshan, and M. Yannakakis. Timing verification by successive approximation. In *Proceedings, Fourth Intern. Conf. on Computer-Aided Verification*. Springer-Verlag, 1993.

[AK86]   B. Auermeier and R. Kemmerer. RT-ASLAN: a specification language for real-time systems. *IEEE Trans. on Software Eng.*, 12(9):879–889, September 1986.

[All83]   J. F. Allen. Maintaining knowledge about temporal intervals. *CACM*, 26(11), November 1983.

[AMBC86]   Ajmone-Marsan, Balbo, and Conte. *Performance Analysis of Multiprocessor Systems*. MIT Press, 1986.

[BB87]   T. Bolognesi and E. Brinksma. Introduction to the ISO specification language LOTOS. *Computer Networks and ISDN Systems*, 14:25–59, 1987.

[BB91]   J. Baeten and J. Bergstra. Real-time process algebra. *Formal Aspects of Computing*, 3(2):142–188, 1991.

[BCM$^+$90] J. Burch, E. Clarke, K. McMillan, D. Dill, and L. Hwang. Symbolic model checking: 10^{20} states and beyond. In *Proceedings, Fifth Conference on Logic in Computer Science*, 1990.

[BD91]   B. Berthomieu and M. Diaz. Modeling and verification of time dependent systems using time petri nets. *IEEE Trans. on Software Eng.*, 17(3):259–273, March 1991.

[Ber91]   G. Berry. Another look at real-time programming. *Proceedings of the IEEE*, 79, 1991.

[BG92]   G. Berry and G. Gonthier. The Esterel synchronous programming language: Design, semantics, implementation. *Science of Computer Programming*, 19(2), 1992.

[BGCL93]   P. Bremond-Gregoire, J. Y. Choi, and I. Lee. The soundness and completeness of ACSR. Technical Report MS-CIS-93-59, Univ. of Pennsylvania, June 1993.

[BK85]   J. Bergstra and J. Klop. Algebra of communicating processes with abstraction. *Journal of Theoretical Computer Science*, 37:77–121, 1985.

[BM88]   R. Boyer and J. Moore. *A Computational Logic Handbook*. Academic Press, New York, 1988.

[Bru95]   G. Bruno. *Model-based Software Engineering*. Chapman-Hall, London, 1995.

[BS93]   J. Bowen and V. Stavridou. Safety-critical systems, formal methods and standards. *Software Engineering Journal*, 8(4):189–209, July 1993.

[BSV93]   F. Balarin and A. Sangiovanni-Vincentelli. A verification strategy for timing constrained systems. In *Proceedings, Fourth Intern. Conf. on Computer-Aided Verification*. Springer-Verlag, 1993.

[CE81]   E. M. Clarke and E.A. Emerson. Synthesis of synchronization skeletons for branching time temporal logic. In *Proceedings, Logic of Programs Workshop*, volume 131 of *Lecture Notes in Computer Science*, Yorktown Heights, NY, 1981. Springer-Verlag.

[CES86]   E.M. Clarke, E. A. Emerson, and A. P. Sistla. Automatic verification of finite-state concurrent systems using temporal logic specifications. *ACM Transactions on Programming Languages and Systems*, 8(2):244–263, 1986.

[CHLR93]   P. Clements, C. Heitmeyer, B. Labaw, and A. Rose. MT: A toolset for specifying and analyzing real-time systems. In *Proceedings, Real-Time Systems Symp.*, Raleigh, NC, December 1993.

[CPKM94]   A. Coen-Porisini, R. Kemmerer, and D. Mandrioli. A formal framework for ASTRAL intralevel proof obligations. *IEEE Trans. on Software Eng.*, 20(8):548–561, August 1994.

[CPS93]   R. Cleaveland, J. Parrow, and B. Steffen. The concurrency workbench: A semantics-based tool for the verification of concurrent systems. *ACM Trans. Programming Languages and Systems*, 15(1):36–72, January 1993.

[DeM78]   T. DeMarco. *Structured Analysis and System Specification*. Yourdon Inc., New York, 1978.

[DWT95]   D. Dill and H. Wong-Toi. Verification of real-time systems by successive over and under approximation. In *Proceedings, Fourth Intern. Conf. on Computer-Aided Verification*. Springer-Verlag, 1995.

[ESA93]   ESA. *HOORA: Hierarchical Object-Oriented Requirements Analysis*, 1993. ESA report E2S/OORA/WP1/METH.

[Flo67]   R. Floyd. Symp. on applied mathematics: Mathematical aspects of computer science, vol. 19. In J. Schwartz, editor, *Assigning meanings to programs*, pages 254–255. American

Mathematical Society, New York, 1967.

[For92]   Formal Systems (Europe) Ltd., Oxford, UK. *Failure Divergence Refinement, User Manual and Tutorial, Version 1.2*, December 1992.

[Gen87]   H. Genrich. Predicate/transition nets. In W. Reisig and G. Rozenberg, editors, *Advances in Petri Nets*, pages 254–255. Springer-Verlag, Berlin-New York, 1987.

[GH93]   J. V. Guttag and J. J. Horning. *Larch: Languages and Tools for Formal Specification*. Springer-Verlag, 1993.

[GMM90]   C. Ghezzi, D. Mandrioli, and A. Morzenti. TRIO, a logic language for executable specifications of real-time systems. *Journal of Systems and Software*, 12(2):107–123, May 1990.

[Gor88]   M. Gordon. Mechanizing programming logics in higher order logic. Technical Report 145, Univ. of Cambridge, Cambridge, UK, 1988.

[Hal93]   N. Halbwachs. *Synchronous programming of reactive systems*. Kluwer Academic Publishers, 1993.

[Har87]   D. Harel. Statecharts: a visual formalism for complex systems. *Science of Computer Programming*, 8(1):231–274, 1987.

[HL94a]   C. Heitmeyer and N. Lynch. The Generalized Railroad Crossing: A case study in formal verification of real-time systems. In *Proceedings, Real-Time Systems Symp.*, San Juan, Puerto Rico, December 1994.

[HL94b]   C. Heitmeyer and N. Lynch. The Generalized Railroad Crossing: A case study in formal verification of real-time systems. Technical Report 7619, Naval Research Laboratory, Wash., DC, 1994. Also Technical Report MIT/LCS/TM-51, Lab. for Comp. Sci., MIT, Cambridge, MA, 1994.

[HLN+90]   D. Harel, H. Lachover, A. Naamad, A. Pnueli, M. Politi, R. Sherman, A. Shtull-Trauring, and M. Trakhtenbrot. Statemate: A working environment for the development of complex reactive systems. *IEEE Transactions on Software Engineering*, 16(4):403–414, 1990.

[Hoa69]   C. A. R. Hoare. An axiomatic basis for computer programming. *Communications of the ACM*, 12(10):576–580, October 1969.

[Hoa85]   C. A. R. Hoare. *Communicating Sequential Processes*. Prentice-Hal, New York, 1985.

[i-L91]   i Logix, Inc., Burlington, MA. *Languages of STATEMATE*, January 1991.

[i-L93]   i-Logix, Inc., Burlington, MA. *STATEMATE: Analyzer Reference Manual, Version 5.0*, June 1993.

[Jef95]   R. D. Jeffords. An approach to encoding the TRIO logic in PVS. Technical Report NRL/MR/5540-95-7777, NRL, Wash., DC, 1995.

[JM86]   F. Jahanian and A.K. Mok. Safety analysis of timing properties in real-time systems. *IEEE Trans. on Software Eng.*, 12(9):890–904, September 1986.

[JM94]   F. Jahanian and A.K. Mok. Modechart: A specification language for real-time systems. *IEEE Trans. on Software Eng.*, 20(10):879–889, October 1994.

[JS88]   F. Jahanian and D.A. Stuart. A method for verifying properties of Modechart specifications. In *Proceedings, Real-Time Systems Symp.*, Huntsville, AL, December 1988.

[Kem85]   R. A. Kemmerer. Testing formal specifications to detect design errors. *IEEE Trans. Softw. Eng.*, SE-11(1):32–43, January 1985.

[Koy90]   R. Koymans. Specifying real-time properties with metric temporal logic. *Real-Time Systems*, 2:255–299, 1990.

[KPS+93]   S. Kromodimoeljo, W. Pase, M. Saaltink, D. Craigen, and I. Meisels. A tutorial on EVES. Technical report, Odyssey Research Associates, Ottawa, Ont., 1993.

[Kro87]   F. Kroeger. *Temporal Logics of Programs*. EATCS Monographs on Theoretical Computer Science, Springer-Verlag, New York-Berlin, 1987.

[LBGG94]   I. Lee, P. Brémond-Grégoire, and R. Gerber. A Process Algebraic Approach to the Specification and Analysis of Resource-Bound Real-Time Systems. *Proceedings of the IEEE*, pages 158–171, Jan 1994.

[LRD95]   F. Lagnier, P. Raymond, and C. Dubois. Formal verification of a critical system written in Saga/Lustre. In *Workshop on Formal Methods, Modelling and Simulation for System Engineering*, St Quentin en Yvelines, France, February 1995.

[LSGL94]   V. Luchangco, E. Söylemez, S. Garland, and N. Lynch. Verifying timing properties of concurrent algorithms. In *Formal Description Techniques VII: Proceedings, FORTE'94*, pages 259–273, Berne, Switzerland, October 1994. IFIP WG6.1, Chapman and Hall.

[Lut93]   R. R. Lutz. Targeting safety-related errors during software requirements analysis. In *Proceedings, First ACM SIGSOFT Symp. on the Foundations of Software Engineering*, Los Angeles, CA, December 1993.

[LV91]   N. Lynch and F. Vaandrager. Forward and backward simulations for timing-based systems. In *Proceedings of REX Workshop "Real-Time: Theory in Practice"*, volume 600 of *Lecture Notes in Computer Science*, pages 397–446, Mook, The Netherlands, June 1991. Springer-Verlag.

[McC62]   J. McCarthy. Towards a mathematical science of computation. In *Proceedings, IFIP*, pages 21–28, 1962.

[McM92]   K. L. McMillan. *Symbolic model checking — an approach to the state explosion problem.* PhD thesis, Carnegie Mellon University, 1992.

[MF76]   P. Merlin and D. Farber. Recoverability of communication protocols. *IEEE Trans. on Communications*, 24(9):1036–1043, September 1976.

[Mil89]   R. Milner. *Communication and Concurrency.* Prentice-Hall, New York, 1989.

[MMT91]   M. Merritt, F. Modugno, and M. Tuttle. Time constrained automata. In J. C. M. Baeten and J. F. Goote, editors, *CONCUR'91: 2nd International Conference on Concurrency Theory*, volume 527 of *Lecture Notes in Computer Science*, pages 408–423, Amsterdam, The Netherlands, August 1991. Springer-Verlag.

[OSR93]   S. Owre, N. Shankar, and J. Rushby. User guide for the PVS specification and verification system (Draft). Technical report, Comp. Sci. Lab, SRI Intl., Menlo Park, CA, 1993.

[Ost89]   J. Ostroff. *Temporal Logic For Real-Time Systems.* Research Studies Press LTD., Taunton, Somerset, England, 1989.

[Ost92]   J. S. Ostroff. Formal methods for the specification and design of real-time safety-critical systems. *Journal of Systems and Software*, 33(60):890–904, April 1992.

[Ost94]   J. Ostroff. Visual tools for verifying real-time systems. In T. Rus and C. Rattray, editors, *Theories and Experiences for Real-Time System Development*, AMAST Series in Computing, Volume 2, pages 83–101, Singapore, 1994. World Scientific Publishing Co.

[Pet62]   C. A. Petri. *Kommunikationen Mit Automaten.* PhD thesis, University of Bonn, Bonn, Germany, 1962.

[Pet81]   J. L. Peterson. *Petri Net Theory and the Modeling of Systems.* Prentice-Hall, Englewood Cliffs, NJ, 1981.

[RR87]   G. Reed and A. Roscoe. Metric spaces as models for real-time concurrency. In *Proceedings, Mathematical Foundations of Computer Science, LNCS*, volume 298, New York, 1987. Springer-Verlag.

[RvH91]   J. Rushby and F. von Henke. Formal verification of algorithms for critical systems. In *Proceedings, ACM SIGSOFT Conf. on Software for Critical Systems*, pages 1–15, December 1991.

[SGW94]   B. Selic, G. Gullekson, and P. Ward. *Real-Time Object Modeling.* John Wiley, 1994.

[Sha93]   N. Shankar. Verification of real-time systems using PVS. In *Proceedings, Fifth International Conference on Computer-Aided Verification*, volume 697 of *Lecture Notes in Computer Science*, pages 280–291, 1993.

[SM88]   S. Shlaer and S. Mellor. *Object oriented system analysis: Modeling the world in data.* Prentice-Hall, Englewood Cliffs, New Jersey, 1988.

[SS94]   J. Skakkebaek and Natarajan Shankar. Towards a Duration Calculus proof assistant in PVS. In *Third Intern. Symp. on Formal Techniques in Real-Time and Fault-Tolerant Systems*, volume 863 of *Lecture Notes in Computer Science*, pages 660–679, 1994.

[WM85]   P. T. Ward and S. J. Mellor. *Structured Development for Real-Time Systems.* Yourdon Press, New York, 1985.

[YMW93]   J. Yang, A.K. Mok, and F. Wang. Symbolic model checking for event-driven real-time systems. In *Proceedings, 14th IEEE Real-Time Systems Symp.*, Raleigh-Durham, December 1993.

2

Specification and Analysis of Real-Time Systems: Modechart Language and Toolset

ALOYSIUS K. MOK and DOUGLAS A. STUART [1]
The University of Texas at Austin

FARNAM JAHANIAN
The University of Michigan

ABSTRACT

This chapter illustrates the use of the Modechart specification language and the MT toolset by using them in the specification and analysis of the control rod system of a nuclear reactor. The specification language and an associated logic, RTL, are introduced, as is a tool for building specifications. Two approaches are then used to analyze the specification. The Modechart simulator is used to exhibit individual behaviors of the system. The Modechart verifier is used to verify global properties of the system.

2.1 INTRODUCTION

Since real-time systems are often safety-critical systems, ensuring the correctness of a real-time system is very important. Since real-time systems are also typically complex systems, with behaviors that depend on the inter-relationships among the timing of the events of the system, testing is inadequate as the sole means for ensuring the correctness of such systems. Formal methods offer the hope of guaranteeing the correct behavior of such systems. In particular, they offer the hope of mechanical techniques which can be used to demonstrate the correctness of a real-time system.

---

[1] Supported in part by a research grant from the Office of Naval Research under ONR contract number N0014-94-1-0582, the Texas Advanced Research Program and the Naval Research Laboratory

---

Formal Methods For Real-Time Computing, Edited by Heitmeyer and Mandrioli
© 1996 John Wiley & Sons Ltd

The ultimate goal of mechanical verification would be to have a system designer give a natural language description of a specification to a verification system, and have the verifier say, 'Yes, the system is correct.' This is not possible with the current state of the art, and is likely to be unattainable for some time. Accordingly, we will attempt to construct an interactive methodology where the system designer would create a formal specification, and then guide a mechanical verification system to the conclusion that the system is correct. The basis of the approach will be to begin with a core mechanical verification tool, and surround it with a (continually expanding) number of "helper" mechanisms, and provide the designer with an (ever more effective) interface for using the helper mechanisms to lead the core tool to the correct conclusion. This chapter will focus on Modechart, one formal specification language, and some of the techniques that make up the basis of the core mechanical verification process. Modechart ([JM94]) is a graphical specification language, influenced by Statechart ([Har87]). Modechart is intended for describing embedded real-time applications, whose control structure can naturally be described as timed hierarchical state machines. This chapter will also provide an introduction to the Modechart Toolset, which has been implemented jointly at the Naval Research Laboratory and the University of Texas at Austin.

One example will be used throughout this chapter to illustrate the techniques and concepts being introduced. This example first appeared in [JM86]. A nuclear reactor has two control rods, which control the pace of the reaction in the reactor core, and therefore the power output of the reactor. Each rod can be either inserted or withdrawn, and it takes between one and fifty time units for the rod to change positions. For safety reasons, at most one of the rods may be moving at any time. Throughout the remainder of this chapter, this example will be developed and extended to illustrate how Modechart may be used to specify such a system, and how the tools available may be used to discover properties about the system.

Modechart represents the control structure of the system being specified by modes and transitions between them. Figure 2.1 shows a modechart specification for part of the nuclear reactor system example (the figure was generated automatically by the Modechart Toolset from a textual description of the specification). This portion of the specification includes only one of the control rods, and its controller. The specification is a single mode, *nuke*, containing two modes. *Controller1* represents the controller of the rod, and cycles between the modes *idle1*, *req1*, *busy1*, and *done1*. *Req1* represents a request to move the rod being present, and *busy1* represents the controller viewing the rod as being in motion. *Rod1* represents the control rod, and is in *rest1*, *move1*, or *reset1*.

There are three types of analysis that can be performed on such a specification. Modechart specifications can be converted into a formal first order logic, RTL ([JM86]), and natural deduction can be used to make inferences about the specification, either by hand, or using a mechanical theorem prover of some kind. Since RTL is a first order logic, the whole panoply of natural deduction and theorem provers may be used with minimal modification. This approach will not be further discussed in this chapter.

Another type of analysis useful to a system designer is to examine a typical computation of the specification. The Modechart Toolset provides a simulator for this purpose. Using the simulator allows the user to examine an individual computation of the specification. While this type of analysis can not provide any guarantees about the correctness of the system, it is often helpful in the process of matching the formal specification with the natural specification. Figure 2.2 shows the the result of simulating the specification of Figure 2.1. The lower two windows indicate when given modes are active. In this case, the top line indicates the intervals when *move1* is active, and the bottom line when *busy1* is active. The active intervals are

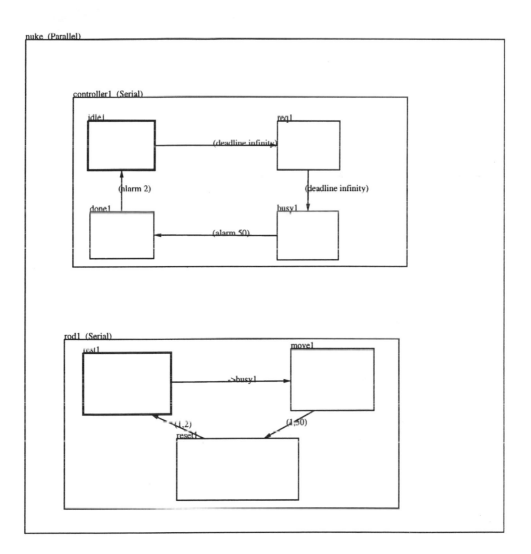

Figure 2.1 Nuclear reactor controller and rod (figure automatically generated)

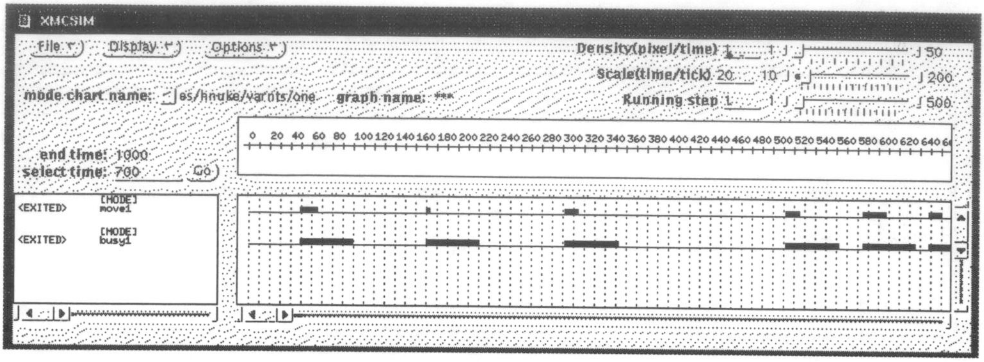

Figure 2.2   Nuclear reactor controller and rod simulation

indicated by a thick bar in the time line to the right of the name of the mode. As an example, the first active interval for *move1* is approximately from time 48 to time 65, while the first active interval for *busy1* is from time 48 to time 98. This particular execution indicates that whenever the rod is moving, its controller is busy. For this computation, then, the modechart specification does appear to be functioning as intended.

The third type of analysis, also supported by the Modechart Toolset, is verification. Although the simulation of Figure 2.2 indicates that the specification does behave as desired in one computation, it can offer no guarantees that the specification is actually correct, since it does not rule out the specification behaving incorrectly in some other computation, or even at some later point in the computation being simulated. To actually prove the correctness of the specification it is necessary to examine all of the computations of the specification. The initial approach to verification provided by the Modechart Toolset is that of model checking. The model checking approach involves constructing a finite model of all of the behaviors of the specification, and then examining that model to ensure the correctness of all of the behaviors so represented. The particular finite model representation used by the Modechart Toolset verifier is the *computation graph*. Figure 2.3 is the computation graph of the specification of Figure 2.1. Each point in the computation graph is a configuration of the specification, and each edge in the graph represents a transition of the specification. Using this computation graph, the Modechart verifier can be used to prove that whenever mode *move1* is active, mode *busy1* is active as well. This ensures that the specification behaves correctly at all times in all computations, while the simulation just indicated the correctness of the specification in a segment of one computation.

This section has provided a brief introduction and overview of the specification language Modechart, and the analysis techniques and tools that can be used to analyze Modechart specifications. The remainder of this chapter will provide a more detailed tutorial introduction. The next section will briefly introduce the computation model used by Modechart. Section 2.3 will introduce Modechart. Sections 2.4 and 2.5 will introduce the Modechart simulator and verifier respectively. Section 2.6 will explore the nuclear reactor example in more detail.

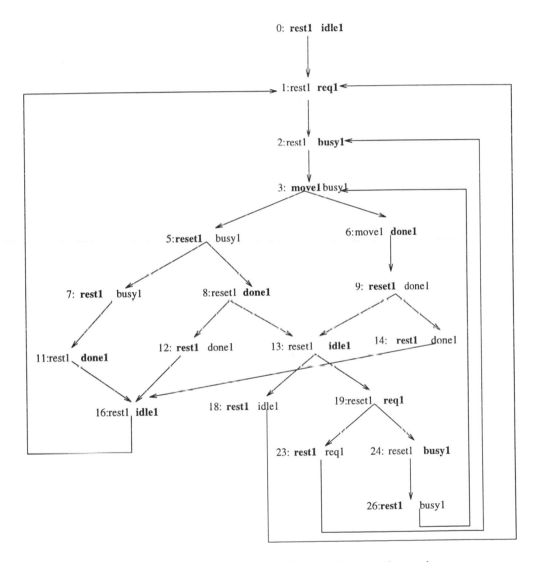

Figure 2.3   Nuclear reactor controller and rod computation graph

2.2   THE MODECHART COMPUTATION MODEL

A specification language such as Modechart provides a means of describing real-time systems in a precise way, and for formally showing that a specification in the language satisfies certain properties. Although some properties may be purely syntactic, such as the size of the specification, or the number of processes or agents, most properties of interest are semantic properties, that is, requirements on the behaviors of the specification. Before proceeding to a more detailed introduction to Modechart, the computation model that will be used to represent the computations of a Modechart specification must first be introduced.

Modechart regards a specification as a collection of events. The building block of a Modechart computation is the event occurrence. An event occurrence is a time-stamped event, representing the occurrence of the event at the indicated time. A computation of a Modechart specification is a set of time-stamped event occurrences. Since each specification is finite, there are only a finite number of events in each specification, so an infinite computation will contain an infinite number of occurrences of at least one event. The formal definition of what it means for a computation to satisfy a modechart can be found in [JM94].

Intuitively, a computation can be regarded as a sequence of sets of event occurrences, where all of the event occurrences in the same set have the same time-stamp. Since Modechart is primarily concerned with timing properties of specifications, in the sense of properties that can be expressed in terms of the times of various event occurrences, the only ordering on the events of a computation considered by Modechart is the ordering introduced by the time-stamps on the individual event occurrences. As a consequence, event occurrences with the same time-stamp are truly considered to be simultaneous, neither is considered to precede the other. This feature of Modechart computations must be borne in mind when writing Modechart specifications, and some of the consequences of this will be seen in subsequent sections.

As a final note on computations of Modechart specifications, Modechart uses a discrete time model. This means that the events in a computation occur at integer times, and more importantly, with a fixed minimum separation between non-simultaneous events. This is in contrast to continuous time, where event occurrences could have real time-stamps, and so non-simultaneous events could be arbitrarily close.

2.3   THE MODECHART SPECIFICATION LANGUAGE

As indicated in section 2.1, Modechart is a hierarchical graphical specification language for real-time systems. The two basic elements from which Modechart specifications are constructed are *modes* and *transitions*. Modes represent the control state of the system being specified. Transitions represent the flow of control of the system being specified.

Each mode in a specification, or modechart, must be one of three types. *Atomic* modes have no internal structure, and are the basic building blocks of a specification. Referring to Figure 2.1, the atomic modes are *rest1*, *reset1*, *move1*, *idle1*, *req1*, *done1*, and *busy1*. Each represents a primitive control state of the system.

Serial modes have internal structure. Each serial mode has at least one child mode, and has a designated child mode which serves as an *initial mode*. A serial mode represents the sequential composition of its children, and the children of a serial mode are considered to be in series. Accordingly, at any time a serial mode is active, exactly one of its child modes must also be active. The initial mode of the serial mode is the mode that is considered to be entered when the serial mode itself is entered, unless some other child of the serial mode is entered explicitly. Referring again to Figure 2.1, the serial modes in the specification are *rod1* with initial mode *rest1*, and *controller1*, with initial mode *idle1*. In figures, the initial mode of a serial mode will be designated with a **bold** outline. In any computation of the specification of Figure 2.1, whenever *rod1* is active, exactly one of *rest1*, *reset1* and *move1* will be active.

Parallel modes also have internal structure. Each parallel mode has a number (possibly zero) of children. Although a parallel mode with zero children is syntactically legal, it is in practice equivalent to an atomic mode. A parallel mode represents the parallel composition of its children, and the children of a parallel mode are considered to be in parallel. Accordingly, at any time a parallel mode is active, all of its child modes must also be active. Turning again to Figure 2.1, there is only a single parallel mode, *nuke*, which represents the entire specification. The children of *nuke* are *rod1* and *controller1*.

While modes represent the control state of a system, the control flow among control states is represented by *transitions*. Graphically, a transition is a directed edge between modes. Each transition therefore has a source mode and a destination mode. Taking a transition from one mode to another represents control leaving the state represented by the source mode and being transferred to the destination mode, and is considered to be instantaneous. Since all of the children of a parallel mode must be active when the parallel mode is itself active, transitions are only possible between children of a serial mode, that is, modes that are in series. However, since Modechart is a hierarchical language, a transition could have its source mode inside one child mode of a serial mode, and its destination inside a different child of the same serial mode. Accordingly, this requirement is more properly that the first common ancestor of the source and destination modes of a transition must be a serial mode, or the transition must be a self loop, and the parent of the source and destination mode must be a serial mode. Recalling the modechart specification in Figure 2.1, there are three transitions among the children of *rod1*, and four transitions among the children of *controller1*. There is a transition in *rod1* with source mode *rest1* and destination *move1*.

Before turning to the question of when transitions can be taken, which is a semantic rather than syntactic issue, it is necessary to provide the link between the syntax of Modechart being described here, and the computation model presented in the preceding section. Since the computation model views a system as a collection of events, it is necessary to identify the events associated with modes and transitions. Since an event is a point in time at which something occurs, a mode being active is not an event. The events associated with modes are the entry and exit of the mode. Syntactically, the entry event for mode M is denoted by $\rightarrow M$, and the exit event for mode M is denoted by $M \rightarrow$. The event associated with a transition is the event of the transition being taken, known as the transition event. The transition event for a transition from mode $M1$ to mode $M2$ is represented as $M1 \rightarrow M2$. Every computation of a modechart will consist solely of mode entry and exit events and transition events. Accordingly, every computation of the modechart of Figure 2.1 will consist of one or more occurrences of each of the 27 distinct events, the 20 entry and exit events of the 10 modes in the modechart, and the 7 transition events of the 7 transitions.

Having defined the events of the specification, in order to define the computations of the specification, it remains only to establish when transitions among modes are taken. Conditions are associated with transitions to govern when they may be taken. Each transition has exactly one condition associated with it, and that condition is in disjunctive normal form. Each disjunct is either a *timing condition* or a *triggering condition*.

A timing condition consists of a *delay* and a *deadline*. The delay and deadline are both non-negative integers, and the deadline must be greater than or equal to the delay. A timing condition with delay r and deadline d is denoted (r,d). There are also a number of abbreviations for some special timing constraints. *(delay r)* is an abbreviation for (r, ∞). *(alarm r)* is an abbreviation for (r, r). *(deadline d)* is an abbreviation for $(0, d)$. Referring again to Figure 2.1, the condition on the transition $move1 \rightarrow reset1$ is the timing constraint *(1, 50)*, representing a delay of 1 and a deadline of 50, and the condition on the transition $done1 \rightarrow idle1$ is *(alarm 2)*, representing a delay and deadline of 2. A timing condition is satisfied if the source mode of the transition with the timing condition has been active at least as long as the delay of the timing condition.

A triggering condition is a conjunction of events and predicates, which is satisfied when all of the events in the triggering condition occur while all of the predicates are also true. A triggering condition is considered to have a deadline of zero with respect to the time at which the condition becomes true. This is in contrast with the deadline (and the delay) of a timing condition, which is with respect to the time at which the source mode is entered. Each conjunct of a triggering condition must be one of the following:

- The event $\rightarrow M$ is satisfied when mode M is entered.
- The event $M \rightarrow$ is satisfied when mode M is exited.
- The event $M1 \rightarrow M2$ is satisfied when the transition $M1 \rightarrow M2$ is taken.
- The predicate $M == true$ is satisfied if mode M is active.
- The predicate $M == false$ is satisfied if mode M is not active.
- The mode list predicate $\{(M1, \ldots, MN)\}$ is satisfied if any of the modes in the list are active.
- The before list predicate $\{< M1, \ldots, MN)\}$ is satisfied if any of the modes in the list are active and have been active for at least one time unit.

Note that at the time instant when a mode is entered or exited, the mode is considered to be both active and inactive. It is important to consider this when constructing triggering conditions on transitions.

The only triggering condition in Figure 2.1 is on the transition $rest1 \rightarrow move1$, and consists of the single event $\rightarrow busy1$, which is the entry event for the mode *busy1*.

A transition may only be taken at a time at which one or more of its condition's disjuncts, of either type, are satisfied. A condition being satisfied is a necessary condition for the transition to be taken, but does not force the transition to be taken. The deadline on a transition does however impose a requirement that the source mode of the transition must be exited at or before the time indicated by the deadline of the condition. The delay on a timing constraint, and the condition of a triggering condition, can therefore be regarded as permitting the transition to be taken, while the deadline on either type of condition is a requirement for the source mode to be exited by some transition, not necessarily the transition with the deadline. This distinction is only relevant, though, if there is more than one transition that exits the source mode. A deadline of infinity therefore imposes no restriction at all, and indicates that the transition need never be taken. Therefore, a timing condition $(0, \infty)$ indicates a transition that may be taken with complete discretion.

Referring to Figure 2.1, $rest1 \rightarrow move1$ may be taken at any time the event $\rightarrow busy1$ occurs, that is when the mode *busy1* is entered, and any time $\rightarrow busy1$ occurs, the source mode of the transition, *rest1*, must be exited. Since there is only the one transition leaving *rest1*, the transition to be taken must be *rest1* → *move1*. Similarly, the transition *move1* → *reset1* may be taken one time unit after mode *move1* is entered, and must be taken no later than 50 time units after *move* is entered.

As indicated, the effect of taking a transition is to exit the source mode of the transition and to enter the destination mode. Taking a transition must maintain the relationships among serial and parallel modes and their children established previously. A transition actually exits the child of the serial mode that is the least common ancestor of the source and destination modes that contains the source mode, and likewise enters the child of the common ancestor that is the ancestor of the destination mode. In addition, a transition exits all active children of any mode that is exited. A transition enters all of the ancestors of the destination mode that are also descendants of the common serial mode. Also, for each parallel mode entered, all of its children are entered (and considered active). For each serial mode entered its initial mode is entered, unless one of its children is an ancestor of the destination mode. A mode that is exited or entered by a transition is said to be *explicitly* exited or entered if the edge representing the transition originates or ends at the mode, or a descendant of the mode. Any other mode exited or entered by the transition is said to be *implicitly* exited or entered. In the case of Figure 2.1, no transition implicitly enters or exits any mode. The transition *rest1* → *move1* explicitly exits the mode *rest1*, and explicitly enters the mode *move1*. In Figure 2.10, *control_fl*, *init_cf*, *rod1_fl*, *init_flr1*, *rod2_fl* and *init_flr2* are all entered implicitly by the transition *ready_ch* → *full*, which explicitly exits *ready_ch*, *control_hf*, and *half*, and implicitly exits *rod1_hf*, *rod2_hf*, and their active children.

Finally, to complete this discussion of the semantics of modechart specifications, the *root mode* is the outermost mode in the specification, and the only mode which has no parent. Each computation begins with the entry of the root mode at time 0, together with those modes that would be entered if the root mode were explicitly entered by a transition, that is, all children of each parallel mode entered, and the initial child of each serial mode entered. The remaining events in the computation are the result of transitions that are taken.

The root mode of the specification in Figure 2.1 is *nuke*. The modes initially entered are *nuke*, *controller1*, *idle1*, *rod1*, and *rest1*, so any computation of this modechart must include the first occurrences of the events → *nuke*, → *controller1*, → *idle1*, → *rod1*, and → *rest1* among those that occur at time zero. The computation that consists solely of the entry events of the initial modes is one computation of this specification, since the only transition that can be satisfied by this collection of events, and has an active source mode, is the transition *idle1* → *req1*. This transition has timing condition (*deadline*∞), therefore no other event need even occur. Another possible computation would result if the transitions *idle1* → *req1*, *req1* → *busy1*, and *rest1* → *move1* all occur at time 100, *move1* → *reset1* and *busy1* → *done1* both occur at time 150, and *reset1* → *rest1* and *done1* → *idle1* both occur at time 152.

The Modechart Toolset, MT, includes a tool for creating, modifying, and browsing Modechart specifications. The tool can also automatically generate Postscript versions of specifications, and this facility has been used to generate the modechart in Figure 2.1. The tool consists of four windows. The Modechart window controls the top level behavior of the tool. The Specification window controls specification level behavior, such as selecting an analysis tool to apply to the specification. The Locator window provides an overview of the entire specification, and serves as a scrollbar. The Work window provides a detailed view of the portion of the specification specified by the Locator window, and is used to manipulate the specification. The nuclear reactor example, a part of which is represented by the modechart

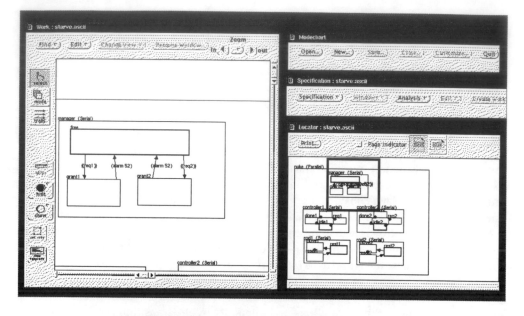

Figure 2.4   The Modechart Toolset

of Figure 2.1, consists of two rods and two controllers, and a manager which ensures that the two rods are not in motion at the same time. Figure 2.4 shows one possible specification for the entire nuclear reactor system loaded into the toolset.

The modechart in Figure 2.4 consists of the parallel root mode *nuke*, which has five serial children. The two rod controller pairs, *controller1* and *rod1* and *controller2* and *rod2* are similar to *controller1* and *rod1* from Figure 2.1, and differ only from the specification in Figure 2.1 in the condition on the transition from *reqi* to *busyi*. The fifth serial mode, *manager*, is new, and its function is to prevent the two rods from moving simultaneously. It does so by granting permission to the controllers to begin moving. The manager consists of three modes. The mode *free* represents neither rod having permission to move. The mode *grant1* represents *rod1* having permission to move, so that the condition on the transition $refor1 \rightarrow busy1$ is $\rightarrow grant1$. Similarly, *grant2* represents *rod2* having permission to move. Since each control rod moves for at most 50 time units once it has permission to move, the condition on the transitions back into *free* is the timing condition *(alarm 52)*. Choosing 52 rather than 50 ensures that there is a one time unit margin before and after a rod's movement during which the other rod does not have permission to move. 50 time units is sufficient to guarantee that there is no positive length interval during which both rods could be moving, but would allow for the possibility that one rod would begin moving the instant that the other stopped moving.

The design decision that must be addressed carefully is the conditions on the transitions into each granting mode. One possibility would be the entry event for the corresponding requesting mode. This is not a good choice, since an event condition of this type is only satisfied at the instant that the requesting mode is entered. Therefore, if a rod requested permission to move when the manager was unable to grant it, that rod would never gain permission to move, since the requesting mode could not be entered again until it had already received permission and moved the rod. In this case, a predicate triggering condition is necessary. There are a number of possible choices, one being a mode list predicate consisting only of the request mode. Accordingly, as in the figure, the condition on the transition $free \rightarrow grant1$ is $\{(req1)\}$, and similarly for the condition on $free \rightarrow grant2$.

2.4   THE MODECHART SIMULATOR

The preceding section concluded by introducing one possible specification for the nuclear reactor system. All of the elements required by the specification, two rods, two controllers, and a manager, are present. What are the behaviors of this specification? The intended behavior is that each rod controller should seek permission to move its individual rod, wait for permission from the manager, begin moving the rod, and then return to the idle state, eventually issuing another request. Also, the manager should ensure that at most one rod is moving at any time. Does the specification in fact exhibit this behavior? The answer to this question requires analysis of the computations of the specification.

As indicated, the Modechart Toolset supports two main semantic analysis tools, a simulator and a verifier. The simulator allows examination of hopefully representative computations, while the verifier considers all computations. First the simulator will be used to generate an individual computation for examination, to see if the computation conforms to the expected behavior.

The Modechart Simulator generates a single execution of the system as specified by a modechart specification. It begins by generating the entry events for all of the initial modes of the specification. Then, each time instant, including time 0, it attempts to take eligible transitions. Each time instant, the set of transitions with satisfied conditions is generated. A transition from this set is chosen and executed, changing the active modes and the current events. After each transition is executed, the set of transitions with satisfied conditions is updated by removing transitions with source modes that are no longer active, and adding transitions with conditions newly satisfied by the events caused by the just executed transitions, and those transitions from newly active modes with satisfied transitions. This process is repeated until either no more transitions with satisfied conditions are available, or no transition with a satisfied condition has a zero deadline, and the simulator elects not to take any of the remaining eligible transitions. In either case, the clock is then incremented to reflect the passage of a single time unit, and the process of taking transitions is begun again.

Since the simulator produces only a single execution, and a modechart specification will generally have more than one execution, the simulator must select a single execution from multiple candidates. As indicated in the preceding section, there are two types of choice the simulator must make. The first is a choice among competing transitions which exit the same source mode. The second is when not to take a transition with a satisfied condition which has an unexpired deadline. This is equivalent to deciding when to schedule a transition with a timing condition.

The simulator accepts as input, in addition to the specification, an *options file*. This file allows the user to give instructions to the simulator on how such non-deterministic choices are to be made. Four choices are available to the user for each transition. The user may designate that a transition is always to be taken as soon as possible (as soon as the delay transpires), as late as possible (only when the deadline is reached), at a specific time (always after 10 time units), or randomly, in which case the simulator makes a choice from a random distribution. The options file is supplied by the user at the beginning of a given run of the simulator.

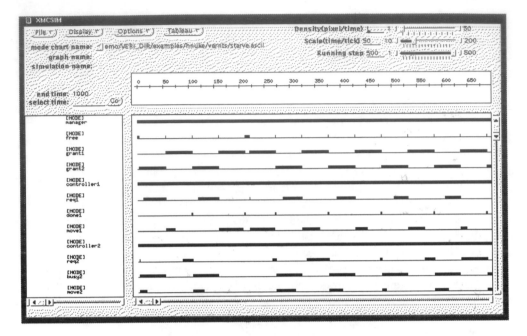

Figure 2.5   Simulating the nuclear reactor

The options file also provides the user with a means for determining the length of the simulation. The user may supply an absolute length, a step size, and breakpoints. The run length determines how long the simulation will run without user direction for further execution. The step size allows the user to step through the execution at a desired time granularity. Breakpoints, analogous to breakpoints in debuggers, allow the user to designate events the occurrence of which will cause the simulation to halt.

Figure 2.5 shows the result of simulating the nuclear reactor specification of Figure 2.4 for 1000 time units. The simulator window contains four major areas. The top area contains the various controls and menus for the simulator. The three display areas show the results of the simulation graphically. The top display area shows a simple time-line, the scale of which can be varied by the user. The bottom two areas display the activity of the system specified during the simulation. The left window is a legend for the main display area. For each mode and transition in the left window there is a line representing the behavior of that mode or transition in the right window. In the case of a transition, the line represents when the transition's condition is satisfied, and when it is taken. For a mode, a thin line indicates that the mode is not active, while a thick line indicates that the mode is active. Which individual modes and events are tracked in the display area is also determined by the options file.

In the case of Figure 2.5, all of the objects being tracked are modes. The top four modes are *manager*, *free*, *grant1*, and *grant2*. Since *manager* is a child of *nuke*, which is the root mode, and a parallel mode, it will always be active, indicated in the figure by the line for the mode being thick throughout the simulation. Accordingly, no information is conferred by including it in the monitored set of modes. However, doing so can be helpful by providing a visual separator. The three lines directly below the first solid line are the lines for the children of that mode. Note that the manager is seldom in *free*, and appears to grant requests by both rods.

The middle four lines in Figure 2.5 represent some of the modes associated with the first rod. The modes in question are *controller1* as a separator, and then *req1*, *done1* and *move1*. Examining this portion of the display, it would appear that the rod only moves following a request, and that all of the requests are being granted, although generally after a delay, that the rod then moves, and only enters done after the rod has finished moving, as intended.

The final four lines in Figure 2.5 represent modes associated with the second rod. In this case the modes in question are *controller2*, again as a separator, *req2*, *busy2*, and *move2*. In this case, examining the display indicates that the second rod also follows the request-move pattern, although it tends not to wait as long as the first rod for its requests to be granted. Also, the controller does move the rod only when mode *busy2* has been entered.

This computation behaves as anticipated. Examining the display in its entirety, each rod moves only while it has been granted permission by the manager, since each move mode is active only while the corresponding grant mode is active. The active intervals for the two move modes do not appear to overlap. Also, each of the rods gets permission to move each time permission is requested; neither control rod appears to starve. All of these, however, are only observations based on examining a single execution. This illustrates the advantages and disadvantages of simulation. It provides insight into the behavior of the system being simulated, and allows for the formation of hypotheses, but it does not make any guarantee about universally valid attributes of the specification, as indicated in the next section.

2.5 THE MODECHART VERIFIER

The previous section used the Modechart simulator to examine the nuclear reactor specification. Although such examination may provide valuable insight into the behavior of the system being specified, and be valuable in other ways, it can not guarantee the correctness of the specification. Simulation produces a single presumably typical execution. Correctness requires the examination of all executions. Since most modecharts have a number of computations, simulation is inadequate for the task of verifying the correctness of a specification. The Modechart Toolset provides a verification tool for this purpose. Figure 2.6 shows the graphical interface to the verification tool.

There are a number of verification techniques available for real-time systems. The Modechart Verifier performs verification using *model checking*. The model checking approach is to construct a finite representation, or model, that encompasses all of the computations of the system being verified. The desired correctness properties are then checked against the model. If the property holds for the model, then it must hold for all of the computations of the specification. Model checking therefore requires both a finite representation of the computations of a specification, and a way of representing the properties to be checked.

As indicated in the introduction, the model for the computations of a Modechart specification is the *computation graph*. A computation graph is a directed graph. The vertices, called *points*, represent points in time at which events occur. Accordingly, points can also be considered to represent the configuration of the system after the occurrence of the event represented by the point. Vertices are labeled with the modes active at the time represented by the point, as in Figure 2.3. Modes that are always active are omitted from the labels of points in the figures. The edges represent the occurrence of transitions. The mode entered at the point, by the transition or transitions entering the point, is indicated in the figure by having its name appear in **bold**. Point number *1* is labeled 1: **req1**, rest1, indicating that in point 1, the modes *req1* and *rest1* are active, and the point represents the entry of *req1* as a result of taking the transition *idle1* → *req1*.

Since transitions are instantaneous, and there may be several transitions at the same time, time must pass in the configurations represented by the points of the computation graph. The amount of time that may be spent in a given point is determined by the *timing constraints* imposed on the transitions which can be taken from the point. These timing constraints include any timing conditions on transitions from the point, and along a sequence of transitions, or path, leading to the point, as well as the effect of the implied deadline on any triggering conditions. For any path through the graph, these cumulative effects are captured using a separation graph, and may be calculated as a path weight in such a graph. Using this information, the transitions which can actually be taken from a given point, and so appear as edges from the point in the computation graph, may be identified. Points may be distinguished by their label, or by being subject to different timing constraints. For example, in Figure 2.3, points 12 and 14 have the same label, but are subject to different timing constraints: point 16 may happen 2 time units after point 12, but only 1 time unit after point 14.

As an example, returning to Figure 2.3, there are two transitions from modes active in point 6, the transition *move1* → *reset1*, which appears in the figure, and the transition *done1* → *idle1*, which does not appear. The reason it does not appear, is that the timing constraints that lead up to point 6 force the transition *move1* → *reset1* to happen at the same time as point 6, while the timing condition on *done1* → *idle1* ensures that it must happen strictly later than point 6, so that *done1* → *idle1* may not happen at point 6, otherwise the transition *move1* → *reset1* would miss its deadline.

Model checking also requires a formal representation for the properties to be checked. The Modechart Toolset uses the first order logic RTL, Real Time Logic ([JM86]), to formally represent properties of Modechart specifications. In fact Modechart was originally developed as a way of organizing system specifications written in RTL. RTL is a first order logic, consisting of the usual first order connectives and quantifiers, plus the relations and operators of integer addition. Multiplication is not allowed, except for multiplication by a constant as an abbreviation for repeated addition.

The link between the logic and the computations of a modechart specification is provided by the *occurrence function*. The occurrence function, denoted by @, is a function with two arguments. The first argument is an event, and the second argument is an integer. The value of the function is the time of the indicated occurrence of the event. For example, $@(\rightarrow req1, i+4)$ is the time of the $i + 4th$ entry into the mode *req1*.

The key correctness property of the nuclear reactor example, that both of the rods may not be in motion at the same time, can be written

$$\forall i \forall j @(move2 \rightarrow, j) \leq @(\rightarrow move1, i) \vee @(move1 \rightarrow, i) \leq @(\rightarrow move2, j).$$

It states that for every interval in which rod one is moving, so that *move1* is active, every interval in which *move2* is active either ends before the activation interval for *move1* begins, or starts after the interval for *move1* has ended. The result of instantiating this formula as a query for the verifier of the Modechart Toolset can be seen in Figure 2.7

The current verifier implements a number of queries which check the computation graph to determine the satisfiability or validity of formulas which match templates supplied by the verifier for modecharts satisfying appropriate technical restrictions. Formula templates provided cover a wide range of useful properties, including mode activation interval exclusion, such as the correctness formula for the nuclear reactor example above (Figure 2.7), mode activation interval inclusion, event minimum and maximum separation, and the minimum and maximum activation intervals of a mode, which will be used to determine the presence or absence of starvation for the nuclear reactor example at the end of this section (Figure 2.8). Future work will extend the subset of RTL for which such templates are provided, although arbitrary RTL formulas can not be checked, since it was shown in [Jah89] that the model checking problem for arbitrary modecharts and arbitrary RTL formulas is undecidable.

Figure 2.6 shows the verifier tool of the Modechart Toolset after constructing the computation graph for the nuclear reactor modechart. The top section of the tool includes the various command menus, and displays information about the specification and the computation graph. The middle section is used to select and identify various elements of the specification and computation graph that can be used to build queries which can be applied to the computation graph. The bottom section is an output window for text output. In the figure, it contains statistical information about the computation graph, including the number of points and edges in the graph, 100 and 334 respectively.

Figure 2.7 shows a query window for the formula template corresponding to the mutual exclusion property for rod movement, instantiated to the formula above, and with the result indicated that the formula is in fact true, as intended, and as indicated by the simulation. Figure 2.8 shows a second query window. This one indicates the minimum and maximum times the mode *req1* may be active. Although the minimum time is 0, the maximum time is infinity, indicating that rod one could starve, contrary to the indications of the simulation. This example illustrates the advantages of simulation, that it can provide insight into the operation of the system being specified, and indications of its correctness, but that it can also be misleading, as in this case, where the simulation did not exhibit starvation that verification did uncover.

2.6   A SPECIFICATION FOR A NUCLEAR REACTOR

The previous sections introduced the Modechart specification language and the Modechart Toolset using the nuclear reactor example. This section will further develop the nuclear reactor specification to illustrate how Modechart and the Toolset can be used to develop a specification.

The nuclear reactor specification of Figure 2.4 was correct in that it prevented both control rods from moving simultaneously. However, as revealed by the verifier in the preceding section, it is possible for the manager to starve either of the control rods. Examining the specification, the reason for this becomes clear. The *manager* is ready to grant permission to a control rod at 52 time unit intervals. It also takes 52 time units for a rod controller to make the cycle from request to request, so that it is possible for a controller to submit a new request at the beginning of every decision cycle for the manager. Since the manager non-deterministically selects between the competing rods, it could forever ignore one of the rods on some computation, because the other rod could continue asking for and receiving permission to move as frequently as possible.

How can a manager be written to prevent starvation? There are several approaches. One approach is for the manager to remember which rod is supposed to next receive permission to move if both are requesting permission. A possible manager modechart that does this is given in Figure 2.9. In this modechart, once permission is granted to move a particular rod, if a request for the other rod arrives before the moving rod is finished, the manager moves to

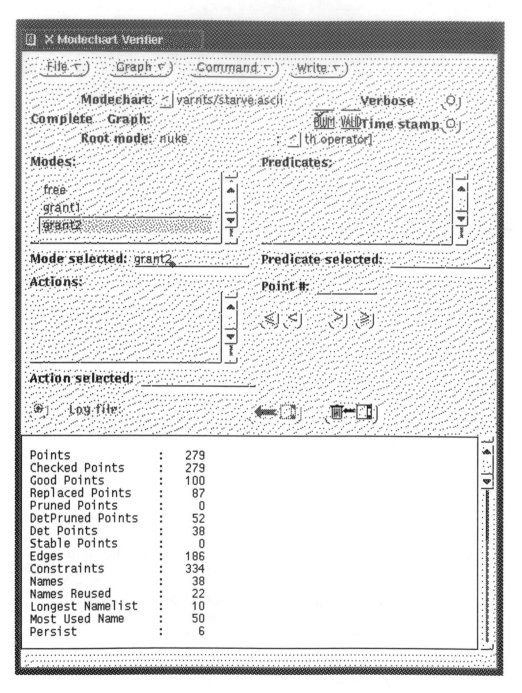

Figure 2.6   The Modechart Verifier

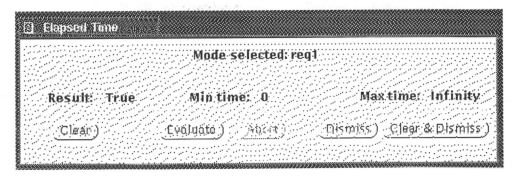

Figure 2.7 The Modechart Verifier

Figure 2.8 The Modechart Verifier

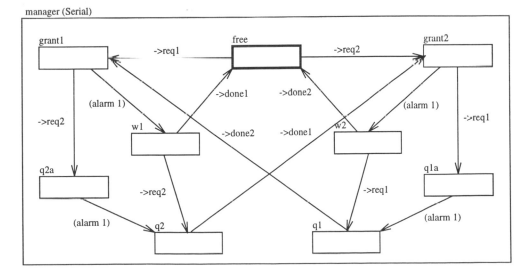

Figure 2.9 A starvation free manager

a mode reflecting the queuing of this request, in the case of a request for rod2 while rod1 is moving, to *q2*. When the moving rod finishes, either the manager returns to *free* if there is no queued request, or to the appropriate grant mode if there is a queued request. The verifier confirms that this solution is still correct, and also does not permit starvation.

This modechart also illustrates a number of unusual features of Modechart that must be considered when writing Modechart specifications. Note that the queuing modes are essentially split in two. For example, there are modes *q2* and *q2a* that both represent a queuing of *req2*. The second is entered directly from *grant1* on the arrival of a request. The first is entered if a request arrives while in *w1*, which is itself entered one time unit after the request is granted, if a request for rod2 does not arrive earlier. The purpose of this construction is to eliminate the possibility of a *zero cycle*. A zero cycle is a sequence of transitions that can be taken simultaneously, such that the destination mode of the final transition is the source mode of the first transition. Such a cycle could require an infinite number of events to happen in zero time, since the cycle could be repeated as often as desired. Such computations are considered illegal, and a purported Modechart containing such a cycle is not considered to be a valid Modechart. In this case, if the *(alarm 1)* transitions were not present, and there was an edge directly from *grant1* to *free* with condition $\rightarrow$ *done1*, and rod1 requested permission to move immediately when it finished, there would be a zero cycle from *grant1* to *free* and back, since both conditions, $\rightarrow$ *done1* and $\rightarrow$ *req1* would be true at that time. Also, if rod1 and rod2 both requested permission at the same time as rod1 finished, the manager could move from *grant1* to *free* to *grant1* to *q2* to *grant2* all at the same time, giving both rods permission to move, violating mutual exclusion of rod movement.

This manager, while it results in a correct and starvation free specification, is complex. It also requires communication between the controllers and the manager both when permission is sought to move a rod, and also when movement is completed, which was not needed by the previous specification. Examining the earlier specification, it can be seen that starvation occurs because a request is granted immediately to any requesting controller, without regard to how long the request has been outstanding. One simple modification to change this results in a specification that is both correct and starvation free. Changing the transition condition on the transition *free* $\rightarrow$ *grant1* to $\{< req1)\}$, and changing the condition on the transition *free* $\rightarrow$ *grant2* to $\{< req2)\}$ accomplishes this. The reasoning behind this change is that when a a controller re-requests permission at the same time it completes the previous move, the request arrives at the same time as the manager enters *free*. However, since a before list requires the mode in the list be active for the preceding time unit, a rod that has been waiting for permission will satisfy the condition, while the new request will not. This specification is smaller and simpler, and may be better than the one in Figure 2.9.

The modecharts in all of the examples to this point have all been *flat*. Each has consisted of a parallel root mode with a number of serial children, each of which had only atomic children. This section will conclude with an example of a modechart which is not flat, which has a more complex hierarchical arrangement. The previous versions of the nuclear reactor example have all dealt only with ensuring the mutual exclusion and non-starvation of the movement of the control rods in the reactor. The causes of requests to move the control rods have been ignored. Each controller decides with complete freedom when to request permission to move its control rod. This final example will add an operator, shown in Figure 2.10, which decides when the control rods will be moved.

Since there are two control rods, the operator has three choices for the power level produced by the reactor. Either no rods are moved in, one rod is moved in, or both rods are moved in. In

operator (Serial)

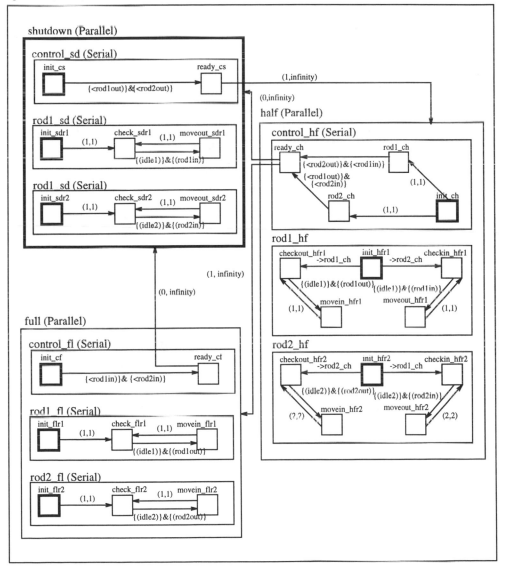

Figure 2.10 Nuclear reactor operator

the first case, the reactor is operating at full power, in the second half power, and if both rods are in, the reactor is shutdown. The operator will therefore be represented by a serial mode with three children, one for each mode of operation of the reactor. In this case, however, these three children will not be atomic, since they must govern the operation of the control rods. Since each mode is responsible for two control rods, as well as deciding what to do, each of these modes will be a parallel mode with three children. Looking first at the *shutdown* mode, each control rod must be inserted, so the modes responsible for each rod must just ensure that its rod is in. The mode *control_sd*, which controls the behavior of the shutdown mode, is just a simple serial mode with an initial mode, and a *ready_cs* mode to be entered when both rods are in. The *full* mode is similar. The *half* mode is slightly more complicated, since the decision mode, *control_hf*, must decide which rod will be in and which will be out. Similarly, the controllers for the individual rods must first find out which position their rod should be in before taking any action. Finally, since the current position of the mode is necessary, not just whether or not it is moving, a serial child of the root mode is added for each rod to monitor its location. The modes required for this are not shown.

Note that there are transitions in *operator* which occur within the lowest level serial modes, but also which come from the lowest level atomic modes, and leave the serial mode that contains them, such as the transition from *ready_cs* to *half*. Such a transition leaves not only the source mode, but also any active modes in parallel with it. In the given example, the transition leaves not only *ready_cs* but also *rod1_sd* and *rod2_sd* and their active children implicitly, and *shutdown* itself explicitly.

This final specification has also been subjected to analysis using the Modechart Toolset. We have used the Verification tool to show that this version of the specification is also correct and without starvation.

2.7   CONCLUSION

This chapter has illustrated how Modechart can be used to specify a real-time system through various stages of refinement. In this process, two powerful analysis techniques, simulation and verification, were used to examine the correctness of the specification. This analysis leads to insights which were used to create a better final specification. This chapter has also provided a brief introduction to the Modechart Toolset, which includes an interface tool for creating, editing, and browsing specifications, a simulation tool, and a verification tool. The toolset was used to mechanically examine the specification, validating expectations about typical behaviors, and verifying the correctness of the specification over all behaviors. More detailed information about the Modechart specification language can be found in [JLM88] and [JM94]. Simulating Modechart specifications is covered in [CHLR93]. The theoretical framework for the verifier is in [JS88] and [Stu90]. Finally, [RPC94] is a detailed user's guide for the Modechart Toolset.

In the introduction, a methodology was proposed envisioning specification, verification and validation as a collaborative process involving the user and mechanical support. What has been outlined in this chapter is the kernel of such an approach, although there are indications of the collaboration even in this introduction. The property that *rod1* was in mode *move1* only while *controller1* is in *busy1* is verified in the introduction. The same property holds for all of the modecharts in this chapter, and for both control rods, and can be established by verification of the property for each of the control rods for each specification. However, the only impact the remainder of the specification has on this property is in the timing of the transitions $idle \rightarrow req$ and $req \rightarrow busy$. The verification performed in the introduction ensures that the property holds if these transitions occur at arbitrary times. Therefore, the property will also hold if the transitions occur only at designated times, since such computations are included in those already checked, and so verification of this property for the modechart of Figure 2.1 is sufficient to guarantee that it also holds for all of the modecharts of this chapter. This technique of considering only those portions of the specification that can affect a particular property under consideration is known as *focussing*. Also, since all of the modecharts are symmetric in the two control rods, it is also sufficient to check the property for a single control rod.

ACKNOWLEDGMENTS

The authors would like to acknowledge the efforts of Connie Heitmeyer's group at NRL and Paul Clements, Alex Ho, Jin Yang, Dennis Chen and Helen Wang at the University of Texas in the design and implementation of the Modechart Toolset.

REFERENCES

[CHLR93] P. C. Clements, C. L. Heitmeyer, B. G. Labaw, and A. T. Rose. MT: A toolset for specifying and analyzing real-time systems. In *Proc. IEEE Real-Time Systems Symposium*, December 1993.

[Har87] D. Harel. Statecharts: A visual formalism for complex systems. *Science of Computer Programming*, (8):231–274, 1987.

[Jah89] F. Jahanian. Verifying properties of systems with variable timing constraints. In *Proceedings of the Tenth Real-Time Systems Symposium*, Santa Monica, California, December 1989.

[JLM88] F. Jahanian, R.S. Lee, and A.K. Mok. Semantics of modechart in real time logic. In *Proc. of 21st Hawaii International Conference on System Sciences*, January 1988.

[JM86] F. Jahanian and A.K. Mok. Safety analysis of timing properties in real-time systems. *IEEE Trans. Software Engineering*, SE-12(9):890–904, September 1986.

[JM94] F. Jahanian and A. K. Mok. Modechart: A specification language for real-time systems. *IEEE Trans. Software Engineering*, 20(12), 1994.

[JS88] F. Jahanian and D. A. Stuart. A method for verifying properties of modechart specifications. In *Proc. IEEE Real-Time Systems Symposium*, pages 12–21, Huntsville, AL, December 1988.

[RPC94] A. Rose, M. Perez, and P. Clements. Modechart toolset user's guide. Technical Report NRL/MRL/5540-94-7427, Center for Computer High Assurance Systems, Naval Research Lab, Washington, D.C., February 1994.

[Stu90] D. A. Stuart. Implementing a verifier for real-time systems. In *Proc. IEEE Real-Time Systems Symposium*, pages 62–71, Orlando, FL, December 1990.

3

Automata-Theoretic Verification of Real-Time Systems

RAJEEV ALUR
AT&T Bell Laboratories, New Jersey

DAVID L DILL
Stanford University, California

ABSTRACT

We propose *timed (finite) automata* to model the behavior of real-time systems over time. Our definition provides a simple, and yet powerful, way to annotate state-transition graphs with timing constraints using finitely many real-valued *clocks*. A timed automaton accepts *timed words* — infinite sequences in which a real-valued time of occurrence is associated with each symbol. We study timed automata from the perspective of formal language theory: we consider closure properties, decision problems, and subclasses. We discuss the application of this theory to automatic verification of real-time requirements of finite-state systems. Finally, we give an overview of the heuristics employed by different tools to alleviate the computational complexity of the verification algorithm.

3.1 INTRODUCTION

Formal methods for specifying, analyzing, and manipulating the behavior of concurrent systems become much more attractive in practical use if they can be automated. A number of methods based on *finite-state* representations have achieved considerable success in practical applications such as protocol and hardware verification, precisely because many problems are decidable for finite-state representations. Finite-state verification methods include checking equivalences (such as bisimulation), preorders (such as simulation), temporal logic properties (eg. CTL model-checking), and inclusion of the language of one automaton in another.

Until recently, temporal logics and finite automata were primarily concerned with *qualitative* temporal reasoning about systems. For example, whether a system deadlocks or livelocks,

---

Formal Methods For Real-Time Computing, Edited by Heitmeyer and Mandrioli
© 1996 John Wiley & Sons Ltd

whether a property is always true, or whether some response eventually occurs. More recently, ways of extending finite-state techniques to timed systems have been discovered, which retain many of the desirable properties of conventional finite representations.

In this chapter, we will concentrate on *linear-time models*, although finite-state real-time techniques can also be applied to *branching-time* problems, such as (timed) CTL model-checking and bisimulation checking. In the *linear time model*, it is assumed that an execution can be completely modeled as a sequence of states or system events, called a *trace*. The *behavior* of the system is a set of such traces. Since a set of sequences is a formal language, this leads naturally to the use of automata for the specification and verification of systems. When the systems are finite-state, we can use finite automata, leading to effective constructions and decision procedures for *automatically* manipulating and analyzing system behavior.

In qualitative models, it is useful to describe non-terminating executions, so that *liveness* properties, such as "if a request occurs infinitely often, so does the response" can be expressed. Consequently many verification theories are based on the theory of ω-regular languages, which reasons about sets of infinite strings, instead of the finite strings usually considered in ordinary regular languages (e.g. the system COSPAN [Kur94] or the system HSIS [ABB+94]). In our linear real-time model, an execution is an infinite trace of events, and time is added by pairing each event of a trace with a time value. Time values are chosen from the set of real numbers. Such a model is called a *dense-time* model. The alternative *discrete-time* model uses integer time values, and requires that continuous time be approximated by choosing some fixed quantum *a priori*, which limits the accuracy with which physical systems can be modeled. Dealing with dense time in a finite-automata framework is more difficult than dealing with discrete time, because the transformation from a set of dense-time traces into an ordinary formal language is not obvious. Instead, we have developed a theory of *timed* formal languages and *timed automata* to support automated reasoning about such systems. The study of timed finite automata has yielded interesting theoretical results, and, if progress continues at its current rate, is likely to succeed in practice just as qualitative finite-state methods have.

Overview

We begin with an overview of ω-automata and verification for untimed systems (Section 2). Then, we define timed automata by augmenting ω-automata with a set of real-valued variables called *clocks*. The clocks can be reset to 0 (independently of each other) with the transitions of the automaton, and keep track of the time elapsed since the last reset. The transitions of the automaton put certain constraints on the clock values: a transition may be taken only if the current values of the clocks satisfy the associated constraints. With this mechanism we can model timing properties such as "the channel delivers every message within 3 to 5 time units of its receipt". Timed automata accept *timed words* — infinite sequences in which a real-valued time of occurrence is associated with each symbol. Timed automata can capture several interesting aspects of real-time systems: qualitative features such as liveness, fairness, and nondeterminism; and quantitative features such as periodicity, bounded response, and timing delays.

We present an overview of the formal language theory for timed automata. Due to the real-valued clock variables, the state space of a timed automaton is infinite. The *untiming* algorithm, discussed in detail in Section 5, constructs a finite quotient of this space, and is the key to algorithmic solutions to decision problems for timed automata.

Section 6 outlines the application of timed automata to verification of timed systems. A timed system is modeled as a collection of timed automata representing the various components of the system. The specification to be checked is given as a deterministic timed automaton representing the correct behaviors. The system satisfies the property if the language of the product of the automata modeling the components is contained in the language of the specification automaton. We present an algorithmic solution to the verification problem. To alleviate the high computational complexity of the verification algorithm, different verification tools use different heuristics. We discuss some of the implemented solutions.

3.2   AUTOMATA-THEORETIC VERIFICATION OF UNTIMED SYSTEMS

In this section we will briefly review the relevant aspects of the theory of ω-regular languages, and its application to modeling and automatic verification of untimed systems. We refer the reader to [Tho90] for a summary of the theory of ω-regular languages, and to [Kur94] for its application to verification.

3.2.1   Büchi automata

The more familiar definition of a formal language is as a set of finite words over some given (finite) alphabet. As opposed to this, an ω-language consists of infinite words. Thus an ω-language over a finite alphabet Σ is a subset of Σ^ω — the set of all infinite words over Σ. ω-automata provide a finite representation for certain types of ω-languages. An ω-automaton is essentially the same as a nondeterministic finite-state automaton, but with the acceptance condition modified suitably so as to handle infinite input words.

A *transition table* $\mathcal{A}$ is a tuple $\langle \Sigma, S, S_0, E \rangle$, where Σ is an input alphabet, S is a finite set of automaton states, $S_0 \subseteq S$ is a set of start states, and $E \subseteq S \times S \times \Sigma$ is a set of edges. The automaton starts in an initial state, and if $\langle s, s', a \rangle \in E$ then the automaton can change its state from s to s' reading the input symbol a. Formally, for an infinite word $\overline{\sigma} = \sigma_1 \sigma_2 \ldots$ over the alphabet Σ, we say that

$$r : \quad s_0 \xrightarrow{\sigma_1} s_1 \xrightarrow{\sigma_2} s_2 \xrightarrow{\sigma_3} \cdots$$

is a *run* of the transition table $\mathcal{A}$ over σ, provided $s_0 \in S_0$, and $\langle s_{i-1}, s_i, \sigma_i \rangle \in E$ for all $i \geq 1$. For such a run, the set $inf(r)$ consists of the states $s \in S$ such that $s = s_i$ for infinitely many $i \geq 0$.

Different types of ω-automata are defined by adding an acceptance condition to the definition of the transition tables. We will use Büchi acceptance condition (alternatives such as Streett acceptance or Muller acceptance lead to expressively equivalent definitions, see [Tho90]). A *Büchi automaton* $\mathcal{A}$ is a transition table $\langle \Sigma, S, S_0, E \rangle$ with an additional set $F \subseteq S$ of accepting states. A run r of $\mathcal{A}$ over a word $\sigma \in \Sigma^\omega$ is an *accepting run* iff $inf(r) \cap F \neq \emptyset$. In other words, a run r is accepting iff some state from the set F repeats infinitely often along r. The language $L(\mathcal{A})$ accepted by the Büchi automaton $\mathcal{A}$ consists of the words $\sigma \in \Sigma^\omega$ such that $\mathcal{A}$ has an accepting run over σ.

Example 3.2.1 Consider the 2-state automaton of Figure 3.1 over the alphabet $\{a, b\}$. Both states are start states and s_1 is the accepting state. The automaton accepts all words with an

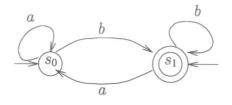

Figure 3.1   Büchi automaton accepting words with infinitely many b's

infinite number of b's. Thus, the automaton expresses the constraint that every a is followed by b. ∎

An ω-language is called ω-*regular* iff it is accepted by some Büchi automaton. The class of ω-regular languages is closed under all the Boolean operations. Language intersection is implemented by a product construction for Büchi automata. There are known constructions for complementing Büchi automata.

When Büchi automata are used for modeling finite-state concurrent processes, the verification problem reduces to that of language inclusion. The inclusion problem for ω-regular languages is decidable. To test whether the language of one automaton is contained in the other, we check for emptiness of the intersection of the first automaton with the complement of the second. Testing for emptiness is easy; we only need to search for a cycle that is reachable from a start state and includes at least one accepting state. In general, complementing a Büchi automaton involves an exponential blow-up in the number of states, and the language inclusion problem is known to be PSPACE-complete. However, checking whether the language of one automaton is contained in the language of a *deterministic* automaton can be done in polynomial time.

A transition table $\mathcal{A} = \langle \Sigma, S, S_0, E \rangle$ is *deterministic* iff there is a single start state, and the number of a-labeled edges starting at s is at most one for all states $s \in S$ and for all symbols $a \in \Sigma$. Thus, for a deterministic transition table, the current state and the next input symbol determine the next state uniquely. Consequently, a deterministic automaton has at most one run over a given word, and this allows an efficient way to complement.

3.2.2   Trace semantics

In trace semantics, we associate a set of observable *events* with each process, and model the process by the set of all its *traces*. A trace is a (linear) sequence of events that may be observed when the process runs. For example, an event may denote an assignment of a value to a variable, or pressing a button on the control panel, or arrival of a message.

In our model, a trace will be a sequence of sets of events. Thus if two events a and b happen simultaneously, the corresponding trace will have a set $\{a, b\}$ in our model. Formally, given a set A of events, a *trace* $\bar{\sigma} = \sigma_1 \sigma_2 \ldots$ is an infinite word over $\mathcal{P}(A)$ — the set of nonempty subsets of A. An *untimed process* is a pair (A, X) comprising of the set A of its observable events and the set X of its possible traces.

Example 3.2.2   Consider a channel P connecting two components. Let a represent the arrival of a message at one end of P, and let b stand for the delivery of the message at the other end of the channel. The channel cannot receive a new message until the previous one has reached the other end. Consequently the two events a and b alternate. Assuming that the messages keep arriving, the only possible trace is $\overline{\sigma}_P = \{a\}, \{b\}, \{a\}, \{b\} \ldots$ Often we will denote the singleton set $\{a\}$ by the symbol a, and infinite repetition $abababa\ldots$ by $(ab)^\omega$. The process P is represented by $(\{a, b\}, (ab)^\omega)$. ■

Various operations can be defined on processes; these are useful for describing complex systems using the simpler ones. We will consider only the most important of these operations, namely, *parallel composition*. The parallel composition of a set of processes describes the joint behavior of all the processes running concurrently.

The parallel composition operator can be conveniently defined using the projection operation. The *projection* of $\overline{\sigma} \in \mathcal{P}(A)^\omega$ onto $B \subseteq A$ (written $\overline{\sigma}\lceil B$) is formed by intersecting each event set in $\overline{\sigma}$ with B and deleting all the empty sets from the sequence. For instance, in Example 3.2.2 $\overline{\sigma}_P\lceil\{a\}$ is the trace a^ω. Notice that the projection operation may result in a finite sequence; but for our purpose it suffices to consider the projection of a trace σ onto B only when $\sigma_i \cap B$ is nonempty for infinitely many i. For a set of processes $\{P_i = (A_i, X_i) \mid i = 1, 2, \ldots n\}$,

$$\|_i P_i = (\cup_i A_i, \{\overline{\sigma} \in \mathcal{P}(\cup_i A_i)^\omega \mid \overline{\sigma}\lceil A_i \in X_i \text{ for } i = 1, \ldots n\}).$$

Thus $\overline{\sigma}$ is a trace of $\|_i P_i$ iff $\overline{\sigma}\lceil A_i$ is a trace of P_i for each $i = 1, \ldots n$. When there are no common events the above definition corresponds to the unconstrained interleavings of all the traces. On the other hand, if all event sets are identical then the trace set of the composition process is simply the set theoretic intersection of all the component trace sets.

Example 3.2.3 Consider another channel Q connected to the channel P of Example 3.2.2. The event of message arrival for Q is same as the event b. Let c denote the delivery of the message at the other end of Q. The process Q is given by $(\{b, c\}, (bc)^\omega)$.

When P and Q are composed we require them to synchronize on the common event b, and between every pair of b's we allow the possibility of the event a happening before the event c, the event c happening before a, and both occurring simultaneously. Thus $[P \parallel Q]$ has the event set $\{a, b, c\}$, and has an infinite number of traces. ■

In this framework, the verification question is presented as a *language inclusion problem*: is the language of the implementation automaton a subset of the language of the specification automaton? Intuitively, the specification automaton gives the set of allowed behaviors, so the implementation is included in the specification if and only if every actual behavior of the implementation is allowed. Both the implementation and the specification are given as untimed processes. The implementation process is typically a composition of several smaller component processes. We say that an implementation (A, X_I) is *correct* with respect to a specification (A, X_S) iff $X_I \subseteq X_S$.

Example 3.2.4 Consider the channels of Example 3.2.3. The implementation process is $[P \parallel Q]$. The specification is given as the process $S = (\{a, b, c\}, (abc)^\omega)$. Thus the specification requires the message to reach the other end of Q before the next message arrives at P. In this case, $[P \parallel Q]$ does not meet the specification S, for it has too many other traces, specifically, the trace $ab(acb)^\omega$. ■

3.2.3 ω-automata and verification

Observe that for an untimed process (A, X), X is an ω-language over the alphabet $\mathcal{P}(A)$. If it is a regular language it can be represented by a Büchi automaton.

We model a finite-state (untimed) process P with event set A using a Büchi automaton $\mathcal{A}_P$ over the alphabet $\mathcal{P}(A)$. The states of the automaton correspond to the internal states of the process. The automaton $\mathcal{A}_P$ has a transition $\langle s, s', a \rangle$, with $a \subseteq A$, if the process can change its state from s to s' participating in the events from a. The acceptance conditions of the automaton correspond to the fairness constraints on the process. The automaton $\mathcal{A}_P$ accepts (or generates) precisely the traces of P; that is, the process P is given by $(A, L(\mathcal{A}_P))$. Such a process P is called an ω-*regular process*.

The user describes a system consisting of various components by specifying each individual component as a Büchi automaton. In particular, consider a system I comprising of n components, where each component is modeled as an ω-regular process $P_i = (A_i, L(\mathcal{A}_i))$. The implementation process is $[\|_i P_i]$. We can automatically construct the automaton $\mathcal{A}_I$ for the implementation I using the construction for language intersection for Büchi automata.

The specification is given as a Büchi automaton $\mathcal{A}_S$ over the alphabet $\mathcal{P}(A)$. The implementation meets the specification iff $L(\mathcal{A}_I) \subseteq L(\mathcal{A}_S)$. In this case, the verification problem reduces to checking emptiness of $L(\mathcal{A}_I) \cap L(\mathcal{A}_S)^c$. The verification problem is provably computationally expensive, namely, PSPACE-complete. The size of $\mathcal{A}_I$ is exponential in the description of its individual components. If $\mathcal{A}_S$ is nondeterministic, taking the complement involves an exponential blow-up, and hence, in practice, either deterministic automata are used for specifications, or the user provides complement of the specification (i.e. the automaton that accepts "bad" traces).

A variety of heuristics are used to implement the verification strategy outlined above. Note that testing language inclusion corresponds to finding cycles in the product of the automata $\mathcal{A}_i$ together with the complement $\mathcal{A}_S^c$. There is no need to explicitly construct the product automaton, and thus the search is done on-the-fly. The search may be done by enumerating states in a depth-first fashion, or by manipulating sets of states in a breadth-first fashion. The latter technique—also called symbolic model checking—sometimes turns out to be effective even for systems with a large number of states (see [McM93] for an overview of symbolic model checking using binary decision diagrams). For complex problems, the verification algorithm is used in conjunction with compositional and hierarchical proof methods that allow a systematic decomposition of the verification problem (see [Dil89b, Kur94, LT87] for some of the methodologies, and also the article by Lynch in this volume).

3.2.4   Train-Gate Controller

We consider an example of an automatic controller that opens and closes a gate at a railroad crossing. The system is composed of three components: TRAIN, GATE and CONTROLLER as shown in Figure 3.2. All of them are modeled as Büchi automata. The example is simplified, however, it suffices to illustrate the basic concepts in automata-theoretic automated verification. Note that, for now, we model only the sequencing of events within each component, and timing will be added to the model later.

The event set for the train automaton is {*approach, exit, in, out, id_T*}. The event id_T represents its idling event; the train is not required to enter the gate. The train communicates with the controller with two events *approach* and *exit*. The events *in* and *out* mark the events

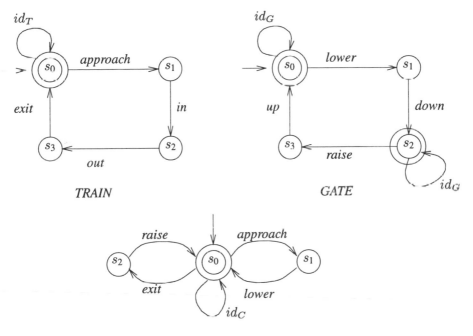

Figure 3.2   Train-gate controller

of entry and exit of the train from the railroad crossing. The event set for the gate automaton is {*raise, lower, up, down, id_G*}. The gate is open in state s_0 and closed in state s_2. It communicates with the controller through the signals *lower* and *raise*. The events *up* and *down* denote the opening and the closing of the gate. The gate can take its idling transition id_G in states s_0 or s_2 forever. Finally, the event set for the controller is {*approach, exit, raise, lower, id_C*}. The controller idle state is s_0. Whenever it receives the signal *approach* from the train, it responds by sending the signal *lower* to the gate. Whenever it receives the signal *exit*, it responds with a signal *raise* to the gate.

The entire system is then TRAIN ‖ GATE ‖ CONTROLLER. The event set is the union of the event sets of all the three components. In this example, all the automata are particularly simple; they are deterministic, and do not have any fairness constraints (every run is an accepting run). The automaton A_I specifying the entire system is obtained by composing the above three automata.

The safety correctness requirement for the system is that whenever the train is inside the gate, the gate should be closed. The safety property is specified by the automaton of Figure 3.3. An edge label *in* stands for any event set containing *in*, and an edge label "*in*, ¬*out*" means any event set not containing *out*, but containing *in*. The automaton disallows *in* before *down*, and *up* before *out*. All the states are accepting states.

To verify the safety requirement, we need to check whether the language of A_I is contained in the language of the safety automaton. This can be done using an automated tool such as

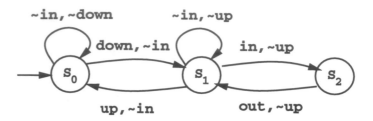

Figure 3.3 Safety property

COSPAN. The desired inclusion does not hold, and the verification tool reports a trace of A_I that violates the safety property (the trace consists of only two events, *approach* followed by *in*). We need to introduce sufficient delay between the events *approach* and *in* so that the safety property is satisfied.

3.3   TIMED LANGUAGES

To introduce time in trace semantics, we define timed words by coupling a real-valued time with each symbol in a word.

3.3.1   Timed languages

The set of nonnegative real numbers, R^+, is chosen as the time domain. A *time sequence* $\bar{\tau} = \tau_1 \tau_2 \cdots$ is an infinite sequence of time values $\tau_i \in \mathsf{R}^+$ with $\tau_i > 0$, satisfying the following constraints:

1. *Monotonicity:* $\bar{\tau}$ increases strictly monotonically; that is, $\tau_i < \tau_{i+1}$ for all $i \geq 1$.
2. *Progress:* For every $t \in \mathsf{R}^+$, there is some $i \geq 1$ such that $\tau_i > t$.

A *timed word* over an alphabet Σ is a pair $(\bar{\sigma}, \bar{\tau})$ consisting of an infinite word $\bar{\sigma} = \sigma_1 \sigma_2 \dots$ over Σ and a time sequence $\bar{\tau}$. A *timed language* over Σ is a set of timed words over Σ. If each symbol σ_i is interpreted to denote an event occurrence then the corresponding component τ_i is interpreted as the time of occurrence of σ_i. The progress requirement ensures that we disallow infinitely many events to occur within a finite interval of time. Let us consider some examples of timed languages.

Example 3.3.1 Let the alphabet be $\{a, b\}$. Define a timed language L_1 to consist of all timed words $(\bar{\sigma}, \bar{\tau})$ such that there is no b after time 5.6. Thus the language L_1 is given by

$$L_1 = \{(\bar{\sigma}, \bar{\tau}) \mid \forall i. \, ((\tau_i > 5.6) \to (\sigma_i = a))\}.$$

Another example is the language L_2 consisting of timed words in which a and b alternate, and for the successive pairs of a and b, the time difference between a and b keeps increasing. The language L_2 is given as

$$L_2 = \{((ab)^\omega, \bar{\tau}) \mid \forall i. \, ((\tau_{2i} - \tau_{2i-1}) < (\tau_{2i+2} - \tau_{2i+1}))\}. \qquad \blacksquare$$

The language-theoretic operations such as intersection, union, complementation are defined for timed languages as usual. In addition we define the *Untime* operation which discards the time values associated with the symbols, that is, it considers the projection of a timed trace $(\overline{\sigma}, \overline{\tau})$ on the first component: for a timed language L over Σ, $Untime(L)$ is the ω-language consisting of words $\overline{\sigma}$ such that $(\overline{\sigma}, \overline{\tau}) \in L$ for some time sequence $\overline{\tau}$. For instance, referring to Example 3.3.1, $Untime(L_1)$ is the ω-language with words that contain only finitely many b's, and $Untime(L_2)$ consists of a single word $(ab)^\omega$.

3.3.2   Adding timing to traces

An untimed process models the sequencing of events but not the actual times at which the events occur. Thus the description of the channel in Example 3.2.2 gives only the sequencing of the events a and b, and not the delays between them. Timing can be added to a trace by coupling it with a sequence of time values.

A *timed trace* over a set of events A is a pair $(\overline{\sigma}, \overline{\tau})$ where $\overline{\sigma}$ is a trace over A, and $\overline{\tau}$ is a time sequence. In a timed trace $(\overline{\sigma}, \overline{\tau})$, each τ_i gives the time at which the events in σ_i occur. In particular, τ_1 gives the time of the first observable event; we always assume $\tau_1 > 0$, and define $\tau_0 = 0$. A *timed process* is a pair (A, L) where A is a finite set of events, and L is a set of timed traces over A.

Example 3.3.2 Consider the channel P of Example 3.2.2 again. Assume that the first message arrives at time 1, and the subsequent messages arrive at fixed intervals of length 3 time units. Furthermore, it takes 1 time unit for every message to traverse the channel. The process has a single timed trace $\rho_P = (a, 1), (b, 2), (a, 4), (b, 5) \ldots$ and it is represented as a timed process $P^T = (\{a, b\}, \{\rho_P\})$. ■

The operations on untimed processes are extended in the obvious way to timed processes. To get the projection of $(\overline{\sigma}, \overline{\tau})$ onto $B \subseteq A$, we first intersect each event set in $\overline{\sigma}$ with B and then delete all the empty sets along with the associated time values. The definition of parallel composition remains unchanged, except that it uses the projection for timed traces. Thus in the parallel composition of two processes, we require that both the processes should participate in the common events at the same time. This rules out the possibility of interleaving: the parallel composition of two timed traces is either a single timed trace or is empty.

Example 3.3.3 As in Example 3.2.3 consider another channel Q connected to P. For Q, as before, the only possible trace is $\overline{\sigma}_Q = (bc)^\omega$. In addition, the timing specification of Q says that the time taken by a message for traversing the channel, that is, the delay between b and the following c, is some real value between 1 and 2. The timed process Q^T has infinitely many timed traces, and it is given by

$$\left[\{b, c\}, \{(\overline{\sigma}_Q, \overline{\tau}) \mid \forall i. (\tau_{2i-1} + 1 < \tau_{2i} < \tau_{2i-1} + 2)\} \right].$$

The description of $[P^T \parallel Q^T]$ is obtained by composing ρ_P with each timed trace of Q^T. The composition process has uncountably many timed traces. An example trace is

$$(a, 1), (b, 2), (c, 3.8), (a, 4), (b, 5), (c, 6.02) \ldots \blacksquare$$

The time values associated with the events can be discarded by the *Untime* operation. For a timed process $P = (A, L)$, $Untime[(A, L)]$ is the untimed process with the event set A and the trace set consisting of traces $\overline{\sigma}$ such that $(\overline{\sigma}, \overline{\tau}) \in L$ for some time sequence $\overline{\tau}$.

Note that

$$Untime(P_1 \parallel P_2) \subseteq Untime(P_1) \parallel Untime(P_2).$$

However, as Example 3.3.4 shows, the two sides are not necessarily equal. In other words, the timing information retained in the timed traces constrains the set of possible traces when two processes are composed.

Example 3.3.4 For the channels of Example 3.3.3, $Untime(P^T) = P$ and $Untime(Q^T) = Q$. The composition $P^T \parallel Q^T$ has a unique untimed trace $(abc)^\omega$, but $P \parallel Q$ has infinitely many traces: between every pair of b events all possible orderings of an event a and an event c are admissible. ∎

The verification problem is again posed as an inclusion problem. The implementation is given as a composition of several timed processes, and the specification is also given as a timed process.

Example 3.3.5 Consider the verification problem of Example 3.2.4 again. If we model the implementation as the timed process $P^T \parallel Q^T$ then it meets the specification S. The specification S is now a timed process $(\{a, b, c\}, \{((abc)^\omega, \overline{\tau})\})$. Observe that, though the specification S constrains only the sequencing of events, the correctness of $P^T \parallel Q^T$ with respect to S crucially depends on the timing constraints of the two channels. ∎

3.4   TIMED AUTOMATA

We augment the definition of ω-automata so that they accept timed words, and use them to develop a theory of timed regular languages analogous to the theory of ω-regular languages.

3.4.1   Transition tables with timing constraints

We extend transition tables to *timed transition tables* so that they can read timed words. When an automaton makes a state-transition, the choice of the next state depends upon the input symbol read. In case of a timed transition table, we want this choice to depend also upon the time of the input symbol relative to the times of the previously read symbols. For this purpose, we associate a finite set of (real-valued) *clocks* with each transition table. A clock can be set to zero simultaneously with any transition. At any instant, the reading of a clock equals the time elapsed since the last time it was reset. With each transition we associate a clock constraint, and require that the transition may be taken only if the current values of the clocks satisfy this constraint. Before we define the timed transition tables formally, let us consider some examples.

Example 3.4.1 Consider the timed transition table of Figure 3.4. The start state is s_0. There is a single clock x. An annotation of the form $x := 0$ on an edge corresponds to the action of resetting the clock x when the edge is traversed. Similarly an annotation of the form $(x < 2)?$ on an edge gives the clock constraint associated with the edge.

The automaton starts in state s_0, and moves to state s_1 reading the input symbol a. The clock x gets set to 0 along with this transition. While in state s_1, the value of the clock x shows the

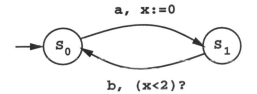

Figure 3.4 Example of a timed transition table

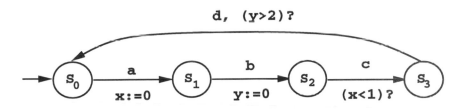

Figure 3.5 Timed transition table with 2 clocks

time elapsed since the occurrence of the last a symbol. The transition from state s_1 to s_0 is enabled only if this value is less than 2. The whole cycle repeats when the automaton moves back to state s_0. Thus the timing constraint expressed by this transition table is that the delay between a and the following b is always less than 2. ∎

Thus to constrain the delay between two transitions e_1 and e_2, we require a particular clock to be reset on e_1, and associate an appropriate clock constraint with e_2. Note that clocks can be set asynchronously of each other. This means that different clocks can be restarted at different times, and there is no lower bound on the difference between their readings. Having multiple clocks allows multiple concurrent delays, as in the next example.

Example 3.4.2 The timed transition table of Figure 3.5 uses two clocks x and y, and accepts the language

$$L_3 = \{((abcd)^\omega, \bar{\tau}) \mid \forall j. ((\tau_{4j+3} < \tau_{4j+1} + 1) \wedge (\tau_{4j+4} > \tau_{4j+2} + 2))\}.$$

The clock x gets set to 0 each time the automaton moves from s_0 to s_1 reading a. The check $(x < 1)$? associated with the c-transition from s_2 to s_3 ensures that c happens within time 1 of the preceding a. A similar mechanism of resetting another independent clock y while reading b and checking its value while reading d, ensures that the delay between b and the following d is always greater than 2. ∎

Notice that in the above example, to constrain the delay between a and c and between b and d the automaton does not put any explicit bounds on the time difference between a and the following b, or c and the following d. This is an important advantage of having multiple clocks

which can be set independently of one another. We remark that the clocks of the automaton
do not correspond to the local clocks of different components in a distributed system. All the
clocks increase at the uniform rate counting time with respect to a fixed global time frame.
They are fictitious clocks invented to express the timing properties of the system. Alternatively,
we can consider the automaton to be equipped with a finite number of stop-watches which can
be started and checked independently of one another, but all stop-watches refer to the same
clock.

3.4.2 Clock constraints and clock interpretations

To define timed automata formally, we need to say what type of clock constraints are allowed
on the edges. An atomic constraint compares a clock value with a time constant, and a clock
constraint is a conjunction of atomic constraints. Any value from Q, the set of nonnegative
rationals, can be used as a time constant. Formally, for a set X of clock variables, the set $\Phi(X)$
of *clock constraints* δ is defined inductively

$$\delta := x \leq c \mid c \leq x \mid x < c \mid c < x \mid \delta_1 \wedge \delta_2,$$

where x is a clock in X and c is a constant in Q.

A *clock interpretation* ν for a set X of clocks assigns a real value to each clock; that is,
it is a mapping from X to R^+. We say that a clock interpretation ν for X satisfies a clock
constraint δ over X iff δ evaluates to true using the values given by ν.

For $t \in R^+$, $\nu + t$ denotes the clock interpretation which maps every clock x to the value
$\nu(x) + t$. For $Y \subseteq X$, $[Y \mapsto t]\nu$ denotes the clock interpretation for X which assigns t to
each $x \in Y$, and agrees with ν over the rest of the clocks.

3.4.3 Timed transition tables

A *timed transition table* $\mathcal{A}$ is a tuple $\langle \Sigma, S, S_0, C, E \rangle$, where

- Σ is a finite alphabet,
- S is a finite set of states,
- $S_0 \subseteq S$ is a set of start states,
- C is a finite set of clocks, and
- $E \subseteq S \times S \times \Sigma \times 2^C \times \Phi(C)$ gives the set of transitions. An edge $\langle s, s', a, \lambda, \delta \rangle$ represents
  a transition from state s to state s' on input symbol a. The set $\lambda \subseteq C$ gives the clocks to
  be reset with this transition, and δ is a clock constraint over C.

Given a timed word $(\bar{\sigma}, \bar{\tau})$, the timed transition table $\mathcal{A}$ starts in one of its start states at
time 0 with all its clocks initialized to 0. As time advances, the values of all clocks change,
reflecting the elapsed time. At time τ_i, $\mathcal{A}$ changes state from s to s' using some transition of
the form $\langle s, s', \sigma_i, \lambda, \delta \rangle$ reading the input σ_i, if the current values of clocks satisfy δ. With this
transition the clocks in λ are reset to 0, and thus start counting time with respect to the time
of occurrence of this transition. This behavior is captured by defining *runs* of timed transition
tables. A run r, denoted by $(\bar{s}, \bar{\nu})$, of a timed transition table $\langle \Sigma, S, S_0, C, E \rangle$ over a timed word
$(\bar{\sigma}, \bar{\tau})$ is an infinite sequence of the form

$$r : \langle s_0, \nu_0 \rangle \xrightarrow[\tau_1]{\sigma_1} \langle s_1, \nu_1 \rangle \xrightarrow[\tau_2]{\sigma_2} \langle s_2, \nu_2 \rangle \xrightarrow[\tau_3]{\sigma_3} \cdots$$

with, for all $i \geq 0$, $s_i \in S$ and ν_i is a clock interpretation for C, satisfying the following requirements:

- *Initiation:* $s_0 \in S_0$, and $\nu_0(x) = 0$ for all $x \in C$.
- *Consecution:* for all $i \geq 1$, there is an edge in E of the form $\langle s_{i-1}, s_i, \sigma_i, \lambda_i, \delta_i \rangle$ such that $(\nu_{i-1} + \tau_i - \tau_{i-1})$ satisfies δ_i and ν_i equals $[\lambda_i \mapsto 0](\nu_{i-1} + \tau_i - \tau_{i-1})$.

The set $inf(r)$ consists of those states $s \in S$ such that $s = s_i$ for infinitely many $i > 0$.

Example 3.4.3 Consider the timed transition table of Example 3.4.2, and the word $(a, 2), (b, 2.7), (c, 2.8), (d, 5) \ldots$ Below we give the initial segment of the run. A clock interpretation is represented by listing the values $[x, y]$.

$$\langle s_0, [0,0]\rangle \xrightarrow[2]{a} \langle s_1, [0,2]\rangle \xrightarrow[2.7]{b} \langle s_2, [0.7, 0]\rangle \xrightarrow[2.8]{c} \langle s_3, [0.8, 0.1]\rangle \xrightarrow[5]{d} \langle s_0, [3, 2.3]\rangle \cdots \blacksquare$$

3.4.4 Timed regular languages

We can couple acceptance criteria with timed transition tables, and use them to define timed languages. A *timed Büchi automaton* (in short TBA) is a tuple $\langle \Sigma, S, S_0, C, E, F \rangle$, where $\langle \Sigma, S, S_0, C, E \rangle$ is a timed transition table, and $F \subseteq S$ is a set of *accepting* states. A run $r = (\bar{s}, \bar{\nu})$ of a TBA over a timed word $(\bar{\sigma}, \bar{\tau})$ is called an *accepting run* iff $inf(r) \cap F \neq \emptyset$. For a TBA $\mathcal{A}$, the language $L(\mathcal{A})$ of timed words it accepts is defined to be the set $\{(\bar{\sigma}, \bar{\tau}) \mid \mathcal{A}$ has an accepting run over $(\bar{\sigma}, \bar{\tau})\}$.

In analogy with the class of languages accepted by Büchi automata, we call the class of timed languages accepted by TBAs timed regular languages: a timed language L is a *timed regular language* iff $L = L(\mathcal{A})$ for some TBA $\mathcal{A}$.

Example 3.4.4 The language L_3 of Example 3.4.2 is a timed regular language (the timed transition table of Figure 3.5 coupled with the acceptance set consisting of all the states, accepts L_3).

For every ω-regular language L over Σ, the timed language $\{(\bar{\sigma}, \bar{\tau}) \mid \bar{\sigma} \in L\}$ is timed regular.

A typical example of a nonregular timed language is the language L_2 of Example 3.3.1. It requires that the time difference between the successive pairs of a and b form an increasing sequence. Another nonregular language is $\{(a^\omega, \bar{\tau}) \mid \forall i. (\tau_i = 2^i)\}$. $\blacksquare$

3.4.5 Properties of Timed Automata

The closure properties and decision problems for timed automata play an important role in their application to verification. We mention the relevant results here, and refer the reader to [AD94] for details.

The class of timed regular languages is closed under intersection. That is, given TBAs $\mathcal{A}_i$, it is possible to construct a TBA that accepts the intersection of $L(\mathcal{A}_i)$'s. The construction is a modification of the product construction for Büchi automata.

Consider TBAs $\mathcal{A}_i = \langle \Sigma, S_i, S_{i_0}, C_i, E_i, F_i \rangle$, $i = 1, 2, \ldots n$ with disjoint clock sets. The set of clocks for the product automaton $\mathcal{A}$ is $\cup_i C_i$. The states of $\mathcal{A}$ are of the form $\langle s_1, \ldots s_n, k \rangle$, where each $s_i \in S_i$, and $0 \leq k < n$. The i-th component of the tuple keeps track of the state of $\mathcal{A}_i$, and the last component is used as a counter for cycling through the accepting conditions

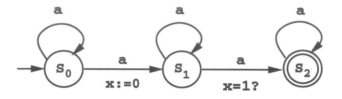

Figure 3.6   Noncomplementable automaton

of all the individual automata. Initially the counter value is 0, and it is incremented from k to $(k + 1)$ (modulo n) iff the current state of the k-th automaton is an accepting state.

The initial states of $\mathcal{A}$ are of the form $\langle s_1, \ldots s_n, 0 \rangle$ where each s_i is a start state of $\mathcal{A}_i$. A transition of $\mathcal{A}$ is obtained by coupling the transitions of the individual automata having the same label. Let $\{\langle s_i, s'_i, a, \lambda_i, \delta_i \rangle \in \mathrm{E}_i \mid i = 1, \ldots n\}$ be a set of transitions, one per each automaton, with the same label a. Corresponding to this set, there is a joint transition of $\mathcal{A}$ out of each state of the form $\langle s_1, \ldots s_n, k \rangle$ labeled with a. The new state is $\langle s'_1, \ldots s'_n, j \rangle$ with $j = (k + 1) \bmod n$ if $s_{k+1} \in F_{k+1}$, and $j = k$ otherwise. The set of clocks to be reset with this transition is $\cup_i \lambda_i$, and the associated clock constraint is $\wedge_i \delta_i$.

The counter value cycles through the whole range $0, \ldots (n - 1)$ infinitely often iff the accepting conditions of all the automata are met. Consequently, we define the accepting set for $\mathcal{A}$ to consist of states of the form $\langle s_1, \ldots s_n, n - 1 \rangle$, where $s_n \in F_n$.

The class of timed regular languages is also closed under union. However, it is not closed under complement.

Example 3.4.5   The language accepted by the automaton of Figure 3.6 over $\{a\}$ is

$$\{(a^\omega, \tau) \mid \exists i \geq 1. \exists j > i. (\tau_j = \tau_i + 1)\}.$$

The complement of this language cannot be characterized using a TBA. The complement needs to make sure that no pair of a's is separated by distance 1. Since there is no bound on the number of a's that can happen in a time period of length 1, keeping track of the times of all the a's within the past 1 time unit, would require an unbounded number of clocks. ∎

In Section 3.5, we give an algorithm for testing whether the language of a TBA is empty. Recall that to test whether the language of one Büchi automaton is contained in another, we test the emptiness of the language of the product of the first automaton with the complement of the latter. This strategy cannot be used for TBAs, as it is not possible to automatically complement a TBA. In fact, there is no algorithm for testing whether the language of one TBA is contained in another (the language inclusion problem is undecidable). The language inclusion problem is solvable if we use deterministic TBAs as specification automata.

3.4.6   Deterministic timed automata

Recall that in the untimed case a deterministic transition table has a single start state, and from each state, given the next input symbol, the next state is uniquely determined. We want a similar criterion for determinism for the timed automata: given an extended state and the next input symbol *along with its time of occurrence,* the extended state after the next transition should be uniquely determined. So we allow multiple transitions starting at the same state with the same label, but require their clock constraints to be *mutually exclusive* so that at any time only one of these transitions is enabled. A timed transition table $\langle \Sigma, S, S_0, C, E \rangle$ is called *deterministic* iff

1. it has only one start state, $|S_0| = 1$, and
2. for all $s \in S$, for all $a \in \Sigma$, for every pair of edges of the form $\langle s, -, a, -, \delta_1 \rangle$ and $\langle v, -, a, -, \delta_2 \rangle$, the clock constraints δ_1 and δ_2 are mutually exclusive (i.e., $\delta_1 \wedge \delta_2$ is unsatisfiable).

A timed automaton is deterministic iff its timed transition table is deterministic. Deterministic timed automata can be easily complemented because a deterministic timed transition table has at most one run over a given timed word. The algorithm for checking emptiness can be used to test whether the language of one TBA is included in the language of a deterministic TBA. More details regarding deterministic TBAs can be found in [AD94].

3.5 CHECKING EMPTINESS

In this section we describe an algorithm for checking the emptiness of the language of a timed automaton. The existence of an infinite accepting path in the underlying transition table is clearly a necessary condition for the language of an automaton to be nonempty. However, the timing constraints of the automaton rule out certain additional behaviors. We will show that a Büchi automaton can be constructed that accepts exactly the set of untimed words that are consistent with the timed words accepted by a timed automaton.

Recall that our definition of timed automata allows clock constraints which involve comparisons with rational constants. If the clock constraints of the given automaton $\mathcal{A}$ involve rational constants, we can multiply each constant by the least common multiple of denominators of all the constants appearing in the clock constraints of $\mathcal{A}$. This transformation leaves the untimed language unchanged. Consequently, for checking emptiness, we can restrict ourselves to timed automata whose clock constraints involve only integer constants.

3.5.1 Clock Regions

At every point in time the future behavior of a timed transition table is determined by its state and the values of all its clocks. This motivates the following definition: for a timed transition table $\langle \Sigma, S, S_0, C, E \rangle$, an *extended state* is a pair $\langle s, \nu \rangle$ where $s \in S$ and ν is a clock interpretation for C. Since the number of such extended states is infinite (in fact, uncountable), we cannot possibly build an automaton whose states are the extended states of $\mathcal{A}$. But if two extended states with the same $\mathcal{A}$-state agree on the integral parts of all clock values, and also on the ordering of the fractional parts of all clock values, then the runs starting from the two extended states are very similar. The integral parts of the clock values are needed to determine whether or not a particular clock constraint is met, whereas the ordering of the fractional parts is needed to decide which clock will change its integral part first. For example, if two clocks x and y are between 0 and 1 in an extended state, then a transition with clock constraint $(x = 1)$ can be followed by a transition with clock constraint $(y = 1)$, depending on whether or not the current clock values satisfy $(x < y)$.

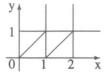

6 Corner points: e.g. $[(0,1)]$

14 Open line segments: e.g. $[0 < x = y < 1]$

8 Open regions: e.g. $[0 < x < y < 1]$

Figure 3.7   Clock regions

The integral parts of clock values can get arbitrarily large. But if a clock x is never compared with a constant greater than c, then its actual value, once it exceeds c, is of no consequence in deciding the allowed paths.

Now we formalize this notion. For any $t \in R^+$, $fract(t)$ denotes the fractional part of t, and $\lfloor t \rfloor$ denotes the integral part of t; that is, $t = \lfloor t \rfloor + fract(t)$. We assume that every clock in C appears in some clock constraint. For each $x \in C$, let c_x be the largest integer c such that x is compared with c in some clock constraint appearing in E.

The equivalence relation $\sim$ is defined over the set of all clock interpretations for C; $\nu \sim \nu'$ iff all the following conditions hold:

1. For all $x \in C$, either $\lfloor \nu(x) \rfloor$ and $\lfloor \nu'(x) \rfloor$ are the same, or both $\nu(x)$ and $\nu'(x)$ exceed c_x.
2. For all $x, y \in C$ with $\nu(x) \leq c_x$ and $\nu(y) \leq c_y$, $fract(\nu(x)) \leq fract(\nu(y))$ iff $fract(\nu'(x)) \leq fract(\nu'(y))$.
3. For all $x \in C$ with $\nu(x) \leq c_x$, $fract(\nu(x)) = 0$ iff $fract(\nu'(x)) = 0$.

A *clock region* for A is an equivalence class of clock interpretations induced by $\sim$.

We will use $[\nu]$ to denote the clock region to which ν belongs. Each region can be uniquely characterized by a (finite) set of clock constraints it satisfies. For example, consider a clock interpretation ν over two clocks with $\nu(x) = 0.3$ and $\nu(y) = 0.7$. Every clock interpretation in $[\nu]$ satisfies the constraint $(0 < x < y < 1)$, and we will represent this region by $[0 < x < y < 1]$. The nature of the equivalence classes can be best understood through an example.

Example 3.5.1 Consider a timed transition table with two clocks x and y with $c_x = 2$ and $c_y = 1$. The clock regions are shown in Figure 3.7. ∎

The role of the region equivalence can be understood by defining a (time-abstract) transition relation over the extended states. For two extended states $\langle s, \nu \rangle$ and $\langle s', \nu' \rangle$, and an alphabet symbol a, define $\langle s, \nu \rangle \xrightarrow{a} \langle s', \nu' \rangle$ iff there exists a time increment $t \in R^+$ and an edge $\langle s, s', a, \lambda, \delta \rangle$ such that $\nu + t$ satisfies δ and $\nu' = [\lambda \mapsto 0](\nu + t)$. Thus, $\langle s, \nu \rangle \xrightarrow{a} \langle s', \nu' \rangle$ iff the automaton in extended state $\langle s, \nu \rangle$ can let some time elapse, and read the input symbol a to transition to $\langle s', \nu' \rangle$. The crucial property of the equivalence relation $\sim$ is the following:

If $\nu_1 \sim \nu_2$ and $\langle s, \nu_1 \rangle \xrightarrow{a} \langle s', \nu_1' \rangle$ then there exists a clock interpretation ν_2' such that $\nu_1' \sim \nu_2'$ and $\langle s, \nu_2 \rangle \xrightarrow{a} \langle s', \nu_2' \rangle$.

Due to this property, the equivalence relation $\sim$ is called a time-abstract bisimulation. Note that there are only a finite number of regions. Also note that for a clock constraint δ

of $\mathcal{A}$, if $\nu \sim \nu'$ then ν satisfies δ iff ν' satisfies δ. We say that a clock region α satisfies a clock constraint δ iff every $\nu \in \alpha$ satisfies δ. Each region can be represented by specifying

(1) for every clock x, one clock constraint from the set

$$\{x = c \mid c = 0, 1, \ldots c_x\} \cup \{c - 1 < x < c \mid c = 1, \ldots c_x\} \cup \{x > c_x\},$$

(2) for every pair of clocks x and y such that $c - 1 < x < c$ and $d - 1 < y < d$ appear in (1) for some c, d, whether $\mathit{fract}(x)$ is less than, equal to, or greater than $\mathit{fract}(y)$.

By counting the number of possible combinations of equations of the above form, we conclude that the number of clock regions is bounded by $\left[|C|! \cdot 2^{|C|} \cdot \Pi_{x \in C}(2c_x + 2)\right]$. Thus, the number of clock regions is exponential in the encoding of the clock constraints.

3.5.2   The region automaton

The first step in the decision procedure for checking emptiness is to construct a transition table whose paths mimic the runs of $\mathcal{A}$ in a certain way. We will denote the desired transition table by $R(\mathcal{A})$, the *region automaton* of $\mathcal{A}$. A state of $R(\mathcal{A})$ records the state of the timed transition table $\mathcal{A}$, and the equivalence class of the current values of the clocks. It is of the form $\langle s, \alpha \rangle$ with $s \in S$ and α being a clock region. The intended interpretation is that whenever the extended state of $\mathcal{A}$ is $\langle s, \nu \rangle$, the state of $R(\mathcal{A})$ is $\langle s, [\nu] \rangle$. The region automaton starts in some state $\langle s_0, [\nu_0] \rangle$ where s_0 is a start state of $\mathcal{A}$, and the clock interpretation ν_0 assigns 0 to every clock. The transition relation of $R(\mathcal{A})$ is defined so that the intended simulation is obeyed. It has an edge from $\langle s, \alpha \rangle$ to $\langle s', \alpha' \rangle$ labeled with a iff $\mathcal{A}$ in state s with the clock values $\nu \in \alpha$ can make a transition on a to the extended state $\langle s', \nu' \rangle$ for some $\nu' \in \alpha'$.

For a timed transition table $\mathcal{A} = \langle \Sigma, S, S_0, C, E \rangle$, the corresponding region automaton $R(\mathcal{A})$ is a transition table over the alphabet Σ.

- The states of $R(\mathcal{A})$ are of the form $\langle s, \alpha \rangle$ where $s \in S$ and α is a clock region.
- The initial states are of the form $\langle s_0, [\nu_0] \rangle$ where $s_0 \in S_0$ and $\nu_0(x) = 0$ for all $x \in C$.
- $R(\mathcal{A})$ has an edge $\langle \langle s, \alpha \rangle, \langle s', \alpha' \rangle, a \rangle$ iff $\langle s, \nu \rangle \xrightarrow{a} \langle s', \nu' \rangle$ for some $\nu \in \alpha$ and some $\nu' \in \alpha'$.

Example 3.5.2 Consider the timed automaton $\mathcal{A}_0$ shown in Figure 3.8. The alphabet is $\{a, b, c, d\}$. Every state of the automaton is an accepting state. The corresponding region automaton $R(\mathcal{A}_0)$ is also shown. Only the regions reachable from the initial region $\langle s_0, [x = y = 0] \rangle$ are shown. Note that $c_x = 1$ and $c_y = 1$. The timing constraints of the automaton ensure that the transition from s_2 to s_3 is never taken. The only reachable region with state component s_2 satisfies the constraints $[y = 1, x > 1]$, and this region has no outgoing edges. Thus the region automaton helps us in concluding that no transitions can follow a b-transition. ∎

Let us establish a correspondence between the runs of $\mathcal{A}$ and the runs of $R(\mathcal{A})$. For a run $r = (\overline{s}, \overline{\nu})$ of $\mathcal{A}$ of the form

$$r \; : \; \langle s_0, \nu_0 \rangle \xrightarrow[\tau_1]{\sigma_1} \langle s_1, \nu_1 \rangle \xrightarrow[\tau_2]{\sigma_2} \langle s_2, \nu_2 \rangle \xrightarrow[\tau_3]{\sigma_3} \cdots$$

define its projection $[r] = (\overline{s}, [\overline{\nu}])$ to be the sequence

$$[r] \; : \; \langle s_0, [\nu_0] \rangle \xrightarrow{\sigma_1} \langle s_1, [\nu_1] \rangle \xrightarrow{\sigma_2} \langle s_2, [\nu_2] \rangle \xrightarrow{\sigma_3} \cdots$$

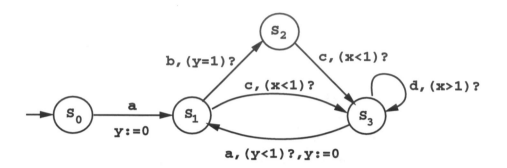

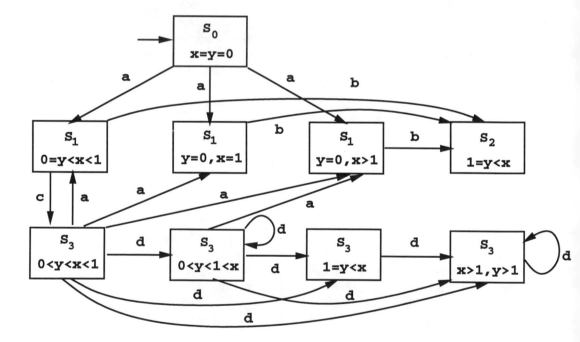

Figure 3.8 Automaton $\mathcal{A}_0$ and its region automaton

From the definition of the edge relation for $R(\mathcal{A})$, it follows that $[r]$ is a run of $R(\mathcal{A})$ over σ. Since time progresses without bound along r, every clock $x \in C$ is either reset infinitely often, or from a certain time onwards it increases without bound. Hence, for all $x \in C$, for infinitely many $i \geq 0$, $[\nu_i]$ satisfies $[(x = 0) \vee (x > c_x)]$. This prompts the following definition: a run $r = (\bar{s}, \bar{\alpha})$ of the region automaton $R(\mathcal{A})$ is *progressive* iff for each clock $x \in C$, there are infinitely many $i \geq 0$ such that α_i satisfies $[(x = 0) \vee (x > c_x)]$. The correspondence between the runs of $\mathcal{A}$ and the runs of $R(\mathcal{A})$ can be made precise now: if r is a progressive run of $R(\mathcal{A})$ over σ then there exists a time sequence τ and a run r' of $\mathcal{A}$ over $(\bar{\sigma}, \bar{\tau})$ such that r equals $[r']$.

Example 3.5.3 Consider the region automaton $R(\mathcal{A}_0)$ of Figure 3.8. Every run r of $R(\mathcal{A}_0)$ has a suffix of one of the following three forms: (i) the automaton cycles between the regions $\langle s_1, [y = 0 < x < 1] \rangle$ and $\langle s_3, [0 < y < x < 1] \rangle$, (ii) the automaton stays in the region $\langle s_3, [0 < y < 1 < x] \rangle$ using the self-loop, or (iii) the automaton stays in the region $\langle s_3, [x > 1, y > 1] \rangle$.

Only the case (iii) corresponds to the progressive runs. For runs of type (i), even though y gets reset infinitely often, the value of x is always less than 1. For runs of type (ii), even though the value of x is not bounded, the clock y is reset only finitely often, and yet, its value is bounded. Thus every progressive run of $\mathcal{A}_0$ corresponds to a run of $R(\mathcal{A}_0)$ of type (iii). ∎

3.5.3 The untiming construction

For a timed automaton $\mathcal{A}$, its region automaton can be used to recognize $Untime[L(\mathcal{A})]$. For this purpose, we need to add acceptance conditions so that only progressive runs satisfy the accepting conditions. This leads to the main theorem for timed automata:

> Given a TBA $\mathcal{A} = \langle \Sigma, S, S_0, C, E, F \rangle$, there exists a Büchi automaton over Σ which accepts $Untime[L(\mathcal{A})]$,

or equivalently,

> If a timed language L is timed regular then $Untime(L)$ is ω-regular

Example 3.5.4 Let us consider the region automaton $R(\mathcal{A}_0)$ of Example 3.5.2 again. Since all states of $\mathcal{A}_0$ are accepting, from the description of the progressive runs in Example 3.5.3 it follows that the transition table $R(\mathcal{A}_0)$ can be changed to a Büchi automaton by choosing the accepting set to consist of a single region $\langle s_3, [x > 1, y > 1] \rangle$. Consequently

$$Untime[L(\mathcal{A}_0)] = L[R(\mathcal{A}_0)] = ac\,(ac)^*\,d^\omega. \blacksquare$$

To check whether the language of a given TBA is empty, we can check for the emptiness of the language of the corresponding Büchi automaton. Given a timed Büchi automaton $\mathcal{A} = \langle \Sigma, S, S_0, C, E, F \rangle$ the emptiness of $L(\mathcal{A})$ can be checked in time $O[(|S| + |E|) \cdot 2^{|\delta(\mathcal{A})|}]$, where $|\delta(\mathcal{A})|$ is the length of the encoding of the clock constraints of $\mathcal{A}$. This blow-up in the length of clock constraints seems unavoidable; technically, the problem of checking emptiness of a TBA is PSPACE-complete. Note that the source of this complexity is not the choice of R^+ to model time. The PSPACE lower bound holds even if we leave the syntax of timed automata unchanged, but use the discrete domain N to model time.

3.6 VERIFICATION

In this section we discuss how to use the theory of timed automata to prove correctness of finite-state real-time systems.

3.6.1 Verification using timed automata

For a timed process (A, L), L is a timed language over $\mathcal{P}(A)$. A *timed regular process* is one for which the set L is a timed regular language, and can be represented by a timed automaton.

Finite-state systems are modeled by TBAs. The underlying transition table gives the state-transition graph of the system. We have already seen how the clocks can be used to represent the timing delays of various physical components. As before, the acceptance conditions correspond to the fairness conditions. Notice that the progress requirement imposes certain fairness requirements implicitly. Thus, with a finite-state process P, we associate a TBA $\mathcal{A}_P$ such that $L(\mathcal{A}_P)$ consists of precisely the timed traces of P.

An implementation is described as a composition of several components. Each component should be modeled as a timed regular process $P_i = (A_i, L(\mathcal{A}_i))$. It is possible to construct a TBA $\mathcal{A}_I$ which represents the composite process $[\|_i P_i]$. However, in the verification procedure we are about to outline, we will not explicitly construct the implementation automaton $\mathcal{A}_I$.

The specification of the system is given as another timed regular language S over the alphabet $\mathcal{P}(A)$, where $A = \cup_i A_i$. The system is *correct* iff $L(\mathcal{A}_I) \subseteq S$. If S is given as a deterministic TBA $\mathcal{A}_S$, then we can solve this algorithmically. Consider TBAs $\mathcal{A}_i = \langle \mathcal{P}(A_i), S_i, S_{i_0}, C_i, E_i, F_i \rangle$, $i = 1, \ldots n$, and the deterministic TBA $\mathcal{A}_S = \langle \mathcal{P}(A), S_0, S_{0_0}, C_0, E_0, F_0 \rangle$. Assume without loss of generality that the clock sets C_i, $i = 0, \ldots n$, are disjoint.

The verification algorithm constructs the transition table of the region automaton corresponding to the product $\mathcal{A}$ of the timed transition tables of $\mathcal{A}_i$ with $\mathcal{A}_S$. The set of clocks of $\mathcal{A}$ is $C = \cup_i C_i$. The states of $\mathcal{A}$ are of the form $\langle s_0, \ldots s_n \rangle$ with each $s_i \in S_i$. The initial states of $\mathcal{A}$ are of the form $\langle s_0, \ldots s_n \rangle$ with each $s_i \in S_{i_0}$. A transition of $\mathcal{A}$ is obtained by coupling the transitions of the individual automata labeled with consistent event sets. The transitions of the region automaton $R(\mathcal{A})$ are defined from the edges of $\mathcal{A}$ as described in Section 3.5. To test the desired inclusion, the algorithm searches for a cycle in the region automaton such that

(1) it is accessible from an initial state of $R(\mathcal{A})$,
(2) it satisfies the progressiveness condition: for each clock $x \in C$, the cycle contains at least one region satisfying $[(x = 0) \vee (x > c_x)]$,
(3) since our definition of the composition requires that we consider only those infinite runs in which each automaton participates infinitely many times, we require that, for each $1 \leq i \leq n$, the cycle contains a transition in which the automaton $\mathcal{A}_i$ participates,
(4) the fairness requirements of all implementation automata $\mathcal{A}_i$ are met: for each $1 \leq i \leq n$, the cycle contains some state whose i-th component belongs to the accepting set F_i,
(5) the fairness condition of the specification is *not* met: the cycle does not contain a state whose 0-th component belongs to the accepting set F_0.

The desired inclusion does not hold iff a cycle with all the above conditions can be found.

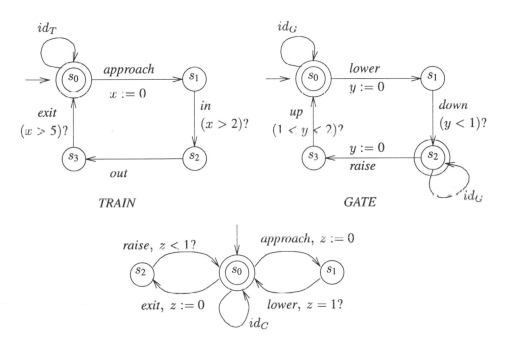

Figure 3.9 Train-gate controller with timing

3.6.2 Verification example

Let us revisit the railroad controller example. We introduce the following timing characteristics to the model of Section 2.4. The train is required to send the signal *approach* at least 2 minutes before it enters the crossing. Furthermore, we know that the maximum delay between the signals *approach* and *exit* is 5 minutes. The gate responds to the signal *lower* by closing within 1 minute, and responds to the signal *raise* within 1 to 2 minutes. The response time of the controller to the *approach* signal is 1 minute, and to the signal *exit* is at most 1 minute. These constraints can easily be expressed using clocks, and the revised model is shown in Figure 3.9. As before, the implementation timed automaton A_I is the parallel composition TRAIN || GATE || CONTROLLER.

In addition to the safety requirement, we can now consider the real-time liveness requirement that the gate is never closed at a stretch for more than 10 minutes. The real-time liveness property is specified by the timed automaton of Figure 3.10. The automaton requires that every *down* be followed by *up* within 10 minutes. Note that the automaton is deterministic, and hence can be complemented. Furthermore, observe that the acceptance condition is not necessary; we can include state s_1 also in the acceptance set. This is because the progress of time ensures that the self-loop on state s_1 with the clock constraint $(x < 10)$ cannot be taken indefinitely, and the automaton will eventually visit state s_0.

The correctness of A_I against the two specifications can be checked separately as outlined

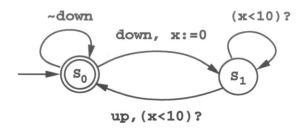

Figure 3.10   Real-time liveness property

in Section 3.6. Observe that though the safety property is purely a qualitative property, it does not hold if we discard the timing requirements. In case of both properties, the region automaton of the product has only a few reachable vertices (approximately 100), and all the tools can verify the property quickly (less than 1 minute).

3.6.3   Heuristics

The number of regions in a region automaton is exponential in the total number of clocks, and is proportional to the magnitudes of constants in the clock constraints. To alleviate this blow-up a variety of heuristics have been proposed.

Manipulating with Zones

The first heuristic attempts to group regions together. Consider a timed transition table $A = \langle \Sigma, S, S_0, C, E \rangle$. A clock zone is a union of one or more clock regions. The zone automaton $Z(A)$ is a transition table over the alphabet Σ

- The states of $Z(A)$ are of the form $\langle s, \alpha \rangle$ where $s \in S$ and α is a clock zone.
- The initial states are of the form $\langle s_0, [\nu_0] \rangle$ where $s_0 \in S_0$ and $\nu_0(x) = 0$ for all $x \in C$.
- $Z(A)$ has an edge $\langle s, \alpha \rangle \xrightarrow{a} \langle s', \alpha' \rangle$ iff the zone α' contains all clock interpretations ν' such that $\langle s, \nu \rangle \xrightarrow{a} \langle s', \nu' \rangle$ for some $\nu \in \alpha$.

Example 3.6.1   Let us revisit the region construction of Example 3.5.2 (see Figure 3.8). The reachable part of the zone automaton is shown in Figure 3.6.3. Note that, unlike the region automaton, in the zone automaton, each vertex has at most one successor per input symbol. The number of vertices of $Z(A_0)$ is less than the number of vertices of $R(A_0)$. ■

The emptiness of the language of a timed automaton A can be checked by searching for cycles in the zone automaton $Z(A)$. Theoretically, the number of zones is exponential in the number of regions, and thus, the zone automaton may be exponentially bigger than the region automaton. However, in practice, the zone automaton has fewer reachable vertices, and thus, leads to an improved performance. Furthermore, while the number of clock regions grows with the magnitudes of the constants used in the clock constraints, experience indicates that the number of reachable zones is relatively insensitive to the magnitudes of constants.

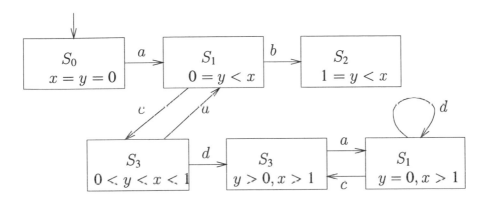

Figure 3.11   Reachable zone automaton

Observe that if the timed transition table A has n clocks, then each zone is a subset of the n-dimensional euclidean space R^{+n}. Each zone can be represented by linear inequalities over the clock variables. Let us call a zone *simple* if it can be described as a conjunction of clock constraints and formulas of the form $x - y \leq c$, $x - y \geq c$, $x - y < c$, and $x - y > c$ for clocks x and y, and constant c. Thus, a simple zone is convex, and is described by comparing either a clock value, or difference of two clocks, with constants. The structure of timed transition tables ensures that

> If a vertex $\langle s, \alpha \rangle$ of the zone automaton $Z(A)$ is reachable from an initial state, then the zone α is a (finite) union of simple zones.

A simple zone can be nicely represented by a structure called *difference-bound-matrix* (DBM) (see [Dil89a] for details). While searching for cycles in the zone automaton, each zone is maintained as a union of DBMs, and the edges of the zone automaton are computed on the fly. The DBM representation allows efficient computation of the successors of a vertex. Furthermore, the DBM representation is canonical, hence, testing equality between two zones is easy.

The tool KRONOS allows verification of timed automata based on search using zones. Instead of deterministic timed automata as specifications, KRONOS uses timed μ-calculus as the specification language. We refer the reader to [HNSY94] for the theory underlying KRONOS, and to [NOSY93] for the description of the tool and its applications.

Approximations

A variety of abstract interpretation techniques can be used to improve the performance of searching in the zone automaton. As we indicated, manipulating with simple zones is efficient. The vertices of the zone automaton contain unions of simple zones. The search can be speeded up by replacing a union of simple zones by the smallest simple zone containing them. For instance, the zone $x < 1 \vee 2 < x < 3$ is replaced by the simple zone $x < 3$.

Formally, for a timed transition table A, the approximate-zone automaton $Z^*(A)$ is a transition table as follows. A state of $Z^*(A)$ is a pair $\langle s, \alpha \rangle$ consisting of a state $s \in S$ and a simple zone α. A state $\langle s, \alpha \rangle$ is initial if $s \in S_0$ and α contains the single clock interpretation that assigns 0 to all clocks. $Z^*(\mathcal{A})$ has an edge $\langle s, \alpha \rangle \xrightarrow{a} \langle s', \alpha' \rangle$ iff the zone α' is the smallest simple zone that contains all clock interpretations ν' such that $\langle s, \nu \rangle \xrightarrow{a} \langle s', \nu' \rangle$ for some $\nu \in \alpha$. In other words, if the zone automaton has the edge $\langle s, \alpha \rangle \xrightarrow{a} \langle s', \alpha'' \rangle$, and α' is the convex hull of α'' then $Z^*(\mathcal{A})$ has the edge $\langle s, \alpha \rangle \xrightarrow{a} \langle s', \alpha' \rangle$.

The transition table $Z^*(\mathcal{A})$ approximates $Z(\mathcal{A})$. The acceptance conditions on $Z(\mathcal{A})$ are translated to the acceptance conditions on $Z^*(\mathcal{A})$. Thus, instead of searching $Z(\mathcal{A})$ we can search for cycles in $Z^*(\mathcal{A})$. Note that searching in the approximate-zone automaton $Z^*(\mathcal{A})$ can be done efficiently manipulating DBMs.

If the language of $Z^*(\mathcal{A})$ is empty then so is the language of $Z(\mathcal{A})$, and so is the language of $\mathcal{A}$ (when $\mathcal{A}$ represents the product of the components together with the complement of the specification, this means that the system satisfies its specification). However, when the language of $Z^*(\mathcal{A})$ is nonempty, we cannot conclude nonemptiness of the language of $Z(\mathcal{A})$. In this case, we may need to perform the search in $Z(\mathcal{A})$. More effective techniques that perform repeated search using only simple zones have been developed. See [Won94] for a variety of approximation techniques for zone automata, and experimental results on its applications.

Iterative Verification

Consider a TBA $\mathcal{A} = \langle \Sigma, S, S_0, C, E \rangle$. The computational complexity of the verification problem depends upon the number of clocks and magnitudes of constants in clock constraints. The iterative approximation strategy considers TBAs $\mathcal{A}_0, \mathcal{A}_1, \mathcal{A}_2, \ldots$ and in iteration i, tests the emptiness of $L(\mathcal{A}_i)$. The approximations satisfy the following property:

- Each TBA $\mathcal{A}_i$ is an approximation of $\mathcal{A}$: $L(\mathcal{A}) \subseteq L(\mathcal{A}_i)$.
- Each TBA $\mathcal{A}_i$ has the same state-transition structure as $\mathcal{A}$, but simpler clock constraints than $\mathcal{A}$ (i.e. the constraints on edges of $\mathcal{A}_i$ use less number of clocks, or constants with smaller magnitudes).
- As i increases, $\mathcal{A}_i$ is a better approximation of $\mathcal{A}$: $L(\mathcal{A}_{i+1}) \subset L(\mathcal{A}_i)$.
- The approximations converge in finite number number of iterations: for some i, $L(\mathcal{A}) = L(\mathcal{A}_i)$.

Specifically, $\mathcal{A}_0$ has the same state-transition structure as $\mathcal{A}$ except that every clock constraint of $\mathcal{A}$ is simplified to true. Testing emptiness of $\mathcal{A}_0$ is easy: we simply need to search for a reachable cycle that contains an accepting state. If $L(\mathcal{A}_0)$ is empty then so is $L(\mathcal{A})$, and we are done. If not, then there is a word $\overline{\sigma}$ and an accepting run $\overline{s}$ of $\mathcal{A}_0$ over $\overline{\sigma}$. The next step is to test whether there exists a time sequence $\overline{\tau}$ such that $\mathcal{A}$ has a run over $(\overline{\sigma}, \overline{\tau})$ that follows the state-sequence $\overline{s}$. This problem is computationally easy, and can be solved efficiently in polynomial-time. If there is such a run, then $\overline{\sigma} \in Untime(L(\mathcal{A}))$, and we can infer that $L(\mathcal{A})$ is nonempty. If not, then the algorithm needs to compute the next approximation $\mathcal{A}_1$. The approximation is computed by adding a minimal set of constraints of $\mathcal{A}$ to $\mathcal{A}_0$ so that $\mathcal{A}_1$ has no run corresponding to $\overline{s}$. A variety of heuristics are used for this purpose. The next example illustrates the ideas.

Example 3.6.2 Consider the TBA $\mathcal{A}$ shown in Figure 3.6.3 (the alphabet is unary, and 5 is the accepting state). The automaton uses 3 clocks, and the largest constant is 20. Thus, the region automaton has large number of vertices. Observe that $L(\mathcal{A})$ is empty.

The first approximation is $\mathcal{A}_0$. The language $L(\mathcal{A}_0)$ is nonempty, and the accepting run is $\overline{s} = 012345^\omega$. This run $\overline{s}$ is checked against the constraints of $\mathcal{A}$, and the run is found

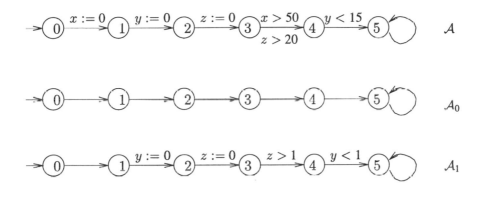

Figure 3.12 Iterative verification

to be inconsistent (i.e. $\mathcal{A}$ cannot follow the run $\bar{s}$). The algorithm then computes a minimal set $C' \subseteq \{x, y, z\}$ of clocks such that thee constraints on the clocks in C' are sufficient for the inconsistency of $\bar{s}$. In this case, $C' = \{y, z\}$. Next, the algorithm attempts to relax the constraints: lower bounds can be decreased, and upper bounds can be increased. In particular, $y < 15$ can be replaced by $y < 20$. Also, it is possible to divide all constants by the greatest common divisor of all the constants. This leads to the approximation $\mathcal{A}_1$. The automaton $\mathcal{A}_1$ has only 2 clocks, and the constants are small. The region automaton of $\mathcal{A}_1$ is used to conclude that $L(\mathcal{A}_1)$ is empty, and this implies $L(\mathcal{A})$ is empty. ∎

Thus at each step of the iteration, either we can conclude the emptiness or nonemptiness of $L(\mathcal{A})$, or need to add additional constraints (with relaxed bounds) to obtain a better approximation. For precise details of the iterative scheme, see [AIKY95]. This heuristic is implemented in the tool COSPAN (see [AIKY95] for experimental results). In many cases, the original emptiness question can be answered in a few iterations. Another advantage of the method is that in many cases the algorithm computes the tight bounds that are needed to prove the specification.

3.7 DISCUSSION

In this chapter, we have shown how to extend the theory of finite automata to incorporate timing, and illustrated its application to verification of real-time systems. Various tools such as COSPAN, HSIS, and KRONOS incorporate timing verification based on these principles. For further details on the implementations and experimental results the reader is referred to [NOSY93, AIKY95, Won94].

Related work

There is an extensive literature on verification of timed systems. Examples of formalisms that admit modeling real-time systems include timed Petri nets [Ram74], timed transition systems [Ost90, HMP91], timed I/O automata [LA92], process algebras such timed CSP [RR88] and

ATP [NRSV90], and Modecharts [JM87]. The algorithmic techniques developed for timed automata apply to these other models also.

In this paper, we used automata not only to describe the system, but also to write correctness requirements. Alternatively, real-time requirements can be written as formulas of timed temporal logics. Model-checking algorithms for various timed temporal logics have been developed: examples include discrete linear-time logics [JM86, Ost90, AH94], dense linear-time logics [AFH91], discrete branching-time logics [EMSS90, CC94], and dense branching-time logics [ACD93, HNSY94]

We have considered only algorithmic methods for verification that can be fully automated, and apply only to finite-state systems. Real-world problems need decomposition of the given verification problem into subproblems to which the verification algorithms can be applied. This decomposition requires a careful modeling that admits compositional and hierarchical reasoning. Such issues are discussed in, for instance, [AL91, LV92, Sha92].

Hybrid systems

Recently, the model of timed automata has been extended so that continuous variables other clocks, such as temperature and imperfect clocks, can be modeled. *Hybrid automata* are useful in modeling discrete controllers embedded within continuously changing environment. Verifying correctness of hybrid automata is computationally more expensive than of timed automata, but in simple cases, such as the railroad controller, it allows reasoning with parametric bounds. We refer the reader to [ACH$^+$95] for an introduction to hybrid automata, and to [HH95] for an introduction to the verifier HyTech.

REFERENCES

[ABB$^+$94]   A. Aziz, F. Balarin, R. Brayton, S. Cheng, R. Hojati, T. Kam, S. Krishnan, R. Ranjan, A. Sangiovanni-Vincetelli, T. Shiple, V. Singhal, S. Tasiran, and H. Wang. HSIS: A BDD-based environment for formal verification. In *Proc. Design Automation Conference*, 1994.

[ACD93]   R. Alur, C. Courcoubetis, and D.L. Dill. Model-checking in dense real-time. *Information and Computation*, 104(1):2–34, 1993.

[ACH$^+$95]   R. Alur, C. Courcoubetis, T. Henzinger, P. Ho, X. Nicollin, A. Olivero, J. Sifakis, and S. Yovine. The algorithmic analysis of hybrid systems. *Theoretical Computer Science*, 138: 3–34, 1995.

[AD94]   R. Alur and D.L. Dill. A theory of timed automata. *Theoretical Computer Science*, 126:183–235, 1994.

[AFH91]   R. Alur, T. Feder, and T.A. Henzinger. The benefits of relaxing punctuality. In *Proceedings of the Tenth ACM Symposium on Principles of Distributed Computing*, pages 139–152, 1991.

[AH94]   R. Alur and T.A. Henzinger. A really temporal logic. *Journal of the ACM*, 41(1):181–204, 1994.

[AIKY95]   R. Alur, A. Itai, R.P. Kurshan, and M. Yannakakis. Timing verification by successive approximation. *Information and Computation*, 118(1):142–157, 1995.

[AL91]   M. Abadi and L. Lamport. An old-fashioned recipe for real time. In *Real-Time: Theory in Practice, REX Workshop*, LNCS 600, pages 1–27. Springer-Verlag, 1991.

[CC94]   S. Campos and E. Clarke. Real-time symbolic model checking for discrete time models. In *Theories and experiences for real-time system development*, AMAST series in computing, 1994.

[Dil89a]   D.L. Dill. Timing assumptions and verification of finite-state concurrent systems. In J. Sifakis, editor, *Automatic Verification Methods for Finite State Systems*, LNCS 407, pages 197–212. Springer–Verlag, 1989.

[Dil89b]   D.L. Dill. *Trace Theory for Automatic Hierarchical Verification of Speed-independent Circuits*. ACM Distinguished Dissertation Series. MIT Press, 1989.

[EMSS90]   E.A. Emerson, A.K. Mok, A.P. Sistla, and J. Srinivasan. Quantitative temporal reasoning. In E.M. Clarke and R.P. Kurshan, editors, *Computer-Aided Verification, 2nd International Conference, CAV'90*, LNCS 531, pages 136–145, 1990.

[HH95]   T. Henzinger and P. Ho. Hytech: The cornell hybrid technology tool. Technical report, Cornell University, 1995.

[HMP91]   T.A. Henzinger, Z. Manna, and A. Pnueli. Temporal proof methodologies for real-time systems. In *Proceedings of the 18th ACM Symposium on Principles of Programming Languages*, pages 353–366, 1991.

[HNSY94]   T.A. Henzinger, X. Nicollin, J. Sifakis, and S. Yovine. Symbolic model-checking for real-time systems. *Information and Computation*, 111(2):193–244, 1994.

[JM86]   F. Jahanian and A.K. Mok. Safety analysis of timing properties in real-time systems. *IEEE Transactions on Software Engineering*, SE–12(9):890–904, 1986.

[JM87]   F. Jahanian and A.K. Mok. A graph-theoretic approach for timing analysis and its implementation. *IEEE Transactions on Computers*, C–36(8):961–975, 1987.

[Kur94]   R.P. Kurshan. *Computer-aided Verification of Coordinating Processes: the automata-theoretic approach*. Princeton University Press, 1994.

[LA92]   N.A. Lynch and H. Attiya. Using mappings to prove timing properties. *Distributed Computing*, 6:121–139, 1992.

[LT87]   N.A. Lynch and M. Tuttle. Hierarchical correctness proofs for distributed algorithms. In *Proceedings of the Seventh ACM Symposium on Principles of Distributed Computing*, pages 137–151, 1987.

[LV92]   N. Lynch and F. Vaandrager. Action transducers and timed automata. In *Proceedings of the Third Conference on Concurrency Theory CONCUR '92*, LNCS 630, pages 436–455. Springer-Verlag, 1992.

[McM93]   K. McMillan. *Symbolic model checking: an approach to the state explosion problem*. Kluwer Academic Publishers, 1993.

[NOSY93]   X. Nicollin, A. Olivero, J. Sifakis, and S. Yovine. Recent results on the description and analysis of timed systems. Technical report, VERIMAG, Grenoble, France, 1993.

[NRSV90]   X. Nicollin, J.-Luc Richier, J. Sifakis, and J. Voiron. ATP: an algebra for timed processes. In *Proceedings of the IFIP TC2 Working Conference on Programming Concepts and Methods, Sea of Galilee, Israel*, 1990.

[Ost90]   J. Ostroff. *Temporal Logic of Real-time Systems*. Research Studies Press, 1990.

[Ram74]   C. Ramchandani. Analysis of asynchronous concurrent systems by Petri nets. Technical Report MAC TR-120, Massachusetts Institute of Technology, 1974.

[RR88]   G.M. Reed and A.W. Roscoe. A timed model for communicating sequential processes. *Theoretical Computer Science*, 58:249–261, 1988.

[Sha92]   A.U. Shankar. A simple assertional proof system for real-time systems. In *Proceedings of the 13th IEEE Real-Time Systems Symposium*, pages 167–176, 1992.

[Tho90]   W. Thomas. Automata on infinite objects. In J. van Leeuwen, editor, *Handbook of Theoretical Computer Science*, volume B, pages 133–191. Elsevier Science Publishers, 1990.

[Won94]   H. Wong-Toi. *Symbolic approximations for verifying real-time systems*. PhD thesis, Stanford University, 1994.

4

Formal Verification of Real-Time Systems Using Timed Automata

CONSTANCE HEITMEYER
Naval Research Laboratory

NANCY LYNCH
Massachusetts Institute of Technology

ABSTRACT

The use of the Lynch-Vaandrager timed automaton model is illustrated with a solution to the Generalized Railroad Crossing problem. The solution shows formally the correspondence between four system descriptions, an axiomatic (i.e., descriptive) specification, an operational specification represented in terms of timed automata, a discrete system implementation, and a system implementation that works with a continuous gate model. Several sample proofs are given. In the development of the solution, a number of guidelines were applied. These guidelines, which should prove useful in applying formal methods to practical systems, are described and illustrated with examples.

4.1 INTRODUCTION

Recently, researchers have proposed many innovative formal methods for use in the development of real-time systems. Such methods are intended to give system developers and customers greater confidence that the systems satisfy their requirements, especially their critical requirements. However, applying formal methods to practical systems raises a number of questions:

1. How can the artifacts produced in applying formal methods (e.g., formal descriptions, formal proofs) be made understandable to the developers?
2. To what extent can software developers use the formal methods (including formal proof methods)?

Formal Methods For Real-Time Computing, Edited by Heitmeyer and Mandrioli
© 1996 John Wiley & Sons Ltd

3. Real-time systems are usually embedded in environments with continuous components. Given that most formal methods usually rely on discrete models, how can continuous models be incorporated into the formal methods?
4. What kinds of tools can aid developers in applying formal methods?

To address these and other questions, a formal methods expert (Lynch) and an applications expert (Heitmeyer) collaborated in a case study to solve the Generalized Railroad Crossing (GRC) problem [HJL93]. This problem is of special interest because it is more complex than other real-time benchmarks, such as Fischer's mutual exclusion algorithm [Fis], and because versions of the GRC problem have been solved using a number of other real-time formal methods. This chapter presents a solution to the GRC based on the Lynch-Vaandrager timed automaton model [LV91, LV], using invariant and simulation mapping techniques. (See [LV] for a description of these methods and [LA92, Lyn94] for some examples of uses of these methods for timed automata.) It also summarizes our experience in developing the solution. Our close collaboration allowed us to quickly identify and correct some deficiencies in the original problem statement. It also led to representations of the problem and its solution that are usable both by application experts, who need to ensure that the specified system is what is needed, *and* by formal methods experts, who need a formal basis for verification.

This chapter, an extended version of reference [HL94a], is organized as follows. Section 4.2 discusses the general guidelines we found useful in using formal methods to solve this problem, introduces the formal model and proof techniques, and summarizes how we applied the formal methods to the GRC problem. Section 4.3 presents our highest-level problem specification, intended to be understood by applications experts; this specification, referred to as the *axiomatic* specification, improves over the original problem statement by resolving some ambiguities. Section 4.4 contains a secondary operational specification, that is, a specification in terms of automata, which is intended to be useful in formal verification. Section 4.5 contains our system implementation. Section 4.6 outlines the main correctness proof, which shows that the system implementation satisfies the operational specification; it includes some details of two proofs to illustrate the proof styles useful in reasoning with this formal method, namely, invariant assertions and simulation mappings. Section 4.7 presents our fourth system description, which substitutes a more realistic continuous gate model for the discrete gate model used in the third system description, and then shows that the results proved in Section 4.6 extend to a system implementation that incorporates the more realistic environment model. Section 4.8 evaluates the formal method with respect to several criteria. The details of the proofs that the operational specification satisfies the axiomatic specification are provided in a technical report [HL94b].

4.2   APPROACH

4.2.1   Applying Formal Methods to Practical Systems

Applying formal methods to real-time systems involves three major steps of the development process: system requirements specification, design of an implementation, and verification that the implementation satisfies the specification. This three-step process has feedback loops, since, once specified, the requirements and implementation must be revised when later steps in the development process expose omissions and errors.

The use of formal methods requires close collaboration between the formal methods expert and the applications expert during all three steps. The role of the formal methods expert is to produce formal descriptions of both the system requirements and the selected implementation and to prove formally that the implementation satisfies the requirements. The role of the applications expert is to work closely with the formal methods expert to identify the "real" requirements and to ensure that the specified implementation is acceptable. In our collaboration, much of the dialogue focused on the system requirements. Once the requirements specification was acceptable, defining and verifying an implementation, while labor-intensive and time-consuming, was relatively straightforward.

A system requirements specification describes the required external behavior of all acceptable system implementations [HM83]. It has two parts: (1) A set of formal models describing the computer system at an abstract level, the environment (here, the trains and the gate), and the interface between them. (2) Formal statements of the properties that the system must satisfy.

In developing the GRC solution, we found the following guidelines useful. The first four concern the requirements specification. The next two concern the implementation and its verification, and the seventh applies to all three steps.

Axiomatic Specifications. *Specify the required system properties in a descriptive, axiomatic style rather than operationally.* In the original problem statement, both the Safety Property and the Utility Property are expressed in an axiomatic style: each is a relationship that must hold between the two components of the system environment, namely, the trains and the crossing gate. Thus, the required system properties are properties of the environment. Neither property mentions the computer system. The two properties are also stated independently, making it easy to modify them individually.

In applying the timed automaton model, the usual approach is to specify properties operationally so that certain standard verification methods can be used. Thus, in our case study, we initially represented the requirements operationally, as a timed automaton. Our formulation incorporated both the Safety and Utility Properties into a single automaton description, thus losing the advantage of independence. Also, our formulation was stronger than the original, specifying some aspects of what the computer system should do rather than just describing properties that the system needed to guarantee in the environment. Finally, the operational style of our formulation was harder for applications experts to understand. Our final version of the system requirements, which appears in Section 4.3, is axiomatic. Like the original problem statement, it describes the two properties as independent axioms about the environment. It is easy to see that the representation of the properties in the axiomatic specification is equivalent to their representation in the original problem statement.

Verification of the Operational Specification. *Provide an operational specification plus a formal proof that the operational specification implements the axiomatic specification.* Although it is desirable to start with a axiomatic specification, the types of proofs used with the timed automata model rest on operational, automaton versions of the specification and implementation. Therefore, we also present a second, operational requirements specification using timed automata and prove that the operational specification implements the original axiomatic specification.

As in many applications of formal methods, we initially neglected to provide a formal proof of the correspondence between the axiomatic specification and the operational specification. Without such a proof, there is no assurance that the properties satisfied by the system implementation are the ones that are required. In our case, while it is immediately obvious that the statement of the Safety Property in our operational specification is equivalent to the original statement of the Safety Property, the correspondence between the axiomatic and operational versions of the Utility Property is not so clear.

Underspecification and Overspecification. *In the system specification, state exactly what is required – nothing more, nothing less.* In developing our solution, we discovered aspects of the original GRC problem statement that were underspecified. Additional notation is needed to specify the parameters of interest and how they are related. For example, if ϵ_1 represents the minimum time a train requires to travel from the region's entry to the crossing's entry and γ_{down} is the maximum time the gate needs to move down. then we require that $\epsilon_1 > \gamma_{down}$, because it must be possible for the gate to move down before a train reaches the crossing. This constraint was missing from the original problem statement.

A specification should also avoid overspecification. For example, a linear model of the gate position is undesirable, because such a model is not sufficiently general: The gate model must also allow the position of the gate with respect to time to be described as a nonlinear function.

Unreasonable behavior. *Make sure the specified system behavior is reasonable.* The original specification requires the system to do useless work. For example, suppose a train exits the crossing at time t and another train enters the crossing at time $t + b$, where b is the maximum time it takes the gate to go up and then to immediately move down. In this situation, there is insufficient time for even one car to travel through the crossing, yet the Utility Property requires the gate to move up. Thus the Utility Property fails to achieve its practical purpose. To rule out such useless activity, the specification of the Utility Property in the axiomatic specification differs slightly from the property given in the original problem statement: The gate is raised only if sufficient time, δ, exists for at least one car to travel through the crossing.

Verification of the Implementation. *Provide a formal model for the implementation and a proof that it implements the operational specification.* The implementation should be described using the same model that is used for the operational specification, or at least one that is compatible. The proof that the implementation meets the specification can be done using a variety of methods—by hand, as in our study, or with computer assistance.

Continuous Models. *If the environmental models are naturally continuous, verify that the solution still works when a continuous model, rather than a discrete model, is used in the proofs.* To make the specification and the proofs more understandable and to simplify the proofs, we initially used a discrete, abstract model of the gate. However, we later showed formally that the system implementation is still valid when a second, more realistic (i.e., continuous) gate model is substituted for the discrete model.

Understandable Proofs and Descriptions. *Express the system requirements specification, the implementation, and the formal proofs so that they are understandable to applications experts.* If the requirements specification and the specification of the implementation are difficult to understand, the applications expert cannot be confident that the right requirements have been specified and that the implementation is acceptable. The applications expert must also be able to understand the formal proofs. This gives the expert a deep understanding of how and why the system works and how future changes are likely to affect system behavior. To increase their understandability, both the formal specifications and the proofs should be based on standard models such as automaton models, standard notations, and standard proof techniques such as invariants and simulation mappings. To the extent feasible, applications experts should not be required to learn new notations or proof techniques.

4.2.2 The Formal Framework

The formal method used to specify the GRC problem and to develop and verify a solution represents both the computer system and the system environment as *timed automata*, according to the definitions of Lynch and Vaandrager [LV91, LV]. A timed automaton is a very general automaton, i.e., a labeled transition system. It need not be finite-state: for example, the state can contain real-valued information such as the current time or the position of a train or crossing gate. This makes timed automata suitable for modeling not only computer systems but also real-world entities such as trains and gates. The timed automaton model describes a system as a set of timed automata, interacting by means of common actions. In solving the GRC problem, we define separate timed automata for the trains, the gate, and the computer system; the common actions are sensors reporting the arrival of trains and actuators controlling the raising and lowering of the gate. Below, we provide some basic definitions.

Timed Automata. A *timed automaton* A consists of four components:[1]

- *states*(A) is a (finite or infinite) set of states.
- *start*(A) $\subseteq$ *states*(A) is a nonempty (finite or infinite) set of start states.
- *acts*(A) is a (finite or infinite) set of actions divided into *internal* and *external* actions. The external actions include special *time-passage* actions $\nu(t)$, where t is a positive real number, and *visible* actions. The visible actions are classified as *input* and *output* actions.
- *steps*(A) $\subseteq$ *states*(A) $\times$ *acts*(A) $\times$ *states*(A) is a set of steps (i.e., transitions).

Figure 4.1 shows the classification of actions in the timed automaton model. Note that output and internal actions are those performed by the automaton, while inputs are performed by the automaton's environment. The automaton can establish conditions on when an output or internal action can occur but can only react passively to an input. An external action is one that can be shared between the automaton and its environment, whereas an internal action is for local computation only and is hidden from the environment.

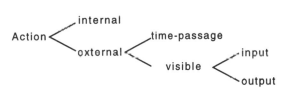

Figure 4.1   The classification of actions in the timed automaton model.

To make the notation more concise, we often write $s \xrightarrow{\pi}_A s'$ as shorthand for $(s, \pi, s') \in$ *steps*(A). Further, in representing a timed automaton A or any of its components, we often suppress the subscript or argument A.

A timed automaton satisfies two axioms. The first says that consecutive time-passage steps can be combined into a single step:

[A1]: If $s \xrightarrow{\nu(t)} s''$ and $s'' \xrightarrow{\nu(t')} s'$, then $s \xrightarrow{\nu(t+t')} s'$.

The second axiom, a kind of converse to [A1], requires the preliminary definition of a *trajectory*, which describes the state changes that can occur during time-passage. (Since

---

[1] There is a slight difference between the model of this chapter and the one used in [HL94a] and [HL94b]. Namely, in those papers, we required the current real time to be represented explicitly in the automaton state. Although this is convenient in many examples, it is not necessary for the general model. The proofs are not changed significantly.

timed automata can be used to model continuous real-world behavior, such changes can be significant.) Namely, if I is a left-closed interval of the reals with left endpoint 0, then an I-trajectory is a function

$$w : I \rightarrow states$$

such that $w(t_1) \xrightarrow{\nu(t_2-t_1)} w(t_2)$ for all $t_1, t_2 \in I$ with $t_1 < t_2$. That is, w assigns a state to each time t in interval I, in such a way that time-passage steps can span between any two states assigned by w. The second axiom says that every time-passage step can be "filled in" with a trajectory:

[A2]: If $s \xrightarrow{\nu(t)} s'$ then there is a $[0, t]$-trajectory w such that $w(0) = s$ and $w(t) = s'$.

Timed Executions and Timed Traces A *timed execution fragment* is a finite or infinite alternating sequence $\alpha = w_0 \pi_1 w_1 \pi_2 w_2 \cdots$, where each w_j is a trajectory and each π_j is a non-time-passage action, and where each π_{j+1} "connects" the final state s of the preceding trajectory w_j with the initial state s' of the following trajectory w_{j+1}, $s \xrightarrow{\pi_{j+1}} s'$. A *timed execution* is a timed execution fragment in which the initial state of the first trajectory is a start state. A state of a timed automaton is defined to be *reachable* if it is the final state of the final trajectory in some finite timed execution of the automaton. In a timed execution, a *time of occurrence* can be associated with each instance of a state or action, in a natural way (by adding up all the preceding amounts of time-passage).

Our examples only use the *admissible* timed executions, i.e., those in which the total amount of time-passage is ∞. We use the notation $atexecs(A)$ for the set of admissible timed executions of timed automaton A.

To describe the problems to be solved by timed automata, we require a definition of their visible behavior. We use the notion of *timed traces*, where the *timed trace* of any timed execution is just the sequence of visible actions that occur in the timed execution, paired with their times of occurrence. Thus the sequence has the form $(\pi_1, t_1), (\pi_2, t_2), \cdots$, where each π_j is a non-time-passage action and each t_j is a nonnegative real-valued time. The *admissible timed traces* of a timed automaton are just the timed traces that arise from all the admissible timed executions. We use the notation $attraces(A)$ for the set of admissible timed traces of timed automaton A. If α is any timed execution, we use the notation $ttrace(\alpha)$ to denote the timed trace of α.

Composition. Let A and B be timed automata that are *compatible*, in the sense that they have no output actions in common, and that no internal action of A is an action of B, and vice versa. Then the *composition* of A and B, written as $A \times B$, is the timed automaton defined as follows:

- $states(A \times B) = states(A) \times states(B)$.
- $start(A \times B) = start(A) \times start(B)$.
- $acts(A \times B) = acts(A) \cup acts(B)$; an action is *visible* in $A \times B$ exactly if it is visible in either A or B, and likewise for *internal* actions; a visible action of $A \times B$ is an *output* in $A \times B$ exactly if it is an output in either A or B and is an *input* otherwise.
- $(s_A, s_B) \xrightarrow{\pi}_{A \times B} (s'_A, s'_B)$ exactly if

  1. $s_A \xrightarrow{\pi}_A s'_A$ if $\pi \in acts(A)$, else $s_A = s'_A$, and
  2. $s_B \xrightarrow{\pi}_B s'_B$ if $\pi \in acts(B)$, else $s_B = s'_B$.

Thus, A and B can proceed jointly on a common input or time-passage action, or on an output of one that is an input of the other.

If α is a timed execution of $A \times B$, then $\alpha|A$ and $\alpha|B$ denote the projections of α on A and B. For instance, $\alpha|A$ is defined by projecting all states in α on the state of A, removing actions that do not belong to A and combining consecutive trajectories. The projection notation is also used for sequences of actions; for example, $\beta|A$ denotes the subsequence of β consisting of actions of A.

MMT Automata. The *MMT automaton model* [MMT91, LA92, Lyn94] provides a convenient way of representing many (but not all) of the timed automata in this chapter. The model is essentially a special case of the general Lynch-Vaandrager timed automaton model, in which the automata have a very simple, stylized structure. In particular, an MMT automaton can be expressed as an *I/O automaton* [LT89] together with upper and lower bounds on the time between certain actions. An I/O automaton is a labeled transition system representing an *asynchronous* (non-real-time) system, in which the output and internal actions are grouped into *tasks*. An MMT automaton includes an upper bound and a lower bound for each task; these are used as bounds on the time between successive actions of the task (when any are enabled). (In this chapter, each task of each automaton consists of only a single action.)

A timed execution of an MMT automaton A is an alternating sequence of the form $s_0, (\pi_1, t_1), s_1, \cdots$, where the π's are input, output or internal actions (but not time-passage actions). For each j, it must be that $s_j \xrightarrow{\pi_{j+1}} s_{j+1}$. The successive times $t_1, t_2, \cdots$ are nondecreasing and required to satisfy the given lower and upper bounds, plus an admissibility requirement. It is easy to transform any MMT automaton A into a naturally-corresponding timed automaton A'. The resulting timed automaton has exactly the same admissible timed traces as the MMT automaton A.

Invariants and Simulation Mappings. An *invariant* of a timed automaton is any property that is true of all reachable states, or equivalently, any set of states that contains all the reachable states. A simulation mapping [LV91, LV, Lyn94] relates the states s of one timed automaton to the states u of another in such a way that admissible timed traces correspond. Let the notation $f[s]$, where f is a binary relation, denote $\{u : (s, u) \in f\}$. Suppose A and B are timed automata and P_A and P_B are invariants of A and B. Then a *simulation mapping* from A to B with respect to P_A and P_B is a relation f over $states(A)$ and $states(B)$ that satisfies:

1. If $s \in start(A)$ then $f[s] \cap start(B) \neq \emptyset$.
2. If $s \xrightarrow{\pi}_A s'$, $s, s' \in P_A$, and $u \in f[s] \cap P_B$, then there exists $u' \in f[s']$ such that there is a timed execution fragment from u to u' having the same timed visible actions and the same total amount of time-passage as the given step.

Note that in the second item of this definition, π can be a visible, internal or time-passage action. If π is a visible action, then there must be exactly one timed visible action in the corresponding timed execution fragment, whereas if π is an internal or time-passage action, there will be no timed visible actions in the fragment.

The most important fact about these simulations is that they imply admissible timed trace inclusion:

Theorem 4.2.1 *If there is a simulation mapping from timed automaton A to timed automaton B, with respect to any invariants, then $attraces(A) \subseteq attraces(B)$.*

This means that each visible behavior of automaton A, that is, each sequence of A's visible actions, together with their times of occurrence, is contained in the set of visible behaviors of automaton B.

4.2.3 Applying Formal Methods to the GRC Benchmark

The four system descriptions that make up our GRC solution are: *AxSpec*, the axiomatic requirements specification; *OpSpec*, the operational requirements specification; *SystImpl*, the discrete system implementation; and *SystImpl'*, a system implementation with a continuous gate model. Figure 4.2 illustrates the four specifications and how they are related.

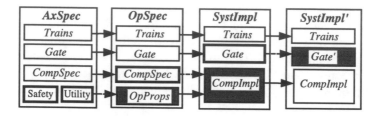

Figure 4.2 The four system descriptions and how they are related. In *OpSpec*, *OpProps* incorporates the Safety and Utility properties into the automaton that results from composing *Trains*, *Gate*, and *CompSpec*.

The top-level requirements specification, *AxSpec*, contains timed automata describing the computer system and its environment (the trains and gate), and axioms expressing the Safety and Utility Properties. The Safety Property states that any time there is a train in the crossing, the gate must be down. The Utility Property states that the gate is up unless there is a train in the vicinity. Formally, these axioms are properties added to the composition of three timed automata: *Trains*, *Gate*, and *CompSpec*, where *CompSpec* is a trivial specification of the computer system interface. Figure 4.3 illustrates *AxSpec*.

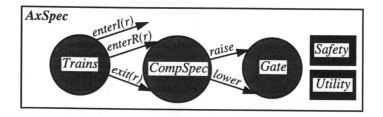

Figure 4.3 *AxSpec* is the composition of *Trains*, *Gate*, and *CompSpec*, constrained by the Safety and Utility properties.

Next, because it is easier to use in proving correctness, we produce a second operational requirements specification in the form of a timed automaton *OpSpec*. In [HL94b], we have shown that *OpSpec* implements *AxSpec*.

Next, we describe our computer system implementation as a timed automaton, *CompImpl*. Correctness means that *CompImpl*, when it interacts with *Trains* and *Gate*, guarantees the Safety and Utility Properties. To show this, we prove that *SystImpl*, the composition of *CompImpl*, *Trains* and *Gate*, provides the same view to the environment components, *Trains* and *Gates*, as the operational specification *OpSpec*. This part of the proof follows well-established, stylized invariant and simulation mapping methods, which is why we moved from the axiomatic style of specification to the operational style. All of these proofs can be verified using current mechanical proof technology.

In both specification automata, *AxSpec* and *OpSpec*, and also in the implementation automaton *SystImpl*, time information is built into the state. Timing information consists of the current time plus some deadline information, such as the earliest and latest times that a train that has entered R will actually enter the crossing.[2] The correctness proof proceeds by first proving by induction some invariants about the reachable states of *SystImpl*. The main work in the proof of the Safety Property is done by means of these invariants. An interesting feature of the proofs is that the invariants involve time deadline information.

Next, we show a "simulation mapping" between the states of *SystImpl* and *OpSpec*, again by induction; this is enough to prove the Utility Property. Like the invariants, the simulations involve time deadline information, in particular, inequalities involving time deadlines.

Finally, our main proofs yield a weaker result that what is needed. We have worked with abstract, discrete models of the trains and gate rather than with realistic models that allow continuous behavior. And we have only shown that the "admissible timed traces", i.e., the sequences of visible actions, together with their times of occurrence, are preserved, rather than all aspects of the environment's behavior. We conclude by showing that we have not lost any generality by proving the weaker results. In particular, preservation of admissible timed traces actually implies preservation of all aspects of the environment's behavior. Further, the results extend to *SystImpl'*, a system implementation with a more realistic environment model. Both extensions are obtained as corollaries of the results for admissible timed traces of the discrete model, using general results about composition of timed automata.

4.3 AXIOMATIC SPECIFICATION

We first define two timed automata, *Trains* and *Gate*, which are abstract representations of the trains and gate, respectively. These two components do not interact directly. We then define a trivial automaton *CompSpec*, which interacts with both *Trains* and *Gate* via actions representing sensors and actuators. *CompSpec* describes nothing more than the interface that the computer system must have with the environment. *AxSpec* is obtained by composing these three automata and then imposing the Safety and Utility Properties on the composition; see Figure 4.3. Formally, the two properties are restrictions on the executions of the composition. The Safety Property is just a restriction on the states that occur in the execution, while the Utility Property is a more complex temporal condition.

4.3.1 Parameters and Other Notation

The symbols r, r', etc., denote trains. The symbols I, R, and P denote the railroad crossing, the region from where a train passes a sensor until it exits the crossing, and the portion of R prior to the crossing, respectively. The following positive real-valued constants are defined:

- ϵ_1, a lower bound on the time from when a train enters R until it reaches I.
- ϵ_2, an upper bound on the time from when a train enters R until it reaches I.

---

[2] Including this time information in the state does not contradict footnote 1. Footnote 1 says that the general timed automaton model does not *require* the inclusion of a *now* component in the state. However, there is nothing to *prevent* us from including such a component in the state of any particular automaton we define.

- δ, the minimum useful time for the gate to be up. (For example, this might represent the minimum time for a car to pass through the crossing safely.)
- γ_{down}, an upper bound on the time to lower the gate completely.
- γ_{up}, an upper bound on the time to raise the gate completely.
- ξ_1, an upper bound on the time from the start of lowering the gate until some train is in I.
- ξ_2, an upper bound on the time from when the last train leaves I until the gate is up (unless the raising is interrupted by another train getting "close" to I).
- β, an arbitrarily small constant used to take care of some technical race conditions.[3]

We need some restrictions on the values of the various constants:

1. $\epsilon_1 \leq \epsilon_2$.
2. $\epsilon_1 > \gamma_{down}$. (The time from when a train arrives until it reaches the crossing is sufficiently large to allow the gate to be lowered.)
3. $\xi_1 \geq \gamma_{down} + \beta + \epsilon_2 - \epsilon_1$. (The time allowed between the start of lowering the gate and some train reaching I is sufficient to allow the gate to be lowered in time for the fastest train, and then to accommodate the slowest train. The time γ_{down} is needed to lower the gate in time for the fastest train, but the slowest train could take an additional time $\epsilon_2 - \epsilon_1$. The β is a technicality.)
4. $\xi_2 \geq \gamma_{up}$. (The time allowed for raising the gate is sufficient.)

4.3.2   Trains

We model the *Trains* component as an MMT automaton with no input or internal actions, and three types of outputs, *enterR(r)*, *enterI(r)*, and *exit(r)*, for each train r. The state consists of a *status* component for each train, just saying where it is.

State:

> for each train r:
> $r.status \in \{not\text{-}here, P, I\}$, initially *not-here*

The state transitions are described by specifying the "preconditions" under which each action can occur and the "effect" of each action. We use s to denote the state before the event occurs and s' the state afterwards. We use the convention that if a state component is not mentioned, it is unchanged (although sometimes, to resolve ambiguities or for emphasis, we say explicitly that a component is unchanged).

Transitions:

enterR(r)	*exit(r)*
Precondition:	Precondition:
$s.r.status = not\text{-}here$	$s.r.status = I$
Effect:	Effect:
$s'.r.status = P$	$s'.r.status = not\text{-}here$

enterI(r)
   Precondition:
      $s.r.status = P$
   Effect:
      $s'.r.status = I$

For this automaton (and for all the other MMT automata in this chapter), we consider each non-input action to comprise a task by itself. For the *Trains* automaton, we specify only trivial

---

[3] These arise because the model allows more than one event to happen at the same real time.

bounds (that is, $[0, \infty]$) for the $enterR(r)$ and $exit(r)$ actions. For each $enterI(r)$ action, we use bounds $[\epsilon_1, \epsilon_2]$. This means that from the time when any train r has reached R, it is at least time ϵ_1 and at most time ϵ_2 until train r reaches I. Note that by not defining an upper bound on the $exit(r)$ actions, we are assuming that a train in the crossing I may never exit. While it is certainly undesirable to have a train remain in I forever, our results do not depend on this not happening.

We use the general construction described in [HL94b] to convert this automaton to a timed automaton. This construction involves adding some components to the state – a current time component *now*, and *first* and *last* components for each task, giving the earliest and latest times at which an action can occur once enabled. The transition relation is augmented with conditions to enforce the bound assumptions, that is, that an event cannot happen before its *first* time, and that time cannot pass beyond any *last* time. In this case, only the state components *now*, and $first(enterI(r))$ and $last(enterI(r))$ for each r contain nontrivial information, so we ignore the other cases. Applying this construction yields the timed automaton with the same actions and the following states and transitions. (In this automaton description, as well as elsewhere in the chapter, we sometimes omit explicit mention of the state where there is no ambiguity.)

State:
    now, a nonnegative real, initially 0
    for each train r:
        $r.status \in \{not\text{-}here, P, I\}$, initially *not-here*
        $first(enterI(r))$, a nonnegative real, initially 0
        $last(enterI(r))$, a nonnegative real or ∞, initially ∞.

Transitions:

$enterR(r)$
    Precondition:
        $s.r.status = not\text{-}here$
    Effect:
        $s'.r.status = P$
        $s'.first(enterI(r)) = now + \epsilon_1$
        $s'.last(enterI(r)) = now + \epsilon_2$

$enterI(r)$
    Precondition:
        $s.r.status = P$
        $now \geq s.first(enterI(r))$
    Effect:
        $s'.r.status = I$
        $s'.first(enterI(r)) = 0$
        $s'.last(enterI(r)) = \infty$

$exit(r)$
    Precondition:
        $s.r.status = I$
    Effect:
        $s'.r.status = not\text{-}here$

$\nu(t)$
    Precondition:
        for all r,
            $s.now + t \leq s.last(enterI(r))$
    Effect:
        $s'.now = s.now + t$

4.3.3 Gate

We model the gate as another MMT automaton, this one with inputs *lower* and *raise* and outputs *down* and *up*. The nontrivial time bounds are *down*: $[0, \gamma_{down}]$, and *up*: $[0, \gamma_{up}]$, where γ_{up} and γ_{down} are upper bounds on the time required for the gate to be raised and lowered. To build time into the state, the state components *now*, $last(up)$, and $last(down)$ are added to produce the following states and transitions.

State:

> $status \in \{up, down, going\text{-}up, going\text{-}down\}$, initially up
> now, a nonnegative real, initially 0
> $last(down)$, a nonnegative real or ∞, initially ∞
> $last(up)$, a nonnegative real or ∞, initially ∞

Transitions:

lower
> Effect:
>> if $s.status \in \{up, going\text{-}up\}$ then
>>> $s'.status = going\text{-}down$
>>> $s'.last(down) = now + \gamma_{down}$
>>> $s'.last(up) = \infty$
>> else unchanged $status, last(down),$
>>> $last(up)$

raise
> Effect:
>> if $s.status \in \{down, going\text{-}down\}$ then
>>> $s'.status = going\text{-}up$
>>> $s'.last(up) = now + \gamma_{up}$
>>> $s'.last(down) = \infty$
>> else unchanged $status, last(down),$
>>> $last(up)$

down
> Precondition:
>> $s.status = going\text{-}down$
> Effect:
>> $s'.status = down$
>> $s'.last(down) = \infty$

up
> Precondition:
>> $s.status = going\text{-}up$
> Effect:
>> $s'.status = up$
>> $s'.last(up) = \infty$

$\nu(t)$
> Precondition:
>> $s.now + t \le s.last(up)$
>> $s.now + t \le s.last(down)$
> Effect:
>> $s'.now = s.now + t$

4.3.4 CompSpec

We model the computer system interface as a trivial MMT automaton *CompSpec* with inputs *enterR(r)* and *exit(r)* for each train r, and outputs *lower* and *raise*. *CompSpec* receives sensor information when a train arrives in the region R and when it leaves the crossing I. Note that *CompSpec* does not have an input action *enterI(r)*; this expresses the assumption that there is no sensor that informs the system when a train actually enters the crossing. *CompSpec* has just a single state. Inputs and outputs are always enabled, and cause no state change. There are no timing requirements. (While not actually required, we include in the specification, for the sake of clarity, the precondition *true* for both the *lower* and *raise* actions.)

Transitions:

enterR(r)
> Effect:
>> none

exit(r)
> Effect:
>> none

lower
> Precondition:
>> *true*
> Effect:
>> none

raise
> Precondition:
>> *true*
> Effect:
>> none

4.3.5 AxSpec

To get the full specification, we compose the three MMT automata given above, *Trains*, *Gate* and *CompSpec*, yielding a new MMT automaton. But this is not enough: we then add constraints to express the two correctness properties in which we are interested. Formally, these constraints are axioms about an *admissible timed execution* α of the composition automaton. We state the Utility Property in terms of the occupancy intervals $[\tau_i, \nu_i]$ used in the original problem statement: that is, $t \in [\tau_i, \nu_i]$ iff at time t there are one or more trains in the crossing. In the statements of these properties and elsewhere in this paper, we include the automaton name, *Trains*, *Gate*, etc., as a prefix to disambiguate similarly named state components. We do not bother to prefix the *now* component, since it must be the same in all the composed automata.

1. **Safety Property**

   All the states in α satisfy the following condition: If *Trains.r.status* $= I$ for some r, then *Gate.status* $=$ *down*.

2. **Utility Property**

   If s is is a state in α with $s.Gate.status \neq up$, then for some i at least one of the following holds.

   (a) $s.now \in [\tau_i - \xi_1, \nu_i + \xi_2]$ or
   (b) $s.now \in [\nu_i + \xi_2, \tau_{i+1} - \xi_1]$ with $\tau_{i+1} - \nu_i \leq \xi_2 + \delta + \xi_1$.

The Safety and Utility properties are stated independently. The Safety Property is an assertion about all the states reached in α, saying that all satisfy the critical safety property. In contrast, the Utility Property is a temporal property with a somewhat more complicated structure, which says that if the gate is not up, then either there is a recent preceding state or an imminent following state in which a train is in the crossing I. The second condition takes care of the special case where there is both a recent state and an imminent state in which some train is in I; although these states are not quite as recent or imminent as required by the first case, there is insufficient time for a car to pass through the crossing.

The composition of *Trains*, *Gate* and *CompSpec* constrained by the two properties form the axiomatic specification *AxSpec*. We define the *admissible timed executions* of *AxSpec*, *atexecs*(*AxSpec*), to be the set of admissible timed executions of the composition automaton that satisfy the Safety and Utility axioms. Also, we define the *admissible timed traces* of *AxSpec*, *attraces*(*AxSpec*), to be the set of timed traces of such executions. These are analogous to the notions of admissible timed execution and admissible timed traces used for timed automata.

4.3.6 Implementation Requirements

An implementation of *AxSpec* uses a new timed automaton, called *CompImpl*, with the same interface as *CompSpec*. *CompImpl* will be composed with the same *Trains* and *Gate* automata given above, yielding a new system *SystImpl*. The system *SystImpl* should produce executions that, when projected on the environment (*Trains* composed with *Gate*), yields behavior that is also allowed by the system specification *AxSpec*. More precisely, for every admissible timed execution α of *SystImpl*, there should be a corresponding admissible timed execution α' of *AxSpec* such that $\alpha'|Trains \times Gate = \alpha|Trains \times Gate$. That is, the two executions project identically on the *Trains* and *Gate* automata.

4.4 OPERATIONAL SPECIFICATION

Unlike *AxSpec*, which consists of a timed automaton together with some axioms that describe restrictions on the automaton's executions, the operational specification, *OpSpec*, is simply a timed automaton – all required properties are built into the automaton itself as restrictions on the state set and on the actions that are permitted to occur. As a result, *OpSpec* is probably harder for an applications expert to understand than *AxSpec*. But it is easier to use in proofs (at least for the style of verification we are using). Thus we regard *OpSpec* as an intermediate specification rather than a true problem specification; we only require that *OpSpec* implement *AxSpec*, not necessarily vice versa, and that all implementations satisfy *OpSpec*.

The two specifications are also different in another respect: the Safety and Utility properties are stated independently in *AxSpec*, whereas they are intertwined in *OpSpec*. When a collection of separate properties is specified by an automaton, the properties usually become intertwined.

4.4.1   The Specification

To obtain *OpSpec*, we first compose *Trains*, *Gate*, and *CompSpec*, and then incorporate the Safety and Utility Properties into the automaton itself. Formally, the modified automaton is obtained from the composition by restricting it to a subset of the state set, then adding some additional state components, and finally modifying the definitions of the steps to describe their dependence on and their effects on the new state components. Although the composition of the three component automata is an MMT automaton, the modified version is not – it is a timed automaton.

First, to express the Safety Property, we restrict the states to be those states of the composition that satisfy the following invariant: "If $Trains.r.status = I$ for any r, then $Gate.status = down$."

Second, the time-bound restrictions expressed by the Utility Property are encoded as restrictions on the steps. The strategy is similar to that used to encode MMT time bound restrictions into the steps of a timed automaton – it involves adding explicit deadline components. We describe the modifications in two parts:

1. *The time from when the gate starts going down until some train enters I is bounded by ξ_1.* To express this restriction formally, we add to the state of the composed system a new deadline $last_1$, representing the latest time in the future that a train is guaranteed to enter I. Initially, this is set to ∞, meaning that there is no such scheduled requirement. To add this new component to *OpSpec*, we include the following new effects in two of the actions:

    Transitions:

lower	*enterI(r)*
Effect:	Effect:
if $s.Gate.status \in \{up, going\text{-}up\}$	$s'.last_1 = \infty$
and $s.last_1 = \infty$ then	
$s'.last_1 = now + \xi_1$	
else unchanged $last_1$	

    As before, we also add a new precondition to the time-passage action $\nu(t)$, that $s.now + t \le s.last_1$. That is, the time-passage action cannot cause time to pass beyond $s.last_1$. This means that whenever the gate starts moving down, some train must enter I within time ξ_1. The new effect being added to the *lower* action just "schedules" the arrival of a train in I.

2. *From when the crossing becomes empty, either the time until the gate is up is bounded by ξ_2 or else the time until a train is in I is bounded by $\xi_2 + \delta + \xi_1$.* Again, we express the condition by adding deadlines, only this time the situation is trickier since there are two alternative bounds rather than just one. We add two new components, $last_2(up)$ and

$last_2(I)$, both initially ∞. The first represents a milestone to be noted – whether or not the gate reaches the *up* position by the designated time – rather than an actual deadline. In contrast, the second represents a real deadline – a time by which a new train must enter I, *unless* the gate reached the *up* position by the milestone time $last_2(up)$. To add these new components to *OpSpec*, we include the following additional effects in three of the actions:

Transitions:

$exit(r)$
    Effect:
        if $s.Trains.r'.status \neq I$ for all $r' \neq r$
        then
            $s'.last_2(up) = now + \xi_2$
            $s'.last_2(I) = now + \xi_2 + \delta + \xi_1$
        else
            unchanged $last_2(up)$
            unchanged $last_2(I)$

up
    Effect:
        if $now \leq s.last_2(up)$ then
            $s'.last_2(up) = \infty$
            $s'.last_2(I) = \infty$
        else
            unchanged $last_2(up)$
            unchanged $last_2(I)$

$enterI(r)$
    Effect:
        $s'.last_2(up) = \infty$
        $s'.last_2(I) = \infty$

Also, as with $last_1$, an implicit precondition is placed on the time-passage action, saying that time cannot pass beyond $last_2(I)$. But no such limitation is imposed for time passing beyond $last_2(up)$, because this is just a milestone to be recorded, not a time-blockage.

4.4.2 Properties

We make some simple claims about *OpSpec*:

Lemma 4.4.1 *In all reachable states of OpSpec:*

1. *If* $Trains.r.status = I$ *for any* r, *then* $Gate.status = down$.
2. $last_2(up) + \delta + \xi_1 = last_2(I)$.

Lemma 4.4.2 *In all reachable states of OpSpec:*

1. $now \leq last_1$.
2. $now \leq last_2(I)$.
3. *If* $last_1 \neq \infty$ *then* $last_1 \leq now + \xi_1$.
4. *If* $last_2(I) \neq \infty$ *then* $last_2(I) \leq now + \xi_2 + \delta + \xi_1$.
5. *If* $last_2(up) \neq \infty$ *then* $last_2(up) \leq now + \xi_2$.

4.4.3 Relationship Between *OpSpec* and *AxSpec*

We show that *OpSpec* implements *AxSpec* in the following sense:

Lemma 4.4.3 *For any admissible timed execution α of OpSpec, there is an admissible timed execution α' of AxSpec such that $\alpha'|Trains \times Gate = \alpha|Trains \times Gate$. (This is the same as saying that α satisfies the two properties given explicitly for AxSpec.)*

Note that the relationship between *OpSpec* and *AxSpec* is only one-way: there are admissible timed executions of *AxSpec* that have no executions of *OpSpec* yielding the same projection. Consider, for instance, the following example. Suppose that after I becomes empty, the system does a very rapid *raise*, *lower*, *raise*. These could conceivably all happen within time ξ_2 after the previous time there was a train in I, which would make this "waffling" behavior legal according to *AxSpec*. However, when this *lower* occurs, there is no following entry of a train into I, which means that this does not satisfy *OpSpec*.

4.5   IMPLEMENTATION

To describe our implementation *SystImpl*, we use the same *Trains* and *Gate* automata but replace the *CompSpec* component in *OpSpec* and *AxSpec* with a new component *CompImpl*, a computer system implementation. *CompImpl* is a timed automaton (not an MMT automaton) with the same interface as *CompSpec*. It keeps track of the trains in R together with the earliest possible time that each might enter I. (This time could be in the past.) It also keeps track of the latest operation that it has performed on the gate and the current time.

State:
>   for each train r:
>> $r.status \in \{not\text{-}here, R\}$, initially *not-here*
>> $r.sched\text{-}time$, a nonneg. real number or ∞, initially ∞
> $gate\text{-}status \in \{up, down\}$, initially *up*
>   *now*, a nonnegative real, initially 0

Transitions:

enterR(r)
>   Effect:
>> $s'.r.status = R$
>> $s'.r.sched\text{-}time = now + \epsilon_1$

exit(r)
>   Effect:
>> $s'.r.status = not\text{-}here$
>> $s'.r.sched\text{-}time = \infty$

lower
>   Precondition:
>> $s.gate\text{-}status = up$
>> $\exists r :\ s.r.sched\text{-}time \le$
>>> $now + \gamma_{down} + \beta$
>   Effect:
>> $s'.gate\text{-}status = down$

raise
>   Precondition:
>> $s.gate\text{-}status = down$
>> $\not\exists r :\ s.r.sched\text{-}time \le$
>>> $now + \gamma_{up} + \delta + \gamma_{down}$
>   Effect:
>> $s'.gate\text{-}status = up$

$\nu(t)$
>   Precondition:
>> if $s.gate\text{-}status = up$ then
>>> $s.now + t < s.r.sched\text{-}time - \gamma_{down}$
>>> for all r
>> if $s.gate\text{-}status = down$ then
>>> $\exists r :\ s.r.sched\text{-}time \le$
>>>> $s.now + \gamma_{up} + \delta + \gamma_{down}$
>   Effect:
>> $s'.now = s.now + t$

Observe that the fact that *CompImpl.gate-status* $=$ *up* does not mean that *Gate.status* $=$ *up* but just that *Gate.status* $\in \{up, going\text{-}up\}$. A similar remark holds for *CompImpl.gate-status* $=$ *down*. Note that *r.sched-time* keeps track of the earliest time that train r might enter I. The system lowers the gate if the gate is currently up (or going up) and some train might soon arrive in I. Here "soon" means by the time the computer system can lower the gate plus a little bit more – this is where we consider the technical race condition mentioned earlier. The system raises the gate if the gate is currently down (or going down) and no train can soon arrive in I. This time, "soon" means by the time the gate can be raised plus the time for a car to pass through the crossing plus the time for the system to lower the gate. The system allows time to pass subject to two conditions. First, if *gate-status* $=$ *up*, then real time is not allowed to reach a time at which it is necessary to lower the gate. Second, if *gate-status* = *down* and the gate should be raised, then time cannot increase at all (until the gate is raised).

The full system implementation, *SystImpl*, is just the composition of the *Trains*, *Gate* and *CompImpl* components. Some basic invariants about *SystImpl* are useful; the next two lemmas say that *CompImpl* has accurate information about the trains and gate, respectively.

Lemma 4.5.1 *The following are true in any reachable state of SystImpl:*

1. *CompImpl.r.status* = R *iff Trains.r.status* $\in \{P, I\}$.
2. *If Trains.r.status* = P, *then CompImpl.r.sched-time* = *Trains.first(enterI(r))*.
3. *If CompImpl.r.status* = R *and CompImpl.r.sched-time* > *now, then Trains.r.status* = P.
4. *If Trains.r.status* = I, *then CompImpl.r.sched-time* $\leq$ *now.*
5. *If CompImpl.r.sched-time* $\neq \infty$, *then Trains.r.status* $\in \{P, I\}$.

Lemma 4.5.2 *The following are true in any reachable state of SystImpl:*

1. *CompImpl.gate-status* = *up if and only if Gate.status* $\in \{up, going\text{-}up\}$.
2. *CompImpl.gate-status* = *down if and only if Gate.status* $\in \{down, going\text{-}down\}$.

4.6   CORRECTNESS PROOF

The main correctness proof shows that every admissible execution of *SystImpl* projects on the external world like some admissible execution of *OpSpec*.

We first state a collection of invariants, leading to a proof of the safety property. All are proved by induction on the length of an execution. The first invariant says that if a train is in the region and the gate is either up or going up, then the train must still be far from the crossing. We include the proof of Lemma 4.6.1 just for illustration; the following proofs follow the same style.

Lemma 4.6.1 *In all reachable states of SystImpl, if Trains.r.status* = P *and Gate.status* $\in \{up, going\text{-}up\}$, *then Trains.first(enterI(r))* > *now* + γ_{down}.

Proof: By induction on the length, i.e., the total number of non-time-passage and time-passage steps, of an execution. After 0 steps, the claim is vacuously satisfied, since *Trains.r.status* = *not-here*. Assume the claim is true after m steps. We must prove it is true after $m + 1$ steps.

Fix any particular train r. We need only consider actions that cause *Trains.r.status* to become equal to P, cause *Gate.status* to change to be in $\{up, going\text{-}up\}$, decrease *Trains.first(enterI(r))*, or increase *now*, namely *enterR(r)*, *raise*, and $\nu(t)$ actions. The other actions do not affect the statement.

1. *enterR(r)*

An effect is s'.*Trains.first(enterI(r))* = *now* + ϵ_1. Since $\epsilon_1 > \gamma_{down}$ by an assumption on the constants, we have s'.*Trains.first(enterI(r))* > *now* + γ_{down}, as needed.

2. *raise*

Assume s'.*Trains.r.status* = P. The precondition implies s.*CompImpl.r.sched-time* >

$now + \gamma_{up} + \delta + \gamma_{down}$, so that $s.CompImpl.r.sched\text{-}time > now + \gamma_{down}$ and therefore $s'.CompImpl.r.sched\text{-}time > now + \gamma_{down}$. By Lemma 4.5.1, Part 2, $s'.CompImpl.r.sched\text{-}time = s'.Trains.first(enterI(r))$. So $s'.Trains.first(enterI(r)) > now + \gamma_{down}$, as needed.

3. $\nu(t)$

Assume $s'.Trains.r.status = P$ and $s'.Gate.status \in \{up, going\text{-}up\}$. Then, Lemma 4.5.2 implies that $s'.CompImpl.gate\text{-}status = up$, and the precondition for time passage implies that $s'.now < s.CompImpl.r.sched\text{-}time - \gamma_{down}$. By Lemma 4.5.1, Part 2, $s.CompImpl.r.sched\text{-}time = s.Trains.first(enterI(r))$. So, $s.Trains.first(enterI(r)) > s'.now + \gamma_{down}$, which implies $s'.Trains.first(enterI(r)) > s'.now + \gamma_{down}$, as needed.

■

The second invariant says that if a train is nearing I and the gate is going down, then the gate is nearing the *down* position. In particular, the earliest time at which the train might enter I is strictly after the latest time at which the gate will be down.

Lemma 4.6.2 *In all reachable states of SystImpl, if Trains.r.status = P and Gate.status = going-down, then Trains.first(enterI(r)) > Gate.last(down).*

These invariants are used in the (inductive) proof of the main safety result:

Lemma 4.6.3 *In all reachable states of SystImpl, if Trains.r.status = I for any r, then Gate.status = down.*

To show the Utility Property, we present the simulation mapping from *SystImpl* to *OpSpec*. Specifically, if s and u are states of *SystImpl* and *OpSpec*, respectively, then we define s and u to be related by relation f provided that:

1. $u.now = s.now$.
2. $u.Trains = s.Trains.$[4]
3. $u.Gate = s.Gate$.
4. $u.last_1 \geq min\{s.Trains.last(enterI(r))\}$.
5. Either $u.last_2(I) \geq min\{s.Trains.last(enterI(r))\}$, or
   $u.last_2(up) \geq now + \gamma_{up}$ and the *raise* precondition holds in s, or
   $u.last_2(up) \geq s.Gate.last(up)$ and $s.Gate.status = going\text{-}up$.

The first three parts of the definition are self-explanatory. The last two parts provide connections between the time deadlines in the specification and implementation. In the typical style for this approach, the connections are expressed as inequalities. The fourth condition bounds the latest time by which some train must enter I, a bound mentioned in the specification, in terms of the actual time it could take in the implementation, namely, the minimum of the latest times for all the trains in P. The fifth condition is slightly more complicated – it bounds the time for *either* some train to enter I or the gate to reach the up position. There are two cases for the gate reaching the up position – one in which the gate has not yet begun to rise and the other in which it has.

---

[4] By this we mean that the entire state of the *Trains* automaton, including the time components, is preserved.

Theorem 4.6.4 f *is a simulation mapping from SystImpl to OpSpec, with respect to the invariant stated in Lemma 3.6.3.*

Proof: We show the two conditions required for a simulation mapping. The first condition is immediate, because the unique start states of the two automata satisfy all the relationships in the definition of f. The interesting condition is the step condition.

Suppose that $s \xrightarrow{\pi}_{SystImpl} s'$, s and s' satisfy the invariants of *SystImpl*, and $u \in f[s]$ satisfies the invariants I'm absolutely useless here... of *OpSpec*. We must produce $u' \in f[s']$ such that there is a timed execution fragment from u to u' having the same timed visible actions and the same total amount of time-passage as the given step. We do this using a case analysis based on π.

Some arguments are similar for all the cases. For example, for each non-time-passage action π, we first argue that π is enabled in u, and then define u' to be the unique state that results from applying the action π from state u. For a time-passage action, we first argue that the same amount of time can pass from u, and then define u' to be the unique state that results from allowing that amount of time to pass.

Then in each case, we must check that $u' \in f[s']$; in each case, Conditions 1-3 are easy to check, so we need only consider Conditions 4 and 5. We only include key details for two illustrative cases. The other cases follow the same style.

1. $\pi = enterR(r)$.

Enabling: Since π is enabled in s, we have $s.Trains.r.status = not\text{-}here$. Since $u \in f[s]$, we have $u.Trains.r.status = not\text{-}here$. This implies that π is enabled in u.

Condition 5: The only alternative that might be falsified by π is the second, and only if $enterR(r)$ falsifies the *raise* precondition. So suppose that $u.last_2(up) \geq now + \gamma_{up}$ and the *raise* precondition holds in s but gets falsified in s'. Then, there exists r such that $s'.CompImpl.r.sched\text{-}time \leq now + \gamma_{up} + \delta + \gamma_{down}$. Since an effect of the action is $s'.CompImpl.r.sched\text{-}time = now + \epsilon_1$, we have $\epsilon_1 \leq \gamma_{up} + \delta + \gamma_{down}$.

It suffices to show that $u'.last_2(I) \geq s'.Trains.last(enterI(r))$, since that would show that the action makes the first alternative of Condition 5 true. We have that $u'.last_2(I) = u.last_2(I)$ and $s'.Trains.last(enterI(r)) = now + \epsilon_2$. So it suffices to show that $u.last_2(I) \geq now + \epsilon_2$.

Since $u.last_2(up) \geq now + \gamma_{up}$, and $u.last_2(I) = u.last_2(up) + \delta + \xi_1$ (this by Part 2 of Lemma 4.4.1), it is enough to show that $now + \gamma_{up} + \delta + \xi_1 \geq now + \epsilon_2$, or, more simply, that $\gamma_{up} + \delta + \xi_1 \geq \epsilon_2$.

But $\gamma_{up} + \delta \geq \epsilon_1 - \gamma_{down}$ as noted above. And we have that $\xi_1 \geq \gamma_{down} + \epsilon_2 - \epsilon_1$, by an assumption about the constants. So, $\gamma_{up} + \delta + \xi_1 \geq \epsilon_2$ as needed.

2. $\pi = \nu(t)$.

Enabling: We must show that time t is allowed to pass in *OpSpec*. This amounts to showing that $s'.now \leq u.last_1$ and $s'.now \leq u.last_2(I)$.

To show $s'.now \leq u.last_1$, we need only consider the case where $u.last_1 \neq \infty$. In this case, Condition 4 implies that $u.last_1 \geq s.Trains.last(enterI(r))$ for some r. The precondition on time-passage in *CompImpl* implies that $s'.now \leq s.Trains.last(enterI(r))$. So $s'.now \leq u.last_1$, as needed.

To show that $s'.now \leq u.last_2(I)$, we only need to consider the case where $u.last_2(I) \neq \infty$. In this case, we consider the three alternatives of Condition 5 for s and u. If the first alternative holds, then the argument is as for $last_1$. If the second alternative holds, then the *raise* precondition holds in s. But this implies that $\nu(t)$ cannot be enabled in s, a contradiction. If the third alternative holds, then $s'.now \leq s.Gate.last(up) \leq u.last_2(up) \leq u.last_2(I)$, which suffices.

Condition 5: The only alternative that the time-passage action might falsify is the second. But this means that the *raise* precondition holds in s, which is impossible since then $\nu(t)$ could not be enabled in s.

■

Theorems 4.6.4 and 4.2.1 together imply that all admissible timed traces of *SystImpl* are admissible timed traces of *OpSpec*. This is not quite what we need, because it does not give us corresponding projections on environment automata. However, we can obtain the needed correspondence between *SystImpl* and *OpSpec* as a corollary, using general results about composition of timed automata:

Corollary 4.6.5 *For any admissible timed execution α of SystImpl, there is an admissible timed execution α' of OpSpec such that $\alpha'|Trains \times Gate = \alpha|Trains \times Gate$.*

Putting this together with Lemma 4.4.3, we obtain the main theorem, which relates the admissible timed executions of *SystImpl* and *AxSpec*:

Theorem 4.6.6 *For any admissible timed execution α of SystImpl, there is an admissible timed execution α' of AxSpec such that $\alpha'|Trains \times Gate = \alpha|Trains \times Gate$.*

4.7   REALISTIC MODELS OF THE REAL WORLD

The models used above for the trains and gate are rather abstract. An applications expert might prefer more realistic models giving, for instance, exact or approximate positions for the trains and gate. However, a formal methods expert would probably not want to include such details, because they would complicate the proofs. Fortunately, we can satisfy both.

For any real world component, it is possible to define a *pair of models*, one abstract and one more realistic. The only constraint is that the realistic model should be an "implementation" of the abstract model, i.e., its set of admissible timed traces should be included in that of the abstract model. All the difficult proofs are carried out using the abstract models, as above. Then corollaries are given to extend the results to the realistic models. This extension is based on general results about composition of timed automata.

For example, we can define a new type of gate component, *Gate'*, similar to the *Gate* defined above, but having a more detailed model of gate position. *Gate'* is also a timed automaton. Fix any constant γ'_{down}, $0 \leq \gamma'_{down} \leq \gamma_{down}$. Define g_d to be a function mapping $[0, \gamma'_{down}]$ to $[0, 90]$. Function g_d is defined so that $g_d(0) = 90$, $g_d(\gamma'_{down}) = 0$, and g_d is monotone nonincreasing and continuous. $g_d(t)$ gives the position of the gate after it has been going down for time t. Similarly, fix a constant γ'_{up}, $0 \leq \gamma'_{up} \leq \gamma_{up}$, and define g_u to be a function mapping $[0, \gamma'_{up}]$ to $[0, 90]$. Function g_u is defined so that $g_u(0) = 0$, $g_u(\gamma'_{up}) = 90$, and g_u is monotone nondecreasing and continuous.

The actions of *Gate'* are the same as for *Gate*. The state is also the same, with the addition of one new component $pos \in [0, 90]$ to represent the gate position, initially 90. The *lower* and *raise* transitions are the same as for *Gate*, except that γ'_{down} and γ'_{up} are used in place of γ_{down} and γ_{up}; they are omitted below. The *up* and *down* transitions contains new preconditions stating that the correct position has been reached. The time-passage transitions adjust *pos*.

Transitions:

down
    Precondition:
        $s.status = going\text{-}down$
        $s.pos = 0$
    Effect:
        $s'.status = down$
        $s'.last(down) = \infty$

up
    Precondition:
        $s.status = going\text{-}up$
        $s.pos = 90$
    Effect:
        $s'.status = up$
        $s'.last(up) = \infty$

$\nu(t)$
    Precondition:
        $t' = now + t$
        $t' \leq s.last(down)$
        $t' \leq s.last(up)$
    Effect:
        $s'.now = t'$
        if $s.status = going\text{-}up$ then
            $s'.pos = \max\{s.pos,$
              $g_u(t' - (s.last(up) - \gamma'_{up}))\}$
        elseif $s.status = going\text{-}down$ then
            $s'.pos = \min\{s.pos,$
              $g_d(t' - (s.last(down) - \gamma'_{down}))\}$
        else unchanged *pos*

Thus, unlike the more abstract automata considered so far, *Gate'* allows interesting state changes to occur in conjunction with time-passage actions. Note that *Gate'* contains a rather arbitrary decision about what happens if a *lower* event occurs when the gate is in an intermediate position. It says that the gate stays still for the initial time that it would take for the gate to move down to its current position if it had started from position 90. Alternative modeling choices would also be possible. A similar remark holds for *raise*.

We relate the new gate model to the old one.

Lemma 4.7.1 $attraces(Gate') \subseteq attraces(Gate)$.

Now, let *SystImpl'* be the composition of *Trains*, *Gate'*, and *CompImpl*, and let *AxSpec'* be the composition of *Trains*, *Gate'*, and *CompSpec*, with Safety and Utility Properties added as in *AxSpec*. Using Theorem 4.6.6 and general results about composition of timed automata, we obtain:

Theorem 4.7.2 *For any admissible timed execution α of SystImpl', there is an admissible timed execution α' of AxSpec' such that $\alpha'|Trains \times Gate' = \alpha|Trains \times Gate'$.*

4.8   CONCLUDING REMARKS

We have applied a formal method based on timed automata, invariants, and simulation mappings to model, solve, and verify the Generalized Railroad Crossing problem. Here, we extrapolate from this experience and attempt to evaluate the method for modeling and verifying other real-time systems.

Generality.   *Can the method be used to describe all acceptable implementations?* It seems so. Timed automata can have an infinite number of states and both discrete and continuous variables. Further, they can express the maximum allowable nondeterminism, use symbolic parameters to represent system constants, and represent asynchronous communication. Thus the method is significantly more general than state exploration approaches, which typically require a finite number of states and constant timing parameters.

Readability.   *Are the formal descriptions easy to understand?* The environment model and the system implementation model are easy to understand, since these are naturally modeled as automata. The requirements specifications do not look so natural when expressed as automata; an axiomatic form seems easier to understand. However, if one starts with an axiomatic specification, then one has to rewrite the specification as an automaton. It may be difficult to determine that the automaton specification is equivalent to (or implements) the axiomatic specification.

Information.   *Does the proof yield information other than just the fact that the implementation is correct? Does it provide insight into the reasons that the implementation works?* Yes. The invariants and simulations that require considerable effort to produce yield payoffs by providing very useful documentation. They express key insights about the behavior of the implementation. In contrast, state exploration techniques yield no such byproducts, only an assertion that the implementation satisfies the desired properties.

Power.   *Can the method be used to verify all implementations?* Simulation methods (extended beyond what is described in this chapter, to include "backward" as well as "forward" simulations) are theoretically complete for showing admissible timed trace inclusion. They also seem to be powerful in practice, although they might sometimes benefit from combination with other verification methods, such as state exploration, process algebra, temporal logic or partial order techniques. State exploration alone is less powerful in practice, since it only checks whether a subfamily of solutions satisfy some specific properties.

Ease of Carrying out the Proof.   *How hard is it to construct a proof using this method? Can typical software developers learn to do this?* Constructing these proofs, though not difficult, required significant work. The hardest parts were getting the details of the models right and finding the right invariants and simulation mapping. This is an art rather than an automatic procedure. The actual proofs of the invariants and the simulation were tedious but routine.

Carrying out such a modeling and verification effort requires the ability to do formal proofs, which most software developers are not trained to do. In contrast, using a state exploration technique, a software developer can check automatically whether a given "model" satisfies the properties of interest. (State exploration techniques, such as model checkers, are already being used in practice by developers to check the correctness of certain implementations, e.g., of circuits.) On the other hand, the proofs developed using the method of this chapter are amenable to mechanical proof checking. So, automated support can be provided to developers attempting to develop formal proofs.

Scalability.   *Does the formalism scale up to handle larger problems?* We do not yet know. Just reasoning about this relatively simple problem was quite complex. A bigger system will mainly add complexity in the form of more system components and more actions, which leads in turn to more invariants, more components in the simulation mapping, and more cases in the proofs. But, in contrast to model checking, the blowup should not be exponential. Nonetheless, use of the method for larger problems should be coupled with various methods of decomposing a problem, so one need not reason about an entire complex system at once. Additional levels of abstraction and use of parallel composition should help.

Ease of Change.   *How easy is it to modify the specifications and the proofs?* Separating the system model from the environment model and splitting the environment model into the individual gate model and train model makes it easy to change the descriptions. Should one want to use a more complex train model (for example, trains move backward as well as forward), one can easily substitute the revised model for the original. Expressing the required properties axiomatically and independently makes it easier to change the requirements.

Changes to the specifications and implementations require, of course, changes to the proofs. If the changes are fairly small, we expect most of the prior work to survive, and the stylized form of the proof provides useful structure for managing the modifications. Here is a place where mechanical aid would be most helpful – proofs could be rerun quickly to discover which parts need to be changed.

Computer Assistance.   *How can mechanical proof systems help?* Currently, we are developing computer assistance to check the proofs of the theorems in Sections 4.3-4.7. We are also investigating the feasibility of automating, at least in part, different proof styles, such as induction proofs and simulation mappings, useful in reasoning about timed automata. Preliminary results of our initial experiments with the proof system PVS [OSR93] confirm that the hand proofs can be checked mechanically. Automating parts of the proof also appears feasible. PVS has been found to be reasonably "user-friendly": its decision procedures lead to easy proofs of "obvious" assertions, and its support of higher-order logic permits more straightforward proofs than systems supporting only first-order logic. Experiments [SAGG ¹ 93, LSGL95] with the proof system Larch [GH93] on other similar invariant and simulation mapping proofs have also been carried out with similar success.

Acknowledgments. Thanks to M. Archer, R. Jeffords, and the anonymous reviewers for their very useful comments.

REFERENCES

[Fis]   Michael Fischer. Re: Where are you? E-mail message to Leslie Lamport. Arpanet message number 8506252257.AA07636@YALE-BULLDOG.YALE.ARPA (47 lines), June 25, 1985 18:56:29EDT.

[GH93]   John V. Guttag and Jim J. Horning. *Larch: Languages and Tools for Formal Specification.* Springer-Verlag, 1993.

[HJL93]   Constance Heitmeyer, Ralph Jeffords, and Bruce Labaw. A benchmark for comparing different approaches for specifying and verifying real-time systems. In *Proc., 10th Intern. Workshop on Real-Time Operating Systems and Software*, May, 1993.

[HL94a]   Constance Heitmeyer and Nancy Lynch. The Generalized Railroad Crossing: A case study in formal verification of real-time systems. In *Proceedings, Real-Time Systems Symposium*, San Juan, Puerto Rico, December 1994.

[HL94b]   Constance Heitmeyer and Nancy Lynch. The Generalized Railroad Crossing: A case study in formal verification of real-time systems. Technical Report 7619, Naval Research Laboratory, Wash., DC, 1994. Also Technical Report MIT/LCS/TM-51, Lab. for Comp. Sci., MIT, Cambridge, MA, 1994.

[HM83]   Constance Heitmeyer and John McLean. Abstract requirements specifications: A new approach and its application. *IEEE Trans. Softw. Eng.*, SE-9(5), September 1983.

[LA92]   Nancy Lynch and Hagit Attiya. Using mappings to prove timing properties. *Distrib. Comput.*, 6:121–139, 1992.

[LSGL95]   Victor Luchangco, Ekrem Söylemez, Stephen Garland, and Nancy Lynch. Verifying timing properties of concurrent algorithms. In Dieter Hogrefe and Stefan Leue, editors, *Formal Description Techniques VII: Proceedings of the 7th IFIP WG6.1 International Conference on Formal Description Techniques* (FORTE'94, Berne, Switzerland, October 1994), pages 259–273. Chapman and Hall, 1995.

[LT89]   Nancy Lynch and Mark R. Tuttle. An introduction to Input/Output automata. *CWI-Quarterly*, 2(3):219–246, September 1989. Centrum voor Wiskunde en Informatica, Amsterdam, The Netherlands.

[LV]   Nancy Lynch and Frits Vaandrager. Forward and backward simulations – Part II: Timing-based systems. Submitted for publication.

[LV91]   Nancy Lynch and Frits Vaandrager. Forward and backward simulations for timing-based systems. In *Proceedings of REX Workshop "Real-Time: Theory in Practice"*, volume 600 of *Lecture Notes in Computer Science*, pages 397–446, Mook, The Netherlands, June 1991. Springer-Verlag.

[Lyn94]   Nancy Lynch. Simulation techniques for proving properties of real-time systems. In *REX Workshop '93*, volume 803 of *Lecture Notes in Computer Science*, pages 375–424, Mook, the Netherlands, February 1994. Springer-Verlag.

[MMT91]   Michael Merritt, Francesmary Modugno, and Mark R. Tuttle. Time constrained automata. In J. C. M. Baeten and J. F. Goote, editors, *CONCUR'91: 2nd International Conference on Concurrency Theory*, volume 527 of *Lecture Notes in Computer Science*, pages 408–423, Amsterdam, The Netherlands, August 1991. Springer-Verlag.

[OSR93]   Sam Owre, N. Shankar, and John Rushby. User guide for the PVS specification and verification system (Draft). Technical report, Computer Science Lab, SRI Intl., Menlo Park, CA, 1993.

[SAGG⁺93]   Jørgen F. Søgaard-Andersen, Stephen J. Garland, John V. Guttag, Nancy A. Lynch, and Anna Pogosyants. Computer-assisted simulation proofs. In Costas Courcoubetis, editor, *Computer-Aided Verification: 5th International Conference, CAV'93* (Elounda, Greece, June/July 1993), volume 697 of *Lecture Notes in Computer Science*, pages 305–319. Springer-Verlag, 1993.

5

Refining System Requirements to Program Specifications

ERNST-RÜDIGER OLDEROG

FB Informatik, Universität Oldenburg

ANDERS P. RAVN and JENS ULRIK SKAKKEBÆK

Technical University of Denmark

ABSTRACT

A coherent and mathematically well-founded approach to the design of real-time and hybrid systems is presented. It covers requirements analysis and specification, design of controlling automata satisfying the requirements, and derivation of occam-like communicating programs from these automata. The generalized railroad crossing due to [HL94] illustrates the approach.

Requirements are analyzed within a conventional dynamic systems model of a plant, where states are functions of the reals, representing time. The requirements are specified in an assumption-commitment style using *Duration Calculus*, a real-time interval logic. Controlling real-time automata are specified in the same formalism by elementary constraints on the plant states for each control state or *phase*. The Duration Calculus is used to verify that the control design refines the requirements.

The real-time automata map smoothly to component descriptions in a systems design language that uses timed trace assertions over state transition events to constrain control flow. Components can under certain conditions be transformed to occam-like communicating programs.

5.1 INTRODUCTION

Development of real-time computing systems that control physical processes is a challenging task. Some of the problems are illustrated by the following fictive story:

Formal Methods For Real-Time Computing, Edited by Heitmeyer and Mandrioli
© 1996 John Wiley & Sons Ltd

A development team has just completed a fully computerized control system for a railroad level crossing. Testing is now under way, and the first incident report comes in: a train passed while the gates were half-open.

The programmers analyze the post-mortem dump of the computer store. Fortunately the *GateDown* signal has been sent, so it is not their fault. It must be the gate actuator that fails. However, the electronic engineer demonstrates, using the block and circuit diagrams, that if just the *GateDown* signal has been sent within 25μ seconds, then the *Down* state is asserted within 3μ seconds on the gate motor interface. The problem must be with this electro-mechanical subassembly.

Reaching the company that produces the gate subassembly takes a day or two, but eventually, a message comes back: Unless *Down* is asserted continually for at least 9 seconds, the gate is not sure to be down.

Back to the programmers: We sent the signal as fast as possible, but is that fast enough? We assumed that the *Approach* signal was sufficiently ahead of the train entering the crossing. What is really the maximal speed of the trains? ...

The reader can surely continue the story to its end, whether the system finally succeeds to pass the tests or the project is discarded. However, the challenge to researchers in computing science and software engineering is clear: Find coherent notations, theories and techniques that can document the different assumptions and design decisions above, and which allows the team to analyze the scenario beforehand.

There are several issues: One is design documentation with associated engineering practices and standards, preferably supported by tools. This is a very relevant and active research area, but it is not the topic here. If the documentation besides informal inspection and review also is used for reasoning using engineering calculations, the contents must be in a formal notation that define objects in a mathematical framework. Such a framework is the theme of this paper.

A simple answer to the issue of notation and underlying mathematics is to choose a universal language like predicate logic. It is certainly expressive enough to specify any relation among quantities, and it also allows the most flexible calculations. However, they are very tedious to do, as anyone who has had to do formal proofs realizes. Furthermore, even for simple systems like a railroad crossing, the number of quantities (trains, gate assembly, sensors, circuits, program variables) in the state space, over which variables would range, is immense. For these reasons, one cannot consider predicate logic a practical specification language.

There are two modifications that make the proposal feasible. The first is to utilize specialized theories, e.g., mathematical analysis or automata theory, to describe some of the phenomena. This modification is well-known, and is applied in science and engineering to cope with the complexity of analyzing mathematical models of given phenomena. The second modification is to make the specification modular. That is, the quantities are collected in local clusters with associated formulas that only speak about these quantities. Informally, such a procedure has been used for decades, however, it is first with the advent of computing with extremely large state spaces that it has become essential to formalize the notion.

A final consideration is whether one specialized notation suffices to cover the large span of technologies in an embedded real-time system: from mechanical or chemical processes down to electronic circuits. Practice seems to indicate that we need conventional mathematical analysis at the top, a design language somewhere below, programming and hardware description languages at the bottom. In order to have a coherent design, the utmost care must be taken to link these descriptions together.

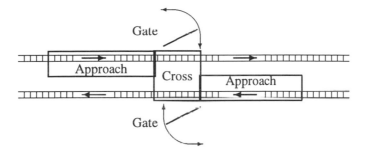

Figure 5.1   Physical components – plant – for the railroad crossing

The objective of the Provably Correct Systems project (ProCoS) [LR94, B+93] is to develop a mathematical basis for development of embedded, real-time, computer systems, therefore the project has investigated one approach to the issues outlined above. This paper introduces the specification languages, verification techniques and links for three levels of development: requirements definition and control design; transformation to a systems architecture with program designs and finally their transformation to programs in an occam-like language. The generalized railroad crossing [HL94] is used as a running example.

The rest of the chapter is organized as follows. Section 5.2 introduces the conventional dynamic systems model with observable states over time. It illustrates the module concept which is taken directly from the Z language [Spi92], and ends with an introduction to the constraint language, Duration Calculus. Section 5.3 shows the formulation of requirements in the form of assumptions and commitments for a controller design.

Section 5.4 introduces some design techniques for systematic decomposition of requirements to elementary commitments for phases of a collection of real-time automata, while Section 5.5 shows variations on the design. In Section 5.6, the automata are transformed to specifications for components in a network of communicating synchronous processes, and these are then in Section 5.7 transformed to programs.

The conclusion points to related and further work, including work on tools to support the approaches.

5.2   SYSTEM MODELS

An embedded computer system is part of a total system that is a physical process, a *plant*, characterized by a state that changes over real time. The role of the computer is to monitor this state through sensors and based on computations from the sensor inputs to change the state through output to actuators. The computer is simply a convenient device that can be instructed to manipulate a mathematical model of the plant. As long as the computations were implemented by electronic or electro-mechanical devices, the technology ensured that the implementations and models were reasonably simple. This is no longer the case; the development of digital computer technology gives an opportunity to implement large, complex programs which are hard to relate to models or even the objectives of systems control.

Our mathematical basis for modeling systems by their observable *states* is identical to the one found in conventional dynamic systems theory [Lue79]. However, in order to deal with complexity we shall immediately introduce a module concept such that the state space can be segmented. Furthermore, specification of constraints cannot be given in the form of differential or difference equations because these will enforce deterministic interaction among components, so we shall introduce a real-time logic, Duration Calculus [ZHR91, ZRH93, Zho93], that formalizes dynamic systems properties. This logic also provides a calculus such that specification of sensors, actuators and controlling state machines can be verified to be a refinement of the requirements [RR91, SRRZ92, RRH93, EKM+93, Ina94].

5.2.1   States

A first step in formalizing properties of a physical system is to agree on a system model with names for observable states. Our basis is the well-known *time-domain model*, where a system is described by a collection of *states* which are functions of time (the real numbers). We illustrate the state concept through the running example: a version of a computer controlled railroad crossing inspired by [HL94]. The railroad crossing has a gate assembly that can raise and lower the gate, and some track monitors that can detect when trains enter and leave the critical section surrounding the crossing. This physical system or plant is illustrated by Figure 5.1.

For the gate assembly it seems obvious to model the gate position by

$$g : Time \rightarrow [0, 90],$$

a continuous-differentiable state function that ranges over values in the interval $[0, 90]$. The domain $Time$ is the non-negative reals. An observation of the gate is thus the angle in degrees to the horizontal (closed) position. Such an observation exists for every point of time, and the movement of the gate is assumed to be continuous and smooth. As usual, we can introduce the state $\dot{g}$ to denote the derivative of g, physically denoting the speed of movement. The position of the gate is controlled by an electro-mechanical assembly which has an input command

$$Down : Time \rightarrow \textbf{Bool}.$$

This is a Boolean state where $Down$ means that the gate shall be closing or closed and $\neg Down$ means that it shall be opening or open. A discrete state like $Down$ cannot be continuous, so we allow sectionally continuous state functions. For a discrete value domain, this means step functions. Real valued functions, like $\dot{g}$, may have discontinuities in isolated points. With g, $\dot{g}$ and $Down$, we have introduced the observables for the gate assembly of this plant.

For the tracks, we shall not bother to model the individual trains, for an example where this is done, see [SRRZ92, Sch94a]. The track monitoring assembly is modeled by

$$Track : Time \rightarrow \{empty, appr, cross\}$$

that ranges over three values:

$empty$:   no trains in the critical section or the crossing,
$appr$:   trains in the critical section, but none in the crossing,
$cross$:   trains in the crossing and maybe in the critical section.

A final component of the railroad crossing is the controller that coordinates the track

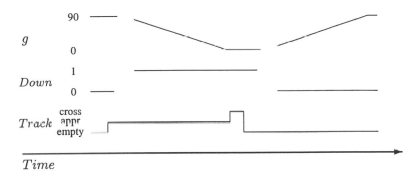

Figure 5.2 A timing diagram. Gaps indicate that a value is unknown

monitors and the gate assembly. The states for this module are introduced during the design, when the requirements constraining the plant states have been formulated.

A *behavior* of a system is an assignment of state functions to the names of elementary states, here g, $Down$ and $Track$. An *observation of a behavior* is a restriction of such an assignment to a bounded interval; it can be illustrated by a timing diagram as in Figure 5.2. Boolean values are represented by 0 (*false*) and 1 (*true*).

5.2.2 Schemas

States and other quantities like parameters denoting constant values might be introduced informally as above. This is the usual approach in mathematics, and works well for a small collection of quantities that are used in a limited context; but in development of a larger system with a modular structure and going through several stages of refinement it is essential to be able to structure declarations corresponding to the specifications of systems and subsystems. Therefore we use a concrete syntax for specifications based on the Z-schema notation [Spi92]. The states for the example can thus be introduced by the following schemas:

```
┌─ Gate ──────────────────────────────────────
  g      :  Time → [0, 90]
  ġ      :  Time → R
  Down   :  Time → Bool
```

```
┌─ TrackMonitor ──────────────────────────────
  Tracks  :  Time → {empty, appr, cross}
```

We shall use the symbol $\overset{\text{def}}{=}$ for definitions, e.g.:

$$Up \quad \overset{\text{def}}{=} \quad \neg Down$$
$$Empty \quad \overset{\text{def}}{=} \quad (Tracks = empty)$$
$$Appr \quad \overset{\text{def}}{=} \quad (Tracks = appr)$$
$$Cross \quad \overset{\text{def}}{=} \quad (tracks = cross)$$

A specification is often parameterized with certain quantities, for instance, an upper bound γ on the time to lower or raise the gates. It is also given by a schema:

$$\boxed{\begin{array}{l} GateParm \\ \hline \gamma : \mathbf{R} \end{array}}$$

Schemas can be composed by inclusion in new schemas, where the collection of named quantities is the union of the ones in the component schemas. If some name denotes different quantities in different component schemas, the composition is not defined. We can thus define the plant state and parameters by the schema

$$\boxed{\begin{array}{l} RailCrossing \\ \hline GateParm \\ Gate \\ TrackMonitor \end{array}}$$

Constraints

The schema $GateParm$ means that the delay constant γ is unconstrained; it can even be non-positive. Such a gate assembly is unthinkable, therefore γ is constrained to be positive by a predicate in a constraint part of the schema

$$\boxed{\begin{array}{l} GateParm \\ \hline \gamma : \mathbf{R} \\ \hline \gamma > 0 \end{array}}$$

This schema denotes exactly the positive γ values. In general, constraints on a schema are given by a predicate over the named quantities. The meaning of a schema with a constraint is then the set of all behaviors satisfying the predicate. Mostly the predicate uses notations of various special theories, here e.g. the mathematical toolkit of Z [Spi92], mathematical analysis, and of course the Duration Calculus. If the predicate is inconsistent, the schema denotes the empty set of behaviors.

The schema $Gate$ describes all possible behaviors of gates, also some undesirable ones, as when $g = 45$ holds throughout. So the allowed behaviors should be further constrained. For that purpose we now consider some observation interval $[b, e]$ of $Time$.

Gate movement. The gate assembly controls the $\dot{g}$ state, and thereby the g state. Mathematical analysis gives a constraint: $g(e) = g(b) + \int_b^e \dot{g}(t)dt$.

Gate closing. Further constraints depend on the input state $Down$. We now analyze a case where $Down$ holds initially, and assume that when the gate is not fully closed, the magnitude of the speed is constant $c > 0$, at least after a short delay $\varepsilon > 0$. Using predicate logic this can be described as follows:

$$\forall m : Time \bullet (m = b + \varepsilon < e) \wedge (\forall t : Time \bullet b < t < m \Rightarrow Down(t)) \Rightarrow$$
$$(\exists m' : Time \bullet (m < m' \le e) \wedge (\forall s : Time \bullet (m < s < m') \Rightarrow$$
$$(g(s) > 0 \Rightarrow \dot{g}(s) = -c) \wedge (g(s) = 0 \Rightarrow \dot{g}(s) = 0)).$$

The point m chops the observation interval into an initial subinterval of length ε where $Down$ holds. At the end of this interval, then for some time up to an m', the velocity $\dot{g}$ is $-c$ when the gate is still closing ($g(s) > 0$) and 0 when the gate is fully closed. Notice that we allow a discontinuous velocity and that the end point values are ignored.

The conjunction of the *Gate movement* and *Gate closing* properties is part of the gate constraints, and these should hold for any observation interval. This is specified by prefixing each of the formulas above with $\forall\, b, e : Time \bullet b \leq e \Rightarrow$.

5.2.3 Duration Calculus

As illustrated above it is possible to formalize properties of hybrid systems (real-time systems with interacting continuous and discrete states) using predicate logic and mathematical analysis. However, formal reasoning is rather cumbersome when all formulas contain several quantifiers. This is the rationale for having a temporal logic: it will implicitly quantify over the time domain. When this domain is discrete, it is very natural to fix a current point, for instance the beginning b of the observation and then specify in terms of the future where e will range over the naturals. Conversely, one may fix e and consider the past. For reasoning with such logics see e.g. the books [MP93, Ost89], the report on TLA+ [Lam91], or as a variation the logic of Jahanian and Mok [JM86]. Further variants can be found in the proceedings [LdRV94, Vyt91, Jos88]. Such logics can be extended to dense time [PH88], either with explicit clocks e.g. [AL92] or with modalities that incorporate a length constraint, e.g. [Koy90]. However, specification of properties depicted in timing diagrams seem conveniently given by interval logics, [SMSV83, Mos85]. In particular, intervals seem appropriate in a dense time setting, because neighborhood properties have to be formalized.

Duration Calculus has evolved from these considerations. The basis is Moszkowski's (discrete time) interval logic (ITL) [Mos85, Mos86] which provides the basic binary modality "chop", written ';'. The contribution of Duration Calculus is to formalize properties of states.

Syntax. The syntax of Duration Calculus distinguishes *(duration) terms*, each one associated with a certain type, and *(duration) formulas*. Terms are built from names of elementary states like g or $Down$, *rigid variables* representing time independent logical variables and are closed under arithmetic and propositional operators. Examples of terms are $\neg Down$ and $y - 0$ (of Boolean type) and $\dot{g} - c$ (of type real).

Terms of type real are also called *state expressions* and terms of Boolean type are called *state assertions*. We use f for a typical state expression and P for a typical state assertion.

Duration terms are built from $\mathbf{b}.f$ and $\mathbf{e}.f$ denoting the *initial* and *final value* of f in a given interval, and $\int f$ denoting the *integral* of f in a given interval. For a state assertion P, the integral $\int P$ is called the *duration* because it measures the time P holds in the given interval.

Duration formulas are built from duration terms of Boolean type and closed under propositional connectives, the chop connective, and quantification over rigid variables and variables of duration terms. We use D for a typical duration formula.

Semantics. The semantics of Duration Calculus is based on an *interpretation* $\mathcal{I}$ that assigns a fixed meaning to each state name, type and operator symbol of the language, and a time interval $[b, e]$. For given $\mathcal{I}$ and $[b, e]$ the semantics defines what domain values duration terms and what truth values duration formulas denote. For example, $\int f$ denotes the integral $\int_b^e f(t)dt$, $\mathbf{b}.f$ denotes the limit from the right in b, and $\mathbf{e}.f$ denotes the limit from the left in e.

A duration formula D *holds* in $\mathcal{I}$ and $[b, e]$, abbreviated $\mathcal{I}, [b, e] \models D$, if it denotes the truth

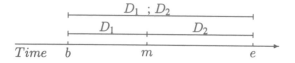

Figure 5.3   Timing diagram for chop

value *true* for $\mathcal{I}$ and $[b, e]$. D is *true* in $\mathcal{I}$, abbreviated $\mathcal{I} \models D$, if $\mathcal{I}, [0, t] \models D$ for every $t \in Time$. A *model* of D is an interpretation $\mathcal{I}$ which makes D true, i.e. with $\mathcal{I} \models D$. The formula D is *satisfiable* if there exists an interpretation $\mathcal{I}$ with $\mathcal{I} \models D$.

A *behavior* is an interpretation restricted to the names of the elementary states.

Examples. Gate movement is an equality between two duration terms:

$$GM \stackrel{\text{def}}{=} \mathbf{e}.g = \mathbf{b}.g + \int \dot{g}.$$

For an assertion P, it is obvious that it holds in the interval, just when the duration $\int P$ is equal to the length of the interval. The length is the duration of the constant function 1 ($\int 1$). This duration is often used, so it is abbreviated (ℓ), pronounced 'the length'. The property that P holds is thus given by the atomic formula $\int P = \ell$. This holds trivially for a point interval, so we consider proper intervals of a positive length. These two properties are combined in the abbreviation

$$\lceil P \rceil \stackrel{\text{def}}{=} \int P = \ell \wedge \ell > 0,$$

read as 'P holds'. The property that *Down* holds is thus denoted by $\lceil Down \rceil$. We also use a variant of this notation when P holds for some time $t \geq 0$:

$$\lceil P \rceil^t \stackrel{\text{def}}{=} \int P = \ell = t.$$

In the *gate closing* constraint we also need to express properties of subintervals. This motivates the chop operator. Given duration formulas D_1 and D_2, the formula $D_1 ; D_2$ holds on the interval $[b, e]$ just when there is a chop point m such that D_1 holds on the initial subinterval $[b, m]$ and D_2 holds on the final subinterval $[m, e]$, see Fig. 5.3. The desired property is now given by

$$GC \stackrel{\text{def}}{=} \lceil Down \rceil^\varepsilon ; \ell > 0 \Rightarrow$$
$$\ell = \varepsilon ; \lceil (g > 0 \Rightarrow \dot{g} = -c) \wedge (g = 0 \Rightarrow \dot{g} = 0) \rceil ; true.$$

Initialization and invariants. Notice that when a behavior satisfies a formula D, then D holds for every prefix $[0, t]$ of time. It means that initialization can be specified by a formula that typically has the form $\ell = 0 \vee D_0 ; true$, where $\ell = 0$ holds for the starting point $[0, 0]$, while D_0 gives initial constraints on the states which will hold for some arbitrarily small but positive time. For example, we suppose that initially there are no trains on the track. This property can be formalized as follows:

$$\ell = 0 \vee \lceil Empty \rceil ; true.$$

The gate properties are, however, *invariants*, so we must express that they hold in any subinterval. For this purpose, the operators "somewhere" ($\Diamond$) and its dual "everywhere" ($\Box$) are introduced: $\Diamond D \overset{\text{def}}{=} true ; D ; true$ and $\Box D \overset{\text{def}}{=} \neg\Diamond\neg D$.

The gate invariants are thus formalized $\Box (GM \wedge GC)$.

Reasoning about properties

The proof system for Duration Calculus is built on four kinds of elementary laws or rules:

Math is a lifting rule that allows any result R about values or integrals which can be proven to hold for any interval using mathematical analysis (MA):

$$\frac{MA\vdash \forall b, e : Time \bullet b \le e \Rightarrow R(f_1(b+), f_1(e-), \int_b^e f_1(t)dt, \ldots, f_n(b+), f_n(e-), \int_b^e f_n(t)dt)}{R(\mathbf{b}.f_1, \mathbf{e}.f_1, \int f_1, \ldots, \mathbf{b}.f_n, \mathbf{e}.f_n, \int f_n)}$$

Lifting is crucial for a smooth interface to other engineering disciplines where mathematical analysis is the standard tool. Some examples from the gate assembly are:

M1. If a state expression is constant then its initial and final values are identical to this constant, e.g., $\lceil g - 0 \rceil \Rightarrow \mathbf{b}.g = \mathbf{e}.g = 0$.

M2. If the derivative of a state is zero then the state assumes a constant value. Thus we have $\lceil \dot{g} = 0 \rceil \Rightarrow \exists r : [0, 90] \bullet \lceil g = r \rceil$.

M3. An integral has a fixed value for any interval, and an integral is zero in any point interval: $\ell = 0 \Rightarrow \int f = 0$.

Interval laws deal with properties of the chop operator. It is associative and monotone w.r.t. implication:

$$\frac{D_1 \Rightarrow D_1'}{(D_1 ; D_2) \Rightarrow (D_1' ; D_2')}$$
$$D_2 \Rightarrow D_2'$$

Monotonicity is very useful in proofs, because it allows us to drop unimportant constraints within a chopped formula.

Chop distributes over disjunction and over conjunction when the chop-point is aligned: $((D_1 \wedge \ell = r) ; D_2) \wedge ((D_3 \wedge \ell = r) ; D_4) \Rightarrow ((D_1 \wedge D_3) ; (D_2 \wedge D_3))$.

Duration-Interval laws link integrals and values over a chop. The use of integrals (durations) is really justified by the additive properties in this link, because they are the basis for a divide and conquer strategy on durations in real-time systems design.

Integral-Chop. $\int f = v_1 ; \int f = v_2 \Rightarrow \int f = v_1 + v_2$.

Sum. $\int f = r_1 + r_2 \Rightarrow (\int f - r_1) ; (\int f = r_2)$ for non-negative r_1, r_2. This uses that $Time$ is dense. A consequence of *Sum* and *Integral-Chop* is: $\lceil P \rceil ; \lceil P \rceil \Leftrightarrow \lceil P \rceil$.

Values. $\mathbf{b}.f = v \Leftrightarrow \mathbf{b}.f = v$; *true* and $\mathbf{e}.f = v \Leftrightarrow true$; $\mathbf{e}.f = v$. This and the interval laws gives: $\mathbf{e}.f = v \Rightarrow true$; $(\ell = 0 \wedge \mathbf{e}.f = v)$ and a similar result for $\mathbf{b}.f$. With *Integral-Chop* and *M3* this is used to prove $\Box\, GM \Rightarrow \Box \exists v \bullet \mathbf{e}.g = v$; $\mathbf{b}.g = v$, indicating continuity of g.

Induction over behaviors is crucial when proving invariant properties. Simple induction over time is not possible, thus it is replaced by induction over discrete state changes. In the following induction rule X denotes a formula letter occurring in a formula $H(X)$, and P is a state assertion.

$$\frac{\vdash H(\ell = 0) \qquad H(X) \vdash H(X \vee X \; ; \; \lceil P \rceil \vee X \; ; \; \lceil \neg P \rceil)}{H(true)}$$

A mirrored rule does backwards induction using $H(X \vee \lceil P \rceil \; ; \; X \vee \lceil \neg P \rceil \; ; \; X)$ as the obligation in the inductive step.

An important consequence is the **P-cover** property $\lceil P \rceil \; ; \; true \vee \lceil \neg P \rceil \; ; \; true \vee \ell = 0$ and its mirror image $true \; ; \; \lceil P \rceil \vee true \; ; \; \lceil \neg P \rceil \vee \ell = 0$.

Example 1. Invariant properties similar to **P-cover** are important for splitting a proof into cases. An example used below is that for any non-point interval: $\lceil P \rceil \vee true \; ; \; \lceil \neg P \rceil \; ; \; (\ell = 0 \vee \lceil P \rceil)$. This is proved by induction.

Example 2

Let us illustrate how to reason in the calculus by proving that the gate assembly has the property that when *Down* holds for $\gamma = \varepsilon + 90/c$ then the gate is down. This can be alternatively stated as "There is no interval when Down holds for γ followed by the gate being open." Adding our assumptions about the gate assembly gives the proof obligation:

$$\Box\, (GM \wedge GC) \Rightarrow \Box \neg (\lceil Down \rceil^\gamma \; ; \; \lceil g > 0 \rceil)$$

Proof. The proof of such a statement is most easily done by contradiction. Assume that there is some interval where $\lceil Down \rceil^\gamma \; ; \; \lceil g > 0 \rceil$. The law *Sum* and arithmetic gives

$$\lceil Down \rceil^\varepsilon \; ; \; \lceil Down \rceil^{\gamma - \varepsilon} \; ; \; \lceil g > 0 \rceil.$$

We split the proof instantiating *Example 1* as $\lceil g > 0 \rceil \vee true \; ; \; \lceil g = 0 \rceil \; ; \; (\ell = 0 \vee \lceil g > 0 \rceil)$ and using it on the middle interval to give two cases:

1. $\lceil Down \rceil^\varepsilon \; ; \; (\lceil Down \rceil^{\gamma - \varepsilon} \wedge true \; ; \; \lceil g = 0 \rceil \; ; \; (\ell = 0 \vee \lceil g > 0 \rceil)) \; ; \; \lceil g > 0 \rceil$,
2. $\lceil Down \rceil^\varepsilon \; ; \; \lceil Down \wedge g > 0 \rceil^{\gamma - \varepsilon} \; ; \; \lceil g > 0 \rceil$.

For case 1 we simplify and rearrange using *Sum*, *Integral-Chop*, and monotonicity to give

$$true \; ; \; (\lceil Down \rceil^\varepsilon \wedge true \; ; \; \lceil g = 0 \rceil) \; ; \; \lceil g > 0 \rceil$$

Applying *GC* gives

$$true \; ; \; (\lceil Down \rceil^\varepsilon \wedge true \; ; \; \lceil g = 0 \rceil) \; ; \; \lceil g > 0 \wedge \dot{g} = -c \rceil \; ; \; true$$

which simplifies via monotonicity to

$$true \; ; \; \lceil g = 0 \rceil \; ; \; \lceil g > 0 \wedge \dot{g} = -c \rceil \; ; \; true.$$

Now rule *M1* gives

$$true \; ; \; \textbf{e.}g = 0 \; ; \; \lceil g > 0 \wedge \dot{g} = -c \rvert \; ; \; true.$$

Applying rule *M2* gives an $r > 0$ in the formula:

$$true \; ; \; \textbf{e.}g = 0 \; ; \; \lceil g = r \rceil \; ; \; true.$$

Finally *M1* and *Values* give $true \; ; \; \textbf{e.}g = 0 \; ; \; \textbf{b.}g = r \; ; \; true.$ in contradiction to the continuity of g (rule *M3*).

For case 2, we have from **Math** that there exists an angle v such that

$$\lceil Down \rceil^{\varepsilon} \; ; \; (\textbf{b.}g = v \wedge \lceil Down \wedge g > 0 \rceil^{\gamma - \varepsilon}) \; ; \; \lceil g > 0 \rceil.$$

The GC constraint will also for the middle interval give

$$\lceil Down \rceil^{\varepsilon} \; ; \; (\textbf{b.}g = v \wedge \lceil Down \wedge g > 0 \wedge \dot{g} = -c \rceil^{\gamma - \varepsilon}) \; ; \; \lceil g > 0 \rceil.$$

The middle interval is split after $s = v/c \le 90/c$ to give

$$true \; ; \; (\textbf{b.}g = v \wedge \lceil \dot{g} = \quad c \rceil^{s}) \; ; \; \lceil g > 0 \rceil.$$

Using GM on the middle interval gives $\textbf{e.}y = 0 \; ; \; \lceil g > 0 \rceil$, thus contradicting the continuity of g, cf. the last steps of case 1. This completes the proof.

This is an outline of the most complex proof needed in this paper. The complexity is caused by the hybrid reasoning: linking mathematical analysis based interval properties together in order to arrive at properties of superintervals.

5.2.4   Standard Form

In principle, constraints can be formulated using arbitrary formulas, but a standard form has turned out to be useful because it simplifies reasoning and checks for feasibility.

The basis is a binary operator ($\longrightarrow$). It expresses that whenever a *pattern* given by a formula D is observed, then it will be "followed by" a *goal* state P:

$$D \longrightarrow \lceil P \rceil \stackrel{\text{def}}{=} \Box \neg (D \; ; \; \lceil \neg P \rceil).$$

This operator is monotone like an implication and has a number of distributive laws. When the pattern is a lifted state assertion, a **Transitive** law holds:

$$\frac{\lceil P_1 \rceil^{t_1} \longrightarrow \lceil P_2 \rceil \quad \lceil P_1 \wedge P_2 \rceil^{t_2} \longrightarrow \lceil P_3 \rceil}{\lceil P_1 \rceil^{t_1 + t_2} \longrightarrow \lceil P_2 \wedge P_3 \rceil}$$

The standard form can be used to formulate the gate movement GC. When an analogous constraint for Up and the GM invariant are added, we have a specification for the gate assembly module.

```
___GateAssembly_____
 Gate
 ε, c : R
_____
 ε > 0 ∧ c > 0
 [Down]ᵉ ⟶ ⌈(g > 0 ⇒ ġ = −c) ∧ (g = 0 ⇒ ġ = 0)⌉
 [Up]ᵉ ⟶ ⌈(g < 90 ⇒ ġ = c) ∧ (g = 90 ⇒ ġ = 0)⌉
 □ (e.g = b.g + ∫ġ)
```

This specification is an example of the information about gates that a development team needs in order to calculate real-time constraints for the controller module and verify that system requirements are met.

5.3 SYSTEM REQUIREMENTS

Requirements constrain the plant state, and thereby define the desired system model. This section first explains the general setting where requirements are composed of commitments that represent a user's expectations and assumptions that record the designer's expectation about the intrinsic behavior of the plant. A design is a specification that constrains the combined plant and controller state in such a way that the requirements are satisfied. The general setting is then illustrated by a requirements analysis for the running example.

5.3.1 General Setting

The constraints are typically a conjunction $\bigwedge R_i$ of individual requirements. A single requirement is a conditional, where the antecedent is the *assumption* and the consequence is the *commitment*, $R_i \overset{\text{def}}{=} A_i \Rightarrow C_i$. The commitments formalize the informal *expectations* for the system.

A design is specified by a formula D that links the plant state and a controller state by specifying constraints on the combined state. Given assumptions A, commitment C and a design D, the verification of the design demonstrates $D \Rightarrow (A \Rightarrow C)$ or equivalently

$$D \wedge A \Rightarrow C.$$

This formula shows that assumptions and designs from a logical point of view are interchangeable.

Requirements analysis is an activity that documents requirements for which a design can be found. There is a tradeoff between assuming some property or ensuring it through a design constraint. Requirements analysis thus easily extends into finding a top-level design. However, although assumptions are formalized at a late stage in requirements analysis, they will in a final documentation be introduced from the start, because they are determined by the plant design and not by the controller design.

Refinement

Another formulation of the link between design, assumption and commitment is that assumptions are plant properties which ensure that a design *refines* the commitments. We shall illustrate the refinement concept by the gate assembly and a more abstract set of gate control commitments.

The specification *GateAssembly* brings discrete and continuous states together in a hybrid specification. It is, however, not simple to use, and the details about the movement of y are really not relevant for the design of a controller for the railroad crossing. Fortunately, we have just proved that there is an abstraction that gives us sufficient details.

$$
\begin{array}{|l}
\underline{GateControl} \\
Gate \\
GateParm \\
\hline
[Up]^{\gamma} \longrightarrow \lceil g = 90 \rceil \\
\lceil Down \rceil^{\gamma} \longrightarrow \lceil g - 0 \rceil \\
\hline
\end{array}
$$

Indeed, the proof outline in the previous section has shown that the *Down* constraints of *GateAssembly* imply the *Down* constraint of *GateControl* for $\gamma = \varepsilon + 90/c$. A law for the standard form can be used to show that the implication is valid for a greater γ as well. By symmetry, we have a similar result for the *Up* constraint. This can then be recorded in a design decision:

$$
\begin{array}{|l}
\underline{GateLink} \\
\gamma, \varepsilon, c : \mathbf{R} \\
\hline
\gamma \geq \varepsilon + 90/c \\
\hline
\end{array}
$$

This design decision links the two sets of parameters such that the implication is preserved.

In terms of models, we have shown that any model for *GateAssembly* is also a model for *GateControl*. This is what we mean, when we write that *GateAssembly* and *GateLink* *refines GateControl*:

$$GateAssembly \wedge GateLink \sqsupseteq GateControl.$$

It is the same as saying that *Gatelink* is a correct design for *GateControl* under the assumption of *GateAssembly*.

Refinement is a semantic issue, but it can be proved using the calculus.

Input and controlled quantities

Assumptions are not for free. At the *end* of the design activity it must be proven that the assumptions in conjunction with the design are feasible, i.e. that the conjunction $A \wedge D$ is satisfiable. If the two formulas A and D are individually satisfiable, a syntactic check for satisfiability of their conjunction is given by the well known technique of dividing the state and parameter names into input and controlled (internal and output) sets, and ensuring that no quantity is controlled by both A and D.

In order to determine whether a state name is an input or controlled, the following syntactical condition suffices: A state name that occurs in the goal of a standard form or occurs in a non-standard form is controlled. State names that are not controlled according to this rule are input.

In the example, g, ε and c are controlled by the *GateAssembly*, and *Down* is an input. Correspondingly, the *GateLink* controls γ while ε and c are inputs.

Intermodule feasibility. The constraints on a module shall also preserve feasibility, and here it is too restrictive to use a division into controlled and input states. A sufficient condition on a conjunction of standard forms is, however, that either the patterns in the forms exclude each other or if the conjunction of their goals is satisfiable.

Validation

While feasibility is a formal property, there is still the question of whether the assumptions, the commitments and the system model are reasonable. This calls for *validation*, i.e. careful experiments to check the mathematical model against reality, a topic outside the scope of this presentation. Work in that direction may for instance use simulation tools that can illustrate expected behaviors.

5.3.2   The Generalized Railroad Crossing

In the following we shall illustrate the concepts introduced above with the generalized railroad crossing. First the informal expectations in [HL94] are recapitulated. Then they are formalized as commitments, and finally we search for a design and some assumptions that will allow us to satisfy the commitments.

Expectations

Two informal expectations are given in [HL94]:

Safety: The gate is down, $g = 0$, during all occupancy intervals. An occupancy interval is an interval where *Cross* holds.

It is obvious that this is easy to satisfy by blocking the crossing, so therefore there is a second expectation that rules out trivial designs.

Utility: The gate is up when no train is in the crossing. This is further qualified in terms of the non-occupancy intervals, where $\neg Cross$ holds. There are given two positive reals ξ_1, ξ_2 such that the gate must be open, $g = 90$, at ξ_2 time after the start of a non-occupancy interval and remain open until ξ_1 time before the end of that interval (i.e. the start of the next occupancy interval). It is fairly straightforward to see that the gate must be opened when a non-occupancy interval is long enough. This is ensured by the ξ_2 parameter. On the other hand, the gate cannot remain closed until the instantaneous transition from $\neg Cross$ to $Cross$, therefore the ξ_1 period is introduced.

The reader may wish to consult the timing diagram in Figure 5.2 to check that *Utility* is indeed a reasonable expectation.

Commitments

The expectations are analyzed for the plant state $RailCrossing$ introduced in the previous section.

The *Safety* expectation is easily formalized as whenever $Cross$ then $g = 0$, leading to the commitment:

Safe
$RailCrossing$

$\lceil Cross \rceil \longrightarrow \lceil g = 0 \rceil$

The reader may want to check that this is stronger than an invariant $\square (\lceil Cross \rceil \rightarrow \lceil g - 0 \rceil)$. The *Utility* property has the parameters

---
GRCParm
$\xi_1, \xi_2 : \mathbf{R}$

$\xi_1 > 0 \wedge \xi_2 > 0$

---

and it can also be expressed very concisely, although not in a standard form:

Utility
$RailCrossing$
$GRCParm$

$\square ((\lceil \neg Cross \rceil \wedge \ell > \xi_1 + \xi_2) \rightarrow \ell = \xi_2 \,;\, \lceil g = 90 \rceil \,;\, \ell = \xi_1)$

It is interesting to note that the utility property as presented in [HL94] leaves it open what should be done before the first train arrives. We have assumed that the same property shall hold.

Assumptions

It is obvious that we cannot satisfy *Safe* by a direct design that immediately forces the gate down, when $Cross$ becomes true. What one needs is to introduce additional assumptions on the trains and track monitoring assembly that will support a reasonable top-level design for the controller. Such an analysis is described below.

Train movement. We assume that the track monitor behaves as a finite state automaton cycling from *Empty* to approaching, *Appr*, to *Cross*, from which it may return to any of the previous states. It corresponds to an assumption that an approaching train will cross. This prohibits shunting of trains in the approaching area. Formally:

$\lceil Empty \rceil \longrightarrow \lceil Empty \vee Appr \rceil$
$\lceil Appr \rceil \longrightarrow \lceil Appr \vee Cross \rceil.$

The constraint $\lceil Cross \rceil \longrightarrow \lceil Cross \vee Empty \vee Appr \rceil$ is left out, because it is equivalent to $\lceil Cross \rceil \longrightarrow \lceil true \rceil$, which is trivially true.

We assume that that the crossing is initially empty:

$$\ell = 0 \vee \lceil Empty \rceil \; ; \; true.$$

The behaviors generated by the automaton gives an opportunity to introduce the concept of a *phase*. It is simply the name of an automaton state, and is determined by a state assertion. The phase constraints on train movement are collectively named $TMoves$.

Fast trains. The former of the two train movement formulas immediately tells us that $Cross$ is preceded by $Appr$. If this approaching phase is long enough, we have time to close the gate. Formally, we assume that for a given $\varepsilon_1 > 0$

$TFast$ _____

   $RailCrossing$

   $\varepsilon_1 : \mathbf{R}$
   _____

   $(\lceil Empty \rceil \; ; \; \lceil Appr \rceil \wedge \ell \leq \varepsilon_1) \longrightarrow \lceil Appr \rceil.$

Intuitively speaking, ε_1 is a lower bound on the time the fastest train spends in the approaching region, cf., the information that the programmers were missing in the story in the introduction.

Analysis of Safe. We can now reason about a violation of the *Safe* commitment with the assumptions about movement and speed given above:

$$true \; ; \; \lceil Cross \rceil \; ; \; \lceil g > 0 \rceil.$$

The movement formulas allow expanding the behavior backward. The formal argument uses laws about "followed-by", which are proved from **P-cover** and the distributive laws. The result is that the behavior must satisfy:

$$true \; ; \; \lceil Empty \rceil \; ; \; \lceil Appr \rceil \; ; \; \lceil Appr \vee Cross \rceil \; ; \; \lceil Cross \rceil \; ; \; \lceil g > 0 \rceil.$$

The train speed assumption means that the $Appr$ interval at the start is at least ε_1 long, thus there is a real value $s > \varepsilon_1$ such that

$$true \; ; \; \lceil Empty \rceil \; ; \; \lceil \neg Empty \rceil^s \; ; \; \lceil g > 0 \rceil.$$

It is now easy to see that we can satisfy the *Safe* constraint by a design satisfying $\lceil \neg Empty \rceil^{\varepsilon_1} \longrightarrow \lceil g = 0 \rceil$, because it will contradict the behavior above.

Before we have the final controller design, we use the $GateControl$ abstraction. Here we simply apply the law **Transitive** and arrive at the controller design commitment

---
$Safe1$ _____

   $RailCrossing$

   $\varepsilon_1 : \mathbf{R}$
   _____

   $\varepsilon_1 > \gamma$

   $\lceil \neg Empty \rceil^{\varepsilon_1 - \gamma} \longrightarrow \lceil Down \rceil$
---

and have outlined a refinement

$$Safe1 \land GateControl \land TMoves \land TFast \sqsupseteq Safe$$

Analysis of Utility. Turning to *Utility*, the $\neg Cross$ phase is analyzed using **P-Cover** and the transition constraint on *Appr* to be either $\lceil Empty \rceil$; ($\lceil Appr \rceil \lor \ell = 0$) or $\lceil Appr \rceil$. The latter case is inconvenient, because we have already decided to close the gate in that phase, so we would not like to open it as well.

Slow trains. An upper bound ε_2 on *Appr* is now a helpful assumption:

$$
\begin{array}{|l|}
\hline
\underline{\;TSlow\;} \\
\quad RailCrossing \\
\quad \varepsilon_2 : \mathbf{R} \\
\hline
\quad \lceil Appr \rceil^{\varepsilon_2} \longrightarrow \lceil \neg Appr \rceil. \\
\hline
\end{array}
$$

It is interpreted as an upper bound on the time the slowest train spends in the approaching region.

A design for Utility. One part of the utility commitment is now discharged by assuming $\varepsilon_2 \le \xi_1 + \xi_2$. This leaves the case where the $\neg Cross$ phase is initially *Empty*. Here we propose a design commitment $\lceil Empty \rceil^{\xi_2} \longrightarrow \lceil g = 90 \rceil$. However, a dangling *Appr* must also be short. Thus we strengthen the constraint on the slowest train to $\varepsilon_2 \le \xi_1$.

Finally, we use *GateControl* to detach the controller design from directly controlling the gate, and arrive at:

$$
\begin{array}{|l|}
\hline
\underline{\;Utility1\;} \\
\quad RailCrossing \\
\quad \varepsilon_2 : \mathbf{R} \\
\hline
\quad \xi_1 \ge \varepsilon_2 \land \xi_2 > \gamma \\
\quad \lceil Empty \rceil^{\xi_2 - \gamma} \longrightarrow \lceil \neg Down \rceil \\
\hline
\end{array}
$$

This is part of the refinement: $Utility1 \land GateControl \land TMoves \land TSlow \sqsupseteq Utility$.

Requirements

The analysis above has lead to assumptions $TMoves$ about train movement, $TFast$ and $TSlow$ about train speeds, and some designs $Safe1$ and $Utility1$ for the controller. These refine the requirements:

$$
\begin{aligned}
ReqSafe &\stackrel{\text{def}}{=} (TMoves \land TFast \land GateControl) \Rightarrow Safe \\
ReqUtility &\stackrel{\text{def}}{=} (TMoves \land TSlow \land GateControl) \Rightarrow Utility
\end{aligned}
$$

These are the requirements that the controller designers have to check with the customer and providers of the gate and track monitoring assembly.

Note that the assumptions have been split carefully between commitments. In negotiations with the user, the *Safe* assumptions are safety critical, while *Utility* assumptions are more a question of convenience.

5.4 CONTROLLER DESIGN

We now design and implement a real-time automaton for controlling the asynchronous plant states *Empty* and *Down*. Notice that *Empty* is an input state and thus can only be observed, whereas *Down* has to be controlled in such a way that the commitments *Safe*1 and *Utility*1 are satisfied. The controller interacts with the plant through sensors and actuators. Here we need a sensor for the observable *Empty* and an actuator for *Down*.

5.4.1 Sensors, Actuators and Main Controller

The sensor for *Empty* updates a controller phase e and the actuator for *Down* changes *Down* according to the value of a another controller phase d. The controller phases e and d play the role of program variables that are read and updated by the controller. The specifications of sensor, actuator and controller introduce further real valued parameters that are summarized in:

```
┌─ Controller ──────────────────────────────────────
│ e, d : Time → Bool
│ ν_s, ν_a, ν_1, ν_2 : R   the sensor, actuator and main controller delays
│ τ_e, τ : R   stability time
└───────────────────────────────────────────────────
```

The Gate Actuator. It sets *Down* when the phase d has been stable for ν_a, and resets *Down* when d has been reset for ν_a:

```
┌─ GateActuator ────────────────────────────────────
│ Down : Time → Bool
│ Controller
├───────────────────────────────────────────────────
│ ⌈d⌉^{ν_a} ⟶ ⌈Down⌉
│ ⌈¬d⌉^{ν_a} ⟶ ⌈¬Down⌉
└───────────────────────────────────────────────────
```

Here d and ν_a are input and *Down* is controlled. Note that an implementation may set the controlled state before ν_a; because the delay ν_a is an upper bound only.

The Track Sensor. It updates e when *Empty* has been stable for ν_s, and maintains the stability of the e and $\neg e$ phases.

```
┌─ TrackSensor ─────────────────────────────────────
│ TrackMonitor
│ Controller
├───────────────────────────────────────────────────
│ ⌈Empty⌉^{ν_s} ⟶ ⌈e⌉
│ ⌈¬Empty⌉^{ν_s} ⟶ ⌈¬e⌉
│ (⌈¬e⌉ ; ⌈e⌉ ∧ ℓ ≤ τ_e) ⟶ ⌈e⌉
│ (⌈e⌉ ; ⌈¬e⌉ ∧ ℓ ≤ τ_e) ⟶ ⌈¬e⌉
│ ν_s > τ_e
└───────────────────────────────────────────────────
```

Note that $Empty$ and τ_e are input, while e and ν_s are controlled. An implementation may react faster than the upper bound ν_s; but it cannot react faster than stability τ_e allows.

The Main Controller. The phases e and d are operated upon by the main controller as follows:

$$\begin{array}{l} \underline{\quad MainController\quad\quad\quad\quad\quad\quad\quad\quad\quad\quad\quad\quad\quad} \\ \quad Controller \\ \overline{\quad\quad\quad\quad\quad\quad\quad\quad\quad\quad\quad\quad\quad\quad\quad\quad\quad} \\ \quad \lceil \neg e \rceil^{\nu_1} \longrightarrow \lceil d \rceil \\ \quad \lceil e \rceil^{\nu_2} \longrightarrow \lceil \neg d \rceil \end{array}$$

For the main controller e is input, while d, ν_1 and ν_2 are controlled.

Altogether we have now decomposed the commitments $Safe1$ and $Utility1$ into three modules: track sensor, gate actuator and main controller. By **Transitive**, we can show that their composition implies $Safe1$ and $Utility1$ provided

$$\nu_s + \nu_a + \nu_1 \leq \varepsilon_1 - \gamma \quad \text{and} \quad \nu_s + \nu_a + \nu_2 \leq \xi_2 - \gamma.$$

These inequalities can be satisfied when the controller is implemented in a technology that makes the stability parameters (τ's) small, because then the delays (ν's) can also be small.

The sensors and actuators can be implemented by suitable hardware. For the main controller we illustrate here how to correctly implement it by a sequential program.

5.4.2 Sequentialization

Since the main controller has to monitor the two phases e and d, their a priori independent changes have to be sequentialized or *interleaved*. Formally, this is done by considering the product space of the values of e and d consisting of all minterms $e \wedge d$, $e \wedge \neg d$, $\neg e \wedge \neg d$, $\neg e \wedge d$. We take into account that the sequential implementation cannot be made arbitrarily fast and assume that each of these states will be stable for at least τ.

We can fix an arbitrary initial state and choose here $e \wedge d$, i.e.

$$\ell = 0 \vee \lceil e \wedge d \rceil; true.$$

To determine the transitions, we take into account that a sequential implementation deals with at most one change of the phases e and d at a time. Therefore we admit as transitions only those expressed by the following sequencing constraints:

$$\begin{array}{l} \lceil e \wedge d \rceil \longrightarrow \lceil e \rceil \\ \lceil e \wedge \neg d \rceil \longrightarrow \lceil \neg d \rceil \\ \lceil \neg e \wedge \neg d \rceil \longrightarrow \lceil \neg e \rceil \\ \lceil \neg e \wedge d \rceil \longrightarrow \lceil d \rceil \end{array}$$

To satisfy the first main controller constraint we require additionally:

$$\lceil \neg e \wedge \neg d \rceil^{\nu_1} \longrightarrow \lceil \neg e \wedge d \rceil$$

and to satisfy the second main controller constraint also:

$$\lceil e \wedge d \rceil^{\nu_2} \longrightarrow \lceil e \wedge \neg d \rceil.$$

We can prove that $MainController$ is refined by this design. However, we have introduced a stability assumption on e. In the worst case e has to be stable for $\nu_2 + \tau$ time with τ referring to the stability of states. A similar argument applies for $\neg e$ and ν_1. To remain feasible the $TrackSensor$ must not demand too fast a change, i.e., $\nu_1 + \tau \leq \tau_e \wedge \nu_2 + \tau \leq \tau_e$.

5.4.3   From Phases to Events

As a programming language for implementing the main controller we consider here an occam-like language. The main concept of such a language is communication. A *communication* is an instantaneous event in which both the program and its environment participate.

Up to now we have only a purely state-based description of the main controller. To switch to the communication paradigm of occam, we identify events with the changes of the phases e and d. More precisely, we introduce events named $e^\downarrow, e^\uparrow, d^\downarrow, d^\uparrow$, where $e^\downarrow$ denotes a change from e to $\neg e$ and $e^\uparrow$ a change from $\neg e$ to e, and likewise for $d^\uparrow$ and $d^\downarrow$.

In a purely event-based description we observe *timed traces*, i.e. finite event sequences that may grow over time. Semantically, we introduce a distinguished state name tr that ranges over finite sequences of events or communications:

$$tr : Time \rightarrow Comm^*$$

where $Comm$ denotes the set of communications, here $\{e^\downarrow, e^\uparrow, d^\downarrow, d^\uparrow\}$. We use λ to denote the empty trace. In the event-based setting a system or system component is described as a *timed language*, a set of timed traces [AD94].

Syntactically we shall employ here *timed regular expressions* similarly to the regular timed agents of [AKLN95]. As usual regular expressions are built from letters of a certain alphabet, here $Comm$, and closed under concatenation, sum and Kleene star operators. For convenience we also allow the operator pref denoting prefix closure. As an example consider the untimed regular expression

$$re = \texttt{pref}(d^\downarrow.e^\downarrow.d^\uparrow.e^\uparrow)^*$$

which denotes the following set of traces

$$\lambda, \ d^\downarrow, \ d^\downarrow.e^\downarrow, \ d^\downarrow.e^\downarrow.d^\uparrow, \ d^\downarrow.e^\downarrow.d^\uparrow.e^\uparrow, \ d^\downarrow.e^\downarrow.d^\uparrow.e^\uparrow.d^\downarrow, \ \ldots$$

In timed regular expressions the occurrence of events can be constrained to certain time intervals $[\alpha, \beta]$ with $\alpha : \mathbf{R}^+$ and $\beta : \mathbf{R}^+ \cup \{\infty\}$. We write $[\alpha, \beta] : ev$ to express that the event ev must at be delayed for at least α (lower time bound) and may be delayed for at most β (upper time bound). We identify an untimed event ev with $[0, \infty] : ev$, i.e., an untimed event may occur at any time.

The following timed regular expression describes the main controller with timed events:

$$MC = \texttt{pref}([\tau, \nu_2] : d^\downarrow.[\tau, \infty] : e^\downarrow.[\tau, \nu_1] : d^\uparrow.[\tau, \infty] : e^\uparrow)^*.$$

This expression denotes the timing diagram of Figure 5.4. Formally, the semantics of MC is a Duration Calculus formula $DC(MC)$ in the observable tr [RRH93, HOS+93].

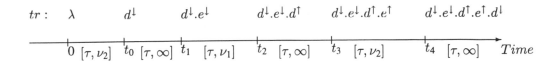

Figure 5.4   Behavior of tr for timed regular expression MC.

5.4.4   Semantic Link

What is the relationship between the timed regular expression MC and the main controller obtained before ? Semantically, switching from the state-based specification of the main controller to its event-based counterpart means replacing the Boolean states e and d by the state tr ranging over timed traces.

The relationship is given by a *linking invariant* which we now explain. For a given event ev we define the duration formula

$$ev \stackrel{def}{=} \exists h \bullet \lceil tr = h \rceil; \lceil tr = h.ev \rceil$$

stating that in a given interval the trace tr has been extended by the event ev. Then the link, $LinkInv$, between e and d and tr is given by the two formulas:

$$(\diamond \underline{e^{\downarrow}} \leftrightarrow \diamond \lceil e \rceil; \lceil \neg e \rceil) \wedge (\diamond \underline{e^{\uparrow}} \leftrightarrow \diamond \lceil \neg c \rceil; \lceil c \rceil)$$

and

$$(\diamond \underline{d^{\downarrow}} \leftrightarrow \diamond \lceil d \rceil; \lceil \neg d \rceil) \wedge (\diamond \underline{d^{\uparrow}} \leftrightarrow \diamond \lceil \neg d \rceil; \lceil d \rceil).$$

This formalizes our intention that $e^{\downarrow}$ denotes a change from e to $\neg e$, and analogously for the other events. Correctness of the event-based specification MC follows from the theorem:

$$DC(MC) \wedge \Box \, LinkInv \Rightarrow MainController.$$

5.5   ENHANCEMENTS

In this section we shall consider some changes and refinements of the design caused either by customer demand or availability of modules.

5.5.1   Gate Up for a Minimal Time

In [HL94] it is noted that the gate may open for so short a time that it is useless for passing vehicles. It would now be easy to formulate an additional stability commitment in the standard form: $(\lceil g \neq 90 \rceil \; ; \; \lceil g = 90 \rceil \wedge \ell \leq \delta) \longrightarrow \lceil g = 90 \rceil$. However, it is difficult to find a gate assembly design that satisfies this, because the *Down* state allows the gate g to bounce a bit during the start of the period. This could easily lead to counterexamples to this naive stability requirement.

An easier solution is to use a propagation property of the commitment in $GateControl$. It means that $\Box (\lceil Up \rceil \Rightarrow \ell \leq \gamma \vee \ell = \gamma \; ; \; \lceil g = 90 \rceil)$. Thus, if Up is stable for $\delta + \gamma$, we shall have a useful period, δ, with the gate up whenever it is raised. We shall therefore consider the following commitment to be a formalization of the expectation

$$(\lceil \neg Up \rceil \; ; \lceil Up \rceil \wedge \ell \leq \delta + \gamma) \longrightarrow \lceil Up \rceil.$$

Using propagation, we can then try to add the design commitment

$$(\lceil d \rceil \; ; \lceil \neg d \rceil \wedge \ell \leq \delta + \gamma + \nu_a) \longrightarrow \lceil \neg d \rceil$$

to the $MainController$. However, this means that any phase which starts with a transition from d to $\neg d$ is stable. In the example, this is the case for exactly the $e \wedge \neg d$ phase which is entered from $e \wedge d$. This forces us to assume that the $TrackSensor$ accepts an e stability of the required length. I.e., $\delta + \gamma + \nu_a < \tau_e$. This constraint may lead to a separate sensor delay and stability parameters for sensing $Empty$ and sensing $\neg Empty$, because the stability constraint given above may be unacceptable for sensing an approaching train via $\neg Empty$.

A further consideration is that the asynchronous $Down$ state may bounce. This can be prevented by adding the constraint:

$$(\lceil \neg Up \rceil \; ; \lceil Up \rceil \wedge \ell \leq 2 \cdot \nu_a) \longrightarrow \lceil Up \rceil$$

and a similar constraint for $Down$ to the $GateControl$. These prevent the $Down$ state from changing more than once when the controller phase d changes.

5.5.2   Polling Sensor

A consideration dictated by engineering is to refine the $TrackSensor$ into a polling from the internal e and $\neg e$ phases. This is achieved by the following protocols that poll the asynchronous state with a period of η:

$$\lceil e \wedge \neg Empty \rceil^\eta \longrightarrow \lceil \neg e \rceil$$
$$(\lceil \neg e \rceil \; ; \lceil e \wedge Empty \rceil \wedge \ell \leq \eta) \longrightarrow \lceil e \rceil$$
$$\lceil e \wedge Empty \rceil^\eta \longrightarrow \lceil e \rceil$$

and

$$\lceil \neg e \wedge Empty \rceil^\eta \longrightarrow \lceil e \rceil$$
$$(\lceil e \rceil \; ; \lceil \neg e \wedge \neg Empty \rceil \wedge \ell \leq \eta) \longrightarrow \lceil \neg e \rceil$$
$$\lceil \neg e \wedge \neg Empty \rceil^\eta \longrightarrow \lceil \neg e \rceil$$

It is a refinement of $TrackSensor$ when $\tau_e \leq \eta \leq \nu_s/2$.

5.6   PROGRAM SPECIFICATIONS

In the main controller a timed regular expression suffices as abstract description of the order and timing of events. In general, however, we need a more flexible description language with structuring operators and the possibility of value-passing and state dependent events.

In the ProCoS project the event-based program specification language SL has been developed to meet these goals. SL can be seen as extending timed regular expressions by parallel composition and concepts of action systems [Rös94, Sch94b, HHF+94]. The advantage of SL is that it comes with a suite of transformation rules that can be applied to refine SL specifications into occam-like programs [OR93, Rös94, Sch94b]. In the following we sketch how to specify components and complete systems in SL; full details can be found in the above references.

5.6.1 Component Specifications

A component specification is of the form SPEC Δ TA CA TR END consisting of an *interface* Δ, a *trace part TA*, a *state part CA* and a *timing part TR*. The desired behavior of the system components is described by the trace, the state, and the timing part.

Interface. The interface declares the communications channels of the component together with their direction and type. For example, for the main controller the interface is given by

```
INPUT OF Signal e↓ , e↑
OUTPUT OF Signal d↓ , d↑
```

The type Signal indicates that no value is transmitted on the channel.

Trace Part. The trace part specifies the sequencing constraints on the channels whereas the communicated values are ignored. This is done by stating one or more *trace assertions* of the form TRACE re.

The regular expression describes sequencing constraints on the channels mentioned in re. By stating several trace assertions, we can specify different aspects of the intended system behavior in a modular fashion. The informal semantics of this part of a specification is that the described behavior must satisfy the sequencing constraints of all trace assertions simultaneously. For the main controller, we have only one trace assertion consisting of the untimed regular expression of Section 5.4.3:

```
TRACE pref (d↓.e↓.d↑.e↑)*
```

Unlike in timed regular expressions the timing constraints are stated separately in SL.

State Part. This part allows us to express communications that depend on (non-finite) states and that carry values. An example where the state part is convenient can be found in [Sch94a]. There a railroad crossing is studied where the length of an approaching train is measured in terms of the number of wheels that have passed a sensor at the track. To model this we would declare a local state variable *wheels* initialized to 0:

```
VAR OF Integer wheels INIT 0.
```

To express the relationship between communications and local state change, we use so-called *communication assertions* which are close to the action notation used for action systems [Bac90] or timed automata [HL94]. For example, we might introduce events *enter* and *exit* with the following communication assertions:

```
COM enter WHEN TRUE THEN wheels ' = wheels + 1
COM exit WHEN wheels > 0 THEN wheels ' = wheels − 1
```

The when-condition describes the precondition under which the the communication can take place and the then-condition describes the effect of the communication on th local state. In the example, an *enter* communication is always enabled and will increment the local variable *wheels* and that an *exit* communication is enabled when the wheel count is positive and will decrement *wheels*. Note that we use the prime notation of Z [Spi92] to refer to the value of a variable at the moment of termination.

Timing Part. A timing part specifies when channels are ready for communication. A lower bound is expressed by

> AFTER *re* WAIT (ch, r)

which means that after the communication of a trace belonging to the language described by the regular expression *re*, the system will not communicate on *ch* before time *r* has elapsed. An upper bound is expressed by

> AFTER *re* READY (ch, r)

which means that after communication of a trace in *re*, the system becomes ready to communicate on *ch* within time *r*.

5.6.2   System Specifications

Component specifications can be named in SL and combined with other components in a parallel construct denoted by the operator SYN (synchronization merge) and channels can be hidden by a HIDE operator.

Altogether SL is a specification language that is close to the programming level. As such it extends Z specifications [Spi92], UNITY programs [CM88] or action systems [Bac90] by explicit communications constrained by regular expressions.

5.7   PROGRAMS

We consider an occam-like programming language PL where parallelism is allowed at the outermost level only [FvK93, HHF+94]. From occam [INM88] we take the following programming operators:

> PAR for the parallel composition of sequential components built from
> SKIP for immediate termination,
> assignment $x := e$, input $ch?x$ and output $ch!e$, and
> WHILE, SEQ, IF for loops, sequential and conditional composition.

In inputs and outputs the input variable x or output value e are omitted if the channel ch is of type Signal.

Additionally there are explicit timing constructs in PL. The wait time of a program segment is specified by an delay statement of the form DELAY r, where r is a non-negative real constant. An upper bound on the computation time of a program segment P is specified by prefixing P with UPPERBOUND r IN, where r is a non-negative real constant. This applies only for the time needed for active computations. Times which are spent in an idle state during a delay are not included. There is also a timed version of occam's alternative composition ALT in PL which is not needed in this paper.

5.7.1 Transformation from SL to PL

The simple structure of SL can be exploited in the development of PL programs. In system specifications the SYN operator together with the HIDE operator is translated into the parallel composition operator PAR of PL. In component specifications the trace part is transformed into a communication skeleton and the state and timing parts complete this skeleton to a sequential PL program.

For simple SL specifications like that of the main controller this transformation can be carried out fully automatic as a language compilation process [HHF+94]. As a result of this process we obtain the following PL program written in the indentation style of occam:

```
SYSTEM MainControl
    CHANNEL OF Signal   d_up, d_down, e_up, e_down :
    WHILE true
      SEQ
        UPPERBOUND nu_2 IN
          d_down !
        e_down ?
        UPPERBOUND nu_1 IN
          d_up !
        e_up ?
END
```

The complete system for monitoring the railroad crossing could then be the parallel composition of three components:

```
SYSTEM GRC
    PAR
        TrackSensor
        MainControl
        GateActuator
END
```

More sophisticated concurrent programs can be developed using transformation rules on syntactic constructs mixing SL and PL [Rös94]. These techniques are an extension of refinement calculi devised for sequential programs [Mor90].

5.8 CONCLUSION

In this paper we have illustrated an approach to the design of real-time systems using the example of the generalized railroad crossing of [HL94]. At the heart of the approach is the use of logic in form of the Duration Calculus. By using suitable abstractions and logical deductions we considerably reduce the complexity of the original commitments: instead of dealing with the track state ranging over the phases *Empty*, *Appr* and *Cross* and the gate state g ranging over a real valued interval we only have to deal with the relationships between Boolean states *Empty* and *Down*.

As a consequence, we only had to introduce sensor, actuator and controller events for these states. By contrast, the solution in [HL94] started by introducing events for all possible changes of the observables like the start of the crossing section. Then all of these events had to be related or controlled.

One emphasis in our approach is to carefully work out the assumptions under which the commitments can be implemented. For example, to refine the original safety and utility commitments we needed the assumptions on the times the fastest and the slowest train spends in the approaching section. These assumptions come out rather clearly in the deductive reasoning in the Duration Calculus. In many other approaches assumptions are not explicitly stated. For example, in [AD94] a similar example of a railroad crossing was tackled in the setting of timed automata. While the proved safety and timed liveness properties are all correct, a side effect of the proposed controller automaton is that it constrains the input event signaling an approaching train. In other words, a tacit assumption is made on the time intervals in between two successive trains. We think that by making logical deductions such hidden assumptions come to surface more clearly.

Another emphasis of our paper and even more of the ProCoS project from which our approach takes its inspiration is on the sound interfaces between different levels of abstraction. In this paper we have related three such levels:

- the hybrid system level where the gate is modeled by a time dependent real-valued function,
- the level of discrete time dependent states,
- the level of timed traces of events.

All three levels were linked in the uniform framework of the Duration Calculus. We believe that to solve realistic control problems, it will be necessary to use several complementary specification techniques. Therefore we need formal methods that guarantee the sound interfacing of such specification techniques.

A final concern is the applicability of the approach. The Duration Calculus is a highly expressive notation and can be used as it is to express safety and quantitative liveness properties. It is subjective whether a notation is readable, but our experience indicates that the timing diagram interpretation helps very much when speaking to the uninitiated. The standard form also seems to encode useful engineering cliches. A key point in the approach is to change notations when more details are added at lower levels of design, we think that this is essential for scalability. The proof system of Duration Calculus is powerful, because it imports reasoning from mathematical analysis, a time honored and highly refined engineering tool. However, the power comes at the cost of decidability. Here it is interesting to note that there are some indications that the standard forms used in the controller design can be checked against timed automata models. For the general calculus, a prototype verification assistant [SS94, Ska94] has been developed, and in fact used to check the refinement steps in Sections 6.3.2 and 6.4.

ACKNOWLEDGEMENTS

Thanks to our colleagues in the ProCoS project, in particular Hans Rischel and Jifeng He, and the reviewers for very useful comments.

This work is partially funded by the Commission of the European Communities (CEC) under the ESPRIT programme in the field of Basic Research Project No. 7071: "ProCoS II: Provably Correct Systems". Anders P. Ravn's work was done while visiting: Christian-

Albrechts-Universität zu Kiel, Institut für Informatik und Praktische Mathematik, funded by the German Research Council (DFG).

REFERENCES

[AD94]   R. Alur and D. Dill. A theory of timed automata. *Theoret. Comput. Sci.*, 126, 1994.

[AKLN95] J.H. Andersen, K.J. Kristoffersen, K.G. Larsen, and J. Niedermann. Automatic synthesis of real time systems. In *Internat. Colloq. on Automata, Languages and Programming, LNCS.* Springer-Verlag, 1995. to appear

[AL92]   M. Abadi and L. Lamport. An old-fashioned recipe for real time. In J. W. de Bakker, C. Huizing, W.-P. de Roever, and G. Rozenberg, editors, *Real-Time: Theory in Practice, REX Workshop*, volume 600 of *LNCS*, pages 1–27. Springer-Verlag, 1992.

[B+93]   J. P. Bowen et al. A ProCoS II project description: ESPRIT Basic Research project 7071. *Bull. Europ. Assoc. for Theoret. Comput. Sci. (EATCS)*, 50:128–137, June 1993.

[Bac90]   R.J.R. Back. Refinement calculus, part II: Parallel and reactive programs. In J.W. de Bakker, W.-P. de Roever, and G. Rozenberg, editors, *Stepwise Refinement of Distributed Systems – Models, Formalisms, Correctness*, volume 430 of *LNCS*, pages 67–93. Springer-Verlag, 1990.

[CM88]   K.M. Chandy and J. Misra. *Parallel Program Design: A Foundation.* Addison-Wesley, 1988.

[EKM+93] M. Engel, M. Kubica, J. Madey, D. L. Parnas, A. P. Ravn, and A. J. van Schouwen. A formal approach to computer systems requirements documentation. In R. L. Grossman, A. Nerode, A. P. Ravn, and H. Rischel, editors, *Hybrid Systems*, volume 736 of *LNCS*, pages 452–474. Springer-Verlag, 1993.

[FvK93]   M. Fränzle and B. v. Karger. Proposal for a programming language core for ProCoS II. ProCoS Project Document [Kiel MF 11/3], 1993.

[HHF+94] J. He, C. A. R. Hoare, M. Fränzle, M. Müller-Olm, E.-R. Olderog, M. Schenke, M. R. Hansen, A. P. Ravn, and H. Rischel. Provably correct systems. In H. Langmaack, W.-P. de Roever, and J. Vytopil, editors, *Formal Techniques in Real-Time and Fault-Tolerant Systems*, volume 863 of *LNCS*, pages 288–335. Springer-Verlag, 1994.

[HL94]   C. Heitmeyer and N. Lynch. The generalized railroad crossing: A case study in formal verification of real-time systems. In *Proc. IEEE Real-Time Systems Symposium*. IEEE Computer Society Press, 1994.

[HOS+93] M. R. Hansen, E.-R. Olderog, M. Schenke, M. Fränzle, B. v. Karger, M. Müller-Olm, and H. Rischel. A duration calculus semantics for real-time reactive systems. Technical Report OLD MRH 1/1, ProCoSII, ESPRIT BRA 7071, Oldenburg Universität, September 1993.

[Ina94]   R. Inal. Modular specification of real-time systems. In *Proceedings of 1994 Euromicro Workshop on Real-Time Systems*. IEEE Computer Society Press, 1994.

[INM88]   INMOS Ltd. *occam 2 reference manual.* Prentice Hall, 1988.

[JM86]   F. Jahanian and A. K L. Mok. Safety analysis of timing properties in real-time systems. *IEEE Trans. Software Eng.*, 12(9):890–904, September 1986.

[Jos88]   M. Joseph, editor. *Proceedings Symp. on Formal Techniques in Real-Time and Fault-Tolerant Systems*, volume 331 of *LNCS*. Springer-Verlag, 1988.

[Koy90]   R. Koymans. Specifying real-time properties with metric temporal logic. *Real-Time Systems*, 2(4):255–299, November 1990.

[Lam91]   L. Lamport. The temporal logic of actions. Technical report, Digital Systems Research Center, 130 Lytton Avenue, Palo Alto, California 94301, USA, 25 December 1991.

[LdRV94] H. Langmaack, W.-P. de Roever, and J. Vytopil, editors. *Proceedings Symp. on Formal Techniques in Real-Time and Fault-Tolerant Systems*, volume 863 of *LNCS*. Springer-Verlag, 1994.

[LR94]   H. Langmaack and A. P. Ravn. The ProCoS project: Provably correct systems. In J. Bowen, editor, *Towards Verified Systems*, volume 2 of *Real-Time Safety Critical Systems*, chapter Appendix B. Elsevier, 1994.

[Lue79]   D. G. Luenberger. *Introduction to Dynamic Systems. Theory, Models & Applications.* Wiley, 1979.

[Mor90]   C. Morgan. *Programming From Specifications*. Prentice-Hall International Series in Computer Science, 1990.

[Mos85]   B. Moszkowski. A temporal logic for multi-level reasoning about hardware. *IEEE Computer*, 18(2):10–19, 1985.

[Mos86]   B. Moszkowski. *Executing Temporal Logic Programs*. Cambridge University Press, 1986.

[MP93]   Z Manna and A. Pnueli. Verifying hybrid systems. In R. L. Grossman, A. Nerode, A. P. Ravn, and H. Rischel, editors, *Hybrid Systems*, volume 736 of *LNCS*, pages 4–35, 1993.

[OR93]   E.-R. Olderog and S. Rössig. A case study in transformational design of concurrent systems. In M.-C. Gaudel and J.-P. Jouannaud, editors, *TAPSOFT '93: Theory and Practice of Software Development*, volume 668 of *LNCS*, pages 90–104. Springer-Verlag, 1993.

[Ost89]   J. S. Ostroff. *Temporal Logic for Real-time Systems*. Advanced Software Development Series. Wiley, 1989.

[PH88]   A. Pnueli and E. Harel. Applications of temporal logic to the specification of real-time systems (extended abstract). In M. Joseph, editor, *Proceedings of a Symposium on Formal Techniques in Real-Time and Fault-Tolerant Systems*, volume 331 of *LNCS*, pages 84–98. Springer-Verlag, 1988.

[Rös94]   S. Rössig. *A Transformational Approach to the Design of Communicating Systems*. PhD thesis, Department of Computer Science, University of Oldenburg, October 1994.

[RR91]   A. P. Ravn and H. Rischel. Requirements capture for embedded real-time systems. In *Proceedings of IMACS-MCTS'91 Symposium on Modeling and Control of Technological Systems, Villeneuve d'Ascq, France, May 7-10, 1991*, volume 2, pages 147–152. IMACS, May 1991.

[RRH93]   A.P. Ravn, H. Rischel, and K. M. Hansen. Specifying and verifying requirements of real-time systems. *IEEE Trans. Software Engineering*, 19(1):41–55, Jan. 1993.

[Sch94a]   M. Schenke. Specification and transformation of reactive systems with time restrictions and concurrency. In H. Langmaack, W.-P. de Roever, and J. Vytopil, editors, *Formal Techniques in Real-Time and Fault-Tolerant Systems*, volume 863 of *LNCS*, pages 605–621. Springer-Verlag, 1994.

[Sch94b]   M. Schenke. A timed specification language for concurrent reactive systems. In D.J. Andrews, J.F. Groote, and C.A. Middelburg, editors, *Semantics of Specification Languages*, Workshops in Computing, pages 152–167. Springer-Verlag, 1994.

[SMSV83]   R. L. Schwartz, P. M. Melliar-Smith, and F. H. Vogt. An interval logic for higher-level temporal reasoning. In *Proceedings of the 2nd. Annual ACM Symposium on Principles of Distributed Computing*, pages 173–186, 1983.

[Spi92]   J. M. Spivey. *The Z Notation: A Reference Manual*. Prentice Hall Int. Series in Computer Science, 2nd edition, 1992.

[SRRZ92]   J. U. Skakkebæk, A. P. Ravn, H. Rischel, and Zhou, Chaochen. Specification of embedded, real-time systems. In *Proceedings of 1992 Euromicro Workshop on Real-Time Systems*. IEEE Computer Society Press, 1992.

[SS94]   J. U. Skakkebæk and N. Shankar. Towards a duration calculus proof assistant in PVS. In H. Langmaack, W.-P. de Roever, and J. Vytopil, editors, *Formal Techniques in Real-Time and Fault-Tolerant Systems*, volume 863 of *LNCS*, pages 660–679. Springer-Verlag, 1994.

[Ska94]   J. U. Skakkebæk. *A Verification Assistant for a Real-Time Logic*. PhD thesis, Dept. Comp. Science, Technical University of Denmark, November 1994.

[Vyt91]   J. Vytopil, editor. *Proceedings Symp. on Formal Techniques in Real-Time and Fault-Tolerant Systems*, volume 571 of *LNCS*. Springer-Verlag, 1991.

[Zho93]   Zhou, Chaochen. Duration calculi: An overview. In D. Bjørner, M. Broy, and I. V. Pottosin, editors, *Proc. Formal Methods in Programming and Their Application*, volume 735 of *LNCS*, pages 256–266. Springer-Verlag, 1993.

[ZHR91]   Zhou, Chaochen, C. A. R. Hoare, and A. P. Ravn. A calculus of durations. *Information Proc. Letters*, 40(5), December 1991.

[ZRH93]   Zhou, Chaochen, A. P. Ravn, and M. R. Hansen. An extended duration calculus for hybrid real-time systems. In R. L. Grossman, A. Nerode, A. P. Ravn, and H. Rischel, editors, *Hybrid Systems*, volume 736 of *LNCS*, pages 36–59. Springer-Verlag, 1993.

6

A Petri Net and Logic Approach to the Specification and Verification of Real-Time Systems

DINO MANDRIOLI, ANGELO MORZENTI, MAURO PEZZÈ, PIERLUIGI SAN PIETRO[1] and SERGIO SILVA[2]
Politecnico di Milano

ABSTRACT

We report on our ongoing research whose long-term goal is to build methods and tools for developing industrial-strength real-time systems. We describe two independent but coordinated approaches, one an operational formalism based on Petri nets and the other a specification language based on logic. Both formalisms are specially designed to deal with time-critical aspects of real-time systems. We also describe our prototype tools and our experience in applying the tools in industrial projects.

In the long term, we plan to integrate the two approaches so that system structure is described formally by a Petri net, whereas system properties are expressed and proved in the logic language. We discuss the advantages of such a "dual language" approach and the barriers to applying the approach to industrial projects in the short term.

6.1 INTRODUCTION

Our group at the Politecnico di Milano is engaged in a long-term research project whose goal is to produce a complete methodology and tool environment supporting the rigorous development of real-time (RT) systems using formal approaches. To achieve results that can be applied in industry, much of the research has been carried out in cooperation with industrial partners. Our main focus is the specification phase of the software life-cycle.

Our early studies of candidate formalisms showed that no single formalism can provide

---

[1] Currently with the Japan Advanced Institute of Science and Technology, Hokuriku
[2] Partially supported by CONACyT-México

Formal Methods For Real-Time Computing, Edited by Heitmeyer and Mandrioli
© 1996 John Wiley & Sons Ltd

optimal solutions to a given problem. In particular, the symmetric pros and cons of operational (abstract machine-based) and descriptive approaches soon became apparent.

As a consequence, we advocate the "dual language" approach, an approach introduced in Chapter 1, as an effective way to achieve the advantages of both the operational and the descriptive approaches. We advocate an operational approach based on Petri nets and a descriptive approach based on a logic language called TRIO. However, achieving the advantages of the dual language approach requires the integration of timed Petri nets and TRIO at the theoretical level, an effort currently in progress at the Politecnico.

To achieve practical results in the short term, we have taken an incremental approach that explores the two approaches separately. A dual language approach that integrates the two remains our long-term objective. The purpose of this chapter is to summarize our main results. First, we describe Cabernet, which is based on a Petri net formalism. Second, we describe TRIO, a logic language explicitly designed for specifying real time systems. We report our experience in applying both approaches in industrial projects. Finally, we give some early results of our application of the dual language approach and summarize our long-term plans for further developing our version of the dual language approach.

Our presentation is largely tutorial and relies heavily on examples rather than technical details. Our examples are based on the Generalized Railroad Crossing (GRC) benchmark described in the preface. First, we begin with a simplified version of the GRC problem called the KRC (Kernel Railroad Crossing), which retains the significant features of the more general problem but leads to an intuitive initial formalization. All of our approaches—Cabernet, TRIO, and the dual language approach—are introduced in our formulation of the KRC problem. For both Cabernet and TRIO, we show next how the KRC specification can be extended to produce a more general formulation of the problem by simply adding more information.[3]

6.2 THE KERNEL RAILROAD CROSSING (KRC) PROBLEM

The KRC consists of a single train which travels through regions R and I according to Figure 6.1.

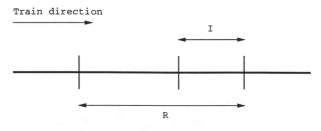

Figure 6.1   Regions R and I in the KRC problem

The train takes a minimum time d_m and maximum time d_M to go from the beginning of R to the beginning of I; it takes a minimum time h_m and maximum time h_M to go from the beginning of I to its end. The gate can be in two stationary positions, *open* and *closed*. It can also be moving up (opening) and moving down (closing) and is operated through commands *go_up* and *go_down*. When the gate receives a command, it requires exactly γ time units to

---

[3] The adopted generalizations, though both based on the original GRC formulation, are not totally aligned. This is to focus attention on some qualifying features of the presented formalisms.

change position. The movement of the gate cannot be interrupted: once it starts moving, say up, it must eventually reach the open position even if meanwhile a *go_down* command is issued.

6.3 PETRI NETS

Traditional Petri nets [Rei82] provide an excellent operational model of the functional behavior of the railroad crossing problem, as shown in [LS87], where a simple railroad crossing is used in a case study. Unfortunately, traditional Petri nets cannot completely model the problem's temporal aspects nor do they scale up to handle generic numbers of trains and/or tracks. Traditional timed Petri net extensions, e.g., Merlin and Farber nets (MF nets) [MF76], provide a good means for describing temporal aspects but cannot identify single train instances apart from their temporal differences; modeling generic numbers of tracks and trains requires this. High-level nets, e.g., Colored nets [Jen87] or Predicate/Transition nets [Gen87], complement timed Petri nets by adding values to tokens and thus allowing trains and tracks to be easily identified, but these approaches do not deal with time. High-level timed Petri nets (HLTPNs) or ER nets, originally proposed in [GMMP91], integrate functional and temporal descriptions in a unique formal framework. The inclusion relation between the different Petri net extensions allows a specification to be built and analyzed incrementally, from a traditional net expressing the functional behavior only, to a timed net adding time, up to a HLTPN providing a complete specification. Each step introduces different details and can be analyzed with different techniques.

6.3.1 Timed Petri Nets and the KRC Problem

In MF nets, each transition is associated with a pair of values, indicating the minimum and maximum firing times. In [MF76], minimum and maximum firing times are expressed as values relative to the enabling time, i.e., the time when the last token is created in the input places. In this chapter, we express minimum and maximum firing times as absolute values, for uniformity with the notation later introduced for HLTPNs. A transition with at least one token in each input place cannot fire before its minimum firing time and must fire no later than its maximum firing time, unless disabled before its maximum firing time by the firing of a conflicting transition.

Large specifications can be modularized by composing subnets. Many approaches have been suggested for achieving this. In this chapter, net composition is achieved using shared places that are input/output places of transitions belonging to different subnets. Examples of MF nets are given in Figures 6.2 and 6.3. They describe the two main components of the KRC problem: the track and the gate. In Figures 6.2 and 6.3, *enab* denotes the enabling time, and double circles indicate shared places.

In the marking shown in Figure 6.2, only transition *Enter_R* is enabled, since it is the only transition with at least one token in all its input places. If we assume that the system starts at time 0, transition *Enter_R* can fire at any time between 0 and infinity. The firing of transition *Enter_R* at time τ removes the token from place *Arrived* and produces new tokens in places *In_R* and *Enter_R_Signal*. The token in place *Enter_R_Signal* contributes to enabling transitions of the subnet corresponding to the gate. The token in place *In_R* enables transition *Enter_I*, which can fire between $\tau + d_m$ and $\tau + d_M$.

A track is described operationally by the different positions of a train and its possible moves. Two signals modeled by the two places *Enter_R_Signal* and *Exit_I_Signal* are sent to the gate. The subnet modeling the gate represents both the physical gate and the controlling device. The physical gate and the controlling device could be modeled with different subnets in a refined version.

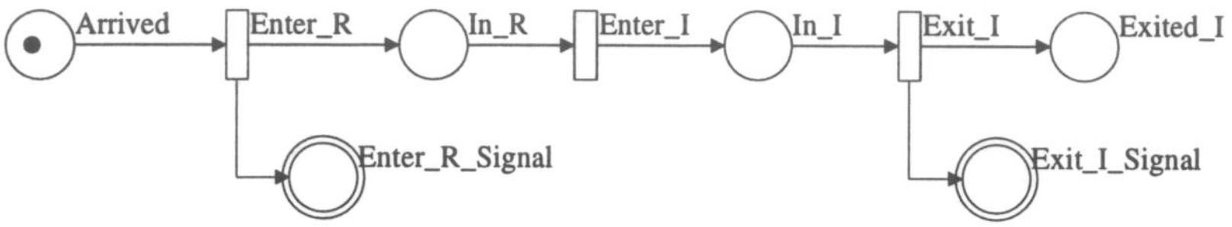

Place	Description
Arrived	Train near region R
In_R	Train in region R, near region I
In_I	Train in region I
Exited_I	Train exited region I (and R)
Enter_R_Signal	Signal to the gate
Exit_I_Signal	Signal to the gate

Transition	Description
Enter_R	Train enters region R
Enter_I	Train enters region I
Exit_I	Train exits region I (and R)

Transition	Minimum firing time	Maximum firing time
Enter_R	enab	enab $+ \infty$
Enter_I	enab $+ d_m$	enab $+ d_M$
Exit_I	enab $+ h_m$	enab $+ h_M$

Figure 6.2   A timed Petri net modeling a KRC track

Figure 6.3, which models the gate, shows the transitions among the *open*, *close*, *opening*, and *closing* states. Places *Enter_R_Signal* and *Exit_I_Signal* denote the signals coming from the sensors on the track.

The timed Petri nets of Figures 6.2 and 6.3 can be combined by joining the *shared* places *Enter_R_Signal* and *Exit_I_Signal* as shown in Figure 6.4. The timing of the MF net of Figure 6.4 is the same as in Figures 6.2 and 6.3. Shared places are represented with double circles, and gray backgrounds identify the component subnets.

Both the safety and utility properties can be proven using the "time reachability tree" in Figure 6.5:

safety   There does not exist a non-zero time interval in which place *In_I* is marked and place *Closed* is not; i.e., a train is never in region I if the gate is not closed.

utility   The gate is closed for the minimum time required to guarantee the safety of the system.

The time reachability tree of Figure 6.5 has been built with Cabernet [Pez94], using the time reachability analysis algorithm described in [GMP94]. Each node of the time reachability tree is described by a symbolic marking: the timestamps of the tokens are indicated by symbolic values, whereas the mutual relations among timestamps are expressed as constraints. For example, the firing sequence $\langle Enter\_R, Go\_Down, Stop\_Down, Enter\_I, Exit\_I \rangle$ ends in

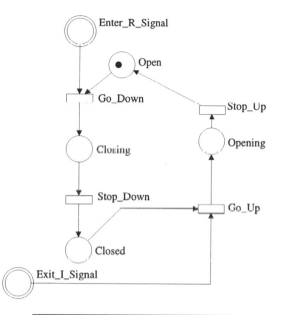

Place	Description
Closing	Gate is closing
Closed	Indicates the state of the gate
Opening	Gate is opening
Open	Indicates the state of the gate

Transition	Description
Go_Down	Starts closing the gate
Go_Up	Starts opening the gate
Stop_Down	Delay for closing completion
Stop_Up	Delay for opening completion

Transition	Minimum firing time	Maximum firing time
Go_Down	$\text{enab} + d_m - \gamma$	$\text{enab} + d_m - \gamma$
Go_Up	enab	enab
Stop_Down	$\text{enab} + \gamma$	$\text{enab} + \gamma$
Stop_Up	$\text{enab} + \gamma$	$\text{enab} + \gamma$

Figure 6.3   A timed Petri net modeling a KRC gate

state $S5$, where places $Closed$, $Exited\_I$, and $Enter\_R\_Signal$ are marked. Places $Exited\_I$ and $Enter\_R\_Signal$ have been marked at the same time. The firing time of transition $Exit\_I$ is denoted by the symbolic value $T5$. Place $Closed$ is marked with a different timestamp indicated by the symbolic value $T3$. The constraint $T1 \geq 0 \wedge T3 = T1 + d_m \wedge T1 + d_m + h_m \leq T5 \leq T1 + d_M + h_M$ denotes the relation among symbolic timestamps.

In this example, we assume that the system starts at time zero, as denoted by the constraint associated with the initial status $S0$ ($T0 = 0$). The first observable event (the firing of transition $Enter\_R$) can happen any time after the system start time, as indicated by the constraint associated with state $S1$ ($T1 \geq T0$).

The time reachability tree of Figure 6.5 symbolically describes all feasible firing sequences with two symbolic sequences, which differ in the sequence of the firings of transitions

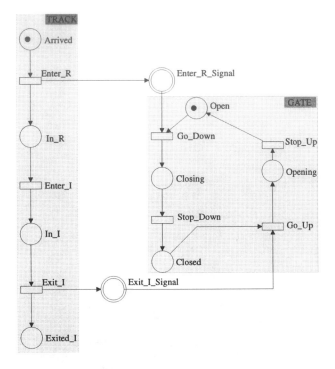

Figure 6.4   A timed Petri net modeling a simplified KRC problem

Stop_Down and *Enter_I*. Both transitions can fire at the same time if the train runs at its maximum speed.

Both properties are verified by examining the symbolic constraints associated with states. The safety property can be proven by comparing the constraints associated with states $S8$ and $S9$. These constraints indicate that state $S8$, the only potentially unsafe state, is entered for zero time units. The utility property can be proven by deducing the maximum time a gate is closed using simple algebraic manipulations of the symbolic constraints associated with the states.

6.3.2   High Level Timed Petri Nets

In this section, we consider the following generalization of the KRC problem to the GRC:

- There are n tracks.
- Each train can travel on a track in either direction (North/South).
- Several trains can be on the same track, given that they are traveling in the same direction and are separated by a minimum safety distance.
- The opening of the gate can be interrupted if a new train enters region R while the gate is opening. Notice that this change would have no impact on the KRC problem, since the KRC assumes at most one train on the only track and thus excludes the case of a new train entering sector R while the gate is still opening.

MF nets do not scale up well from the KRC to the GRC problem, since they do not provide a means for identifying tokens and time can be expressed only as a relative interval. This limitation of the MF model can be overcome using HLTPNs.

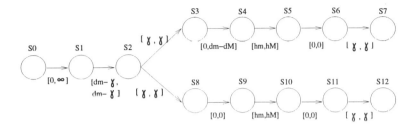

Symbolic state	Last fired transition	Symbolic marking	Constraint
S0		m(Arrived)=T0; m(Open)=T0;	$T0 = 0$
S1	Enter_R	m(Open)=T0; m(In_R)=T1; m(Enter_R_Signal)=T1;	$T0 = 0 \wedge T1 \geq T0$
S2	Go_Down	m(Closing)=T2; m(In_R)=T1;	$T1 \geq 0 \wedge T2 = T1 + d_m - \gamma$
S3	Stop_Down	m(Closed)=T3; m(In_R)=T1;	$T1 \geq 0 \wedge T3 = T1 + d_m$
S4	Enter_I	m(In_I)=T4; m(Closed)=T3;	$T1 \geq 0 \wedge T3 = T1 + d_m \wedge T1 + d_m \leq T4 \leq T1 + d_M$
S5	Exit_I	m(Closed)=T3; m(Exited_I)=T5; m(Exit_I_Signal)=T5;	$T1 \geq 0 \wedge T3 = T1 + d_m \wedge T1 + d_m + h_m \leq T5 \leq T1 + d_M + h_M$
S6	Go_Up	m(Opening)=T6; m(Exited_I)=T5;	$T1 \geq 0 \wedge T1 + d_m + h_m \leq T5 \leq T1 + d_M + h_M \wedge T6 = T5$
S7	Stop_Up	m(Open)=T7; m(Exited_I)=T5;	$T1 \geq 0 \wedge T1 + d_m + h_m \leq T5 \leq T1 + d_M + h_M \wedge T7 = T5 + \gamma$
S8	Enter_I	m(Closing)=T2; m(In_I)=T8;	$T1 \geq 0 \wedge T2 = T1 + d_m - \gamma \wedge T8 = T1 + d_m$
S9	Stop_Down	m(In_I)=T8; m(Closed)=T9;	$T1 \geq 0 \wedge T8 = T1 + d_m \wedge T9 = T8$
S10	Exit_I	m(Closed)=T9; m(Exited_I)=T10; m(Exit_I_Signal)=T10;	$T1 \geq 0 \wedge T9 = T1 + d_m \wedge T1 + d_m + h_m \leq T10 \leq T1 + d_m + h_M$
S11	Go_Up	m(Opening)=T11; m(Exited_I)=T10;	$T1 \geq 0 \wedge T1 + d_m + h_m \leq T10 \leq T1 + d_m + h_M \wedge T11 = T10$
S12	Stop_Up	m(Open)=T12; m(Exited_I)=T10;	$T1 \geq 0 \wedge T1 + d_m + h_m \leq T10 \leq T1 + d_m + h_M \wedge T12 = T10 + \gamma$

Figure 6.5 Time reachability tree of the net of Figure 6.4

A high-level timed Petri net is a Petri net in which

- places are associated with types, that denote the type of the tokens that can mark the place.
- tokens are associated with

  - a data structure indicating the data associated with the tokens. The data structure associated with a token must be of the type associated with the place containing the token.
  - a timestamp indicating the "birth date" of the token, i.e., when the token was created.

- transitions are associated with

  - a predicate that determines the enabling of the transition according to data structures and timestamps of the tokens in the input places.

- an action that indicates the data to be associated with the tokens produced by the firing as a function of the data and the timestamps of the tokens removed by the firing.
- a time function that indicates the minimum and maximum firing times as functions of the data and the timestamps of the tokens removed by the firing.

A HLTPN for the GRC problem is shown in Figure 6.6. Arrows connecting two nodes in both directions overlap, thus giving the graphical effect of double arrows. Figure 6.7 shows the types of the places and the predicates, actions, and firing times of the transitions. The definitions of the types are listed in Figure 6.7. For simplicity, time is omitted if it was already described for the KRC problem, and predicates, actions, and times of the symmetric transitions ($N\_\ldots$ and $S\_\ldots$) are described only once. Predicates and actions of transitions $Arrive\_S$ and $Checkout\_S$ are reported, since they differ significantly for the symmetric transitions. Tokens are referred to by the name of the place.

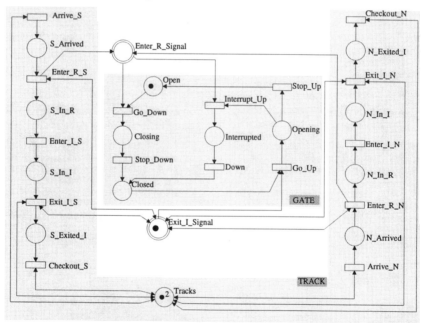

Figure 6.6   A HLTPN model of the GRC problem

A track alternatively used in both directions (North-South/South-North, by convention) is modeled by duplicating the subnet of Figure 6.2, one subnet for each direction. A few controls on trains entering the track are added to ensure the direction and guarantee the minimum distance between two consecutive trains (i.e., place *Tracks*, which indicates the availability of the track, and transitions *Arrive_S*, *Checkout_S*, *Arrive_N*, and *Checkout_N*, which control trains entering tracks in either direction). To model n tracks, n tokens are inserted in place *Tracks*. The gate model has been extended with transitions *Interrupt_Up* and *Down* and place *Interrupted* to handle closing requests during the opening process. (This is caused by the presence of several trains). If a train enters region R before the gate is completely open, transition *Interrupt_Up* aborts the opening and starts closing the gate. The timing of transitions *Interrupt_Up* and *Down* guarantee that the gate will be closed in a time proportional to the reached height. In this case, the modeling of the temporal behavior is straightforward using

Type	Attributes
Track	`(time:real, track_number:int, Trains_count:int, available:int)`
Train	`(time:real, track_number:int)`
Interruption	`(time:real, delta:real)`
Counter	`(time:real, counter:int)`

Place	Type	Meaning of tokens
N_Arrived	Train	A train has entered a track in the system
N_In_R	Train	A train has entered region R
N_In_I	Train	A train is present in region I
N_Exited_I	Train	A train has exited region I (and R)
Tracks	Track	A track in the system
Enter_R_Signal	Void	Request to close the gate
Exit_I_Signal	Counter	Request to open the gate
Closing	Void	The gate is being closed
Closed	Void	The gate is closed
Opening	Void	The gate is being opened
Open	Void	The gate is open
Interrupted	Interruption	Opening aborted

Transition	Predicate	Action
Arrive_N	`(Tracks.trains_count >= 0 && Tracks.available == 1)`	`N_Arrived.track_number = Tracks.track_number; Tracks.trains_count ++; Tracks.available = 0;`
Arrive_S	`(Tracks.trains_count <= 0 && Tracks.available == 1)`	`S_Arrived.track_number = Tracks.track_number; Tracks.trains_count --; Tracks.available - 0;`
Enter_R_N	TRUE	`N_In_R = N_Arrived; Exit_I_Signal.counter ++ ;`
Enter_I_N	TRUE	`N_In_I = N_In_R;`
Exit_I_N	TRUE	`N_Exited_I = N_In_I; Tracks.available = 1; Exit_I_Signal.counter --`
Checkout_N	`(N_Exited.track_number == Tracks.track_number)`	`Tracks.trains_count --;`
Checkout_S	`(S_Exited.track_number == Tracks.track_number)`	`Tracks.trains_count ++;`
Go_Down	TRUE	;
Stop_Down	TRUE	;
Go_Up	TRUE	;
Stop_Up	TRUE	;
Interrupt_Up	TRUE	`Interrupted.delta = Interrupted.time - Opening.time;`
Down	TRUE	;

Transition	Minimum firing time	Maximum firing time
Arrive_N	enab	enab $+ \infty$
Enter_R_N	$N\_Arrived + j_m$	$N\_Arrived + j_M$
Enter_I_N	$N\_In\_R.time + d_m$	$N\_In\_R.time + d_M$
Exit_I_N	$N\_In\_I.time + h_m$	$N\_In\_I.time + h_M$
Checkout_N	`N_Exited_I.time`	`N_Exited_I.time`
Go_Down	$Enter\_R\_Signal.time + d_m - \gamma$	$Enter\_R\_Signal.time + d_m - \gamma$
Stop_Down	γ	γ
Go_Up	`Exit_I_Signal.time`	`Exit_I_Signal.time`
Stop_Up	γ	γ
Interrupt_Up	`Enter_R_Signal.time`	`Enter_R_Signal.time`
Down	`Interrupted.time + Interrupted.delta`	`Interrupted.time + Interrupted.delta`

Figure 6.7 Types, predicates, actions and time-functions of the HLTPN of Figure 6.6

specific features of HLTPNs, namely, relating the timing of transition *Down* to a value that indicates the time interval during which the gate has been opening before having been stopped, computed by the firing of transition *Interrupt_Up*.

The data structures associated with tokens and the predicates and actions associated with transitions limit access to the track to avoid trains on the same track traveling in opposite directions.

Place *Exit_I_Signal*, which is of type counter, keeps track of the number of trains that enter and leave the region R, thus detecting opening signals that must not be processed due to the presence of another train in the region. Place *Tracks* avoids collisions between trains on the same track (traveling in the same direction) by enforcing a minimum safety distance between trains.

Figure 6.8 illustrates the dynamic semantics of HLTPNs by showing the state before and after the firing of transition *Arrive_N*. In this case, a single track is considered. After the firing, no transition is enabled due to the constraints on transitions.

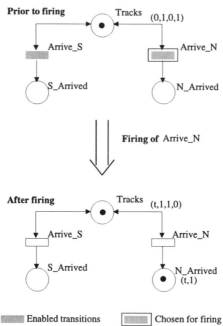

Figure 6.8   State before and after the firing of transition *Arrive_N*

The HLTPN of Figure 6.6 has been analyzed using Cabernet to prove the safety and utility properties. Such an analysis, which is not reported here for brevity, provides deeper insight than the analysis of the KRC problem.

6.3.3   Cabernet: Its Future and Applications

The availability of suitable tools is vital for the specification and validation of large systems. The success of notations and methodologies in industry largely depends on the quality of available tools. Petri nets are supported by some tools, e.g., DESIGN/CPN for hierarchical Colored Petri nets, DSPNexpress for deterministic and stochastic Petri nets, and LOOPN which supports an object-oriented extension to Colored nets. Most available tools support editing, execution, and graphical animation of nets. Additionally, some provide clustering and composition facilities for complex layouts. Analysis and validation facilities are often limited to syntactic checks. A few tools, e.g., Product Net Machine and QPN-Tool, also perform reachability analysis, but this analysis is usually limited to traditional, untimed, reachability analysis. Few tools deal specifically with timed Petri nets.

The solution to the GRC problem described in this chapter has been proven using Cabernet, which supports specification and validation of real-time systems based on HLTPNs. Cabernet, which is fully described in [Pez94], is unique in many respects: It is the only tool that fully supports high-level timed Petri nets, i.e., supports the specification of control, time, data and functionality in an integrated notation. It can also perform timed reachability analysis and thus prove automatically important temporal properties, such as deadline satisfaction. It provides decomposition and customization facilities with a sound formal basis.[4] Below, we briefly summarize the most notable features of Cabernet and survey the case studies we have conducted using Cabernet.

Cabernet provides a kernel engine that allows high level timed Petri nets to be edited, executed and formally analyzed. Execution techniques range from a simple firing model that ignores data, time, and functionality to execution of the complete model. Analysis is based on exploration of a time reachability tree. As illustrated above, each node of the time reachability tree corresponds to a set of markings that differ only in the timestamps associated with the tokens.

The use of symbolic execution techniques and the axiom that requires that time eventually increases guarantees the finiteness of the set of states of the timed reachability tree to be explored for proving properties stated within a finite deadline. Both safety and liveness properties limited to a finite time interval can be proven. Looking for execution paths that guarantee the termination of all tasks within their deadlines is an example of a liveness property stated within a finite time (the largest deadline). Guaranteeing that an alarm is never followed by a catastrophe before entering a normal functioning state is an example of safety property. The interval between an alarm and the next normal functioning state is the range of the safety property. If a normal functioning state is reached in a finite time, as in most safety-critical applications, the safety property can be expressed over a finite time interval.

The complexity of time reachability analysis techniques can be partially overcome by using the net decomposition facilities provided by Cabernet. A high level specification can be refined to a detailed one through property-preserving transformations. Cabernet automatically verifies the correctness of the applied transformations in constant time. Thus, extensive use of decomposition can lead to a more efficient analysis.

Cabernet also provides sophisticated customization mechanisms that allow the end-user notation to be formally adapted to the needs of experts and of specialized applications. Cabernet customization facilities, described in [GP93], are currently being used as part of the ESPRIT project IDERS. The aim of this effort is to apply Cabernet customization technology to Software through Pictures, a popular commercial tool for developing real-time systems [Pic94], and using this approach to validate large industrial applications.

Cabernet has been validated on several practical industrial cases: a gas burner [CP95], a node of an electricity network, the control system of a robot arm, and a diagnostic process [PGCP94]. In each case, the use of Cabernet revealed ambiguities and errors in the original

---

[4] Cabernet can be obtained free of charge from ftp-se.elet.polimi.it via anonymous login. Presently, Cabernet has been licensed free of charge to more than 30 institutions.

Operator	Definition	Comment
$Futr(F, d)$	$d \geq 0 \wedge Dist(F, d)$	Future
$Past(F, d)$	$d \geq 0 \wedge Dist(F, -d)$	Past
$futr(t, d)$		A short notation for the value of the term t at d instants in the future
$past(t, d)$		Similarly for the past
$Lasts(F, d)$	$\forall d'(0 < d' < d \rightarrow Dist(F, d'))$	F holds over a period of length d
$Lasted(F, d)$	$\forall d'(0 < d' < d \rightarrow Dist(F, -d'))$	F held over a period of length d in the past
$Until(A1, A2)$	$\exists t(t > 0 \wedge Futr(A2, t) \wedge Lasts(A1, t))$	$A1$ holds until $A2$ becomes true
$Since(A1, A2)$	$\exists t(t > 0 \wedge Past(A2, t) \wedge Lasted(A1, t))$	$A1$ held since $A2$ became true
$Alw(F)$	$\forall d\, Dist(F, d)$	F always holds
$AlwF(F)$	$\forall d(d > 0 \rightarrow Dist(F, d))$	F will always hold in the future
$AlwP(F)$	$\forall d(d < 0 \rightarrow Dist(F, d))$	F always held in the past
$SomF(F)$	$\exists d(d > 0 \wedge Dist(F, d))$	Sometime in the future F will hold
$Som(F)$	$\exists d\, Dist(F, d)$	Sometime F held or F will hold
$UpToNow(F)$	$\exists \delta(\delta > 0 \wedge Past(F, \delta) \wedge Lasted(F, \delta))$	F held for a nonzero time interval that ended at the current instant
$Becomes(F)$	$F \wedge UpToNow(\neg F)$	F holds at the current instant but did not hold for a nonzero interval that preceded the current instant
$LastTime(F, t)$	$Past(F, t) \wedge (Lasted(\neg F, t))$	F occurred for the last time t units ago

Table 6.1 A sample of derived temporal operators

informal specifications. Most ambiguities were detected by using a formal notation. Most errors were detected by animating and executing the specifications. However, in many cases, time reachability analysis provided a level of confidence that could not be achieved by simple execution and animation.

6.4   TRIO: A SHORT LANGUAGE OVERVIEW

TRIO is a first-order theory augmented with a temporal domain that includes basic arithmetic and the temporal operator $Dist$. For a given formula W, $Dist(W, t)$ means that W is true at a time instant whose distance is exactly t time units from the current instant, i.e., the instant when the sentence is claimed. The current instant is implicit in TRIO formulas.

The attribute TD (time-dependent) means that a given variable or predicate may assume different values at different time instants. TI (time-independent) means the opposite.

On the basis of the fundamental operator $Dist$, many other temporal operators can be defined as derived operators. In this chapter, we use the operators listed in Table 6.1.

For the operators expressing a duration over a time interval (for example, $Lasts$), we give definitions which exclude the endpoints of the specified time interval; i.e. the interval is open. Operators including either one or both of the endpoints can be easily derived from the basic ones. For notational convenience, to indicate inclusion or exclusion of the endpoints, we append to the operator's name suitable subscripts, "i" or "e", respectively. A few examples using the operators $Lasts$, $Since$, $Since$, $AlwP$, and $SomP$ follow.

$$Lasts_{ie}(A, d) \quad := \forall d(0 \le d < t \to Dist(F, d))$$
$$Lasted_{ie}(A, t) \quad := \forall d(0 < d \le t \to Dist(F, -d))$$
$$Since_{ii}(A1, A2) \quad := \exists t(t \ge 0 \land Past(A2, t) \land Lasted_{ii}(A1, t))$$
$$Since_{ie}(A1, A2) \quad := \exists t(t > 0 \land Past(A2, t) \land Lasted_{ie}(A1, t))$$
$$Until_{ie}(A1, A2) \quad := \exists t(t > 0 \land Futr(A2, t) \land Lasts_{ie}(A1, t))$$
$$AlwF_i(F) \quad := \forall d(d \ge 0 \to Dist(F, d))$$
$$SomP_i(A) \quad := \exists d(d \ge 0 \land Dist(F, d))$$

TRIO has been given a formal semantics through the interpretation schema in [GMM92]. A deductive system for TRIO is given in [FMM94]. The proofs below, however, should be easily understood without referring to TRIO's formal semantics.

6.4.1 Axiomatization of the Kernel Railway Crossing

To formalize the train movement inside the crossing region, we define several predicates. $Enter\_R$, $Enter\_I$, and $Exit\_I$ are TD predicates (with no argument) representing the events of a train entering region R, entering region I, or exiting region I (and hence R), respectively. Predicates In_R and In_I represent the state of a train being in region R (i.e., it has entered the region but it did not exit yet) or in region I, respectively. Since, in the KRC, we consider only a single train, each of the events $Enter\_R$, $Enter\_I$, and $Exit\_I$ occurs at most once.

(k1) $Enter\_R \to AlwP(\neg Enter\_R) \land AlwF(\neg Enter\_R)$

(k2) $Enter\_I \to AlwP(\neg Enter\_I) \land AlwF(\neg Enter\_I)$

(k3) $Exit\_I \to AlwP(\neg Exit\_I) \land AlwF(\neg Exit\_I)$

The following axioms model the train movement in regions R and I.
It takes the train a time between d_m and d_M to travel from region R to region I.

(k4) $Enter\_R \to \exists l(d_m \le t \le d_M \land Futr(Enter\_I, t))$

It takes the train a time between h_m and h_M to exit region I once it has entered I.

(k5) $Enter\_I \to \exists t(h_m \le t \le h_M \land Futr(Exit\_I, t))$

Also, an exit event occurs only after the corresponding enter event.

(k6) $Enter\_I \to \exists t(d_m \le t \le d_M \land Past(EnterR, t))$

(k7) $Exit\_I \to \exists t(h_m \le t \le h_M \land Past(Enter\_I, t))$

The above time bounds on train movement satisfy the following obvious relation.

(k8) $d_M \ge d_m > 0 \land h_M \ge h_m > 0$

A train is inside region R or I if it did not exit that region since it entered it.

(k9) $In\_R \leftrightarrow Since_{ii}(\neg Enter\_I, Enter R)$

(k10) $In\_I \leftrightarrow Since_{ii}(\neg Exit\_I, Enter\_I)$

To complete the specification, we state the axioms describing the gate movements. Up and down commands to the gate are formalized by the mutually exclusive predicates, $go(up)$ and $go(down)$, while the state of the gate is modeled by four mutually exclusive predicates, $open$, $closed$, $mvUp$, and $mvDown$, with the obvious meaning.

We consider here a gate that, after a $go(down)$ or $go(up)$ command (the two commands are mutually exclusive), reaches the final position in γ time units (we assume $\gamma < d_m$ and an equal velocity of the gate motion in the two directions). When the gate is moving, any command is ignored: the gate will continue its movement until the final position is reached. Only then is the gate ready to accept a new command. Notice that the above model of the gate is not completely consistent with the timed Petri net model provided in Figure 6.3. We adopt this model for the sake of simplicity, since it is sufficient to ensure the desired safety and utility properties.

The gate movements, which depend on the state and the issued command, are modeled by the axioms given below.

Axioms M1 & M2: when the gate in the *closed* state receives a $go(up)$ command, it will move upwards for γ time units and will remain in the open position until the next command $go(down)$ is issued. A symmetrical axiom holds for the opposite position and direction of movement.

(M1) $UpToNow(closed) \land go(up) \rightarrow$

$$Lasts_{ie}(mvUp, \gamma) \land Futr(Until_{ie}(open, go(down)), \gamma).$$

(M2) $UpToNow(open) \land go(down) \rightarrow Lasts_{ie}(mvDown, \gamma) \land$

$$Lasts_{ie}(mvDown, \gamma) \land Futr(Until_{ie}(closed, go(up)), \gamma).$$

Axiom M3: initially, i.e., before any operation takes place, the gate is open (we assume here that the gate is installed before any train arrives).

(M3) $AlwP_i(\neg go(down)) \rightarrow open$

Operations on the gate are specified by the following intuitive axioms.

(c1) $go(down) \leftrightarrow Past(Enter R, d_m - \gamma)$

(c2) $go(up) \leftrightarrow Exit\_I$

The constant $d_m - \gamma$ in axiom (c1) takes into account the time γ necessary to reach the closed position once the gate movement has started and conservatively considers the minimum time d_m necessary for any train to reach region I once it has entered region R. On the other hand, the gate is immediately raised upon a train's exit from region I.

These commands are carefully defined to guarantee safety and utility, i.e., to ensure that the gate will be closed at any time when a train is inside region I, but at the same time they guarantee that the gate is not closed for too long. These properties are formalized in TRIO as follows. (The two constants γ and $d_M - d_m + \gamma$ in the Utility property take care of the delay in the gate rising upon train exit from I and from the advance in gate lowering upon train entrance to R.)

Safety: $In\_I \rightarrow closed$

Utility: $Lasted_{ii}(\neg In\_I, \gamma) \wedge Lasts_{ii}(\neg In\_I, d_M - d_m + \gamma) \rightarrow open$

In a completely formalized setting, these properties would be derived, possibly with the aid of some (semi)automatic tool, as theorems in a deductive system which includes the axioms given above. For the sake of brevity, we only provide an outline of a proof for the Safety property, the interested reader can refer to [MMP95] for complete proofs and a more complete discussion.

Proof of Safety.
   The structure of the proof simply mirrors the chain of cause-effect relations among the events occurring as the train approaches the crossing. If the train is currently in region I, then it must have entered region R no less than d_m time units ago. But $d_m - \gamma$ time units after the train entered region R (therefore no less than γ time units ago), a $go(down)$ command was issued to the gate; after that it took the gate γ time units to reach the closed state, and no $go(down)$ command was issued since then, because the train is still in region I; therefore the gate is currently in the *closed* state.
   More formally, In_I is equivalent, by (k10), to $Since_{ii}(\neg Exit\_I, Enter\_I)$ which, by the definition of the $Since_{ii}$ operator, implies that $Past(Enter\_I, t)$ for some $t \geq 0$. This in turn by (k6) ensures that $Past(EnterR, t')$ for some $t' \geq d_m$ and then, by (c1), that $Past(go(down), t'')$ for some $t'' \geq \gamma$, i.e, the gate was lowered at least γ time units ago. Now by (k2), (c1), and (M3) this implies $Past(UpToNow(open), t'')$, so that at a time t'' before now the premise of (M2) is satisfied, hence its conclusion holds at that time, i.e.,

($\bullet$) $Past(Until_{ie}(closed, go(up)), t'' - \gamma)$, with $t'' - \gamma \geq 0$.

But (k10) together with (c2) ensures that the first (and only) $go(up)$ command occurs strictly after now, so that *closed* holds now.   **QED**

6.4.2   Description of the Generalized Railway Crossing

We now further develop the case study and pursue more generality by adopting the following, less restrictive assumptions.

1. Any finite number of trains can enter or leave the same region at the same time instant.
2. In every finite time interval, only a finite number of trains can enter R.
3. The number of tracks is unbounded. (This is consistent with assumption 1.)
4. A more sophisticated kind of gate, whose movement in the up direction can be interrupted by an opposite $go(down)$ command, is used.

We base our formalization of the generalized case on the following predicates:

$RI(k)$: the kth train is entering R;

$II(k)$: the kth train is entering I;

$IO(k)$: the kth train is leaving I (and, therefore, R)

All of the above predicates denote unique events; i.e., they can be true at most in a single instant within the time axis. Formally, any predicate E that is classified as a unique event must satisfy the following axiom:

(E1) $\forall k(E(k) \rightarrow (AlwP(\neg E(k)) \wedge AlwF(\neg E(k))))$

Furthermore, it must satisfy a (weak) monotonicity of parameter k with respect to time, i.e.:

(E2) $\forall k(E(k) \wedge k > 1 \rightarrow SomPi(E(k-1)))$

By convention

(E3) $Alw(\neg E(0))$

Although TRIO has no formal definition of input and output, $RI(k)$ and $IO(k)$ will be treated as input events since these are the only events that are signaled by external sensors. Thus, our formalization will assume the occurrence of input events and will specify how the system reacts to such stimuli. In such a formalization, the occurrence of other events will be deduced from the occurrence of the input ones.

Notice that argument k in predicates $RI(k)$, $II(k)$, and $IO(k)$ does not identify a given train but simply acts as a counter. For instance, if at some point in time $RI(k)$ holds and some time later the event $II(k)$ takes place, these two events do not necessarily describe the entering of regions R and I by the same train: since trains can pass each other, the kth train entering R need not be the same train as the kth train entering I.

This approach to the formalization of the train movements was preferred to another, perhaps more intuitive one, where each train would be uniquely identified by, say, a natural number, and a more external view of the system would be adopted where the trip of each single train would be described separately. The proposed axiomatization is closer to a view of the crossing "from inside" its control system: a sensor cannot identify the train that is crossing a given boundary, and the system can therefore only count the number of event occurrences. The adoption of the internal view of the system is the result of a process that started with the external view and ended with the present formalization because of reasons of simplicity in the description and effectiveness in reasoning about the system behavior. As will become apparent below, to control the crossing, precise knowledge of which trains are, say, inside region I at a given time is unnecessary: only their number is relevant, and such a number can be computed as the difference among counters of events II and IO, thus abstracting away from train identity.

6.4.3   Axioms and first properties of the railway system

First, we introduce the following TD variables to count the occurrences of the corresponding events: CRI, CII, and CIO.

The following axioms state that such variables are counters. A counter is a time-dependent variable, which increases for every occurrence of a given event, starting with an initial value zero.

(A1) $Counter(C, E) := Alw(\forall k(k \geq 1$ $((C = k) \leftrightarrow$

$\qquad (SomP_i(E(k)) \wedge \neg SomP_i(E(k+1)))))) \wedge Som(C = 0 \wedge AlwP(C = 0))$

(A2) $Counter(CRI, RI) \wedge Counter(CII, II) \wedge Counter(CIO, IO)$

The following property is an obvious consequence of (A1):

(P1) If C is a counter, $Alw(C \leq futr(C, t))$ (monotonicity of counters)

As in the KRC, the real constants, $d_M, d_m, h_M, and h_m$, represent time bounds among events RI, II, and IO. The geometry of the region R and the behavior of the trains are described by the following axioms.

Axiom B1: if the kth train enters region R at the current instant, then the kth train (not necessarily the same) will enter I at a time in the future between d_m and d_M time units from now.

(B1) $\forall k(RI(k) \rightarrow \exists t \, (d_m \leq t \leq d_M \wedge Futr(II(k), t)))$

Axiom B2: if the kth train enters region I at the current instant, then the kth train has entered R at a time in the past between d_m and d_M time units from now. Similar axioms B3 and B4 describe relations among enter and exit times of region I.

(B2) $\forall k(II(k)$ $\exists t \, (d_m \leq t \leq d_M \wedge Past(RI(k), t)))$

(B3) $\forall k(II(k) \rightarrow \exists t \, (h_m \leq t \leq h_M \wedge Futr(IO(k), t)))$

(B4) $\forall k(IO(k) \rightarrow \exists t \, (h_m \leq t \leq h_M \wedge Past(II(k), t)))$

It is easy to prove the following properties (which are used as lemmas in the proof of the main properties):

(L1) $Alw(CRI \geq CII \geq CIO)$

Proof: We prove only that $CRI \geq CII$, since the other cases can be dealt with analogously. If $CRI < CII$ then by (A1) this implies that for some i an event of type $II(i)$ occurred in the past without any corresponding event $RI(i)$ taking place before then. This contradicts axiom (B2).   **QED**

(L2) $Alw(past(CRI, d_M) \leq CII \leq past(CRI, d_m))$

The proof of (L2) is based on an argument similar to that used for (L1): for instance, if $CII < past(CRI, d_M)$, then in the past, at a distance $d \geq d_M$, an event $RI(k)$ occurred. Since then no corresponding event $II(k)$ occurred, we have a contradiction of (B1). **QED**

The proofs of the following properties L3 and L4 are straightforward or analogous to the proof of L2.

(L3) $Alw(past(CII, h_M) \leq CIO \leq past(CII, h_m))$

(L4) $Alw(past(CRI, d_M + h_M) \leq CIO \leq past(CRI, d_m + h_m))$

(L5) $(CII = CIO) \rightarrow (CII = past(CII, h_m))$

Proof: By (L3) $CIO \leq past(CII, h_m)$ and by monotonicity $CII \geq past(CII, h_m)$.

QED

Recalling that now the gate can be interrupted in its upward movement, we model its motion through the following axioms. (The predicates $go(up)$, $go(down)$, $open$, $closed$, $mvUp$, and $mvDown$, have the same meanings as before.)

Axiom M1: when the gate in the closed state receives a $go(up)$ command, it will move upwards for γ time units or until a $go(down)$ is issued. In the axiom, the Until subformula requires that the gate be in the $mvUp$ state from the present time until the time when its second argument becomes true, which can occur either because an opposite command $go(down)$ is issued or because γ time units have passed.

(M1) $UpToNow(closed) \wedge go(up) \rightarrow Until_{ie}(mvUp, go(down) \vee Past(go(up), \gamma))$

Axiom M2: movement in the down direction will not be interrupted, so that when the gate in the open state receives a $go(down)$ command, it will move downwards for γ time units and then stay closed until a $go(up)$ command is issued.

(M2) $UpToNow(open) \wedge go(down) \rightarrow Lasts_{ie}(mvDown, \gamma) \wedge Futr(Until_{ie}(closed, go(up)), \gamma)$

Axiom M3: when the gate moving up receives a $go(down)$ command, it inverts its motion, at the same speed reaches again the closed position, and stays there until the next $go(up)$.

(M3) $UpToNow(mvUp) \wedge go(down) \wedge LastTime(go(up), t) \rightarrow$

$$Lasts_{ie}(mvDown, t) \wedge Futr(Until_{ie}(closed, go(up)), t)$$

Axiom M4: after moving up for γ time units, if there is no $go(down)$ command, the gate stays open until the next $go(down)$ command.

(M4) $Lasted_{ie}(mvUp, \gamma) \wedge \neg go(down) \rightarrow Until_{ie}(open, go(down))$

Axiom M5: initially, i.e., before any operation takes place, the gate is open (we assume here that the gate is installed before any train arrives).

(M5) $AlwP_i(\neg go(down)) \rightarrow open$

The following Lemma can be immediately derived from axioms (M1-M4):

(L6) $go(down) \wedge Lasts_{ii}(\neg go(up), t) \wedge t \geq \gamma \rightarrow Futr(Lasts_{ii}(closed, t - \gamma), \gamma)$.

The method adopted by the control system to manage the crossing can be informally described as follows: the system computes the number of trains that potentially are in I and whenever this number becomes greater than 0 it issues a $go(down)$ command, while whenever it becomes 0 it issues a $go(up)$ command. Formally, we introduce $CTPI :=$ $past(CRI, d_m) - CIO$: $CTPI$ is the maximum number of trains that can possibly be in region I given the inputs RI and IO from the sensors that occurred up to the present time: the length of time d_m in the past operator is derived from the pessimistic assumption of maximum speed of trains moving from region R to region I. Let $CTPI_\gamma := past(CRI, d_m - \gamma) - CIO$: $CTPI_\gamma$ takes into account a forward shift γ in time necessary to issue the command $go(down)$ to lower the gate due to the nonzero duration of the gate movement.

The commands issued to the gate are then defined by the following axioms:

(C1) $go(down) \leftrightarrow Becomes(CTPI_\gamma > 0)$

(C2) $go(up) \leftrightarrow Becomes(CTPI = 0)$

6.4.4 Safety of the generalized railway system

Following the same argument used in the KRC example, the properties of safety and utility can also be stated and proved for the GRC. For the sake of simplicity, we only sketch the safety property: complete statements and proofs of both safety and utility properties are reported in [MMP95]. Informally, the proof of the safety property is based on the following reasoning: assuming that $CTPI$ represents a pessimistic estimation of the number of trains in the region I (i.e., at any time the number of trains that are in region I is not greater than $CTPI$), we first state and prove that whenever $CTPI > 0$, the gate is closed. The next step in the proof shows that any increase of $CTPI$ from 0 to a value greater than 0 is always anticipated γ time units, by an equal change of $CTPI_\gamma$, so that the gate is given, due to axiom (C1), sufficient time to reach the closed position.

First, we state and prove the following property, called semisafety.

Semisafety: $CTPI > 0 \rightarrow closed$

The proof of semisafety is based on the following additional lemma.

(L7) $Becomes(CTPI_\gamma > 0) \leftrightarrow Futr(Becomes(CTPI > 0), \gamma)$

Proof of L7. We prove only $Becomes(CTPI_\gamma > 0) \rightarrow Futr(Becomes(CTPI > 0), \gamma)$ the other implication being proved in a similar way.

$Becomes(CTPI_\gamma > 0) \rightarrow$

(i) $\exists h \, (Past(RI(h), d_m - \gamma) \wedge \forall j(j < h \rightarrow SomP_i(IO(j))))$

(at time $d_m - \gamma$ the hth train entered R and all preceding trains already exited I by the current time)

Thus

(ii) $Past(Lasts_{ie}((\neg \exists k(IO(k), d_m + h_m), d_m - \gamma)$

(i.e., since $d_m - \gamma$ time units ago no train will exit I for at least $d_m + h_m$) which implies

(iii) $Lasts_{iii}(\neg \exists kIO(k), \gamma)$

(i.e., no train will exit I from now for at least γ time units).

On the other hand (i) implies

(iiii) $\exists h Futr(Past(RI(h), d_m), \gamma)$

(iiii) and (iii) together imply $Futr(Becomes(Past(CRI, d_m) > CIO), \gamma)$, i.e., the second part of the thesis.   **QED**

An immediate corollary of L7 is the following additional lemma (it can be derived from (iii) in the above proof of L7):

(L8) $Becomes(CTPI_\gamma > 0) \rightarrow$

$$Lasts_{ie}(CTPI = 0, \gamma) \wedge Lasts_{ii}(\neg Becomes(CTPI = 0), \gamma).$$

We can now prove the semisafety property.

Proof of semisafety: If $CTPI > 0$ holds now, then there is a non-empty interval (including at least the present time) such that $CTPI > 0$ became true at the beginning of this interval, and it lasted until now. This is formalized as follows.

$CTPI > 0 \rightarrow \exists t(Past(Becomes(CTPI > 0), t) \wedge (Lasted_{ii}((CTPI > 0), t))$

Thus, by (L7),

(i) $Past(Past(Becomes(CTPI_\gamma > 0), \gamma), t)$

By (L8) we have

(ii) $Past(Lasts_{ii}(\neg Becomes(CTPI = 0), \gamma), t + \gamma)$

(ii) and $Lasted_{ii}(CTPI > 0, t)$ imply $Lasted_{ii}(\neg Becomes(CTPI = 0), t + \gamma)$

Now $Past(Becomes(CTPI_\gamma > 0), t + \gamma)$ implies $Past(go(down), t + \gamma)$ by (C1) and $Lasted_{ii}(Becomes(CTPI = 0), t + \gamma)$ implies $Lasted_{ii}(\neg go(up)), t + \gamma)$ by (C2). Finally, the implication follows by (L6).   **QED**

We can now prove that the railway system is safe, that is, if there are trains in I (i.e., $CII - CIO > 0$), then the gate is closed.

Safety: $(CII > CIO) \rightarrow closed$

Proof: $CTPI = past(CRI, d_m) - CIO \geq$ (by L2) $CII - CIO > 0$. Thus, $CTPI > 0$, and the safety statement holds by Semisafety.   **QED**

6.4.5 Specifying in the large with TRIO+

TRIO supports the production of formal, unambiguous specifications. It lacks, however, structuring mechanisms, and therefore the management of large specifications which are typical of real-life systems may become a difficult task. Also, it does not support incremental development, since there is no mechanism to facilitate the construction of complex formulas through several versions at increasing levels of precision and formality. In some sense, TRIO is similar to a Pascal-like toy programming language, which is suitable for describing algorithms but not for building large programs. In other words, TRIO is a *specification language in the small*, whereas we need a *specification language in the large*.

To support specification in the large, a higher level language, TRIO+, has been defined as an extension of the basic language TRIO [MP94]. TRIO+ exploits the concepts and constructs of the object-oriented (OO) methodology. TRIO+ also supports the writing of specifications in a natural way through a simple graphical notation. It is widely acknowledged that an appropriate use of graphical interfaces enhances user friendliness and readability.

The main features of TRIO+ are illustrated below using the GRC example: it will be shown how the specification can be structured into modules connected via abstract interfaces, each module corresponding to one of the "objects" that can be naturally identified in the system we are specifying.

A TRIO+ specification is built by defining suitable *classes*. A class is a set of axioms describing a system, constructed in a modular, independent way. Classes may be *simple* or *structured* and may be organized into *inheritance* hierarchies.

A simple class is a group of TRIO axioms, preceded by the declaration of all occurring predicates, variables, and functions. As an example of a simple class, consider the class $CrossingGate$ shown in Figure 6.9, which includes all the axioms regarding the gate and the declarations of the related predicates, variables, and constants.

A class may be graphically represented as a box, with its name written at the left top; the names of the items are written on lines internal to the box; if an item is visible externally,

```
class CrossingGate;              -- class header
   visible γ, go, state;         -- class interface: exported items can be referenced outside the class
   temporal domain real;              -- the temporal domain to be considered in the specification
   TD items                             -- declaration of time dependent predicates, variables and functions
         predicates   go({up, down});        -- predicate on a domain defined by enumeration
         vars         state: {open, closed, mvUp, MvDown};  -- variable of a type defined by enumeration
   TI items                             -- declaration of time independent predicates, functions, and constants
         consts       γ: real;       -- a real constant
   axioms                      -- class axioms, implicitly preceded by an Alw operator, prefixed by a name for reference
         vars t: real;             -- the time independent variables, implicitly universally quantified
```

-- comments in the form of natural language sentences are highly recommended

positiveγ: $\gamma > 0$

-- when the gate moving up receives a go(down) command it inverts its motion,

-- at the same speed reaches again the closed position and stays there until the next go(up)

M3: $\text{UpToNow(mvUp)} \wedge \text{go(down)} \wedge \text{LastTime(go(up),t)} \rightarrow$

$$\text{Lasts}_{ie}(\text{mvDown,t}) \wedge \text{Futr}(\text{Until}_{ie}(\text{closed,go(up))),t})$$

... axioms M1, M2, M4, and M5 are reported similarly ...

end CrossingGate.

Figure 6.9   Declaration of the class CrossingGate

then the corresponding line continues outside the box. Class *CrossingGate* is represented graphically in Figure 6.10

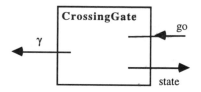

Figure 6.10   Graphic representation of the class CrossingGate

Classes containing components, called *modules*, of other classes are called *structured classes*. Structured classes permit the construction of TRIO+ modular specifications, which are specially designed to describe systems in which *parts* can be easily recognized. In our example, the structured class *Crossing*, whose graphical representation is in Figure 6.11, models the railway crossing: it includes modules for the gate, the sensors at the R and I boundaries, and the control system.

Each of these components corresponds to a module declared in a suitable *modules* clause by indicating its class (the classes *Sensor* for modules *sensorRI* and *sensorIO* and *Control* for module *control* would be declared separately). Items of the structured class, such as II, d_m, d_M, h_m, and h_M in this example, and visible items of the local modules, denoted by using a dot notation, may appear in axioms of the enclosing class.

The oriented arcs joining visible items of the enclosed modules and local items are called *connections*. They specify identity between pairs of items in the scope of the current class and may often be interpreted as information flows between components. In the example, the semantics of the connection $(gate.state, control.gateState)$ is: $Alw(gate.state = control.gateState)$. This asserts that the value of the position of the gate is instantly known to the controller.

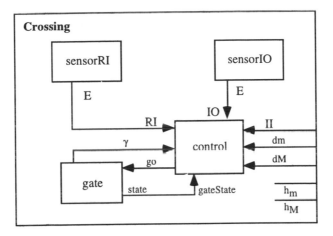

Figure 6.11 Graphical representation of the structured class *Crossing*

TRIO+ supports another object-oriented notion, namely, the inheritance construct, whereby a subclass receives attributes from its superclasses. In TRIO+, a specifier is allowed to add new elements in a super class and, to a certain extent, to modify the inherited one; in particular, one can completely redefine axioms, which implies altering the semantics of the superclass. This flexibility is useful because modeling and requirements specification are often exploratory activities.

For instance, let us assume that class *Sensor*, as used in the above example, contains an axiom called *nonZeno* specifying that at any time only a finite (though *apriori* unbounded) number of trains will cross any region boundary. We could then define a class *sensorWithNTracks* modeling a kind of sensor to be used in a crossing, where the number of tracks is assumed to be equal to a given constant *nTracks*. The class *sensorWithNTracks* would inherit from class *Sensor*. It would also add the constant item *nTracks* modeling the number of distinct tracks in the crossing and would redefine axiom *nonZeno* by stating that no more than *nTracks* simultaneous events of type E can occur at any time, thus imposing this number as a limit on the number of trains that can simultaneously cross any region boundary.

6.4.6 The TRIO environment: experiences in its use

In the last few years, the research on the TRIO and TRIO+ languages was performed in conjunction with the construction of a tool environment for the development of real-time systems and with the application of the languages and tools to industrial projects of increasing complexity. The TRIO environment presently includes the following tools:

- an interactive, graphical editor for TRIO and TRIO+. The editor supports the incremental writing of TRIO-based specifications by checking them for syntactic incompleteness and inconsistency but allowing continued editing activity after appropriate warning messages have been displayed. It also allows for semiformality in the sense that informal comments can replace or be integrated with pure TRIO formulas. In principle, it should support the editing of specifications both in textual and in graphical notations in a completely interchangeable manner. The present prototype, however, supports automatic translation of graphical specifications into textual specifications but provides only limited help in the opposite direction. The present prototype runs on VAX-VMS and UNIX workstations.

- a test case editor. This tool helps to produce testing documentation (test cases, testing results, comments of any type, etc.) associated with a TRIO+ specification. It is already integrated with the specification editor.
- a translator from TRIO+ to TRIO.
- A test case generator [MMM95]. This tool supports the (semi)automatic, user-driven generation of functional test cases associated with a given TRIO specification against which the designer can check implementation correctness. The core of the tool generates models of the axioms specifying the system, using a specialized interpreter of the TRIO language. Such models are used as test cases by separating input and output events. The problem of testing nondeterministic systems is solved by means of an a posteriori verification performed by a specialized and efficient interpreter of the language called the *history checker* [FM94b].

The language and its related techniques and tools have been applied to several real-world case studies, some performed in cooperation with industrial partners. These include:

- a pondage power station;
- a "new generation" digital energy and power meter;
- a system to monitor a voltage signal by means of digital sampling; and
- a hardware device, called a "synchronizer", which performs synchronization and check operations on byte sequences. It has an asynchronous input and a synchronous output and is widely used in communication subsystems.

In each of the above case studies, our tools revealed subtle errors that were not discovered by human inspection and by using more traditional techniques.

TRIO was also adopted as the principal formalism for specification, validation, and verification of real-time systems in a project aimed at technology transfer supported by the European Union in the ESSI framework. In this project, an industrial application was developed to balance the load of the generators in a pondage power plant. This system, considered of average complexity by the standards of ENEL, the Italian electric energy board, was specified in TRIO+ using tools of the environment for validating the specification. Starting from such a specification, the design and implementation were performed, in parallel with the production of test plans, for the acceptance of the final product. This project, which took place from 1994 through the beginning of 1995, is currently reaching a satisfactory conclusion (the experience is reported in [BCC+95]) and confirms the usefulness of TRIO, especially for end-users of large automated systems who specify and order large series of equipment, and who must apply rigid formal procedures for performance evaluation, contract issuing, end-product verification, and acceptance.

We are currently developing another language in the TRIO family. This language will include predefined application-related concepts, such as properties ensured by other axioms of the specification, and notions of state, event, and process. These new features should help the specifier write complete, consistent specifications.

6.5   TOWARDS EXPLOITING THE DUAL-LANGUAGE APPROACH

In this section, we give an initial description of how we would apply the dual-language approach using Petri nets as an operational formalism and TRIO as a descriptive formalism. This requires:

- stating a formal correspondence between the syntax and semantics of the two formalisms. This is often called an *axiomatization* of the operational formalism.
- using the given axiomatization to prove that a system that is modeled by the operational formalism does indeed exhibit the properties in the descriptive formalism.

Accordingly, we provide an axiom system for Petri nets in terms of TRIO formulas. For the sake of simplicity, we make the following simplifying assumptions:

- We consider only 1-bounded Petri nets, where time is formalized according to the Merlin and Farber approach (i.e., minimum and maximum firing times are associated with each transition);
- We consider only nets such that the pre-set and the post-set of every place have at most one element each. These nets are often called *marked graphs*
- We consider only nets with no loops of transitions whose minimum firing times are all 0. In practice, this assumption is no restriction at all since it simply prevents the possibility of unbounded firing sequences occurring in zero time (i.e., the non-Zeno hypothesis).

The simplifications above avoid ambiguities when referring to a token that is in a given place (if there are several tokens the times at which they have been produced are not obvious). The result is a fairly simple axiom system.

Then, we will apply the axiomatization to prove the safety property of the KRC formulation of figure 6.4, which satisfies the above restrictions. The proof of the utility property of the KRC is similar.

It is not difficult, however, to verify that the presented method does indeed scale up to more general cases of Petri nets and sample systems. The interested reader is referred to [FMM94] for more details and examples.

6.5.1   (Restricted) Petri Net Axiomatization

Our approach associates suitable TRIO axioms with given Petri net fragments in such a way that the semantics of a whole net can be derived as a set of theorems that are consequences of the basic axioms.

In the same way, the classical axiomatization of Pascal-like languages associates the backwards substitution axiom with the assignment statement, the **if-then-else** rule and the invariant proof rule with the conditional and **while** statements, respectively, in such a way that a program specification consisting of a pair of pre- and post-conditions can be derived through a suitable proof based on the above axiom and inference rules.

Given the above simplification, we need only consider Petri net fragments of the two types depicted in Figures 6.12.(a) and 6.12.(b): in fact, the KRC formalization given in Figure 6.4 can be obtained by composing fragments of the above types (apart from the "initial" place *Arrived* which has an impact only for its initial marking).

The TRIO axioms use two basic predicates: $fire$ and $marked$. $fire(r)$ holds iff transition r fires at the current instant; $marked(P)$ holds iff place P is marked at the current instant.

A first axiom states that the predicate $fire$ is instantaneous:

(Ist) $fire(r) \rightarrow UpToNow(\neg fire(r))$

Another axiom relates the property of a marked place to the firing of its input and output

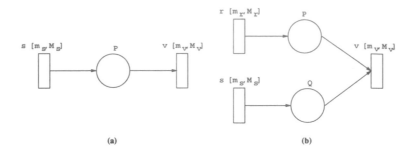

(a)   (b)

Figure 6.12

transitions: if s is the (unique) input transition of a place P and v is its (unique) output transition, then

(Mar) $marked(P) \leftrightarrow (fire(s) \vee Since_{ie}(\neg fire(v), fire(s)))$,
That is, place P is marked iff at the present time or at some time in the past its input transition

fired and since then its output transition did not fire yet.

Notice that $marked$ is a predicate that can hold only in closed intervals.[5]

Furthermore, the following axioms formalize the firing relations for the transitions belonging to the fragments of Figures 6.12.(a) and 6.12.(b):

(LB.(a)) $fire(v) \rightarrow Lasted_{ii}(marked(P), m_v)$

(UB.(a)) $Lasted_{ii}(marked(P), M_v) \rightarrow fire(v)$

(LB.(b)) $fire(v) \rightarrow Lasted_{ii}(marked(P) \wedge marked(Q), m_v)$

(UB.(b)) $Lasted_{ii}(marked(P) \wedge marked(Q), M_v) \rightarrow fire(v)$

LB.(a) formalizes the lower bound for the firing of transition v in the fragment (a): v can fire (at the current instant) only if P was marked for at least m_v instants. UB.(a) states that if P was marked for the last M_v instants, then v must fire at the current instant. Similar explanations hold for the remaining axioms.

The following lemmas are straightforward consequences of the axioms. They illustrate how the above axioms formalize the behavior of timed Petri nets and will be useful in the proof of the properties of the GRC system.

Lemma 1: With reference to Figure 6.12.(a):

---

[5] This fact could cause some trouble. In fact, when transition v connecting place P and place W fires, both places are marked (in our example both $Closed$ and $Opening$ could be marked simultaneously, though for just one instant). This slightly surprising convention has been adopted to deal adequately with zero-time firings, i.e., cases when transition v fires immediately after transition s, and, therefore, the place in between is marked for a single instant. From an intuitive point of view, we could interpret such a phenomenon as a sequence of "almost simultaneously" events and markings; from a mathematical point of view, our axioms can still be applied safely thanks to the simplifying assumptions: since the net is 1-bounded and there are no loops of 0-time transitions, it cannot happen that the same transition fires twice, i.e., the same place is marked twice in the same instant. For a more thorough and general treatment of this issue the reader is referred to [FMM94]

(A) $marked(P) \rightarrow \exists d \ Past(fire(s), d) \wedge d \leq M_v$

(B) $fire(v) \rightarrow \exists d \ Past(fire(s), d) \wedge m_v \leq d \leq M_v$

(C) $fire(s) \rightarrow \exists d \ Futr(fire(v), d) \wedge m_v \leq d \leq M_v$

Lemma 2: With reference to Figure 6.12.(b):

(A) $fire(s) \wedge marked(P) \rightarrow \exists d \ Futr(fire(v), d) \wedge m_v \leq d \leq M_v$

That is, if s fires at the current time and P is marked, then v will fire no earlier than m_v and no later than M_v. A symmetric lemma holds with respect to place Q and transition r.

(B) $fire(v) \rightarrow SomP_i(fire(s)) \wedge SomP_i(fire(r))$

6.5.2 Safety proof of KRC

Let us now formalize the safety property as a TRIO formula. With reference to the Petri net shown in Figure 6.4, we can express the property in the following intuitive way:

(saf) $SomP(marked(Open)) \wedge marked(InI) \rightarrow marked(Closed)$

i.e., if initially the train is outside of R and the gate is open, then, whenever the train is in region I, the gate is closed.

Our job is therefore to prove that (saf) is a theorem in the above axiom system.

The proof of (saf) is derived using the previous lemmas and the following one which states, without proof, an obvious property of the net shown in Figure 6.4.

Lemma 3: Every transition of the net of Figure 6.4 can fire at most once.

We can now prove the safety theorem:

Assume that at the current instant $marked(In\_I)$ holds. Then,

$marked(In\_I) \rightarrow$ (by Lemma 1A)

$\exists t \ Past(fire(Enter\_I), t) \wedge t \leq h_M \rightarrow$ (by Lemma 1B)

$\exists t \ Past(fire(Enter\_I) \wedge \exists p \ Past(fire(Enter\_R), p), t) \wedge d_m \leq p \leq d_M \wedge t \leq h_M \rightarrow$

(by properties of past operator)
$\exists q \ Past(fire(Enter\_R), q) \wedge d_m \leq q \leq h_M + d_M.$

Since, by Lemma 2B, Go_Down could not fire before a firing of $Enter\_R$, then when $Enter\_R$ fired q instants in the past, the place Open was marked. By Lemma 2A, this implies:

$Past(fire(Go\_Down), q - (d_m - \gamma))$, that is, by Lemma 1C:

(*) $Past(fire(Stop\_Down), q - d_m)$.

Notice that $q - d_m \geq 0$, that is $Stop\_Down$ fired in the past.

By definition, $marked(In\_I) \leftrightarrow (fire(Enter\_I) \vee Since_{ie}(\neg fire(Exit\_I), fire(Enter\_I))$ Since $Past(fire(Enter\_I), t)$, with $t \leq h_M$, then $SomF_i(fire(Exit\_I))$, and by Lemma 3 $AlwP(\neg fire(Exit\_I))$. That is, by Lemma 1B:

(**) $AlwP(\neg fire(Go\_Up))$

By (*) and (**) it follows that, in case $q - d_m = 0$, $fire(Stop\_Down)$ holds, in case $q - d_m > 0$, $Since_{ie}(\neg fire(Go\_Up), fire(Stop\_Down))$ holds, that is $marked(Closed)$ holds.   **QED**

Notice the similarity, from a mathematical point of view, between the above proof and the corresponding proof based exclusively on the TRIO language. The dual language proof, however, closely parallels the informal analysis that one could carry out on the basis of a simple inspection of Figure 6.4. In our opinion, this is a major argument in favor of the dual language approach: it combines the advantages of an intuitive analysis, typical of operational models, with the formal rigor of mathematical deduction.

6.6   CONCLUDING REMARKS

We have presented the main features of our two different and complementary approaches to the development of RT systems: Cabernet, based on Petri nets, and TRIO, based on mathematical logic. In the short term our major efforts will be devoted to exploiting the practical use of the two approaches independently. This means:

- Giving priority to training and consulting with industrial users in developing new original results. Our experience, in fact, has shown that much effort should be devoted to technology transfer in all its aspects: the best way to teach new methods on the one hand and to gain inspiration for new developments and improvements on the other hand is to participate in cooperative efforts between academia and industry.
- Devoting considerable effort to improving the supporting tools. (TRIO tools are weak compared to Cabernet, whose tool environment is at a more advanced stage of engineering.) The lack of satisfactory tools in fact, may hamper any practical application of design methods no matter how good the methods are conceptually.
- Focusing attention on a single life cycle phase—specification and verification—rather than trying to cover the whole life cycle.

Concentrating attention and resources on short-term objectives, however, does not mean neglecting longer term goals: for these goals, our efforts will be mainly in the conceptual framework.

Among them, exploiting the dual language approach is certainly one of the most promising directions. As suggested above, we believe that this approach is the most natural way to exploit the complementary features of operational and descriptive approaches.

In the early phases of system analysis and specification, one should describe both the overall structure of the system and its essential properties: in our opinion, the modeling and analysis of the GRC example confirms that system structure is most naturally formalized as an abstract machine (in our case, a Petri net), whereas system properties are most naturally represented using descriptive formulas (in our case, TRIO formulas).

Ideally, the various phases of the entire development process should be integrated so that a smooth transition exists from specification to design and verification. The availability of an operational formalism from the very beginning will naturally lead to a refinement process in which the implementation is described in terms of an operational programming language.[6] For instance, several refinement methods for a smooth transition from a Petri net system description to a complete implementation are already available [FGP93, FM94a].

Finally, we have already noticed that a formal analysis based on the dual language approach is probably closer to an informal analysis based on intuition than pure mathematical deduction. We do acknowledge, however, that issues such as "naturalness" and "understandability", though quite relevant for the success of a formalism, are also a matter of personal taste, and we are far from proposing any formalism as the ultimate choice for the practical application of formal methods in the industrial world.

To exploit the dual language approach and to make it useful in practice, the following major steps must be performed:

- Extending the toy axiom system that has been presented here to the general model of HLTPN. Most conceptual difficulties associated with this task have already been solved [FMM94], but some technical details are still to be completed.
- Building new tools supporting the construction of fully formal correctness proofs. Such tools should exploit both deductive and model checking approaches and should be integrated with existing tools.
- Training users in the application of the approach. This is the most challenging problem and the main reason why we have given lower priority to this objective. We have found, in fact, that proficiency in the construction of formal proofs can be obtained only after specifiers are capable of expressing the system structure and its properties in a formal notation.

In summary, we believe that putting formal methods to work in the industrial world will have a greater chance of succeeding if a realistic, step-by-step path towards such a goal is carefully designed and pursued.

It is widely acknowledged that the most critical phases of the software life cycle are the early ones (see also Chapter 1); furthermore, we are deeply convinced that a major improvement of the present state of the practice can be obtained just by producing high quality specifications without exploiting other potential advantages of formal methods in the early phases. Thus, we decided to concentrate, initially, on single phases of the life cycle and on single formalisms to avoid burdening the user with too much investment both from a cultural and from an economical point of view. Our own experience and some independent findings [FL95] confirm the correctness of this conservative approach.

---

[6] We do not consider here exceptional cases, such as functional or logic programming languages.

ACKNOWLEDGMENTS

A number of people, both in the academic and in the industrial world, took part in the research that is the subject of this chapter. These include: Carlo Ghezzi, Miguel Felder, Sandro Morasca, Elena Ratto, Emanuele Ciapessoni, Ernani Crivelli, Manlio Migliorati, Alfonso Fuggetta, Luciano Baresi, Carlo Bellettini, Paolo Brunasti, Dario Galbiati, Elia Guerriero, Serena Manca, Alessandro Orso, Roberto Palmer, Kim Portman, Roberto Zambetti, Piero Zanchi, and Marco Zoccolante.

We appreciate the suggestions from the anonymous reviewers and Connie Heitmeyer, for improving the presentation.

REFERENCES

[BCC+95] M. Basso, E. Ciapessoni, E. Crivelli, D. Mandrioli, A. Morzenti, E. Ratto, and P. San Pietro. Experimenting a logica-based approach to the specification and design of the control system of a pondage power plant. *ICSE-17 Workshop on industrial application of formal methods*, 1995.

[CP95]   F. Calzolari and M. Pezzè. Property decomposition to speed up analysis. In *Proceedings of the 7th Euromicro Workshop on Real-Time Systems*. IEEE Computer Society Press, 1995.

[FGP93]   M. Felder, C. Ghezzi, and M. Pezzè. Analyzing refinements of state based specifications: the case of TB nets. In *Proceedings of the 1993 International Symposium on Software Testing and Analysis (ISSTA)*, Cambridge (Massachusetts), June 1993.

[FL95]   J. Fitzgerald and P. G. Larsen. Formal specification in the commercial development process. In *Workshop on Formal Methods Application in Software Engineering Practice at the 17th ICSE*, April 1995.

[FM94a]   M. Felder and A. Morzenti. A temporal logic approach to implementation and refinement in timed petri nets. In *Proceedings of ICTL'94: 1st International Conference on Temporal Logic*, pages pp.365–381, Bonn, Germany, July 1994. Lecture Notes in Artificial Intelligence (Subseries of Lecture Notes in Computer Science).

[FM94b]   M. Felder and A. Morzenti. Validating real-time systems by history checking TRIO specifications. *ACM-TOSEM - Transactions on Software Engineering and Methodologies*, 3(4), October 1994.

[FMM94]   M. Felder, D. Mandrioli, and A. Morzenti. Proving properties of real-time systems through logical specification and Petri net models. *IEEE Transactions on Software Engineering*, 20(2):127 – 141, February 1994.

[Gen87]   H. Genrich. Predicate/Transition nets. In W. Reisig and G. Rozemberg, editors, *Advances in Petri Nets*, LNCS 254-255. Springer-Verlag, Berlin-New York, 1987.

[GMM92]   C. Ghezzi, D. Mandrioli, and A. Morzenti. TRIO, a logic language for executable specifications of real-time systems. *Journal of Systems and Software*, 12(2), 1992.

[GMMP91] C. Ghezzi, D. Mandrioli, S. Morasca, and M. Pezzè. A unified high-level Petri net model for time-critical systems. *IEEE Transactions on Software Engineering*, 17(2), February 1991.

[GMP94]   C. Ghezzi, S. Morasca, and M. Pezzè. Timing analysis of time basic nets. *Journal of Systems and Software*, 27(7):97–117, November 1994.

[GP93]   C. Ghezzi and M. Pezzè. Towards extensible graphical formalisms. In *Proceedings of the 7th International Workshop on Software Specification and Design*. IEEE-CS, December 1993.

[Jen87]   K. Jensen. Coloured Petri nets. In W. Reisig and G. Rozemberg, editors, *Advances in Petri Nets*, LNCS 254-255. Springer-Verlag, Berlin-New York, 1987.

[LS87]   N. Leveson and J. Stolzy. Safety analysis using Petri nets. *IEEE Transactions on Software Engineering*, SE-13(3):386–397, March 1987.

[MF76]   P. M. Merlin and D. J. Farber. Recoverability of communication protocols - implications of a theoretical study. *IEEE Transactions on Communications*, September 1976.

[MMM95]   D. Mandrioli, S. Morasca, and A. Morzenti. Generating test cases for real-time systems
            from logic specifications. *ACM-TOCS, Transactions On Computer Systems*, 1995. To
            appear.
[MMP95]   D. Mandrioli, A. Morzenti, and P. San Pietro. Specification of a railway crossing system
            using TRIO. Technical Report 95-011, Politecnico di Milano, 1995.
[MP94]   A. Morzenti and P. San Pietro. Object-oriented logic specifications of time critical systems.
            ACM TOSEM - Transactions on Software Engineering and Methodologies, 3(1), January
            1994.
[Pez94]   M. Pezzè. Cabernet: A customizable environment for the specification and analysis of
            real-time systems. Technical report, Politecnico di Milano, TR 54-94, 1994.
[PGCP94]   M. Pezzè, A. Gargiulo, T. Catarci, and M Di Paola. A formal model for quality assurance
            in coloproctologic surgery. In *Proceedings of Medinfo 94*, 1994.
[Pic94]   Software Through Pictures. *Structure Environment: Using the StP/SE Editors*. Interactive
            Development Environments, February 1994. Release 5.
[Rei82]   W. Reisig. *Petri Nets, An Introduction*. Springer-Verlag, 1982.

7

A Process Algebraic Method for the Specification and Analysis of Real-Time Systems

INSUP LEE, HANENE BEN-ABDALLAH and JIN-YOUNG CHOI
University of Pennsylvania

ABSTRACT

This chapter describes a timed process algebra, called ACSR, which supports time-consuming actions and instantaneous events. Actions model the usage of shared resources and the passage of time, whereas events allow synchronization between processes. To be able to specify real-time systems accurately, ACSR supports static priorities that can be used to arbitrate between actions competing for shared resources and between events that are ready for synchronization. ACSR also offers different notions of equivalence that can be used to verify that two processes behave the same. ACSR is illustrated through the specification and analysis of a scheduler example, as well as three variants of the railroad crossing problem.

7.1 INTRODUCTION

Process algebras, such as CCS [Mil89], CSP [Hoa85] and ACP [Ber85], have been developed to describe and analyze communicating, concurrently executing systems. A process algebra consists of a concise language, a precisely defined semantics and a notion of equivalence. The language is based on a small set of operators and a few syntactic rules for constructing a complex process from simpler components. The semantics describes the possible execution steps a process can take. The notion of equivalence indicates when two processes behave the same, i.e., the two processes have the same execution steps. To verify a system using a

Formal Methods For Real-Time Computing, Edited by Heitmeyer and Mandrioli
© 1996 John Wiley & Sons Ltd

process algebra, one writes a requirements specification as an *abstract* process and a design specification as a *detailed* process. The correctness can then be established by showing that the two processes are equivalent.

There are two aspects that make the process algebraic approach attractive. One is that both design and requirements specifications are described using the same language. A requirements specification is an abstract description of the system that naturally represents required properties. For instance, it need not describe the system architecture, and rather focuses on describing the desired behavior of the system. On the other hand, a design specification is a more detailed description of the system where the components and their synchronizations are explicitly represented. The details in a design specification help to guide the realization of the system.

Another attractive aspect is that a process algebra allows modular verification and hierarchical development of large scale systems if its equivalence relation is also a congruence relation. A design specification can be verified by showing that each of its components is correct with respect to a component in the requirements specification. This reduces the complexity of verifying a large specification to the verification of smaller components. Furthermore, process algebras support the hierarchical design methodology by allowing one to replace any component of a requirements specification by an equivalent component, and retain any correctness proved using the same equivalence. Thus, one can develop a design specification by a series of component-wise design, starting with a requirements specification and gradually replacing its components with detailed components until a desired design specification is realized.

Process algebras without a notion of time have been used widely in specifying and verifying concurrent systems. To expand their usefulness to real-time systems, several real-time process algebras have been developed by adding the notion of time and including a set of timed operators to untimed process algebras [Ace93, Bae91, Hen91, Mol90, Nic94, Ree87, Yi91]. This chapter provides an overview of the Algebra of Communicating Shared Resources (ACSR) [Lee94], which is a discrete real-time process algebra that we have developed. ACSR has several notions, such as resources, static priorities, exceptions, and interrupts, which are essential in modeling real-time systems.

It is well-known that the execution of a real-time system depends not only on delays due to process synchronization, but also on the availability of shared resources. Although real-time process algebras adequately capture delays due to process synchronization, they abstract out resource-specific details by assuming idealized operating environments in two extreme ways. One extreme is to assume the unlimited amount of resources so that the execution of a process is never delayed unless it is waiting for communication. This view of concurrency is known as *maximum parallelism*. The other extreme is to assume that there is only one processor and thus all executions of processes are interleaved. We take a more realistic view in ACSR, and assume that a system has a limited number of shared resources, each of which is capable of executing one action at a time.

When a real-time system has a limited number of shared resources, the timed behavior of the system is affected by their scheduling. There has been much work on schedulability analysis that addresses the problem of determining whether or not a real-time system under a particular scheduling discipline will meet its deadlines [Liu94, Bur94]. The salient aspect of schedulability analysis is its ability to capture contention and scheduling of shared resources. However, the computation models used by the scheduling work ignore the effect of process synchronization except for simple precedence relations or interactions between processes. Although real-time process algebras are particularly effective in modelling synchronization between processes, most of them lack the explicit notion of priority, which makes it difficult to capture the effect of scheduling. ACSR supports the notion of priorities in addition to the notion of resources, and thus, provides a unifying framework that extends the theory of process algebra with notions of real-time scheduling. One can use ACSR to reason about real-time systems that are sensitive to deadlines, communication, synchronization and resource availability.

The ACSR language is carefully designed to facilitate the modular and hierarchical specification of real-time systems. It provides a small set of operators that can be used to build a large specification in incremental and modular fashion. One can first specify the components of a system as processes, and then combine them using operators such as *choice*, *parallel* and *scope* to describe the whole system as a process. The scope operator is unique to ACSR and provides the exception, timeout and interrupt features which are essential for succinct description of large scale systems. ACSR also provides two additional operators– *restriction* for encapsulation and *hiding* for abstraction. The former is to localize a set of events so that they are not visible outside and the latter is to observe only timing properties, ignoring resources used in a system.

ACSR offers several notions of equivalence for comparing two processes. Equivalence compares possible behaviors that processes can exhibit. Different notions of equivalence capture different degrees of detail in behavior. An important use of equivalence is to verify the correctness of a design specification with respect to a requirements specification. There are two general strategies for showing that two processes, an abstract process and a detailed process, are equivalent using ACSR. One verification strategy is syntax-based; the technique is to rewrite these processes, using equational laws, until they become syntactically identical. Another verification strategy is semantics-based; here, we consider all possible executions of both processes and check whether they are equivalent or not.

The rest of the chapter is organized as follows. Section 2 introduces the ACSR language and its computation model. We also introduce a rate-monotonic scheduling example used throughout the paper. Section 3 describes the operational semantics of ACSR using two labelled transition systems: one for unprioritized transitions and another for prioritized transitions. Section 4 defines the notions of equivalence and analysis techniques in ACSR. The rate-monotonic scheduling example is revisited in this section to illustrate the use of the analysis techniques in proving that a specification is correct. Section 5 illustrates the ACSR specification and analysis method through three variants of the railroad crossing system [Hci93]. Section 6 concludes with a brief description on extensions to ACSR on which we have worked.

7.2   THE ACSR LANGUAGE

The computation model of ACSR is based on the view that a real-time system is a set of communicating processes that compete for shared resources. Each execution step is the execution of either an *action* or an *event*. An action is a set of (resource-name, priority) pairs and represents the consumption of named resources for one time unit. Resource names are drawn from the set $\mathcal{R}$ and priorities are drawn from the set N^+ of non-negative integers. The execution of an action is subject to the availability of the named resources and the contention for resources is arbitrated according to the priorities of competing actions. As an example, the action $\{(cpu, 1)\}$ denotes the use of the *cpu* resource at the priority level 1, whereas the action $\{(cpu, 1), (memory, 2)\}$ denotes the use of the *cpu* resource at the priority level 1 as well as the *memory* resource at the priority level 2. The action $\emptyset$ represents the passage of one time unit without consuming any resources, that is, idling for one time unit. We use $\mathcal{D}_R$ to denote a set of actions. We let I, H range over $\mathcal{R}$; n, m, p range over $\mathbf{N}^+$; A, B, C range over $\mathcal{D}_R$.

An event is denoted by a pair (event-label, priority). Event labels are drawn from the set $\mathcal{L} \cup \bar{\mathcal{L}} \cup \{\tau\}$, where $\mathcal{L}$ is the set of event names and $\bar{\mathcal{L}}$ is their inverses. For example, for a given label a, we say that $\bar{a}$ is its *inverse* label. We stipulate that $\bar{\bar{a}} = a$. As in CCS, the special identity label, τ, arises when two events with inverse labels are executed in parallel. Events provide a basic mechanism for synchronization and communication between processes, and they can also be used for observation from outside the system. The execution of an event is assumed to be instantaneous and never consume any resource. Processes execute events asynchronously except when two processes synchronize through matching events. Priorities are used to arbitrate the choice when several events are possible at the same time. We use $\mathcal{D}_E$ to denote a set of events, and let a, b range over $\mathcal{L} \cup \bar{\mathcal{L}} \cup \{\tau\}$ and $(a, n), (b, n)$ range over $\mathcal{D}_E$. When we do not want to distinguish whether it is an action or an event, we use α and β.

A timed behavior is a sequence of actions, in which a sequence of events may appear between any two actions. Figure 7.1 shows an example of a timed behavior in the ACSR computation model. The behavior is described as a possibly infinite sequence of execution steps. At time 0, the events $(a_1, 1)$ and $(a_2, 2)$ occur in that order and then the *cpu* resource is used for one time unit at priority 1. At time 1, the events $(a_2, 3), (a_3, 4)$ happen in sequence and then the *cpu* and *bus* resources are used for one time unit at priorities 1 and 2, respectively. At time 2, the event $(a_4, 2)$ occurs and the system idles for one time unit, and so on.

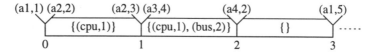

$$
\begin{array}{ccccc}
(a1,1)\ (a2,2) & & (a2,3)\ (a3,4) & & (a4,2) & & (a1,5) \\
& \{(cpu,1)\} & & \{(cpu,1),\ (bus,2)\} & & \{\} & \text{-----} \\
0 & & 1 & & 2 & & 3
\end{array}
$$

Figure 7.1 An example real-time behavior

7.2.1   Syntax

ACSR provides a set of operators that are similar to the common set of operators found in other process algebras: *prefix* for sequencing of actions and events; *choice* for choosing between alternatives; *parallel* for composing two processes to run in parallel; *restriction* and *hiding* for abstracting communication details or resource names; and *recursion* for describing infinite processes. In addition, ACSR supports a variety of operators that deal with time. They are basically to *delay* execution for t time units, to *timeout* while waiting for some actions to occur, and to *bound* the time it takes to execute a sequence of actions. Above all, ACSR provides two operators, *interrupt* and *exception*, that are extremely useful in modeling real-time systems but are not present in other real-time process algebras. The interrupt operator makes it easy to specify reaction to asynchronous actions or events. The exception operator allows an exception to be raised any place inside a process and handled by an exception handling process.

The syntax of ACSR processes is described by the following grammar, where we use P, Q, R, and S to denote ACSR processes, t for a non-negative integer, I, H for subsets of $\mathcal{R}$, and F for a subset of $\mathcal{L} \cup \bar{\mathcal{L}}$:

$$
P ::= \text{NIL} \mid A : P \mid (a, n).P \mid P + P \mid P \| P \mid \\
P \triangle_t^a (Q, R, S) \mid [P]_I \mid P \backslash F \mid P \backslash\backslash H \mid rec\ X.P \mid X
$$

NIL is a process that executes no action (i.e., it is initially and forever deadlocked). There are two prefix operators, corresponding to actions and events, respectively. The first, $A \cdot P$, executes a resource-consuming action A at the first time unit, and proceeds to the process P. On the other hand, $(a, n).P$, executes the event (a, n), and proceeds to P. The difference here is that we consider no time to pass during the event execution. The construct $P + Q$ represents a choice between the two processes P and Q. That is, this process will either behave like P or like Q. The choice is made based on the first execution steps of P and Q. The construct $P \| Q$ represents the parallel composition of the two processes P and Q whereby they may proceed independently or may synchronize.

The Scope construct $P \triangle_t^a (Q, R, S)$ binds the process P by a temporal scope [Lee85], and incorporates both the features of timeouts and interrupts. We call t the *time bound*, where $t \in \mathbf{N}^+ \cup \{\infty\}$ (i.e., t is either a non-negative integer or infinity). The scope may be exited in a number of ways. First, if P successfully terminates before t time units by executing an event labelled with $\bar{a}$, then control proceeds to the "success-handler" Q (here, a may be any label other than τ.) Note that the process Q does not interact with the process P through a. On the other hand, R is a timeout exception-handler; that is, if P fails to terminate before t time units, then control proceeds to R. Lastly, at any time while P is executing it may be interrupted by S, and the scope is then departed.

The Close operator, $[P]_I$, produces a process P that uses exclusively the resources in the set I. The Restriction operator, $P \backslash F$, limits the behavior of P. Here, no events with labels in F are permitted to execute. The Hiding operator, $P \backslash\backslash H$, conceals the identity of resources in the set H from the behavior of the process P. The construct $rec\ X.P$ denotes a recursive process. This allows specification of infinite behaviors.

To simplify the description of large systems, we augment the ACSR syntax with a definition operator as well as indexed processes and events. We use $X \stackrel{\text{def}}{=} P$ to refer to the process expression P by the process name X. We use subscripts to define indexed processes and events, e.g., P_1 and (a_2, p). Note that this definition mechanism can be used to define recursive processes without the use of the rec operator. Thus, for example,

$$P \stackrel{\text{def}}{=} (a, 1).P$$

is the same as the process $rec\ X.(a, 1).X$.

7.2.2 Preemptive Static Priority Scheduler

To illustrate the expressiveness of ACSR, we describe a set of periodic tasks with hard deadlines equal to the task periods, and which execute on a single processor. The deadline of a task defines the latest time by which the execution of the task must finish. To resolve contention over the processor, a rate-monotonic scheduler, for instance, assigns to each task a static priority that is inversely proportional to its period [Liu73]; that is, a task with a shorter period is assigned a higher priority than a task with a longer period. Figure 7.2 shows the ACSR specification of an instance of such systems. To make the example more readable, we use the following notation:

$$A^n = \underbrace{A : A : \cdots : A}_{n \text{ times}} \qquad (n \geq 1)$$

The system consists of a dispatcher, $Dispatch$, and three tasks, T_1, T_2 and T_3. The dispatcher instantiates the tasks at the beginning of their periods. Each task, T_i, is characterized by two

172

LEE, BEN-ABDALLAH, and CHOI

constants: the computation time, c_i, and the period, p_i. We assume task T_i has a longer period than task T_{i+1}, i.e., $p_1 \geq p_2 \geq p_3$. Consequently, task T_i is assigned the priority i, for $i = 1, 2, 3$. Furthermore, to simplify the presentation, we use the following assumptions about the system: tasks become ready at the beginning of their periods, and they can be preempted instantly with no preemption overhead. These assumptions simplify the dispatcher process and the computation processes $C_{i,j}$ shown in Figure 7.2.

$$System \stackrel{def}{=} [(Dispatch \,||\, T_1 \,||\, T_2 \,||\, T_3) \backslash \{s_1, s_2, s_3\}]_{\{cpu\}}$$

$$Dispatch \stackrel{def}{=} D_1 \,||\, D_2 \,||\, D_3$$
$$D_1 \stackrel{def}{=} (\overline{s_1}, 1).\emptyset^{p_1} : D_1$$
$$D_2 \stackrel{def}{=} (\overline{s_2}, 1).\emptyset^{p_2} : D_2$$
$$D_3 \stackrel{def}{=} (\overline{s_3}, 1).\emptyset^{p_3} : D_3$$

$$T_1 \stackrel{def}{=} (s_1, 1).C_{1,0}$$
$$T_2 \stackrel{def}{=} (s_2, 2).C_{2,0}$$
$$T_3 \stackrel{def}{=} (s_3, 3).C_{3,0}$$

$$C_{1,j} \stackrel{def}{=} \emptyset : C_{1,j} + \{(cpu, 1)\} : C_{1,j+1} \qquad 0 \leq j < c_1$$
$$C_{1,c_1} \stackrel{def}{=} \emptyset : C_{1,c_1} + T_1$$

$$C_{2,j} \stackrel{def}{=} \emptyset : C_{2,j} + \{(cpu, 2)\} : C_{2,j+1} \qquad 0 \leq j < c_2$$
$$C_{2,c_2} \stackrel{def}{=} \emptyset : C_{2,c_2} + T_2$$

$$C_{3,j} \stackrel{def}{=} \emptyset : C_{3,j} + \{(cpu, 3)\} : C_{3,j+1} \qquad 0 \leq j < c_3$$
$$C_{3,c_3} \stackrel{def}{=} \emptyset : C_{3,c_3} + T_3$$

Figure 7.2 Prioritized multitask system

The dispatcher periodically instantiates a task T_i using a process D_i as follows: D_i first signals the task T_i to start by sending the event $\overline{s_i}$. It then idles for the duration of the task's period p_i before sending $\overline{s_i}$ again. Once signaled to start, each task T_i tries to compute for c_i time units using the *cpu* resource. This is described by the processes $C_{i,j}$ which keep track of how much computation time is used. When a task T_i does not have access to the *cpu* resource, it idles by executing the process $\emptyset : C_{i,j}$. This means that T_i is preempted. When it finishes its computation, T_i idles waiting for the next periodic instantiation; this is described by process C_{i,c_i}. On the other hand, if T_i does not finish its computation within its period p_i, it will not be able to synchronize with the dispatcher which tries to send the starting event $\overline{s_i}$. Such a missed synchronization leads the process D_i of the dispatcher to deadlock. This in turn leads the whole system to deadlock. We revisit this example in the next section to illustrate the ACSR semantics and again in Subsection 7.4.4 where we address the schedulability analysis problem. We note that because ACSR associates priorities with actions, it is straightforward to change the rate-monotonic scheduler to another scheduler by modifying action priorities.

7.3 THE SEMANTICS OF ACSR

The executions of a process are defined by a labelled transition system. For example, a process P_1 may have the following execution steps:

$$P_1 \xrightarrow{\alpha_1} P_2 \xrightarrow{\alpha_2} P_3 \xrightarrow{\alpha_3} \cdots$$

That is, P_1 first executes α_1 and evolves into P_2, which executes α_2, etc. P_i represents the process's state at the ith step of an execution, while α_i represents the ith step, or *action* taken in the execution. This is a common way of describing a process behavior in most models of computation [Plo81]. In a process algebra, however, the states P_i are typically described by a concrete syntax, i.e., a process. Furthermore, there is a finite set of transition rules which infer the execution steps of the process behavior.

The semantics of ACSR is defined in two steps. First, we develop the *unconstrained* transition system, where a transition is denoted as $P \xrightarrow{\alpha} P'$. Within "$\rightarrow$" no priority information is used to prune impossible executions; we subsequently refine "$\rightarrow$" to define our prioritized transition system, "$\rightarrow_\pi$."

7.3.1 The Structured Transition System

The meaning of the various operators of ACSR are defined by operational rules. Each rule defines an execution step in the labelled transition system which describes the behavior of a process. The rules are read as follows: if the transitions above the line can be inferred, i.e., valid, then the transition below the line can be inferred. A special case is when there are no transitions above the line. In this case the transition below the line can be inferred unconditionally. Such a rule is called an *axiom*.

ACSR has two axioms – one for action prefix and the other for event prefix.

$$\text{ActT} \quad \frac{-}{A:P \xrightarrow{A} P} \qquad\qquad \text{ActI} \quad \frac{-}{(a,n).P \xrightarrow{(a,n)} P}$$

For example, consider the right hand branch of the process $C_{1,0} \stackrel{\text{def}}{=} \emptyset : C_{1,0} + \{(cpu, 1)\} : C_{1,1}$ in the scheduler example in Figure 7.2; the process $\{(cpu, 1)\} : C_{1,1}$ can use the *cpu* resource at priority level 1 for one time unit and proceeds to the process $C_{1,1}$. Alternatively, the task process $T_1 \stackrel{\text{def}}{=} (s_1, 1).C_{1,0}$ can execute the event $(s_1, 1)$ and proceeds to the process $C_{1,0}$.

The rules for Choice are identical for both actions and events (and hence we use "α" as the label).

$$\text{ChoiceL} \quad \frac{P \xrightarrow{\alpha} P'}{P+Q \xrightarrow{\alpha} P'} \qquad\qquad \text{ChoiceR} \quad \frac{Q \xrightarrow{\alpha} Q'}{P+Q \xrightarrow{\alpha} Q'}$$

As an example, the process $C_{1,c_1} \stackrel{\text{def}}{=} \emptyset : C_{1,c_1} + (s_1, 1).C_{1,0}$ from the scheduler example may choose between idling for one time unit or executing the event $(s_1, 1)$. The former behavior is deduced from rule **ChoiceL**, while the latter is deduced from **ChoiceR**.

The Parallel operator provides the basic constructor for concurrency and communication. The first rule, **ParT**, is for two time-consuming transitions.

$$\textbf{ParT} \quad \frac{P \xrightarrow{A_1} P', Q \xrightarrow{A_2} Q'}{P\|Q \xrightarrow{A_1 \cup A_2} P'\|Q'} \quad (\rho(A_1) \cap \rho(A_2) = \emptyset)$$

where $\rho(A)$ is the set of resources used by the action A; e.g., $\rho(\{(cpu, 1), (buffer, 2)\}) = \{cpu, buffer\}$. Note that timed transitions are synchronous, in that the resulting process advances only if both of the constituents take a step. The condition $\rho(A_1) \cap \rho(A_2) = \emptyset$ mandates that each resource is truly sequential, and that only one process may use a given resource during any time step.

The next three laws are for event transitions. As opposed to actions, events may occur asynchronously.

$$\textbf{ParIL} \quad \frac{P \xrightarrow{(a,n)} P'}{P\|Q \xrightarrow{(a,n)} P'\|Q} \qquad\qquad \textbf{ParIR} \quad \frac{Q \xrightarrow{(a,n)} Q'}{P\|Q \xrightarrow{(a,n)} P\|Q'}$$

$$\textbf{ParCom} \quad \frac{P \xrightarrow{(a,n)} P', Q \xrightarrow{(\bar{a},m)} Q'}{P\|Q \xrightarrow{(\tau,n+m)} P'\|Q'}$$

The first two rules show that events may be arbitrarily interleaved. The last rule is for two synchronizing processes; that is, P executes an event with the label a, while Q executes an event with the inverse label $\bar{a}$. Note that when the two events synchronize, their resulting priority is the sum of their constituent priorities. The reason for this will become clear in Example 7.3.2. Also, having multiple rules for an operator introduces branching in the associated labelled transition system.

Example 7.3.1 Consider the following two processes:

$$P \stackrel{\text{def}}{=} (s, 3).P_1 + \{(cpu_1, 8)\} : P_2$$

$$Q \stackrel{\text{def}}{=} (\bar{s}, 5).Q_1 + \{(cpu_2, 7)\} : Q_2$$

The compound process $P\|Q$ admits the following four transitions:

$$P\|Q \xrightarrow{(s,3)} P_1\|Q \qquad \text{[by \textbf{ParIL}]}$$
$$P\|Q \xrightarrow{(\bar{s},5)} P\|Q_1 \qquad \text{[by \textbf{ParIR}]}$$
$$P\|Q \xrightarrow{(\tau,8)} P_1\|Q_1 \qquad \text{[by \textbf{ParCom}]}$$
$$P\|Q \xrightarrow{\{(cpu_1,8),(cpu_2,7)\}} P_2\|Q_2 \quad \text{[by \textbf{ParT}]}$$

Note that an event transition always executes before the next "tick" of the global clock. □

The construction of **ParCom** ensures that the *relative* priority ordering among events with the same labels remains consistent even after communication takes places. The following example shows how the ordering is preserved.

Example 7.3.2 Consider the following variant of our static priority scheduler where the dispatcher D has the choice between instantiating two tasks T_1 and T_2:

$$D \stackrel{\text{def}}{=} (\bar{s}, 5).D_1 + (\bar{s}, 3).D_2$$
$$T \stackrel{\text{def}}{=} (s, 2).T_1 + (s, 3).T_2$$

Thus, in T the second choice is preferred, while in D the first choice is preferred. There are eight possible transitions for $D\|T$:

$$D\|T \xrightarrow{(\bar{s},5)} D_1\|T \qquad\qquad D\|T \xrightarrow{(\bar{s},3)} D_2\|T$$
$$D\|T \xrightarrow{(s,2)} D\|T_1 \qquad\qquad D\|T \xrightarrow{(s,3)} D\|T_2$$
$$D\|T \xrightarrow{(\tau,7)} D_1\|T_1 \qquad\qquad D\|T \xrightarrow{(\tau,5)} D_2\|T_1$$
$$D\|T \xrightarrow{(\tau,8)} D_1\|T_2 \qquad\qquad D\|T \xrightarrow{(\tau,6)} D_2\|T_2$$

While there are now four possible transitions labelled with τ, the addition of priorities in **ParCom** ensures that the original relative orderings are maintained. Note that the τ-transition with the highest priority is that associated with the derivative $D_1\|T_2$. These transitions had the highest priorities in their original constituent processes. □

The Scope operator possesses a total of five transition rules, which describe the various behaviors induced by a temporal scope. The first two rules show that as long as $t > 0$ and P does not execute an event labelled with $\bar{b}$, the executions of P continue.

$$\textbf{ScopeCT} \qquad \frac{P \xrightarrow{A} P'}{P \, \Delta^b_t \, (Q, R, S) \xrightarrow{A} P' \, \Delta^b_{t-1} \, (Q, R, S)} \qquad (t > 0)$$

$$\textbf{ScopeCI} \qquad \frac{P \xrightarrow{(a,n)} P'}{P \, \Delta^b_t \, (Q, R, S) \xrightarrow{(a,n)} P' \, \Delta^b_t \, (Q, R, S)} \qquad (\bar{a} \neq b, t > 0)$$

The **ScopeE** (for "end") shows how P can depart the temporal scope by executing an event labelled with $\bar{b}$. Upon exit, the label $\bar{b}$ is converted to the identity label τ (however, the same priority is retained).

$$\textbf{ScopeE} \qquad \frac{P \xrightarrow{(\bar{b},n)} P'}{P \, \Delta^b_t \, (Q, R, S) \xrightarrow{(\tau,n)} Q} \qquad (t > 0)$$

The next rule, **ScopeT** (for "timeout"), is applied whenever the scope times out; that is, when $t = 0$. At this point, control proceeds to the timeout exception-handler R.

$$\textbf{ScopeT} \qquad \frac{R \xrightarrow{\alpha} R'}{P \, \Delta^b_t \, (Q, R, S) \xrightarrow{\alpha} R'} \qquad (t = 0)$$

Finally, **ScopeI** shows that the process S may interrupt (and kill) P while the scope is still active.

$$\textbf{ScopeI} \qquad \frac{S \xrightarrow{\alpha} S'}{P \, \Delta^b_t \, (Q, R, S) \xrightarrow{\alpha} S'} \qquad (t > 0)$$

Example 7.3.3 Consider the following specification: "Execute P for a maximum of 100 time units. If P executes an event labelled with $\bar{b}$ in that time, then stop the system. However, if P fails to finish within 100 time units, then start executing R. At any time during the execution of P, allow interruption by an event $(c, 3)$, which will halt P, and initiate the interrupt-handler S." This system may be realized by the following process:

$$P \triangle_{100}^{b} (\text{NIL}, R, (c, 3).S).$$

□

The Restriction operator defines a subset of events that are excluded from the behavior of the system. This is done by establishing a set of labels, F ($\tau \notin F$), and deriving only those execution steps that do not involve events with those labels. Actions, on the other hand, remain unaffected.

$$\textbf{ResT} \quad \frac{P \xrightarrow{A} P'}{P \backslash F \xrightarrow{A} P' \backslash F} \qquad\qquad \textbf{ResI} \quad \frac{P \xrightarrow{(a,n)} P'}{P \backslash F \xrightarrow{(a,n)} P' \backslash F} \quad (a, \bar{a} \notin F)$$

Example 7.3.4 Restriction is particularly useful in "forcing" the synchronization between concurrent processes. In Example 7.3.1, synchronization on s and $\bar{s}$ is not forced, since $P\|Q$ has transitions labelled with s and $\bar{s}$. On the other hand, $(P\|Q)\backslash\{s\}$ has only two transitions:

$$(P\|Q)\backslash\{s\} \xrightarrow{(\tau,8)} (P_1\|Q_1)\backslash\{s\} \quad \text{and} \quad (P\|Q)\backslash\{s\} \xrightarrow{\{(cpu_1,8),(cpu_2,7)\}} (P_2\|Q_2)\backslash\{s\}$$

In effect, the restriction declares that s and $\bar{s}$ define a "local channel" between P and Q. □

While Restriction assigns local channels to processes, the Hiding operator conceals resource usage information from the outside environment. Events remain unaffected.

$$\textbf{HideT} \quad \frac{P \xrightarrow{A} P'}{P \backslash\!\backslash H \xrightarrow{A'} P' \backslash\!\backslash H} \qquad \text{where } A' = \{(r, n) \in A \mid r \notin H\}$$

$$\textbf{HideI} \quad \frac{P \xrightarrow{(a,n)} P'}{P \backslash\!\backslash H \xrightarrow{(a,n)} P' \backslash\!\backslash H}$$

In Example 7.3.1, the process P has the following two transitions:

$$P \xrightarrow{(s,3)} P_1 \quad \text{and} \quad P \xrightarrow{\{(cpu_1,8)\}} P_2.$$

If we hide the cpu_1 resource from the executions of P, we obtain the following two transitions:

$$P \backslash\!\backslash \{cpu_1\} \xrightarrow{(s,3)} P_1 \backslash\!\backslash \{cpu_1\} \quad \text{and} \quad P \backslash\!\backslash \{cpu_1\} \xrightarrow{\emptyset} P_2 \backslash\!\backslash \{cpu_1\}.$$

The Close operator assigns dedicated resources. When a process P is embedded in a closed context such as $[P]_I$, we ensure that there is no further sharing of the resources in I. Assume that P executes an action A. If A utilizes less than the full resource set I, the action is augmented with $(r, 0)$ pairs for each unused resource $r \in I - \rho(A)$.

$$\textbf{CloseT} \quad \frac{P \xrightarrow{A_1} P'}{[P]_I \xrightarrow{A_1 \cup A_2} [P']_I} \quad (A_2 = \{(r, 0) \mid r \in I - \rho(A_1)\})$$

$$\textbf{CloseI} \quad \frac{P \xrightarrow{(a,n)} P'}{[P]_I \xrightarrow{(a,n)} [P']_I}$$

The operator $rec\ X.P$ denotes recursion, allowing the specification of infinite behaviors.

$$\textbf{Rec} \quad \frac{P[rec\ X.P/X] \xrightarrow{\alpha} P'}{rec\ X.P \xrightarrow{\alpha} P'}$$

where $P[rec\ X.P/X]$ is the standard notation for substitution of $rec\ X.P$ for each free occurrence of X in P.

As an example, consider $rec\ X.(\{(cpu, 1)\} : X)$, which indefinitely executes the action "$\{(cpu, 1)\}$." By **ActT**,

$$\{(cpu, 1)\} : (rec\ X.(\{(cpu, 1)\} : X)) \xrightarrow{\{(cpu,1)\}} rec\ X\ (\{(cpu, 1)\} : X),$$

so by **Rec**,

$$rec\ X.(\{(cpu, 1)\} : X) \xrightarrow{\{(cpu,1)\}} rec\ X.(\{(cpu, 1)\} : X).$$

We define the unprioritized labelled transition system "$\rightarrow$" as follows: $P \xrightarrow{\alpha} P'$ if the transition on α is derivable by one of the rules described in this section.

7.3.2 The Prioritized Transition System

The prioritized transition system is based on *preemption*, which incorporates our treatment of synchronization, resource-sharing and priority. We use "$\prec$" to denote the preemption relation. For two actions or events, α and β, if $\alpha \prec \beta$, then we say that "α is preempted by β." This means that in any real-time system, if there is a choice between executing either α or β, it will always execute β. Informally, there are three cases for $\alpha \prec \beta$: 1) α and β are events with the same label and β has a higher priority; 2) α and β are actions and β uses a subset of resources with the following two conditions: all resources in β have at least the same priority as in α and at least one at a higher priority than in α, and every resource in α that is not in β must have a zero priority; or 3) β is a τ event with a non-zero priority while α is an action. We note that the case in which τ has a zero priority is treated differently. This is to allow the specification of nondeterministic behaviors where processes can communicate at any time rather than at the earliest possible time.

Definition 7.3.1 (Preemption Relation) *For two actions, α, β, we say that β preempts α ($\alpha \prec \beta$), if one of the following cases hold:*

(1) Both α and β are events in $\mathcal{D}_E$, where $\alpha = (a, p)$, $\beta = (a, p')$, and $p < p'$
(2) Both α and β are actions in $\mathcal{D}_R$, where

$$(\rho(\beta) \subseteq \rho(\alpha)) \wedge$$
$$(\forall (r, p) \in \alpha . (((r, p') \in \beta \Longrightarrow p \le p') \wedge ((r, p') \notin \beta \Longrightarrow p = 0))) \wedge$$
$$(\exists (r, p') \in \beta \exists (r, p) \in \alpha . p < p')$$

(3) $\alpha \in \mathcal{D}_R$ and $\beta \in \mathcal{D}_E$, with $\beta = (\tau, p)$ and $p > 0$.   □

Example 7.3.5 The following examples show some comparisons made by the preemption relation, "$\prec$."

  a. $\{(r_1, 2), (r_2, 5)\} \prec \{(r_1, 7), (r_2, 5)\}$
  b. $\{(r_1, 2), (r_2, 5)\} \not\prec \{(r_1, 7), (r_2, 3)\}$
  c. $\{(r_1, 2), (r_2, 0)\} \prec \{(r_1, 7)\}$
  d. $\{(r_1, 2), (r_2, 1)\} \not\prec \{(r_1, 7)\}$
  e. $(\tau, 1) \prec (\tau, 2)$
  f. $(a, 1) \not\prec (b, 2)$ if $a \ne b$
  g. $(a, 2) \prec (a, 5)$
  h. $\{(r_1, 2), (r_2, 5)\} \prec (\tau, 2)$ □

We next define the prioritized transition system "$\rightarrow_\pi$," which simply refines "$\rightarrow$" to account for preemption.

Definition 7.3.2 *The labelled transition system "$\rightarrow_\pi$" is defined as follows:* $P \xrightarrow{\alpha}_\pi P'$ *if*

a) $P \xrightarrow{\alpha} P'$ *is an unprioritized transition, and*

b) *There is no unprioritized transition* $P \xrightarrow{\beta} P''$ *such that* $\alpha \prec \beta$.   □

Example 7.3.6 In Example 7.3.2, prioritized transition eliminates five of the eight possible transitions, leaving the following:

$$D\|T \xrightarrow{(s,3)}_\pi D\|T_2 \qquad\qquad D\|T \xrightarrow{(\bar{s},5)}_\pi D_1\|T$$
$$D\|T \xrightarrow{(\tau,8)}_\pi D_1\|T_2$$

since $(s, 2) \prec (s, 3)$, and $(\bar{s}, 3) \prec (\bar{s}, 5)$, and $(\tau, p) \prec (\tau, 8)$ for $p = 5, 6, 7$.   □

Example 7.3.7 In the scheduler example, the process *System* is forced to synchronize the events s_1, s_2 and s_3 since they are restricted. After the three synchronization events s_1, s_2 and s_3 are executed, task T_3 will be selected to execute first. Let the processes *Dispatch'* and *System'* correspond to *Dispatch* and *System* after synchronization is done, respectively. And let *Dispatch''* correspond to *Dispatch'* after idling one time unit. That is,

$$Dispatch' \stackrel{\text{def}}{=} \emptyset^{p_1} : D_1 \| \emptyset^{p_2} : D_2 \| \emptyset^{p_3} : D_3$$
$$System' \stackrel{\text{def}}{=} [(Dispatch' \| C_{1,0} \| C_{2,0} \| C_{3,0}) \backslash \{s_1, s_2, s_3\}]_{\{cpu\}}$$
$$Dispatch'' \stackrel{\text{def}}{=} \emptyset^{p_1-1} : D_1 \| \emptyset^{p_2-1} : D_2 \| \emptyset^{p_3-1} : D_3$$

Using the unprioritized transition system, $System'$ has three possible transitions:

$$System' \xrightarrow{\{(cpu,1)\}} [(Dispatch''\|C_{1,1}\|C_{2,0}\|C_{3,0})\backslash\{s_1, s_2, s_3\}]_{\{cpu\}}$$

$$System' \xrightarrow{\{(cpu,2)\}} [(Dispatch''\|C_{1,0}\|C_{2,1}\|C_{3,0})\backslash\{s_1, s_2, s_3\}]_{\{cpu\}}$$

$$System' \xrightarrow{\{(cpu,3)\}} [(Dispatch''\|C_{1,0}\|C_{2,0}\|C_{3,1})\backslash\{s_1, s_2, s_3\}]_{\{cpu\}}$$

However, $System'$ has one transition in the prioritized transition system:

$$System' \xrightarrow{\{(cpu,3)\}}_\pi [(Dispatch''\|C_{1,0}\|C_{2,0}\|C_{3,1})\backslash\{s_1, s_2, s_3\}]_{\{cpu\}}$$

since $\{(cpu, 1)\} \prec \{(cpu, 2)\} \prec \{(cpu, 3)\}$.   □

7.4   ANALYSIS TECHNIQUES

As pointed out in the introduction, there are various techniques to verify that a design specification is correct with respect to a requirements specification. In ACSR, verification techniques
are based on process equivalence, where one attempts to show that a design specification
is equivalent to a requirements specification. There are two approaches to show that two
processes are equivalent.

One approach is to formulate a general set of equational laws, which syntactically charac-
terizes the congruence equivalence relation. This approach is similar to the way we manipulate
arithmetic expressions; for example, we frequently use the law, $3 * (x + y) = 3 * x + 3 * y$
without consciously thinking about the meanings of $3 * (x + y)$ and $3 * x + 3 * y$. The same
approach can be applied to ACSR processes.

The other approach is to compare the semantics, i.e., behaviors, of the two processes. Since
all possible behaviors of a process can be captured by a prioritized labelled transition system,
this approach is based on a technique for determining whether or not two labelled transition
systems are equivalent.

7.4.1   Equivalence Relations

Equivalence between two ACSR processes is based on the concept of *bisimulation* [Par81],
which compares the execution trees of the two processes. We use two common notions of
bisimulation, *strong bisimulation* and *weak bisimulation*.

Definition 7.4.1 *For a given transition system "$\longrightarrow$", any binary relation r is a strong
bisimulation if, for $(P, Q) \in r$ and for any action or event α,*

1. if $P \xrightarrow{\alpha} P'$ then, for some Q', $Q \xrightarrow{\alpha} Q'$ and $(P', Q') \in r$, and
2. if $Q \xrightarrow{\alpha} Q'$ then, for some P', $P \xrightarrow{\alpha} P'$ and $(P', Q') \in r$.   □

In other words, if P (or Q) can take a step on α, then Q (or P) must also be able to take a
step on α with both of the next states also bisimilar. There are some very obvious bisimulation
relations which certainly adhere to the above rules, e.g., $\emptyset$ or syntactic identity. However,
using the theory found in [Mil89], it is straightforward to show that there exists a largest such
bisimulation over "$\longrightarrow$," which we denote as "$\sim$." A relation r_1 is *larger* than a relation r_2 if r_1

is contained in r_2. The largest relation $\sim$ is an equivalence relation, and is a congruence with respect to the operators of ACSR [Ger91]. Similarly, $\sim_\pi$ is the largest strong bisimulation over "$\rightarrow_\pi$," and is also a congruence with respect to the operators of ACSR. We call $\sim_\pi$ a *prioritized strong equivalence* or just a *strong equivalence*. When $(P, Q) \in \sim_\pi$, also written as $P \sim_\pi Q$, we say that P and Q are (prioritized) strongly equivalent. One way to show that P and Q are strongly equivalent is to find a strong bisimulation relation r such that $(P, Q) \in r$. Since $\sim_\pi$ is the largest strong bisimulation, any strong bisimulation, including r, is a subset of $\sim_\pi$. Therefore, we can conclude that $P \sim_\pi Q$.

Example 7.4.1 Consider the following three processes, P, Q, R:

$$
\begin{aligned}
P &\stackrel{\text{def}}{=} \{(buf, 1)\} : P1 + \{(cpu, 2)\} : P \\
P1 &\stackrel{\text{def}}{=} (\tau, 1).P \\
Q &\stackrel{\text{def}}{=} \{(buf, 1)\} : Q1 + \{(cpu, 2)\} : Q2 \\
Q1 &\stackrel{\text{def}}{=} (\tau, 1).Q \\
Q2 &\stackrel{\text{def}}{=} \{(buf, 1)\} : Q3 + \{(cpu, 2)\} : Q \\
Q3 &\stackrel{\text{def}}{=} (\tau, 1).Q \\
R &\stackrel{\text{def}}{=} \{(buf, 1)\} : R + \{(cpu, 2)\} : R
\end{aligned}
$$

P and R are not strongly equivalent, because $P \stackrel{\{(buf,1)\}}{\longrightarrow} P1$ and $R \stackrel{\{(buf,1)\}}{\longrightarrow} R$, but $P1$ and R are not strongly equivalent. The reason $P1$ and R cannot be strongly equivalent is that R can take a step on either the action $\{(buf, 1)\}$ or the action $\{(cpu, 2)\}$; but, $P1$ can take a step on only the event $(\tau, 1)$. However, P and Q are strongly equivalent, which can be explained as follows: Let the relation r be defined as follows:

$$ r = \{(P, Q), (P1, Q1), (P, Q2), (P1, Q3)\}. $$

P (or Q) can take a step on $\{(buf, 1)\}$ and evolves into the state $P1$ (or $Q1$), and $(P1, Q1)$ is in r. When P (or Q) executes the action $\{(cpu, 2)\}$, P (or Q) evolves to P $(Q2)$ and $(P, Q2)$ is also in r. Since r is a strong bisimulation relation and (P, Q) is in r, P and Q are strongly equivalent. $\square$

We often find that different objectives were pursued in formulating the processes for requirements and design specifications; for example, simplicity for the requirements and efficiency for the design. Such differences may result in the internal synchronization events of the two processes that are not identical, even though the two processes may display identical "external" behavior. In particular, there may be τ events in one process that do not correspond directly to τ events in the other since synchronization replaces the complementary event labels with a τ event. For those situations where matching of external behaviors is sufficient, a weaker form of equivalence, *weak bisimulation* [Mil89] is sufficient. The following definitions are needed to define weak bisimulation.

Definition 7.4.2 *Let the set $\mathcal{D}$ denote the set of ACSR actions and events. If $t = \alpha_1 \cdots \alpha_n \in (\mathcal{D} - \{\tau\})^*$, then $E \stackrel{t}{\Rightarrow} E'$ if*

$$ E (\xrightarrow{(\tau,-)})^* \xrightarrow{\alpha_1} (\xrightarrow{(\tau,-)})^* \cdots (\xrightarrow{(\tau,-)})^* \xrightarrow{\alpha_n} (\xrightarrow{(\tau,-)})^* E', $$

where $(\tau, -)$ represents τ with an arbitrary priority value. $\square$

Definition 7.4.3 *If $t \in \mathcal{D}^*$, then $\hat{t} \in (\mathcal{D} - \{\tau\})^*$ is the sequence derived by deleting all occurrences of τ from t.* □

Example 7.4.2 The process P of Example 7.4.1 can execute the following steps:

$$P \xrightarrow{\{(buf,1)\}} \xrightarrow{(\tau,1)} \xrightarrow{\{(cpu,2)\}} P$$

Let $t = \{(buf, 1)\}(\tau, 1)\{(cpu, 2)\}$. Then, we have $\hat{t} = \{(buf, 1)\}\{(cpu, 2)\}$ and

$$P \overset{\hat{t}}{\Rightarrow} P.$$

□

Definition 7.4.4 *For a given labelled transition system "$\longrightarrow$", any binary relation r is a weak bisimulation if, for $(P, Q) \in r$ and $\alpha \in \mathcal{D}$,*

1. *if $P \xrightarrow{\alpha} P'$ then, for some Q', $Q \overset{\hat{\alpha}}{\Rightarrow} Q'$ and $(P', Q') \in r$, and*
2. *If $Q \xrightarrow{\alpha} Q'$ then, for some P', $P \overset{\hat{\alpha}}{\Rightarrow} P'$ and $(P', Q') \in r$.* □

In other words, if P (or Q) can take a step on $\alpha \in \mathcal{D}$, then Q (or P) must also be able to take a step or sequence of steps on $(\tau, -)^*\alpha(\tau, -)^*$. And if P (or Q) can take a step on $(\tau, -)$, then Q (or P) may or may not take a step (or steps) on $(\tau, -)^+$. It is possible to prove the existence of a largest weak bisimulation over "$\longrightarrow_\pi$", which we denote as $\approx_\pi$, in a manner analogous to the case of prioritized strong equivalence. We call the relation $\approx_\pi$ a *prioritized weak equivalence* or just a *weak equivalence*. When $(P, Q) \in \approx_\pi$, also written as $P \approx_\pi Q$, we say that P and Q are (prioritized) weakly equivalent. We note that it is well-known that any strong bisimulation is also a weak bisimulation, and hence, the weak equivalence contains the strong equivalence.

Example 7.4.3 The processes P and R in Example 7.4.1 are weakly equivalent although they are not strongly equivalent. Since $P \overset{\{(buf,1)\}}{\Longrightarrow} P$ and $R \overset{\{(buf,1)\}}{\Longrightarrow} R$, as well as $P \overset{\{(cpu,2)\}}{\Longrightarrow} P$ and $R \overset{\{(cpu,2)\}}{\Longrightarrow} R$, we can conclude that P and R are weakly equivalent. Note that the processes P and Q in Example 7.4.1 are obviously weakly equivalent since strong equivalence implies weak equivalence. □

7.4.2 Syntax Based Analysis

The main distinguishing feature of process algebras over other state-transition models is that a relatively small set of laws can be used to prove strong equivalence in many different situations. As an example, two processes, $P + \text{NIL}$ and P, can be proved equivalent by a law which is common to almost every process algebra – $P + \text{NIL} = P$. This law is true for *any* process P and thus, it can be used in many different instances.

Table 7.1 presents our strong equivalence-preserving laws for ACSR except the Hiding operator. We assume that ACSR processes used in the rest of this section are processes without Hiding operators. In Table 7.1, the laws with italic names represent laws that are common to CCS-like process algebras; the other laws are specific to ACSR. In the sequel, wherever we use the equality symbol "=" in showing that two processes are strongly equivalent, it means that we have used our laws to construct the proof. The equivalence of the processes follows from the soundness of the laws.

Note the use of the summation symbol $\sum$ in Par(3). The interpretation is as follows: Let I be an index set representing processes, such that for each $i \in I$, there is some corresponding process P_i. If $I = \{i_1, \ldots, i_n\}$, because of Choice(4) we are able to neglect parentheses and use the following notation:

$$\sum_{i \in I} P_i \stackrel{\text{def}}{=} P_{i_1} + \ldots + P_{i_n}.$$

When $I = \emptyset$, $\sum_{i \in \emptyset} P_i \stackrel{\text{def}}{=} NIL$.

Par(3) is representative of many of the laws, in that its objective is to "undo" a constructor. That is, it reduces the "$\|$" operator to a simpler form – in this case, a process whose initial steps can be determined by the Prefix and Choice constructors.

Soundness and Completeness.   The ACSR proof system, $\mathcal{A}$, augmented with standard laws for substitution, is sound with respect to prioritized strong equivalence. That is, if we use the laws in the proof system $\mathcal{A}$ to syntactically rewrite a process P to a process Q, then $P \sim_\pi Q$. The soundness can be proved by constructing a bisimulation to show that $P \sim_\pi Q$ for each law $P = Q$ in $\mathcal{A}$.

We also have extended the ACSR proof system, $\mathcal{A}$, with additional laws to form a complete proof system, $\mathcal{A}'$, for the important and useful subset of finite-state ACSR processes. Thus, if two processes in that subset are strongly equivalent, then the laws of the proof system $\mathcal{A}'$ can be used to show their equivalence. The details of the soundness and completeness proof can be found in [Bré93].

7.4.3   Semantics Based Analysis

Instead of using the above laws, it is also possible to determine whether any two finite-state processes are equivalent or not by directly comparing their labelled transition systems. The basic idea of this approach is as follows: Given a finite-state ACSR process, its behavior can be completely captured by a labelled transition system. To decide whether two processes, P and Q, are bisimilar, one first combines the labelled transition system for P and the labelled transition system for Q. Then, the largest bisimulation relation is computed for this combined labelled transition system [Cle93, Kan90].

Recall that weak equivalence was introduced to ignore the occurrences of τ events which are considered important in strong equivalence. ACSR also includes several other attributes such as priorities and resources where requiring strict identification between them is not practically useful. For example, although precise priority values are required in matching events and actions, it frequently is the case that relative priorities are more important than the exact priority values. Another example is that it is also useful to ignore the identity of resources used in actions, especially when a requirements specification is in terms of timing constraints between observable events. This usually results in a much simpler ACSR process as a requirements specification. This technique is illustrated in the following example.

Table 7.1 The Set of ACSR Laws, $\mathcal{A}$

Choice(1)	$P + \text{NIL} = P$
Choice(2)	$P + P = P$
Choice(3)	$P + Q = Q + P$
Choice(4)	$(P + Q) + R = P + (Q + R)$
Choice(5)	$A_1 : P_1 + A_2 : P_2 = A_2 : P_2$ if $A_1 \prec A_2$
Choice(6)	$(a_1, n_1).P_1 + (a_2, n_2).P_2 = (a_2, n_2).P_2$ if $(a_1, n_1) \prec (a_2, n_2)$
Choice(7)	$A : P + (\tau, n).Q = (\tau, n).Q$ if $n > 0$
Par(1)	$P\|Q = Q\|P$
Par(2)	$(P\|Q)\|R = P\|(Q\|R)$

Par(3)

$$\left(\sum_{i \in I} A_i : P_i + \sum_{i \in J}(a_j, n_j).Q_j \right) \| \left(\sum_{k \in K} B_k : R_k + \sum_{l \in L}(b_l, m_l).S_l \right)$$

$$= \begin{bmatrix} \displaystyle\sum_{\substack{i \in I, k \in K, \\ \rho(A_i) \cap \rho(B_k) = \emptyset}} (A_i \cup B_k) : (P_i \| R_k) \\ + \displaystyle\sum_{j \in J} (a_j, n_j).(Q_j \| (\sum_{k \in K} B_k : R_k + \sum_{l \in L}(b_l, m_l).S_l)) \\ + \displaystyle\sum_{l \in L} (b_l, m_l).((\sum_{i \in I} A_i : P_i + \sum_{j \in J}(a_j, n_j).Q_j)) \| S_l \\ + \displaystyle\sum_{\substack{j \in J, l \in L, \\ a_j = b_l}} (\tau, n_j + m_l).(Q_j \| S_l) \end{bmatrix}$$

Scope(1)	$A : P \overset{b}{\triangle}_t (Q, R, S) = A : (P \overset{b}{\triangle}_{t-1} (Q, R, S)) + S$ if $t > 0$
Scope(2)	$(a, n).P \overset{b}{\triangle}_t (Q, R, S) = (a, n).(P \overset{b}{\triangle}_t (Q, R, S)) + S$ if $t > 0 \wedge \bar{a} \neq b$
Scope(3)	$(a, n).P \overset{b}{\triangle}_t (Q, R, S) = (\tau, n).Q + S$ if $t > 0 \wedge \bar{a} = b$
Scope(4)	$P \overset{b}{\triangle}_0 (Q, R, S) = R$
Scope(5)	$(P_1 + P_2) \overset{b}{\triangle}_t (Q, R, S) = P_1 \overset{b}{\triangle}_t (Q, R, S) + P_2 \overset{b}{\triangle}_t (Q, R, S)$
Scope(6)	$(\text{NIL}) \overset{b}{\triangle}_t (Q, R, S) = S$ if $t > 0$
Res(1)	$\text{NIL} \backslash F = \text{NIL}$
Res(2)	$(P + Q) \backslash F = (P \backslash F) + (Q \backslash F)$
Res(3)	$(A : P) \backslash F = A : (P \backslash F)$
Res(4)	$((a, n).P) \backslash F = (a, n).(P \backslash F)$ if $a, \bar{a} \notin F$
Close(1)	$[\text{NIL}]_I = \text{NIL}$
Close(2)	$[P + Q]_I = [P]_I + [Q]_I$
Close(3)	$[A_1 : P]_I = (A_1 \cup A_2) : [P]_I$ where $A_2 = \{(r, 0) | r \in I - \rho(A_1)\}$
Close(4)	$[(a, n).P]_I = (a, n).[P]_I$
Rec(1)	$recX.P = P[recX.P/X]$

Example 7.4.4 Consider the following processes:

$$P \stackrel{def}{=} \{(cpu1, 1)\} : P + \{(cpu2, 1)\} : P$$
$$Q \stackrel{def}{=} \{(cpu2, 1)\} : Q + \{(cpu3, 1)\} : Q$$
$$R \stackrel{def}{=} P \parallel Q$$

Suppose we want to prove that the process R does not reach a deadlock state. One way is to construct such an ACSR requirements specification R' and to show that R and R' are bisimilar. Since any two of the three resources $cpu1, cpu2, cpu3$ can be used during each time unit, R' must explicitly enumerate all possible resource use patterns. However, such an R' is cumbersome to specify and we are not interested in the patterns of resource usage. Thus, the requirements specification can be rephrased as to show that the process $R\backslash\backslash\{cpu1, cpu2, cpu3\}$ never deadlocks. Since the resource information of R is hidden, we can use an ACSR requirements specification, $rec \ X. \ \emptyset : X$. Note that this process essentially runs forever, which means that it does not deadlock. Hence, the correctness of R can be proved by showing that

$$R\backslash\backslash\{cpu1, cpu2, cpu3\} \approx_\pi rec \ X. \ \emptyset : X.$$

$\square$

7.4.4 Example: Schedulability Analysis

A typical question in real-time scheduling is whether a set of tasks is *schedulable* or not; that is, one is interested in verifying that none of the tasks misses its deadline. In the rate-monotonic scheduler of Section 7.2.2, if a task misses its deadline, then the whole system deadlocks. Thus, we can verify that the tasks are schedulable by verifying that the system never deadlocks. Furthermore, at a more abstract level where resource usage and synchronization are irrelevant, the tasks are schedulable if the system idles forever. The schedulability question therefore becomes that of verifying

$$System\backslash\backslash\{cpu\} \approx_\pi rec \ X.\emptyset : X$$

We assume that the computation times and periods of the tasks, T_1, T_2 and T_3 in Figure 7.2 are as follows: $c_1 = 3, p_1 = 15; c_2 = 3, p_2 = 12;$ and $c_3 = 5, p_3 = 10$. Then, *System* becomes

$$System \stackrel{def}{=} [(Dispatch \parallel T_1 \parallel T_2 \parallel T_3) \backslash \{s_1, s_2, s_3\}]_{\{cpu\}}$$

$$\stackrel{def}{=} [(\ (\overline{s_1}, 1).\emptyset^{15} : (\overline{s_1}, 1).D_1 \parallel (\overline{s_2}, 1).\emptyset^{12} : (\overline{s_2}, 1).D_2 \parallel (\overline{s_3}, 1).\emptyset^{10} : (\overline{s_3}, 1).D_3 \parallel$$
$$(s_1, 1).C_{1,0} \parallel (s_2, 2).C_{2,0} \parallel (s_3, 3).C_{3,0}$$
$$)\backslash\{s_1, s_2, s_3\}]_{\{cpu\}}$$

We can apply the parallel composition Par(3) to expand the process *System* and synchronize the start events s_1, s_2, and s_3.

$$System = (\tau, 4).(\tau, 3).(\tau, 2).[(\ \emptyset^{15} : (\overline{s_1}, 1).D_1 \parallel \emptyset^{12} : (\overline{s_2}, 1).D_2 \parallel \emptyset^{10} : (\overline{s_3}, 1).D_3 \parallel$$
$$C_{1,0} \parallel C_{2,0} \parallel C_{3,0}$$
$$)\backslash\{s_1, s_2, s_3\}]_{\{cpu\}}$$

We can use the parallel composition Par(3) again and then Choice(5) to select the branch with $\{(cpu, 3)\}$, since as we saw in Example 7.3.7 it preempts all others.

$$
\begin{aligned}
System \quad = \quad & (\tau, 4).(\tau, 3).(\tau, 2).\{(cpu, 3)\}: \\
& [(\ \emptyset^{14} : (\overline{s_1}, 1).D_1 \,\|\, \emptyset^{11} : (\overline{s_2}, 1).D_2 \,\|\, \emptyset^9 : (\overline{s_3}, 1).D_3 \,\| \\
& \quad C_{1,0} \,\|\, C_{2,0} \,\|\, C_{3,1} \\
& \ )\backslash\{s_1, s_2, s_3\}]_{\{cpu\}}
\end{aligned}
$$

$$\vdots$$

$$
\begin{aligned}
\quad = \quad & (\tau, 4).(\tau, 3).(\tau, 2).\{(cpu, 3)\}^5 : \\
& [(\ \emptyset^{10} : (\overline{s_1}, 1).D_1 \,\|\, \emptyset^7 : (\overline{s_2}, 1).D_2 \,\|\, \emptyset^5 : (\overline{s_3}, 1).D_3 \,\| \\
& \quad (\emptyset : C_{1,0} + \{(cpu, 1)\} : C_{1,1}) \,\| \\
& \quad (\emptyset : C_{2,0} + \{(cpu, 2)\} : C_{2,1}) \,\| \\
& \quad (\emptyset : C_{3,5} + T_3) \\
& \ )\backslash\{s_1, s_2, s_3\}]_{\{cpu\}} \\
\overset{\mathrm{def}}{=} \quad & System_1
\end{aligned}
$$

Similarly, we can repeatedly apply Par(3) and Choice(5) on $System_1$ to rewrite it as follows:

$$
\begin{aligned}
System_1 \quad = \quad & (\tau, 4).(\tau, 3).(\tau, 2).\{(cpu, 3)\}^5 : \{(cpu, 2)\}^3 : \{(cpu, 1)\}^2 : \\
& [(\ \emptyset^5 : (\overline{s_1}, 1).D_1 \,\|\, \emptyset^2 : (\overline{s_2}, 1).D_2 \,\|\, (\overline{s_3}, 1).D_3 \,\| \\
& \quad (\emptyset : C_{1,2} + \{(cpu, 1)\} : C_{1,3}) \,\|\, C_{2,3} \,\|\, (\emptyset : C_{3,5} + (s_3, 1).C_{3,0}) \\
& \ )\backslash\{s_1, s_2, s_3\}]_{\{cpu\}} \\
= \quad & (\tau, 4).(\tau, 3).(\tau, 2).\{(cpu, 3)\}^5 : \{(cpu, 2)\}^3 : \{(cpu, 1)\}^2 : (\tau, 4). \\
& [(\ \emptyset^5 : (\overline{s_1}, 1).D_1 \,\|\, \emptyset^2 : (\overline{s_2}, 1).D_2 \,\|\, D_3 \,\| \\
& \quad (\emptyset : C_{1,2} + \{(cpu, 1)\} : C_{1,3}) \,\|(\emptyset : C_{2,3} + T_2) \,\|\, C_{3,0} \\
& \ )\backslash\{s_1, s_2, s_3\}]_{\{cpu\}} \\
= \quad & (\tau, 4).(\tau, 3).(\tau, 2).\{(cpu, 3)\}^5 : \{(cpu, 2)\}^3 : \{(cpu, 1)\}^2 : \\
& (\tau, 4).\{(cpu, 3)\}^2 : \\
& [(\ \emptyset^2 : (\overline{s_1}, 1).D_1 \,\|\, (\overline{s_2}, 1).D_2 \,\|\, \emptyset^8 : (\overline{s_3}, 1).D_3 \,\| \\
& \quad (\emptyset : C_{1,2} + \{(cpu, 1)\} : C_{1,3}) \,\|\, (\emptyset : C_{2,3} + (s_2, 1).C_{2,0}) \,\|\, C_{3,2} \\
& \ )\backslash\{s_1, s_2, s_3\}]_{\{cpu\}} \\
\overset{\mathrm{def}}{=} \quad & System_2
\end{aligned}
$$

The last two steps describe when task T_3 is started and preempts T_1. They use Par(3) to expand the process and Choice(7) to eliminate choices. We can apply Par(3) and Choice(5) to rewrite $System_2$ as follows:

$$
\begin{aligned}
System_2 \quad = \quad & (\tau, 4).(\tau, 3).(\tau, 2).\{(cpu, 3)\}^5 : \{(cpu, 2)\}^3 : \{(cpu, 1)\}^2 : \\
& (\tau, 4).\{(cpu, 3)\}^2 : (\tau, 3).\{(cpu, 2)\}^3 : \\
& [(\quad (\overline{s_1}, 1).D_1 \parallel \emptyset^7 : (\overline{s_2}, 1).D_2 \parallel \emptyset^5 : (\overline{s_3}, 1).D_3 \parallel \\
& (\emptyset : C_{1,2} + \{(cpu, 1)\} : C_{1,3}) \parallel C_{2,0} \parallel C_{3,5} \\
&)\backslash\{s_1, s_2, s_3\}]_{\{cpu\}} \\
\overset{\text{def}}{=} \quad & System_3
\end{aligned}
$$

At this stage, process D_1 can only send event $\overline{s_1}$ to instantiate task T_1. Since event s_1 is a restricted event, the receiving process, T_1, must at this point be ready to receive s_1. However, this is not the case. We can therefore use Par(3) to rewrite $System_3$ as follows:

$$
\begin{aligned}
System_3 \quad = \quad & (\tau, 4).(\tau, 3).(\tau, 2).\{(cpu, 3)\}^5 : \{(cpu, 2)\}^3 : \{(cpu, 1)\}^2 : \\
& (\tau, 4).\{(cpu, 3)\}^2 : (\tau, 3).\{(cpu, 2)\}^3 : [\,\text{NIL}\backslash\{s_1, s_2, s_3\}]_{\{cpu\}} \\
= \quad & (\tau, 4).(\tau, 3).(\tau, 2).\{(cpu, 3)\}^5 : \{(cpu, 2)\}^3 : \{(cpu, 1)\}^2 : \\
& (\tau, 4).\{(cpu, 3)\}^2 : (\tau, 3).\{(cpu, 2)\}^3 : \text{NIL}
\end{aligned}
$$

The deadlock is due to T_1 missing its deadline during its first period: At time 10 when T_3 is instantiated for the second time, T_1 is preempted after executing 2 time units only, and T_3 is allocated the cpu since it has a higher priority. At time 15 when T_3 finishes its computation, the period of T_1 expires while it needs the cpu for one more unit of computation. Thus, T_1 is not ready to accept the start event s_1 from the dispatcher which leads the system to a deadlock state – a state where time does not progress any longer.

Hiding the cpu resource from $System_3$, we get

$$
\begin{aligned}
System_3\backslash\backslash\{cpu\} \quad &\sim_\pi \quad (\tau, 4).(\tau, 3).(\tau, 2).\emptyset^5 : \emptyset^3 : \emptyset^2 : (\tau, 4).\emptyset^2 : (\tau, 3).\emptyset^3 : \text{NIL} \\
&\sim_\pi \quad (\tau, 4).(\tau, 3).(\tau, 2).\emptyset^{10} : (\tau, 4).\emptyset^2 : (\tau, 3).\emptyset^3.\text{NIL} \\
&\approx_\pi \quad \emptyset^{15} : \text{NIL} \\
&\not\approx_\pi \quad rec\,X.\emptyset : X
\end{aligned}
$$

We therefore conclude that T_1, T_2 and T_3 are not schedulable.

On the other hand, if we decrease the computation time of T_2 to $c_2 = 1$, we can show that the tasks are schedulable, *i.e.*, the system does not deadlock. More specifically, we can use the ACSR analysis techniques to prove that

$$
System\backslash\backslash\{cpu\} \quad \approx_\pi \quad \emptyset^{60} : (System\backslash\backslash\{cpu\})
$$

We can therefore conclude that

$$
System\backslash\backslash\{cpu\} \quad \approx_\pi \quad rec\,X.\emptyset : X
$$

7.5   RAILROAD CROSSING SYSTEMS

The railroad crossing system [Hei93] has been a benchmark example for real-time formal methods. In this section, we illustrate how ACSR can be used to model three versions of the railroad crossing system: the *Generalized Railroad Crossing* [Hei94] which has multiple tracks in the crossing; the *Standard Railroad Crossing* which is an instance of the Generalized Railroad Crossing with a single-track crossing; and the *Busy Railroad Crossing* which augments the Standard Railroad Crossing with cars. We also illustrate how ACSR can be used to verify some properties of the Standard Railroad Crossing and Busy Railroad Crossing.

To make the ACSR specifications easier to read, we adopt the following naming convention: synchronization events start with lower-case letters and observable events start with upper-case letters.

7.5.1   Informal Description And Parameters

The system to be developed controls a gate at a railroad crossing. The railroad crossing lies in a region delimited by entry and exit sensors that detect the entry and exit of trains. The goal is to develop a system that operates the crossing gate subject to *safety* and *utility* properties [Hei94]. The safety property states that when a train is in the crossing, the gate is down. The utility property states that when no train is in the crossing, the gate is up as much as possible.

Our designs contain three main components: *train* and *gate* which describe the environment, and *control* which describes the computer system. These components execute concurrently, produce *observable* events to mark the status of critical activities, and coordinate with one another through *synchronization* events. Tables 7.2 and 7.3 describe the names of events that we use in our designs.

Table 7.2   Observable events

Train		Gate	
Nc :	near crossing	Up :	is up
Ic :	in crossing	$Down$:	is down
Pc :	past crossing		

Table 7.3   Synchronization events

Train → Control		Control → Gate	
ns :	signal entry sensor	$raise$:	signal gate to move up
ps :	signal exit sensor	$lower$:	signal gate to move down

Train. We model a train as a process that sends three observable events, Nc, Ic, and Pc, to mark the train's critical positions, and that coordinates with the control component through two synchronization events, ns and ps. When a train approaches the crossing region, it marks this activity by sending Nc. At this time, the train is detected by the entry sensor and the train sends the event ns to the control component. When a train enters the crossing, it sends Ic. Finally, when a train passes the crossing, it sends Pc and sends the exit-sensory event ps to control.

Gate. We model the gate, which is initially up, as a process that receives signals from the control component. When it receives *lower*, it moves down and marks the end of this activity by the event $Down$. When gate receives *raise*, it moves up and marks the end of this activity by the event Up.

Control. We model the control component as a process that synchronizes the train activities with the gate: When the control receives ns from the train, it sends *lower* to the gate; and when it receives ps, it sends *raise* to the gate.

Being part of a safety-critical system, the components of the railroad crossing system operate under timing assumptions. The timing assumptions are expressed in terms of delays between observable events in the system. Table 7.4 shows the timing assumptions we use in our designs of the railroad crossing system. Note that, in this paper, we elected to use single valued delays, as oppose to intervals, to keep the examples simple; however, we can describe in ACSR any interval delay through the Prefix and Scope operators.

Table 7.4   Timing assumptions

	Bounds	From Event$_1$ to Event$_2$
Train	ni	$Nc \rightarrow Ic$
	ip	$Ic \rightarrow Pc$
	$[\delta, \infty]$	$Pc_i \rightarrow Nc_{i+1}$
Gate	γ	to move up or down

7.5.2   Generalized Railroad Crossing

The Generalized Railroad Crossing, GRC, contains n tracks in the crossing. Thus, at any time, there can be up to n trains approaching, leaving, or in the crossing. Figure 7.3 shows our design specification of the GRC system.

Each $Train_i$ process can be either far from the crossing region, which is indicated by the idle action, or it can be near the crossing region, which is marked by the event Nc_i. The $Control$ process idles while waiting to receive events from trains that approach or leave the crossing. This process remembers the number of trains that consecutively enter the crossing region and sends a *lower* event to the $Gate$ process when the first train enters the crossing region and a *raise* event when the last train passes the crossing region. The $Gate$ process idles while waiting for events from the $Control$ process to move down or up. Note that in our design of the gate if a train enters the crossing before the gate is fully raised, the gate-raising activity is interrupted and the gate-closing activity is started. On the other hand, if no train is near the crossing before the gate is fully raise, the gate-raising activity signals its completion by sending the event $\overline{open}$ after which the gate returns to the initial state. This is described by the Scope operator in the process GU of Figure 7.3.

$$GRC \stackrel{\text{def}}{=} (Trains \parallel Control \parallel Gate) \setminus \{ns, ps, lower, raise\}$$

$$Trains \stackrel{\text{def}}{=} Train_1 \parallel \cdots \parallel Train_n$$

$$Train_1 \stackrel{\text{def}}{=} \emptyset : Train_1 +$$
$$(\overline{Nc_1}, 1).(\overline{ns}, 1).\emptyset^{\text{ni}} : (\overline{Ic_1}, 1).\emptyset^{\text{ip}} : (\overline{Pc_1}, 1).(\overline{ps}, 1).\emptyset^{\delta} : Train_1$$

$$\vdots$$

$$Train_n \stackrel{\text{def}}{=} \emptyset : Train_n +$$
$$(\overline{Nc_n}, 1).(\overline{ns}, 1).\emptyset^{\text{ni}} : (\overline{Ic_n}, 1).\emptyset^{\text{ip}} : (\overline{Pc_n}, 1).(\overline{ps}, 1).\emptyset^{\delta} : Train_n$$

$$Control \stackrel{\text{def}}{=} \emptyset : Control + (ns, 1).(\overline{lower}, 1).Control_1$$

$$Control_1 \stackrel{\text{def}}{=} \emptyset : Control_1 + (ns, 1).Control_2 + (ps, 1).(\overline{raise}, 1).Control$$

$$Control_2 \stackrel{\text{def}}{=} \emptyset : Control_2 + (ns, 1).Control_3 + (ps, 1).Control_1$$

$$\vdots$$

$$Control_n \stackrel{\text{def}}{=} \emptyset : Control_n + (ps, 1).Control_{n-1}$$

$$Gate \stackrel{\text{def}}{=} \emptyset : Gate + (lower, 1).GD$$

$$GD \stackrel{\text{def}}{=} \emptyset^{\gamma} : (\overline{Down}, 1).rec\,X.(\emptyset : X + (raise, 1).GU)$$

$$GU \stackrel{\text{def}}{=} (\emptyset^{\gamma} : (\overline{Up}, 1).(\overline{open}, 1).NIL) \triangle_{\infty}^{open} (Gate, NIL, (lower, 1).GD)$$

Figure 7.3 Generalized railroad crossing

7.5.3 Standard Railroad Crossing

The Standard Railroad Crossing, SRC, is a special instance of the GRC with only one track in the crossing; that is, at any time, there is at most one train in the crossing region. We can therefore instantiate the GRC specification of Figure 7.3 for $n = 1$ and a fixed set of timing assumptions. Figure 7.3 shows an example of SCR for the timing assumptions in Table 7.5.

Table 7.5 Instances of timing assumptions

δ	= 15	γ	= 20
ni	= 25	ip	= 10

To verify formally that the design specification SRC satisfies the safety and utility properties, we construct a requirements specification that is simpler to inspect for the two properties. Figure 7.5 shows two requirements specifications for the SRC: $Spec_1$ describes all possible actions including synchronized events which are represented by the internal event τ, while $Spec_2$ abstracts out the internal events.

In both requirements specifications, the idling for 20 time units corresponds to the time to

$SRC \stackrel{def}{=} (Train \parallel Control \parallel Gate) \backslash \{ns, ps, lower, raise\}$

$Train \stackrel{def}{=} \emptyset : Train + (\overline{Nc}, 1).(\overline{ns}, 1).\emptyset^{25} : (\overline{Ic}, 1).\emptyset^{10} : (\overline{Pc}, 1).(\overline{ps}, 1).\emptyset^{15} : Train$

$Control \stackrel{def}{=} \emptyset : Control + (ns, 1).(\overline{lower}, 1).Control + (ps, 1).(\overline{raise}, 1).Control$

$Gate \stackrel{def}{=} \emptyset : Gate + (lower, 1).GD$

$GD \stackrel{def}{=} \emptyset^{20} : (\overline{Down}, 1).rec\, X.(\emptyset : X + (raise, 1).GU)$

$GU \stackrel{def}{=} (\emptyset^{20} : (\overline{Up}, 1).(\overline{open}, 1).NIL) \triangle_{\infty}^{open} (Gate, NIL, (lower, 1).GD)$

Figure 7.4   Standard railroad crossing

$Spec_1 \stackrel{def}{=} \emptyset : Spec_1 + Spec'_1$

$Spec'_1 \stackrel{def}{=} (\overline{Nc}, 1).(\tau, 2).(\tau, 2).\emptyset^{20} : (\overline{Down}, 1).\emptyset^5 : (\overline{Ic}, 1).\emptyset^{10} : (\overline{Pc}, 1).(\tau, 2).(\tau, 2).$
$\emptyset^{15} : ((rec\, X.\emptyset : X) \triangle_5 (NIL, (\overline{Up}, 1).(\tau, 2).Spec_1, \ Spec'_1))$

$Spec_2 \stackrel{def}{=} \emptyset : Spec_2 + Spec'_2$

$Spec'_2 \stackrel{def}{=} (\overline{Nc}, 1).\emptyset^{20} : (\overline{Down}, 1).\emptyset^5 : (\overline{Ic}, 1).\emptyset^{10} : (\overline{Pc}, 1).$
$\emptyset^{15} : ((rec\, X.\emptyset : X) \triangle_5 (NIL, (\overline{Up}, 1).Spec_2, \ Spec'_2))$

Figure 7.5   Requirements specification for the standard railroad crossing

lower the gate. The idling for 5 time units $(5 = 25 - 20)$ corresponds to the time it remains for a train to actually enter the crossing after signaling its approach. The idling for 10 time units is the time for a train to pass the crossing. The idling for 15 time units is the minimum delay between consecutive trains. Finally, the time-out of 5 time units in the scope operator corresponds to the remaining time to fully raise the gate after a train exits the crossing.

In both requirements specifications, one can see that any occurrence of the event Ic is preceded by a $Down$ event. In addition, any occurrence of the event Up is preceded by the event Pc. The gate is, therefore, down whenever there is a train in the crossing. Furthermore, one can easily inspect that in both requirements specifications, if no event Nc ever occurs, the gate remains in its initial state which is, by assumption, up. On the other hand, if no event Nc occurs within 20 time units of the last occurrence of Pc, the event Up occurs. The gate is therefore up when no train is in the crossing, as much as possible taken the time to raise the gate.

We can use the ACSR analysis techniques to prove that the design specification of the standard railroad crossing, SRC, satisfies the safety and utility properties by showing it is equivalent to the requirements specifications in Figure 7.5. More precisely, we can prove that

$$SRC \quad \sim_\pi \quad Spec_1 \text{ and}$$
$$SRC \quad \approx_\pi \quad Spec_2$$

7.5.4 Busy Railroad Crossing

To illustrate the use of resources and priorities of ACSR, we augment the SRC system with cars. We call this version the *Busy Railroad Crossing*, BRC.

Figure 7.6 shows our design specification of the BRC. (The *Control* process is the same as in Figure 7.4.) The specification of the train in Figure 7.6, $Train'$, differs from $Train$ in Figure 7.4 in the use of the *crossing* resource when the train enters the crossing. We modify the *Gate* process of Figure 7.4 to signal *up* while the gate is up. This event is used by the *Car* process to find out the status of the gate. We assume that a car takes three time units to pass the crossing and returns to the crossing immediately afterward. When a car passes the crossing, it uses the *crossing* resource. To arbitrate resource conflict, we assign a higher priority to the train than to the car on their use of the *crossing* resource. To simplify the requirements specification, we use the same event Nc for a car and a train that signal their arrival to the crossing with a car having a higher priority.

$$BRC \stackrel{\text{def}}{=} [(Train' \| Control \| Gate' \| Car) \backslash \{ns, ps, lower, raise, up\}]_{\{crossing\}}$$

$$Train' \stackrel{\text{def}}{=} \emptyset : Train' + (\overline{Nc}, 1).(\overline{ns}, 1).\emptyset^{25} : TC$$

$$TC \stackrel{\text{def}}{=} (\overline{Ic}, 1).\{(crossing, 5)\}^{10} : (\overline{Pc}, 1).(\overline{ps}, 1).\emptyset^{15} : Train'$$

$$Gate' \stackrel{\text{def}}{=} \emptyset : Gate' + (\overline{up}, 1).Gate' + (lower, 1).GD$$

$$GD \stackrel{\text{def}}{=} \emptyset^{20} : (\overline{Down}, 1).rec\, X.(\emptyset : X + (raise, 1).GU)$$

$$GU \stackrel{\text{def}}{=} (\emptyset^{20} : (\overline{Up}, 1).(\overline{open}, 1).\text{NIL}) \triangle_\infty^{open} (Gate', \text{NIL}, (lower, 1).GD)$$

$$Car \stackrel{\text{def}}{=} (\overline{Nc}, 2).rec\, X.(\emptyset : X + (up, 1).\{(crossing, 2)\}^3 : Car)$$

Figure 7.6 Busy railroad crossing

In addition to the safety and utility properties of the SRC, the BRC system must satisfy an additional safety property: a train and a car never collide into each other. This additional safety property is satisfied if the design specification, BRC, never reaches a deadlock state that is due to the concurrent execution of the action $\{(crossing, 5)\}$ and the action $\{(crossing, 2)\}$ as the only possible actions for $Train$ and Car, respectively.

To verify our claims about the safety and utility of BRC formally, we use the requirements specification $Spec_3$ of Figure 7.7. The requirements specification $Spec_3$ is a purely sequential process that abstracts out synchronization and resource usage. It is simple to inspect for the

$$Spec_3 \stackrel{\text{def}}{=} (\overline{Nc}, 2).Spec'_3$$

$$Spec'_3 \stackrel{\text{def}}{=} (\overline{Nc}, 1).\emptyset^{20} : TPass$$
$$+\emptyset : ((\overline{Nc}, 1).\emptyset^2 : (\overline{Nc}, 2).\emptyset^{18} : TPass$$
$$+\emptyset : ((\overline{Nc}, 1).\emptyset : (\overline{Nc}, 2).\emptyset^{19} : TPass$$
$$+\emptyset : Spec_3))$$

$$TPass \stackrel{\text{def}}{=} (\overline{Down}, 1).\emptyset^5 : (\overline{Ic}, 1).\emptyset^{10} : (\overline{Pc}, 1).Spec''_3$$

$$Spec''_3 \stackrel{\text{def}}{=} (rec\, X.\emptyset : X) \triangle_5 (NIL, (\overline{Up}, 1).Spec'_3, (\overline{Nc}, 1).\emptyset^{20} : TPass)$$

Figure 7.7   Requirements specification of the busy railroad crossing

safety and utility properties. Furthermore, it is obvious that $Spec_3$ never deadlocks due to resource contention. Thus $Spec_3$ describes the desired behavior of the BRC. We can use the ACSR analysis techniques to prove that

$$BRC\backslash\!\backslash\{crossing\} \approx_\pi Spec_3.$$

We can therefore conclude that our design specification BRC satisfies the augmented safety property and the utility property.

7.6   CONCLUSIONS

We have described the ACSR process algebra which allows the specification and analysis of real-time systems. ACSR supports the notions of resources and priorities which make it a unifying framework that combines the areas of process algebra and real-time scheduling. The ACSR computation model is based on the view that the components of a real-time system execute synchronously time and resource consuming actions and communicate through instantaneous events asynchronously, except when two components synchronize through matching events.

ACSR offers notions of equivalence based on prioritized strong and weak bisimulations to allow the verification of the correctness of a design specification with respect to a requirements specification. These notions of equivalence can be used in either a syntax-based analysis that uses a set of algebraic laws or a semantics-based analysis that compares the behaviors described as prioritized labelled transition systems. Furthermore, ACSR notion of prioritized strong equivalence together with its various operators make it possible to construct and analyze a specification in a modular and hierarchical fashion. This is essential for a large scale system which, in practice, is specified and analyzed incrementally in terms of its components.

We have implemented a toolkit based on ACSR, called *VERSA* [Cla95], which has three major functions: rewriting, equivalence testing, and interactive execution. The rewrite system facilitates the rewriting of ACSR processes according to ACSR laws that preserve prioritized strong equivalence. At the direction of the user, the rewrite system applies predefined algebraic laws to produce a new, equivalent process. This allows the user to develop interactively algebraic proofs of the equivalence of processes.

For semantics-based analysis and interactive execution, the equivalence tester converts an ACSR process to a labelled transition system. This tester also prunes transitions made unreachable by the semantics of the prioritized transition system. We have found that this pruning significantly reduces the time required for state space explorations. Once a labelled transition system has been generated, the user can query its size and the presense of deadlock. In addition, processes can be tested for the different notions of ACSR equivalence.

The interactive execution feature allows user-directed execution of process specifications. The user may interactively step through the labelled transition system one action at a time, produce traces from random executions of the labelled transition system, and save process configurations to a stack for later analysis while an alternate path is explored.

We have found that VERSA greatly facilitates the task of using ACSR for non-trivial examples through computer assistance for checking syntax and carrying out analysis automatically. To facilitate the use of ACSR by novice programmers, we are currently developing a graphical specification language based on ACSR and plan to extend VERSA with a graphical user interface.

ACSR is an extension of another real-time process algebra, called CCSR, which shares all the aspects of ACSR except for instantaneous synchronization events [Ger90, Ger94]. In particular, it was the first process algebra to support the notions of both resources and priorities. CCSR was in turn motivated by our previous work on a real-time process algebra without the notions of resources and priorities [Zwa88a, Zwa88b].

We are extending the capability of ACSR in three areas. The first extension is to support dynamic priorities. ACSR supports only static priority; i.e., action and event priorities cannot change during the execution of a process. Since modeling of many real-time scheduling algorithms, such as earliest deadline first, first-come first-served, priority-inheritance protocol, etc., requires dynamic priorities, it is useful to support dynamic priority in timed process algebras. The second extension is to allow dense time so that a timed action can take an arbitrary non-zero amount of time [Bré94]. In addition, it should be possible to specify the value of time using a variable and then derive the range of time values that ensure the correct timing of a process. The third extension is to support data variables and value-passing through messages during communication. This will allow the succinct specifications of real-time systems where data is involved in communication.

Acknowledgement. The authors gratefully acknowledge the comments and suggestions made by the two referees, as well as Vijay Gehlot and Hong-Liang Xie, in improving the quality of this paper. The work described in this paper was strongly influenced by criticisms from the members of Real-Time Systems Group at the University of Pennsylvania. This research was supported in part by NSF CCR 93-11622 and ARO DAAH04-95-1-0092.

REFERENCES

[Ace93] L. Aceto and D. Murphy. On the ill-timed but well-caused. In *Proc. CONCUR'93, International Conference on Concurrency Theory.* LNCS 715, Springer-Verlag, August 1993.

[Bae91] J.C.M. Baeten and J.A. Bergstra. real time process algebra. *Formal Aspects of Computing,* 3(2):142–188, 1991.

[Ber85] J. A. Bergstra and J. W. Klop. Algebra of communicating processes with abstraction. *Journal of Theoretical Computer Science,* 37:77–121, 1985.

[Bré94] P. Brémond-Grégoire. *A Process Algebra of Communicating Shared Resources with Dense Time and Priorities.* PhD dissertation, University of Pennsylvania, Department of Computer and Information Science, 1994.

[Bré93] P. Brémond-Grégoire, J.Y. Choi, and I. Lee. The soundness and completeness of ACSR (Algebra of Communicating Shared Resources). MS-CIS-93-59, University of Pennsylvania, Computer and Information Science Department, Philadelphia, Pennsylvania, June 1993.

[Bur94] A. Burns. Preemptive priority-based scheduling: an appropriate engineering approach. In S. H. Son, editor, *Advances in Real-Time Systems*, chapter 10, pages 225–248. Prentice Hall 1994.

[Cla95] Duncan Clarke, Insup Lee, and Hong-Liang Xie. VERSA: a tool for the specification and analysis of resource-bound real-time systems. *Journal of Computer and Software Engineering*, 3(2), 1995.

[Cle93] R. Cleaveland, J. Parrow, and B. Steffen. The Concurrency Workbench: a semantics-based verification tool for the verification of concurrent systems. *ACM Transactions on Programming Languages and Systems*, 15(1):36–72, January 1993.

[Ger91] R. Gerber. *Communicating Shared Resources: A Model for Distributed Real-Time Systems*. PhD dissertation, University of Pennsylvania, Department of Computer and Information Science, 1991.

[Ger90] R. Gerber and I. Lee. CCSR: a calculus for communicating shared resources. In *Proc. CONCUR'90, International Conference on Concurrency Theory*. LNCS 458, Springer-Verlag, August 1990.

[Ger94] R. Gerber and I. Lee. A resource-based prioritized bisimulation for real-time systems. *Information and Computation*, 113(1):102–142, 1994.

[Hei93] C. Heitmeyer, R. Jeffords, and B. Labaw. Comparing different approaches for specifying and verifying real-time systems. In *Proc. Tenth IEEE Workshop on Real-Time Operating Systems and Software*, pages 122–129, New York, May 1993.

[Hei94] C. Heitmeyer and N. Lynch. The generalized railroad crossing: a case study in formal verification of real-time systems. In *Proc. of Real-Time Systems Symposium (RTSS' 94)*, 1994.

[Hen91] M. Hennessy and T. Regan. A process algebra for timed systems. Technical Report 5/91, University of Sussex, UK, April 1991.

[Hoa85] C.A.R. Hoare. *Communicating Sequential Processes*. Prentice-Hall, 1985.

[Kan90] P. C. Kanellakis and S. A. Smolka. CCS Expressions, Finite State Processes, and Three Problems of Equivalence. *Information and Computation*, 86:43–68, 1990.

[Lee85] I. Lee and V. Gehlot. Language constructs for distributed real-time programming. In *Proc. of Real-Time Systems Symposium (RTSS' 85)*, 1985.

[Lee94] I. Lee, P. Brémond-Grégoire and R. Gerber. A process algebraic approach to the specification and analaysis of resource-bound real-time systems. *Proceedings of the IEEE*, 82(1): 158–171, 1994.

[Liu94] J. W. S. Liu and R. Ha. Efficient methods of validating timing constraints. In S. H. Son, editor, *Advances in Real-Time Systems*, chapter 9, pages 199–224. Prentice Hall 1994.

[Liu73] C.L. Liu and J.W. Layland. Scheduling algorithms for multi-programming in a hard-real-time environment. *Journal of the ACM*, (1):46–61, 1973.

[Mil89] R. Milner. *Communication and Concurrency*. Prentice-Hall, 1989.

[Mol90] F. Moller and C. Tofts. A temporal calculus of communicating systems. In *Proc. of CONCUR '90*, pages 401–415. LNCS 458, Springer-Verlag, August 1990.

[Nic94] X. Nicollin and J. Sifakis. The algebra of timed processes ATP: theory and application. *Information and Computation*, 114(1):131–178, October 1994.

[Par81] D. Park. A timed failure semantics for extended communicating processes. In *Proc. of Fifth GI Conference*, LNCS 104, 1981. Springer-Verlag.

[Plo81] G. Plotkin. A structural approach to operational semantics. Technical Report DAIMI FN-19, Aarhus University, Computer Science Department, 1981.

[Ree87] G.M. Reed and A.W. Roscoe. Metric spaces as models for real-time concurrency. In *Proc. of Math. Found. of Computer Science*. LNCS 298, Springer Verlag, 1987.

[Yi91] Wang Yi. CCS + Time = an interleaving model for real-time systems. In *Proc. of Int. Conf. on Automata, Languages and Programming*, July 1991.

[Zwa88a] A. Zwarico and R. Gerber and I. Lee. A complete axiomatization of real-time processes. Technical Report MS-CIS-88-88, University of Pennsylvania, Department of Computer and Information Science, November 1988.

[Zwa88b] A. Zwarico. *Timed Acceptance: An Algebra of Time Dependent Computing*. PhD dissertation, University of Pennsylvania, Department of Computer and Information Science, 1988.

8

Constraint-Oriented Specification Style for Time-Dependent Behaviours

TOMMASO BOLOGNESI

C.N.R., CNUCE Institute, Pisa

ABSTRACT

In this chapter we emphasize human-oriented usage of formal specifications, and insist that these be not only amenable to automated analysis but also appealing to human intuition and understanding. We concentrate on a specification style called 'constraint-oriented', which is meant to simplify the writing and reading of formal descriptions by approximating, in some aspects, the style of informal descriptions as expressed in natural language. The constraint-oriented style has already been applied succesfully to specifications in standard LOTOS; in this chapter we show how it naturally extends to the specification of time-dependent behaviours in a *timed* LOTOS. The approach is illustrated by the Generalized Railroad Crossing example.

8.1 INTRODUCTION

The most typical and frequently mentioned benefits expected from the adoption of formal specification techniques and formal methods for developing (real-time) systems include support for:

- mechanically proving properties and detecting errors early in the life cycle;
- verifying the correctness of specification and design refinement steps;
- producing the final code or, at least, program skeletons;
- deriving test suites for checking the implementation.

Formal Methods For Real-Time Computing, Edited by Heitmeyer and Mandrioli
© 1996 John Wiley & Sons Ltd

In all four cases above the machine-oriented usage of formal specifications is emphasized – a specification is input to an automated or semi-automated procedure for obtaining the desired result. Indeed, it has been frequently stated that crucial to the industrial-scale success of a formal specification language is the availability of tool environments alleviating as much as possible designers and programmers from the error-prone tasks of the software development process, thus reducing effort and chance of human error.

However, the very first formal specification in a development process cannot be produced but by a human being: it should therefore be easy to write and to read. A reader-friendly formal specification improves transparency of communication and common understanding among members of the specification team; it also represents an adequate interface between this team and the design team on one side, and the customer on the other.

In particular, the customer is typically not acquainted with formal methods and notations, while his comments on the early outputs of the formal specification team would represent valuable feedback to the latter. Thus, a reader-friendly formal specification lending itself to the understanding and approval of the customer, and perhaps close to his informal description of the desired system, is a highly desirable starting point of the (formally-based segment of the) development process.

In this chapter we emphasize the human-oriented usage of formal specifications, and insist that these be not only amenable to automated or semi-automated elaboration, but also appealing to human intuition and understanding. We shall concentrate on a specification style which is meant to simplify the writing and reading of formal descriptions by approximating, in some aspects, the style of informal descriptions as expressed in natural language.

More specifically, in this chapter we discuss the extent to which the conceptually appealing constraint-oriented style, which has already been applied succesfully to specifications in standard (un-timed) LOTOS, can be extended to the specification of time-dependent behaviours in a timed LOTOS.

The chapter is organized as follows. In Section 8.2 we describe the concept of constraint-oriented specification in general terms. In Section 8.3 we illustrate how that specification style can be supported by the standard LOTOS specification language. In Section 8.4 we show how any 'reasonable' timed extension of LOTOS can still support the constraint-oriented specification style, by the introduction of *timing constraints*. In Section 8.5 we provide a constraint-oriented specification, in a timed LOTOS, of the requirements for the Generalized Railway Crossing (GRC) system, an example which is used frequently in the present volume. In Section 8.6 a system is specified (still in timed LOTOS) which is meant to satisfy the given GRC-requirements. In Section 8.7 we summarize the benefits and limitations of constraint-oriented specification in timed LOTOS, and argue that it offers advantages, at least in terms of readability, over alternative, state-based approaches. Some familiarity with LOTOS is beneficial. In particular, we shall use the following LOTOS constructs:

- action prefix, for sequencing actions, with the so-called input symbol '?', output symbol '!', and selection predicate '[. . .]',
- parallel composition '| [. . .] |', the binary operator including, as a parameter, a list of synchronization gates,
- interleaving '| | |', the special case of parallel composition without synchronization gates,
- the guard '[. . .] ->', expressing a condition for enabling a behaviour,
- the binary choice operator ' [ ] ' for offering the choice between two alternative behaviours,

- the generalized choice operator 'choice x:s [] B(x)' for offering the choice among multiple instances of a parameterized behaviour,
- the LOTOS successful termination process 'exit', which enables the execution of any process composed in sequence with the terminating process, and
- sequential composition '>>' for specifying sequences of processes.

We shall further recall the meanings of these constructs at their first occurrences in the subsequent examples.

8.2   SPECIFICATION BY COMPOSITION OF CONSTRAINTS

In this section we introduce the general, simple ideas at the basis of the constraint-oriented descriptive style, without referring to any particular specification language.

A constraint-oriented specification can be most generally defined as one where the global picture of the described object is obtained by composing constraints on (subsets of) its elementary components.

Suppose we want to formally specify a problem by characterizing its solution space (the 'global picture'). Assuming that a solution is an assignment of n real values to n variables (the 'elementary components'), a constraint-oriented specification would consist of a collection of relations (the 'constraints'), each involving a different subset of the variables: the solution space consists of all the assignments that simultaneously satisfy all the given relations.

Consider, for example, three real-valued variables

```
leave_up, up_lower, lower_enter
```

In the context of the Generalized Railroad Crossing system (GRC), frequently used in this volume, and fully illustrated only later in this chapter, these can be understood as time delays between the events named in the identifiers, where leave refers to a train leaving the crossing, up indicates that the Gate has reached its vertical position, lower is the command for lowering the Gate, and enter refers to a train entering the crossing. For example, leave_up is the delay between a train leaving the crossing and the Gate reaching its vertical position. Then we may characterize a set of assignments to these variables by composing the following constraints:

```
Utility1   := 0 < leave_up < c2
Utility2   := 0 < lower_enter < c1
Utility3   := leave_up + up_lower + lower_enter > c2 + d + c1
```

where $c1$, $c2$ and d are predefined constants (incidentally, these constraints correspond, collectively, to the so called *Utility* requirement of the GRC system). The composition is plain logical conjunction, with the obvious understanding that equal identifiers in different constraints must refer to the same value, and is depicted in Figure 8.1.

Suppose now that we want to formally specify a behaviour by characterizing the set of possible event sequences (the 'global picture'). Here the 'elementary components' are the individual events, and a constraint-oriented specification would consist of a collection of constraints on their relative orderings: the global behaviour is formed by all the event sequences that simultaneously satisfy all the given constraints.

As an example, consider again the GRC system, restricting, for our illustrative purposes,

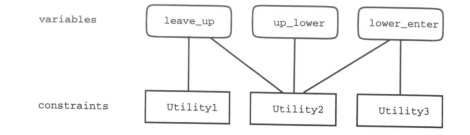

Figure 8.1 Network of constraints on variables

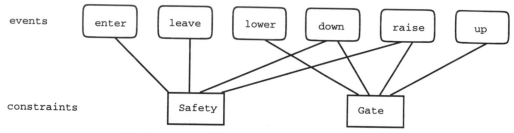

Figure 8.2 Network of constraints on events

to the case of just one train passing only once. Consider the event set {*lower, down, raise, up, enter, leave*}, where the first four events refer to commands (*lower, raise*) and reached positions (*up, down*) of the Gate, while the *enter* and *leave* events refer to the train entering and leaving the crossing. We may characterize the legal sequences of these events by composing the following ordering constraints, which can be themselves expressed as sequences of events:

```
Gate       :=    lower; down; raise; up
Safety     :=    down; enter; leave; raise
```

The composition here is a sort of logical conjunction, with the understanding that equal identifiers in different constraints refer to the same event. In other words, any legal sequence must precisely yield a constraint sequence, when restricted to the appropriate subset of events. The unique sequence of events that simultaneously satisfies the two constraints is: `lower, down, enter, leave, raise, up`. The composition is depicted in Figure 8.2.

Some analogies exist between constraint-oriented formal specifications and informal descriptions in natural language. A (clear) informal description is frequently structured as a sequence of relatively short sentences which share some elements; each sentence adds some information to the global picture by enforcing some constraints on some of those elements. One consequence of this analogy is that one can maintain in a relatively easy way, and in parallel, a set of formalized constraints on one hand, and a set of associated informal explanations on the other. The latter, then, can be naturally composed into a single informal description, virtually without the need to provide further 'textual glue'. The cost of consistently modifying the informal and formal descriptions, e.g. after interaction with the customer, is thus minimised. Note that we do not pretend to push the analogy also to the internal structure of individual formal/informal constraints, but we primarily refer to the simple way in which they are composed in the two cases. We hope that the reader will be further convinced by these observations after reading the constraint-oriented specification provided in Section 8.5, or other specifications in that style.

8.3   CONSTRAINT-ORIENTED STYLE IN LOTOS

We illustrate here the way in which the general idea of constraint-oriented specification is supported by the ISO standard specification language LOTOS [BB87, Bri89]. LOTOS (Language Of Temporal Ordering Specification) is a formal specification language in the family of process algebras, like CCS [M80] and CSP [H85]. It integrates two components, one for specifying the temporal ordering of events, which is largely inspired by the two above mentioned process algebras, and one for expressing data structures, which basically consists of the abstract data type specification language ACT-ONE [EM85].

Application of the LOTOS language started long before the publication of the ISO standard in 1989, first dealing with services and protocols of the ISO-OSI (Open Systems Interconnection) communication network architecture, and then spreading to various other application areas. After about ten years of experience with LOTOS, three main and well consolidated specification styles have emerged, namely the *constraint-oriented, resource-oriented* and *state-oriented styles* [VSVS88]. We briefly recall the main ideas behind the second and third, and then illustrate to a greater extent the first one.

A resource-oriented LOTOS specification is meant to describe directly the actual components of the final system, be they hardware or software pieces, and their interconnections and interactions. Each component is modelled by a LOTOS process, interaction patterns are specified via the parallel composition operator, while the hiding operator is used for shielding these interactions from participation of other processes in the environment. Thus, the resource-oriented style is particularly convenient for implementation-oriented specifications.

In a state-oriented LOTOS specification the behaviour of the system is specified by explicitly identifying the state and the allowed state transitions. The state is modelled by a list of LOTOS variables, which appear as parameters of a LOTOS process. Each transition is modelled as a LOTOS action, which is associated with a LOTOS guard, expressing the enabling conditions in terms of the current state, and is followed by a new instantiation of the process, with parameters describing the effect of the transition on the state. A state-oriented LOTOS process is readily converted into a state transition table and, as such, it is a convenient basis for implementation. Typically the resource-oriented and state-oriented styles are combined in large, implementation-oriented LOTOS specifications, where resources are modelled as interacting state machines.

The constraint-oriented LOTOS specification style represents, in our opinion, one of the most effective conceptual tools available to the users of the language. In a constraint-oriented LOTOS specification one first identifies the set and types of the actions that characterize the system behaviour, and then specifies the latter by composing constraints on

- the ordering of (subsets of) these actions, and on
- the tuples of values associated with them.

This can be made clear only if we explain the structure of LOTOS actions. An action is characterized by

- a gate identifier, indicating the gate (an abstract location) where the action is imagined to occur;
- a tuple of values, possibly of different types, that are 'established' by the action (which may mean 'offered' or 'accepted').

For example, action

$$g < 2, 5 >$$

takes place at gate g, and establishes a pair consisting of two natural values. What we have shown is a *semantic* action, that is, a label in the labelled transition system (LTS) which represents the semantics of the specification. (Every LOTOS specification ultimately describes a LTS, which is a possibly infinite tree where arcs are labelled by actions and paths correspond to 'runs' of behaviour.) The action above could have been generated, at the syntax level, by an *action prefix* behaviour expression such as: g ?x:nat !5 [x < 3]; .... The LOTOS process whose behaviour is described by this expression can indeed perform any one of the three actions:

$$g < 0, 5 >,\ g < 1, 5 >,\ g < 2, 5 >$$

and can synchronize with any other process ready to perform at least one of these actions. Indeed, the exclamation mark sets a precise value for the interaction to occur, while the question mark indicates a set of possible values of a named type; these values may then be constrained by a *selection predicate* – [x < 3], in this example.

Different processes synchronising (or 'insisting') on the same gate can constrain different elements of the tuple, while acting as 'don't care' conditions on the remaining elements. The effect on the tuple of values finally established in the interaction is the logical conjunction of the individual constraints.

For example, consider the three processes insting on gate g, with behaviours:

```
P1 := g      ?x:nat  !5        [x < 3];          STOP
P2 := g      ?x:nat  ?y:nat    [y > 3];          STOP
P3 := g      ?x:nat  ?y:nat    [x MOD 2 = 1];    STOP
```

each offering just one action, and assume that they are required to synchronize on g-actions, as specified by the parallel behaviour expression:

```
P1  |[g]|  P2  |[g]|  P3 .
```

They can agree only on establishing the action $g < 1, 5 >$.

Besides constraining the values at a given gate, the processes insisting on it may constrain the relative orderings of action occurrences. Consider, for example, the three processes:

```
P1 := e;  g ?x:nat !5 [x < 3];              STOP
P2 := f;  g ?x:nat ?y:nat [y > 3];          STOP
P3 := g ?x:nat ?y:nat [x MOD 2 = 1];  h;    STOP
```

These have been obtained by adding to the previously considered behaviours three 'pure' actions e, f and h, that is, actions that occur at gates e, f and h without establishing any value. Besides constraining the values established at gate g, the parallel composition above would induce a relative ordering, at the global level, which is not apparent if the constraints are considered in isolation: actions e and f, taken in either order, must occur before action h.

The two small examples above should have given to the uninitiated reader an informal idea on the meanings of the LOTOS action prefix and parallel composition operators. In summary, by the action prefix one can specify a sequence of actions that terminates with a STOP or, in general, with the instantiation of any other process (STOP is conceived as the process unable to perform any action). An action may establish one or more values at a gate, or just represent the occurrence of an event at that gate, with no value involved. In the first case, the values can be either unconstrained, as done with the '?' symbol, or partially constrained by an additional selection predicate, or completely defined, as done by the '!' symbol. Constrained and unconstrained values can be combined in the same action prefix. By the binary, right-associative operator of parallel composition, two processes can be required to synchronize on the actions occurring at a given set of gates, which is specified in the operator itself. Actions at gates other than the synchronization gates can occur independently in the two processes, that is, their occurrences are freely interleaved.

Of course we have shown here only elementary examples of constraints, consisting exclusively of short action sequences. In general a constraint can be expressed by complex LOTOS processes making use of the full set of LOTOS operators. The interested reader may find several published examples of LOTOS specifications in constraint-oriented style, ranging from the small specification of the Daemon Game [BB87] or of the switching device known as 'Al's Node' to the large specifications of the ISO-OSI Session and Transport Services; these, and other examples of various sizes can be found in [EVD89], in [T93], and in the recent 'LotoSphere book' [BLV95].

8.4   COMPOSING ORDERING AND TIMING CONSTRAINTS IN A TIMED LOTOS

The LOTOS standard does not primitively support any notion of event timing, that is, no constructs are available for specifying the time delay between two events or the absolute time at which an event happens. The need to enhance the language in this respect has been recognized even before the publication of the Standard and has originated a relatively large number of contributions on timed-LOTOS, such as [QF87, BLT90, HTZ90, BL92, L92, QDA93, MFV93, LL94, BL95]. We are not interested here in a survey and comparison of these proposals. In fact, rather than insisting on their differences, we shall rely upon some of the features that most of them share, based on which our discussion of constraint-oriented specification in timed-LOTOS can be kept as general and widely applicable as possible.

When timing information comes into play, the previously illustrated concept of constraint-oriented specification can be quite naturally extended by considering a third type of constraint, dealing with time. Thus, the system behaviour is now characterized by a composition of constraints on

- the ordering of (subsets of) the system actions, on
- the tuples of values associated with them, and on
- action timings.

The most elementary form of timing constraint, essentially adopted by all current timed LOTOS variants, is a time interval associated to an action. Thus, an action at gate g can occur *at some instant t* if at that time:

- all processes insisting on that gate have evolved into behaviours that admit a g-action as a first possible action (matching the ordering), *and*
- all these g-actions are *enabled*, meaning that at time t each one of them has been available for an amount of time falling into its associated time window (matching the timing), *and*
- all the g-actions can agree on establishing a common tuple of values (matching the values).

202   BOLOGNESI

As before, constraints are embedded into LOTOS processes, each process possibly expressing constraints of all three types, and constraint composition is achieved by the parallel composition operator.

Concerning the time domain, most existing proposals agree in requiring that it be at least *dense*, a *discrete* time domain being considered as insufficient for realistic specifications of a variety of systems. A distinction can then be made between conceiving the time domain as a user defined data type, or assuming it as primitive, e.g. the real numbers. There are advantages and disadvantages in both cases (for a discussion, see [BL95]). However, the reader should not be concerned about these two alternatives, since the timed LOTOS examples in the rest of the chapter can be well understood independently of these choices. We shall simply refer to a predefined sort called 'Time'; just for fixing ideas, the reader may safely think of time values as real numbers.

A time interval can be associated to an action by adding a new attribute to the action prefix construct, turning it into what we may call the *time-bounded action prefix*. An example:

```
g ?x:nat !5 [x < 3] {t1, t2};   STOP
```

The closed time interval {*t1, t2*} (we use braces because square brackets are already taken by the selection predicate) bounds the time at which the action is allowed to occur. All timed LOTOS proposals agree in adopting a *relative* timing policy: the aging of an action offer is measured relative to the first instant, say t_0, when the action has been made available. In our example, consisting of only one action, t_0 is the time when the behaviour is instantiated (started). For an action which is not the first one in a sequence, the reference time t_0 would be the time of occurrence of the immediately preceding action.

Consider, for example, the following refinements of the already introduced processes $P1$, $P2$, $P3$:

```
P1:    e;    g ?x:nat !5 [x < 3] {10, 20};              STOP
P2:    f;    g ?x:nat ?y:nat [y > 3];                   STOP
P3:    g ?x:nat ?y:nat [x MOD 2 = 1] {10, 20}; h;    STOP
```

and assume, again, that they are composed in parallel on the g-action. According to $P1$, the g-action is available between 10 and 20 time units after the occurrence of e; according to $P2$, a g-action is possible any time after the occurrence of f (a {0, ∞ } interval being implicitly assumed); and $P3$ is ready to synchronize on g any time between 10 and 20 time units after system startup. The global effect is that, under the conditions $t_f \leq 20$ and $t_e + 10 \leq 20$, where t_f and t_e are the occurrence times of actions f and e, respectively, the g-action is possible any time in the interval $[max\{t_f, t_e + 10\}, 20]$, with values for x and y established as in the previous, untimed case.

What happens when an availability interval expires and the action to which it is associated has not occurred yet? In the current proposals two possibilities are contemplated:

- **Strong timing**
  The action *must* occur within the upper time bound, unless disabled by the occurrence of another action. This is the approach we have adopted in all our proposals (see, e.g., [BL95]), inspired by the timing policy of Merlin and Farber's Time Petri Nets [MF76].
- **Weak timing**
  The action *may* occur; if it does, it takes place at some time instant within the interval. And, when the action has not taken place (has not been observed) within the specified time

interval, the behaviour offering that action turns into the idling process *STOP*, which is only able to let time pass. This is the approach of [MFV93] and [LL94], among others.

Having illustrated some basic elements for the formulation and composition of timing constraints we proceed by showing a typical behavioural scenario that can be easily expressed by them (and that occurs in a specification in the next section), namely the time spacing of non-consecutive actions. Two non-consecutive actions in a sequence are to be spaced in time according to some time constraints. Given the sequence of actions $a_1, a_2, \ldots, a_n$, we can specify that the delay between the occurrence of the first and last action must fall in the closed time interval $[t_1, t_2]$ by writing the parallel expression:

```
a1; a2; ...; an; EXIT (* ordering constraint *)
|[a1, an]|
a1; an {t1, t2}; EXIT (* timing constraint *)
```

We have structured our expression into two subexpressions, dealing, respectively, with an ordering and a timing constraint. Both subexpressions are formed by a sequence of actions followed by the special LOTOS process 'EXIT', also called *successful termination*, which, unlike the process 'STOP', is able to perform the successful termination action δ. The two parallel subexpressions must indeed synchronize on their final, implicit δ-actions, yielding a successful termination of the parallel composition itself. (In the context of the sequential composition 'P >> Q' only when the first process P terminates successfully, by turning into an EXIT rather than a STOP, can the subsequent process Q be enabled.) The semantics of the expression depends on our choice of weak vs. strong timing. In the first case we can only be sure that *if* a_n occurs, it will happen in the interval $[t_{a_1} + t_1, t_{a_1} + t_2]$. However, nothing prevents some initial subsequence of actions to be too slow and pass the $t_{a_1} + t_2$ limit before reaching action a_n, which then becomes unexecutable. The timing requirement is met only in a weak, or conditional sense. In the second case we are guaranteed that none of the actions $a_2, \ldots, a_n$ is allowed to occur later than time $t_{a_1} + t_2$, because the strong timing semantics implies that at time $t_{a_1} + t_2$ further time transitions (delays) are not admitted until a_n has taken place. Thus, the only possible evolution at that time is the (instantaneous) forced occurrence of all the actions left, up to a_n, which unblocks the flow of time. In light of the scenario above, we shall assume a strong timing policy in the subsequent examples.

The few time-related constructs and concepts that we have introduced so far are a sufficient basis for developing constraint-oriented specifications of time-dependent systems, as illustrated in the next section.

8.5 CONSTRAINT-ORIENTED SPECIFICATION OF THE GRC REQUIREMENTS IN A TIMED LOTOS

The GRC system (Generalized Railroad Crossing) is a frequently used example in this volume (see also [HL94]). The system operates a *Gate* (we shall always write it with upper-case initial, for distinguishing it from the LOTOS concept of 'gate') at a railroad crossing I, which lies in a region R. A set of trains travel through I on multiple tracks (in both directions). The Gate at the crossing is to be operated so that some *Safety* and *Utility* requirements be met. We do not provide a separate, informal description of the system and of its requirements because the constraint-oriented specification given below, with its informal comments, is (hopefully) self-contained and readable in a quite natural way – properties which we have claimed to be well promoted by the constraint-oriented style – and is deliberately adopted as our *unique* initial description of the system. Of course our formal description implies a somewhat arbitrary view of the system, but this is true of any other *informal* description (see also discussion on considering further events in the requirements specification, later in this section).

Before providing the LOTOS specification of the GRC system, we list the observable events involved. Note that we use the LOTOS syntax for denoting event sets. Thus, when we write 'leave ?n:nat' we refer to a set of LOTOS events characterized by the gate name *leave* and some natural number *n*.

The events that are essential for our specification of the *Safety* and *Utility* requirements of the GRC are listed below.

- **enterI** - Some train enters the crossing.
- **leave ?n:nat ?x:s** - Some train leaves the crossing. The variable *n*, a natural number, is meant to record the number of trains left in the crossing *after* this exit, while the variable *x*, of a sort *s* corresponding to the set of values {*raising, nonraising*} indicates whether or not the raising of the Gate is to be expected after this event. Thus, after event *leave !0 !raising* or event *leave !0 !nonraising* the crossing is (momentarily) clear.
- **lower** - A command to the Gate, which starts moving down.
- **down** - The Gate reaches its horizontal position.
- **raise** - A command to the Gate. which starts moving up.
- **up** - The Gate reaches its vertical position.

For conciseness, in the specification we shall take the liberty of not always repeating the list of actual gates in process instantiations, when the list is the same as the list of formal gates appearing in the header of the corresponding process definition. For example, process instantiation 'Safety[enterI, leave, down, raise]' can be simply written as 'Safety'. We shall also omit the keywords 'process' and 'endproc' delimiting process definitions, and the *functionality indicators* ':exit' and ':noexit' in specification and process headers.

The next subsection contains the complete formal specification of the GRC requirements. We shall interleave informal descriptions and their formalisations, using a special font for the latter. The prose fragments can be also understood as LOTOS comments inserted in the body of the formal specification, and as an integral part of the latter, although the special enclosing parentheses '(*' and '*)' are omitted.

8.5.1 Specification

```
specification GRC-requirements
[enterI, leave, lower, down, raise, up]
```

The specification involves two main requirements, called *Safety* and *Utility*, which deal, respectively, with the event sets {*down, enterI, leave, raise*} and {*leave, up, lower, enterI*} (note the slight notational abuse: *leave* is an event set itself, due to its associated parameters *n* and *x*, and set union is implied). The requirements are viewed as constraints on the ordering and (for *Utility* only) the timing of events, and are specified as LOTOS processes. A third process is introduced, called *Gate*, involving events *lower, down, raise, up*; it constrains the ordering and timing of the events that characterize the behaviour of the *Gate*. The three processes are

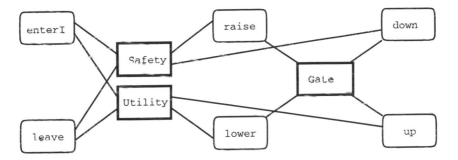

Figure 8.3   Process composition for GRC-requirements

composed in parallel, with synchronization on the shared gates. The composition is illustrated by the diagram in Figure 8.3. In G-LOTOS, the graphical syntax of LOTOS (see [BLV95], Chapter 20), diagrams like this are called *process-gate nets*.

```
behaviour

(Safety[down, enterI, leave, raise]
    |[enterI, leave]|
Utility[leave, up, lower, enterI]
)
    |[lower, down, raise, up]|
Gate[lower, down, raise, up]

where    (* opening the list of process definitions *)
```

The *Safety* requirement is understood as a constraint on the ordering of events *down*, *enterI*, *leave*, *raise*, without being concerned with their relative timings. A system behaviour is safe when its projection to the set of these actions appears as the endless iteration of event *down* (the gate reaching its horizontal position), followed by a nonempty burst of intermixed and eventually balanced *enterI* and *leave* actions (trains entering and leaving the crossing), during which the crossing is never clear, followed by either another burst of trains or by event *raise* (the gate leaving its horizontal position). Essentially, safety is achieved by making sure that the *enter* and *leave* activity is bracketed within a *down-raise* pair. A count is kept of the number of trains currently in the crossing, via natural number n. The *leave* event is enriched by a parameter indicating the number of trains left in the crossing *after* the event. Thus, the last train leaving the crossing is signalled by a *leave!0 ?x:s* event. The *x* parameter, with $x = raising$ or $x = nonraising$, is used for discriminating between *leave* events that are, respectively, not followed or followed by the raising of the Gate. This distinction would not be strictly necessary for expressing the *Safety* requirement in itself, but it is introduced for a correct matching of the latter with the formalization of the *Utility* requirement, where the same distinction is indeed necessary. We are assuming that the system starts with the gate in its upright position.

Recall that the symbol '[]' in expressions such as 'B1 [] B2' stands for the LOTOS *choice* operator, by which one can specify a behaviour as a pair of alternative behaviours *B1* and *B2*. Multiple alternatives can be composed by multiple occurrences of this binary operator. The occurrence of the first action of an alternative resolves the choice: the other alternatives are immediately eliminated. The guard operator preceding the behaviour *B* in expression '[<condition>]->B' specifies that B is enabled only if <condition> is met. Frequently the choice and guard operators are used jointly as in the *Safety* process; in this case, the conditions are not required to be disjoint.

```
Safety[down, enterI, leave, raise] :=
    down; enterI; Burst(1).

Burst[down, enterI, leave, raise](n : nat)      :=
        [n >= 1]->    enterI;                         Burst(n+1
    [] [n >  1]->    leave !(n-1) !nonraising;        Burst(n-1
    [] [n  = 1]->    (leave !0 !raising;       raise;  Safety
                     [] leave !0 !nonraising;  enterI; Burst(1)
                     ).
```

The Utility requirement is understood as a constraint on the ordering and relative timings of events *leave*, *up*, *lower* and *enterI*, and is concerned with assuring that the system be fair to the waiting cars. The Gate is lowered only if a train is arriving early enough. The Gate should not stay closed when the traffic of trains has terminated enough time before, and is expected to restart enough time later. However, the gate raises only if it can stay open enough time for a car to cross it. Note that car crossing is expected only between events *up* and *lower*, since immediately before the *up* event, and immediately after the *lower* event, the gate is moving and cars are supposed to stop (perhaps a red light is turned on for this purpose in the interval between events *lower* and *up*.)

```
Utility[leave, up, lower, enterI] :=
```

When the Gate is lowered, it must be the case that a train enters the crossing within c_1 time units.

```
    lower;   enterI {0, c1};      Utility
```

When the train leaving the crossing is the last one in a burst and the Gate is to be raised (as signalled by event *leave!0!raising*), then the latter must reach the *up* position within c_2 time units after the *leave*, the lower event must occur at most c_1 time units before a new *enter*, and the time delay between the last *leave* and the first new *enter* must be at least c_2+d+c_1, where d is a time sufficient for a car to go through the crossing. We use here the same solution illustrated by the example of Section 8.4. Two parallel sub-behaviours synchronize on events *leave* and *enterI*, then immediately terminate together (EXIT{0}), enabling a recursive instantiation of process *Utility*.

```
[] ((leave !0 !raising;   up {0, c2};   lower;   enterI {0, c1};
        EXIT{0})
    |[leave; enterI]|
    (leave !0 !raising;   enterI{c2 + d + c1, infinity};
        EXIT{0})
   )
    >>   Utility
```

When the train leaving the crossing is the last one in a burst but the Gate is not subsequently raised (as signalled by event *leave!0!nonraising*) then the time delay between the last *leave* and the first new *enter* is less than, or equal to $c2 + d + c1$ (for the meaning of these constants, see previous comment).

```
[]     leave !0 !nonraising;   enterI{0, c2 + d + c1};   Utility
```

Don't care conditions: when not interested by the constraints expressed in the three alternatives above, the events *leave* (other than a last exit), *up* and *enterI* should be potentially allowed to occur in any order.

```
[]     leave ?n:nat !nonraising [n /= 0];   Utility
[]     up;                                   Utility
[]     enterI;                               Utility
```

The *Gate* process constrains the ordering and timing of the events *lower, down, raise, up* that characterize the behaviour of the *Gate*. Once the *lower* command has been issued, the *Gate* is expected to reach its horizontal position (event *down*) in at most *gdown* time units, unless a *raise* command is issued in the meantime. In the symmetric case, once the *raise* command has been issued, the Gate is expected to reach its vertical position (event *up*) in at most *gup* time units, unless a *lower* command is issued in the meantime.

```
Gate[lower, down, raise, up] :=
    lower; (down{0, gdown}; Gate1   []   Gate1) .

Gate1[lower, down, raise, up] :=
    raise; (up{0, gup}; Gate   []   Gate) .


endspec (* GRC-requirements *)
```

8.5.2 Remarks

8.5.2.1 ON THE CONSTRAINT-ORIENTED NATURE OF THE SPECIFICATION

The constraint-oriented nature of the specification above has been already pointed out to some extent in the comments to its three topmost processes/constraints. One can appreciate further the benefits of this descriptive style by taking an alternative reading of the specification, by gates rather than by processes. This can be done by considering one gate at a time, and by identifying the different constraints imposed on the actions occurring at that gate by the processes insisting on it. Consider for example gate *enterI*. Process *Safety* requires that these actions be eventually bracketed within *down* and *raise* events, while it is liberal w.r.t. their timings: it enforces a pure ordering constraint. Process *Utility* requires that an *enterI* following a *lower* event do so at most within time $c1$ – a timing constraint. The process is not restrictive about the time between a last *leave* and the next *enterI* event, because the intervals that enforce two alternative time spacings between these events, namely $[c2 + d + c1, \text{infinity}]$ and $[0, c2 + d + c1]$ are complementary. However, the choice between these two timings corresponds to a choice between two different event sequences: only one of them includes the *up* and *lower* events between a last *leave* and a new *enterI*. This is a constraint where timing and ordering concerns are intertwined. Note that this specification includes only ordering and timing constraints; constraints on values are unnecessary.

8.5.2.2   ON CONSIDERING FURTHER EVENTS IN THE REQUIREMENTS

In [HL94] the axiomatic requirements specification ('AxSpec') involves also the entering of a train into a region R (*enterR*), an event which is imagined to be detected by sensors. Indeed, one could have provided an explicit description of the system of trains, in terms of LOTOS processes, with the understanding that the trains and the Gate represent the predefined 'physical components' of the system, as opposed to the *Safety* and *Utility* processes, which formalize the logical requirements that the design should meet. A process *Trains*, describing also the sensor-detected entrance into region R, can be found in the design presented in the next section. We have not included it here because we do not consider the detection of a train entering region R as necessary for formulating the system *requirements*. The latter can be conveniently concerned only with what happens at the crossing, and should express the ordering and timing conditions to be met by the events taking place there.

8.5.2.3   VALUE MISMATCH VS. TIMING MISMATCH IN CONSTRAINT COMPOSITION

When composing timing constraints we must be aware of an important difference from the 'static' case of composing constraints just on values. Consider the three natural variables a, b, and b', and the system of constraints:

$$2 \leq a \leq 4$$

$$2 \leq b \leq 4$$

$$8 \leq b' \leq 10$$

$$a + b = b'$$

Overall the system admits only one solution, namely $a = 4$, $b = 4$, $b' = 8$. The individual constraint for, say, a would admit $a = 2$ and $a = 3$ as 'local' solutions, but these 'tentative' partial solutions are immediately ruled out when considering the global picture. When dealing with timing constraints in composing event sequences, and building the global picture – a labelled transition system – incrementally, tentative partial solutions can not be readily ruled out, but may be temporarily considered as legal, until it is discovered that they lead to mismatched synchronizations, that is, to time deadlocks. An example of this fact is the following timed LOTOS parallel composition:

```
a{2,4}; b{2,4}; EXIT
|[b]|
b{8,10}; EXIT
```

which reuses the numerical constraints of the previous example in a dynamic setting. The execution of action a at times 2 or 3 prevents the synchronization on action b, and leads to a time deadlock, while executing a at time 4 leads to a successful completion of the specified composition.

Our timed LOTOS specification of the GRC-requirements does exhibit event sequences with timing mismatch. For example, the specification would admit the sequence of actions *lower, down, enterI, leave!0!raising, raise, up, lower, down*, all taking place at time 0, that is, without delays between them. After this sequence, process *Utility* would be in the middle of behaviour:

```
((leave !0 !raising;   up {0, c2};   lower;   enterI {0, c1};
     EXIT{0})
|[leave; enterI]|
  (leave !0 !raising;   enterI{c2 + d + c1, infinity};
     EXIT{0})
)
```

and, more precisely, at the point where the two instances of the *enterI* action are expected to synchronize. However, the instantaneous execution of actions *leave!0!raising, up, lower* leads to a mismatch between time intervals [0, c1] and [c2 + d + c1, infinity] associated to action *enterI*. Only the introduction of non-zero delays between some of the actions in this sequence may avoid the mismatch and allow the behaviour to proceed.

In conclusion, a side effect of using the constraint-oriented style in a timed setting is the potential generation of traces leading to mismatches between local timing conditions. These deadlocks represent 'solutions' that appear as locally feasible but globally unfeasible; as such, they must be considered as illegal, and disregarded. Thus, the correct system behaviour is understood as the one including all the traces that are never blocked by a timing mismatch.

8.6   DESIGN OF THE GRC SYSTEM IN A TIMED LOTOS

We shall now use timed LOTOS for designing a system which is meant to satisfy the GRC-requirements described in the previous section. The new specification allows us to illustrate a useful, recently proposed time-related construct (see, e.g., [LL94]) that was not necessary in the previous specification, namely the detection of action ages. The *age detector* is a variable associated to the action-prefix construct; when the action occurs the variable is bound to a value representing the amount of time during which the action has been continuously on offer. The age detecting variable is introduced by using the '@' symbol, as in the expression:

```
f; g ?x:nat {t1, t2} @t; B(x, t)
```

When the g action occurs, the time variable t is bound to the value $t_g - t_f$, where t_g and t_f are the absolute occurrence times of, respectively, actions g and f. This time value can be referred to, via variable t, in the behaviour following the g-action, much in the same way as the natural value established by the g-action can be referred to via variable x. These facts are put in evidence by the notation '$B(x, t)$', which stands for a generic behaviour expression with free occurrences of the x and t variables.

The observable events of the new specification, called 'GRC-design', are listed below.

- **enterR ?r:train-id** - Some train r enters the region R around the crossing, its passage being detected by a sensor.
- **enterI ?r:train-id** - Some train r enters the crossing.
- **leave ?r:train-id** - Some train r leaves the crossing.
- **lower** - The Gate starts moving down.
- **down** - The Gate reaches its horizontal position.
- **raise** - The Gate starts moving up.
- **up** - The Gate reaches its vertical position.

With respect to the requirements specification, we have introduced the new event *enterR*, which is crucial for the designed system to be aware in time of train arrivals and to operate the

Gate accordingly. Furthermore, the events *enterR*, *enterI* and *leave* are enriched by an attribute
r which identifies the train performing these actions. Notice also that event *leave* no longer
requires the parameters *n* and *x*.

In the formal specification we shall use some simple data structures and operations. For
conciseness, and because they are irrelevant to the purposes of this chapter, we do not provide their (slightly tedious) specification in ACT-ONE, but describe them informally in the
comments closest to their first occurrences.

8.6.1 Specification

```
specification GRC-design
    [enterR, enterI, leave, lower, down, raise, up]
    (n : nat)
```

The specification involves three main processes, called *Trains*, *Gate* and *Control*. Processes
Trains and *Gate* describe the movements of trains and the behaviour of the Gate, and represent
the system environment. Process *Control* is the actual object of our design: it monitors the
train moves and operates the *Gate* so that the Safety and Utility requirements of the previous
specification are met. The three processes are composed in parallel, with synchronization
on the shared events. The number of circulating trains is a parameter of the specification,
called *n*. The diagram in Figure 8.4 illustrates the process composition defined by the parallel
composition expression below. We remind briefly the meaning of the LOTOS symbol '| | |'.
The *interleaving* operator '| | |' is a limit case of the already introduced parallel composition
operator '|S|', where the set of synchronization gates *S* is empty: all the actions of the
composed processes are freely interleaved. Processes *Trains* and *Gate* are here composed
by the interleaving operator because they do not share any action, while they both must
independently offer some of their actions for synchronization with process *Control*.

```
behaviour

    (Trains[enterR, enterI, leave](n)
    |||
    Gate[lower, down, raise, up]
    )
    |[enterR, leave, raise, lower]|
    Control[enterR, leave, raise, lower](0, empty-time-table)

where   (* opening the list of process definitions *)
```

The system of circulating trains is modelled by process *Trains*, which is parameterized by
the number *n* of trains. The process consists of a set of *n Train* processes composed by the
interleaving operator, each being parameterized by a different train identifier *r*, with $1 \leq r \leq n$.

```
Trains[enterR, enterI, leave](n: nat)  :=

    [n > 0] ->
        (     Train[enterR, enterI, leave](n)
        |||   Trains(n-1)
        )
```

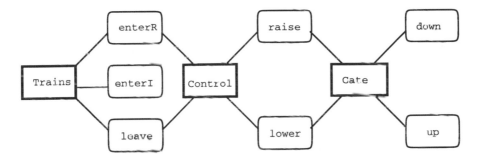

Figure 8.4 Process composition for GRC-design

A single train can perform three types of action: enter the region (*enterR*), enter the crossing (*enterI*) and leave the crossing (*leave*). Each one of these actions is enriched by the train identifier r. The time delay between entering the region and the crossing is bound by the interval $[e1, e2]$, the precise time value being chosen by an internal action i which takes place at the very first moment when the train appears in the system, namely when it enters the region (*enterR*). Note that the notation '$\{t\}$' is a shorthand for '$\{t, t\}$' – a degenerate closed time interval. The time delay between entering and leaving the crossing is unconstrained. Recall that the LOTOS generalized choice construct choice x:s [] B(x) allows one to specify multiple instances of behaviour B, one for each value of parameter x, and to offer the choice among them. In the process below the generalized choice operator is used for selecting the delay between the *enterR* and *enterI* actions. According to the LOTOS semantics, this value is chosen precisely when the urgent internal action i takes place.

```
Train[enterR, enterI, leave](r: nat)  :=

    enterR !r;
        choice t:Time [] [e1 =< t =< e2)] -> i {0};
            enterI !r  {t};    leave !r ;    Train(r)
```

The *Gate* process is unchanged with respect to the previous specification *GRC-requirements*.

```
Gate[lower, down, raise, up]  :=
    lower; (down{0, gdown}; Gate1    []   Gate1) .

Gate1[lower, down, raise, up]  :=
    raise; (up{0, gup}; Gate    []   Gate) .
```

Process *Control* monitors the trains by detecting their entering the region (*enterR*) and their leaving the crossing (*leave*), and operates the Gate via commands *lower* and *raise*. Note that this process is not required to be aware of trains entering the crossing (*enterI*). The process maintains the current absolute time *now* and a *time-table* associating to each known train the minimum absolute time at which it is expected to enter the crossing.

```
Control [enterR, leave, raise, lower]
    (now:Time, time-table:time-table-sort)   :=
```

When a train enters the region, the time-table is updated by adding (operation *add*) pair $(r, now + t + e1)$, where r is a train-id and $now + t + e1$ is the minimum absolute time at which train r may enter the crossing. The age t of action *enterR* is detected, and used also for updating the absolute time *now* when *Control* is re-instantiated.

```
enterR ?r:train-id @t;
    Control(now + t, add(time-table, (r, now + t + e1)))
```

The Gate must be down at the time of the earliest train arrival recorded in the *time-table*. This time is extracted from the table via the *min* operation, the *min* of an empty table being conventionally infinite. Thus, the *lower* command must be issued precisely *gdown* time units earlier than the earliest potential arrival, which accounts for the Gate lowering time in the worst case. (The current time *now* is subtracted for turning absolute time into relative time.) Age detection is used as in the previous branch of this multiple choice.

```
[]    lower {min(time-table) - gdown - now} @t;
          Control(now + t, time-table)
```

When a train leaves the crossing the time-table is updated by the operation *remove*, which eliminates its entry (the pair where the train identifier appears as a first element), and the minimum train arrival time in the updated table is considered: if this time is sufficient for accomodating the worst-case raising time of the gate (*gup*), plus the minimum time for a car to go through the crossing (*d*), plus the worst-case lowering time of the gate (*gdown*), then the gate is raised, otherwise it is not. Note that when the last train in a burst leaves, the time-table becomes empty, if no other train has entered region R in the meantime. Since the *min* of an empty time-table is infinite, the condition for raising the Gate are in this case always met. (We assume $e1 \geq gdown$: a train entering the region R can not reach the Gate faster than the worst Gate lowering time.) Age detection is used as in the previous branches.

```
[] leave ?r:train-id @t;
        (   [min(remove(time-table, r)) > now+t+gup+d+gdown]->
                raise{0}; Control(now+t, remove(time-table, r))
        []  [min(remove(time-table, r)) =< now+t+gup+d+gdown]->
                Control(now+t, remove(time-table, r))
        )

endspec (* GRC-design *)
```

8.6.2 Remarks

The top behaviour expression of the GRC-design is a parallel composition of processes, without hidden gates. The specification could in principle be considered both a resource-oriented and a constraint-oriented one, but it is not a strong representative of either style. We may consider it as resource-oriented, although, out of three processes, one defines the environment (*Trains*) another is perhaps a 'resource' (*Gate*), but is predefined and may also be understood as part of the environment, and only the *Control* is a designed 'resource'. We may consider it as constraint-oriented, in light of the fact that the three main processes cooperate in defining the orderings, the timings and also, in this case, the data attributes of the observable events, although all three processes have the strong flavour of physical, mechanical or electronic components, rather than abstract, logical constraints. Ultimately, the identification of the specification style is, in this case, of little importance.

8.7 CONCLUSIONS

The main purpose of this chapter has been to show that the constraint-oriented specification style is beneficial for human-oriented usage of formal specifications. It seems interesting to compare, in this respect, the constraint-oriented and state-oriented styles, without necessarily referring to the LOTOS language (which supports both), since the latter style in particular has been adopted by a number of approaches in the last decades, including the Z notation [S89], the *Estelle* Formal Description Technique [BD87] developed in ISO in parallel with LOTOS, up to the Timed Automata used for specifying the GRC system elsewhere in this volume. In Section 8.3 we have considered the (LOTOS) state-oriented style as appropriate for the late phases of the design and implementation trajectory, and for 'machine-oriented' usage. When the behaviour to be described is not too complex, a state-oriented approach may yield a reader-friendly document, essentially consisting of a case analysis: if in state s condition c is met, then event a is possible and state s' is reached, with some side-effects. A state-oriented specification is amenable of a 'random access' reading and writing policy, since one can start asking questions like "what if I am at state s and event a occurs?" and then specify the answer, or spot it in the specification, without the need to follow a predefined writing or reading path. One could perhaps go as far as considering the state-oriented approach as *declarative*, since it does support the explicit declaration of the rules which account for the elementary behavioural steps – the state transitions. However, one problem that we envisage in this approach is that the overall system behaviour is left implicit in the game of pre-conditions and post-conditions; while this is acceptable when the complexity of the system is confined to the structure of the global state, it becomes a limitation when it extends to the temporal patterns of events. Such complexity can already be handled more conveniently by the process algebraic approach in itself, which supports the explicit description of behavioural fragments of different sizes, rather than just of unitary size, and their composition by the various behavioural operators for sequencing, choice, disabling, etc.; advantages are then amplified when the parallel composition is used in a constraint-oriented setting. Composing constraints is like accumulating views about the system behaviour; each view focuses on one functional aspect and is correspondingly restrictive about some event orderings, timings, and data exchange opportunities, while being liberal about others. The structuring, or 'stratification' of a description into partial views might very well be considered as a particularly effective instantiation, in the context of specification languages, of the divide-and-conquer strategy that has earlier led, for programming, to block-structured languages such as PASCAL. We believe that, in this respect, state-based specification approaches can not be as successful as constraint-oriented ones.

Further comparison between the state-oriented and constraint-oriented approaches is possible if we look at the specific ways in which they handle the time dimension. For space reasons we simply point to one aspect in which the state-oriented approach seems weaker. For fixing ideas about the two styles, we refer, respectively, to the Timed Automata used in [HL94] (and elsewhere in this volume), and to our timed LOTOS. In Timed Automata one has to specify pre-conditions and post-conditions also for pure time passing transitions. Pre-conditions can in this case be used for ruling out excessively long time delays that would blur the eventual urgency of some event. However, the urgent event is described somewhere else in the specification, in a way which does not reveal any urgency: the time and action dimensions are somehow orthogonal, leaving to the reader the burden of tracing their interplay. Also in our timed LOTOS the time and action dimensions are orthogonal, but only at the semantic level, while at the syntactic level they are well integrated; for example, the time when an action becomes urgent can be spotted immediately. Again, the abstraction level of the state-oriented approach appears to be excessively low, with respect to the readability requirements of a specification language.

In this chapter we have deliberately ignored analysis and verification issues, that are often regarded as the central, if not unique purposes of adopting formal specification languages. Of course, once specifications *GRC-requirements* and *GRC-design* have been written, the obvious question is whether the latter is a correct implementation of the former, according to some formal implementation relation. Although research on behavioural equivalences and preorders has produced, starting around the early eighties, a wide variety of proposals, we are not aware of any semantic relation for dealing with full, timed process algebras (handling time and data) that has emerged as a 'standard', at least in the same way as bisimulation equivalence or testing-equivalence are considered 'standard' relations for untimed process algebras. One source of difficulty is that the notion of observation in time appears to be more tricky than that of observation in a time-less world, which is at the basis of the fundamental behavioural equivalences. Another, related source of difficulty is that, in the timed case, there exist some options in defining the underlying labelled transition systems, which, for example, may or may not include pure time-passing transitions. In case these are included, equivalences and preorders have to deal with transitions of quite different types (action-tansitions, including the special case of internal actions, and time-transitions, which might also be considered as a form of internal action...). There are of course various ways to rephrase the standard equivalence definitions by including time-related aspects (see, e.g., the *weak timed bisimulation equivalence* of [MFV93]) but the resulting relations are often less intuitive than their untimed counterparts.

The other fundamental factor in formal analysis and verification is of course tool support. Several such tools exist today for process algebras in general, and for LOTOS in particular; a remarkable example is the LotoSphere symbolic simulator called *SMILE*, which accepts full LOTOS specifications (including data) and avoids the combinatorial explosion of transition systems by handling data at a symbolic level and by applying 'narrowing' techniques (see [BLV95], Chapter 11). Unfortunately, equivalently effective tools for the analysis and simulation of timed LOTOS specifications are not yet available.

In conclusion, it is hard to predict when and how effectively the application of Timed LOTOS will be supported by adequate semantic relations (equivalences and preorders) and associated verification techniques and tools. Nevertheless, we wish to indicate a few reasons that justify some optimism. The ISO cycle for the revision of the LOTOS standard has not yet been completed, although convergence of the existing proposals for timed enhancements is at hand. Once the revised standard is delivered, it is likely that more effort will be put forth by academic and industrial environments (e.g., by national and international projects) in the development of analysis and simulation techniques and tools, similar to what has happened after the publication ot the LOTOS standard in 1989. The revised standard shall precisely define the timed transition system supporting the operational semantics for the timed case, and, on this basis, it shall eventually identify some useful semantic relations for the timed language, in analogy with the untimed standard; efforts for building verification tools would then conveniently concentrate on these relations.

Of course, the wide experience gained by several research groups in developing LOTOS tools is an excellent basis for the development of enhanced, timed LOTOS tools. For example, it seems quite reasonable to try and extend the symbolic manipulation approach of the above mentioned *SMILE* simulator to the treatment of time variables.

Another quite different and promising topic to be investigated is the translation from timed LOTOS into existing timed models, such as Timed Graphs [ACD90] and Timed Automata [LV92]. In our opinion these models offer complementary advantages w.r.t. timed process algebras: they come with effective analytical techniques, such as model checking, but appear relatively weak in terms of expressive flexibility. In this respect, the superimposition of a rich linguistic layer on top of them can only be beneficial. An example of a mapping from a timed process algebra into timed-graphs, for analytical purposes, is described in [BHKR94].

REFERENCES

[ACD90]   R. Alur, C. Courcoubetis, D. Dill. Model-checking for real-time systems. In *Proc. IEEE fifth annual symposium on Logics In Computer Science*, pages 414–425, 1990.

[BB87]   T. Bolognesi, E. Brinksma. Introduction to the ISO Specification Language LOTOS. *Computer Networks and ISDN Systems*, 14:25-59, 1987.

[BLT90]   T. Bolognesi, F. Lucidi, S. Trigila. From timed Petri Nets to Timed LOTOS. In L. Logrippo, R. L. Probert, H. Ural editors, *Proc. IFIP WG6.1 Tenth International Symposium on Protocol Specification, Testing, and Verification*, pages 395–408, North-Holland, 1990.

[BLT94]   T. Bolognesi, F. Lucidi, S. Trigila. Converging towards a timed LOTOS standard. *Computer Standards & Interfaces*, 16:87-118, 1994.

[BLV95]   T. Bolognesi, J. vd. Lagemaat, A. Vissers. *LotoSphere - Software development with LOTOS*. Kluwer Academic Publishers, 1995.

[BL92]   T. Bolognesi, F. Lucidi. Timed process algebras with urgent interactions and a unique powerful binary operator. *Lecture Notes in Computer Science*, number 600, pages 124-148. Springer-Verlag. 1992.

[BL95]   T. Bolognesi, F. Lucidi. A Timed Full LOTOS with Time/Action Tree Semantics. In T. Rus, C. Rattray editors, *Theories and Experiences for Real-Time System Development - AMAST Series in Computing - Chapter 8*. World Scientific Publishing Co., 1995.

[BHKR94]   S. Bradley, W. D. Henderson, D. Kendall, A. P. Robson. Application-Oriented Real-Time Algebra. *Software Engineering Journal*, 9(5):201-212, 1994.

[Bri89]   E. Brinksma (editor). ISO - Information Processing Systems - Open Systems Interconnection - LOTOS - A Formal Description Technique Based on the Temporal Ordering of Observational Behaviour. ISO International Standard IS8807, 1989.

[BD87]   S. Budkowski, P. Dembinski. An Introduction to Estelle: A Specification Language for Distributed Systems. *Computer Networks and ISDN Systems*, 14:3–23, 1987.

[EM85]   H. Ehrig, B. Mahr. *Fundamentals of Algebraic Specification 1 - Equations and Initial Semantics*, vol. 6 of *EATCS Monographs on Theoretical Computer Science*. Springer-Verlag, 1985.

[EVD89]   P. H. J. Van Eijk, C. A. Vissers, M. Diaz editors. *The Formal Description Technique LOTOS*. Elsevier Science Publishers B. V., North-Holland 1989.

[HL94]   C. Heitmeyer, N. Lynch. The Generalized Railroad Crossing: a Case Study in Formal Verification of Real-Time Systems. In *Proc. IEEE Real-Time Systems Symposium*, 1994.

[HTZ90]   W. H. P. van Hulzen, P. A. J. Tilanus, H. Zuidweg. LOTOS extended with clocks. In S. Vuong, editor, *Proc. Second International Conference on Formal Description Techniques (FORTE)*, North-Holland, 1990.

[H85]   C. A. R. Hoare. *Communicating Sequential Processes*. Prentice-Hall, 1985.

[LL94]   L. Leonard, G. Leduc. An enhanced version of Timed LOTOS and its application to a case study. In R. L. Tenney, M. Ümit Uyar editors, *Formal Description Techniques VI - Proc. IFIP WG6.1 Sixth International Conference on Formal Description Techniques (FORTE) - IFIP Transactions C-22*, pages 483–500, North-Holland, 1994.

[L92]   G. Leduc. An upward compatible timed extension to LOTOS. In K. R. Parker, G. A. Rose editors, *Formal Description Techniques IV - Proc. IFIP WG6.1 Fourth International*

Conference on Formal Description Techniques (FORTE) - IFIP Transactions C-2, pages 217–232, North-Holland, 1992.

[LV92]   N. Lynch, F. Vandraager. Forward and backward simulations for timing-based systems. *Lecture Notes in Computer Science*, number 600, pages 397–446. Springer-Verlag. 1992.

[MFV93]   C. Miguel, A. Fernández, L. Vidaller. Extending LOTOS towards performance evaluation. In M. Diaz, R. Groz, editors, *Formal Description Techniques V - Proc. IFIP WG6.1 Fifth International Conference on Formal Description Techniques (FORTE) - IFIP Transactions C-10*, pages 103–118, North-Holland, 1993.

[MF76]   P. Merlin, D. J. Farber. Recoverability of communication protocols - Implications of a theoretical study. *IEEE Trans. Commun., COM-24*, pages 1036-1043, 1976.

[M80]   R. Milner. *A Calculus of Communicating Systems*, vol. 92 of *Lecture Notes in Computer Science*. Springer-Verlag, 1980.

[QDA93]   J. Quemada, D. De Frutos, A. Azcorra. TIC: A TImed Calculus. *Formal Aspects of Computing*, 5:224–252, 1993.

[QF87]   J. Quemada, A. Fernández. Introduction of Quantitative Relative Time into LOTOS. In L. Logrippo, H. Rudin, C. H. West, editors, *Proc. IFIP WG6.1 Seventh International Symposium on Protocol Specification, Testing, and Verification*, pages 105–121, North-Holland, 1987.

[S89]   J. M. Spivey. *The Z Notation - A Reference Manual*. Prentice-Hall, 1989.

[T93]   K. J. Turner. *Using Formal Description Techniques*. Wiley, 1993.

[VSVS88]   C. A. Vissers, G. Scollo, M. Van Sinderen. Architecture and specification style in formal descriptions of distributed systems. In S. Aggarwal and K. Sabnani, editors, *Proc. IFIP WG6.1 Eighth International Symposium on Protocol Specification, Testing, and Verification*, pages 189–204, North-Holland, 1988.

9

Analysis of Real-Time Systems Using Symbolic Techniques

SÉRGIO CAMPOS, EDMUND CLARKE and MARIUS MINEA
Carnegie Mellon University

ABSTRACT

The chapter presents the use of symbolic model checking for the verification of real-time systems. This method automatically determines whether a temporal logic specification is satisfied for a finite state model. Symbolic techniques use a representation based on binary decision diagrams, which allow extremely large state spaces to be handled. Real-time logics have been introduced that allow the expression of time-bounded properties. In addition, we have introduced quantitative reasoning in the verification process. The algorithms that we have developed produce quantitative information about a real-time system, in addition to determining its correctness. This information allows a more detailed analysis than possible with previous methods. These techniques have been applied to the verification of a number of real-world system, of which we present a few examples: an aircraft controller, a robotics system, a medical monitoring system and the PCI local bus. These examples demonstrate that the techniques are able to verify complex, realistic systems.

9.1 INTRODUCTION

Determining the correctness of a real-time system is a complex task. Temporal logic model checking is a technique for performing this task efficiently. In this method an exhaustive search of a finite-state model is performed and all its execution sequences are explored automatically. A large number of real-time systems can be modeled by finite-state representations, making it possible to use this technique in their verification. Moreover, model checking has proved to be efficient enough to be applicable to systems of industrial size. This chapter presents the model checking method and how it can be used in the verification of real-time systems.

The system being verified is modeled as a state-transition graph, and specifications are

---

Formal Methods For Real-Time Computing, Edited by Heitmeyer and Mandrioli
© 1996 John Wiley & Sons Ltd

expressed as formulas of a propositional temporal logic. The model is searched to determine whether it satisfies the formula. In case the formula is not satisfied, a counterexample is produced. It consists of an execution trace that shows why the formula is violated. Counterexamples help the designer locate the source of the error and correct it.

Symbolic techniques have been developed that increase the efficiency of the model checker significantly [BCM$^+$90, McM92]. A symbolic model checking algorithm is one in which the transition relation is represented implicitly by binary decision diagrams (BDDs) [Bry86], and states are not explicitly enumerated. BDDs eliminate redundancy from the model, allowing extremely large state spaces to be represented. Models with up to 10^{30} states can often be verified in minutes. Our work is based on the symbolic model checking system SMV (Symbolic Model Verifier), developed at Carnegie Mellon University [McM92]. SMV has been used extensively in the verification of industrial designs, including the Futurebus+ cache coherence protocol [CGH$^+$93].

In the original system, however, timing properties cannot be directly expressed. Properties are represented by formulas in the temporal logic CTL (Computation Tree Logic). This logic can express properties such as "event p will happen sometime in the future". However, the property that "event p will happen in at most x units of time" can only be expressed using nested next-time operators. In real-time systems properties of the latter type appear frequently, because the execution time has to be bounded in order to make the system predictable. CTL has been augmented to express real-time properties using the *bounded until operator* [EMSS90], and the algorithms have been extended to check formulas involving operators of this type. The new notation allows a much more compact and convenient way of expressing bounded properties.

These algorithms assume that timing constraints are given explicitly in the formula. The designer provides a constraint on response time for some operation, and the verifier automatically determines if it is satisfied or not. However, these operators do not provide any information about how well the system actually performs in comparison to the given constraint, although this information can be extremely useful in analyzing the behavior of the system. We have developed algorithms to compute quantitative timing information, such as exact upper and lower bounds on the time between a request and the corresponding response. Our algorithms provide insight into *how well* a system works, rather than just determining whether it works at all. They enable a designer to determine the timing characteristics of a complex system given the timing parameters of its components. This information is especially useful in the early phases of system design, when it can be used to establish how changes in a parameter affect the global behavior of the system.

Several other techniques for analyzing the behavior of a real-time system exist. The rate monotonic scheduling theory (RMS) [LSST91, LL73, SKG91] is one example. The RMS theory consists of two components, the first being an algorithm for assigning priorities to tasks in order to maintain predictability. This algorithm assigns higher priorities to processes with shorter periods. Optimal response time with respect to static priority algorithms is guaranteed by the RMS theory if priorities are assigned according to this rule [LL73]. The second component of the RMS theory is a schedulability test based on total CPU utilization; a set of processes (which have priorities assigned according to RMS) is schedulable if the total utilization is below a computed threshold. If the utilization is above this threshold, schedulability is not guaranteed. Moreover, this analysis imposes a series of restrictions on the set of processes. Only certain types of processes are considered with limitations, for example, on periodicity and synchronization. Recent work has extended this theory to more general classes of processes [HKL94], but limitations still exist.

Another approach to schedulability analysis uses algorithms for computing the set of reachable states of a finite-state system [FC93, GL90]. A model for the real-time system is constructed with the added constraint that whenever an exception occurs (e.g. a deadline is missed) the system transitions to a special exception state. Verification consists of computing the set of reachable states and checking whether the exception state is in this set. No restrictions are imposed on the model in this approach, but the algorithm only checks if exceptions can occur or not. Other types of properties cannot be verified, unless encoded in the model as exceptions. Symbolic model checking techniques have also been extended to handle real-time systems [YMW93]. However, this method as well as the others mentioned only determines if the system satisfies a given property, and does not provide any more information on its behavior. In [CHLR93] a tool for analyzing real-time systems is presented that generates quantitative information. This tool uses simulation and model checking techniques. However, the quantitative information produced by the model checker is less general than the information generated by our method.

All of our algorithms use a discrete model of time. In recent years, there has been considerable research on continuous time models [ACD90, AD90, HNSY92, Lew90, NSY92, HHWT95]. Most of these models use a transition relation with a finite set of real-valued clocks and constraints on times when transitions may occur. It can be argued that such models lead to more accurate results than discrete time models. However, continuous time models require an infinite state space because the time component in the states can take arbitrary real values. Most verification procedures based on this type of model depend on constructing a finite quotient space called a *region graph* out of the infinite state space. Unfortunately, the region graph construction is very expensive in practice and current implementations of algorithms that use it can only handle at most a few thousand states. Because we use a discrete model of time, we are able to take advantage of *symbolic* techniques [BCM+90, McM92] in which the transition relation is represented by a binary decision diagram (BDD). This enables us to handle systems that are several orders of magnitude larger than can be handled using continuous time techniques.

To demonstrate how our techniques work, we have applied them to a number of real-time systems. We have analyzed an aircraft controller and have been able to determine its schedulability as well as the response time for critical components. In other examples such as a robotics system and a medical monitoring system we have even been able to pinpoint inefficiencies, suggest improvements to the design and analyze their effects. We have also analyzed the performance of the PCI local bus and bounded transaction latency in several system configurations.

9.2 TEMPORAL LOGIC MODEL CHECKING

Extensive simulation is currently the most widely used verification technique. However, simulation does not exhaust all possible behaviors of a computing system. Exhaustive simulation is too expensive, and non-exhaustive simulation can miss important events, especially if the number of states in the system being verified is large. Other approaches for verification include theorem provers, term rewriting systems and proof checkers. These techniques, however, are usually very time consuming, and require user intervention to a large degree. Such character-istics limit the size of the systems they can verify in practice.

Temporal logic model checking [CE81, CES86] is an alternative approach that has achieved significant results recently. Efficient algorithms are able to verify properties of extremely large systems. In this technique, specifications are written as formulas in a propositional temporal logic and computer systems are represented by state-transition graphs. Verification is accomplished by an efficient breadth first search procedure that views the transition system as a model for the logic, and determines if the specifications are satisfied by that model.

There are several advantages to this approach. An important one is that the procedure is completely automatic. The model checker accepts a model description, specifications written as temporal logic formulas and determines if the formulas are true or not for that model. Another advantage is that, if the formula is not true, the model checker will provide a counterexample. The counterexample is an execution trace that shows why the formula is not true. This is an extremely useful feature because it can help locate the source of the error and speed up the debugging process. Another advantage is the ability to verify partially specified systems. Useful information about the correctness of the system can be gathered before all the details have been determined. This allows the verification of a system to proceed concurrently with its design. Consequently verification can provide valuable hints that will help designers eliminate errors earlier and define better systems.

Properties to be verified are described as formulas in a propositional temporal logic. The system for which the properties should hold is given as a state transition graph. It defines a model for the temporal logic since the semantics of the logic are given in terms of state transition graphs. The model checker traverses this graph and verifies if the model satisfies the formula. Checking that a single model satisfies a formula is much simpler than proving that a formula is valid for all possible models. Because of this fact model checkers can be more efficiently implemented than theorem provers. Clarke and Emerson [CE81] developed the first algorithm. This algorithm used adjacency lists to represent the transition graph and had a complexity that was polynomial in the size of the model and in the length of the formula. This and other equivalent systems were able to handle graphs with up to 10^5 states.

Around 1987, however, the concept of *symbolic model checking* was introduced [BCM+90, McM92]. In the new approach the transition relation is represented implicitly by boolean formulas, and implemented by *ordered binary decision diagrams* [Bry86]. This usually results in a much smaller representation for the transition relation, allowing the size of the models being verified to increase up to more than 10^{30} states. The symbolic model checking approach will be explained in more detail later.

9.3 BINARY DECISION DIAGRAMS

Ordered binary decision diagrams (BDD) are an efficient way to represent boolean formulas. BDDs often provide a much more concise representation than traditional representations like conjunctive normal form or disjunctive normal form. They can also be manipulated very efficiently [Bry86]. Another advantage offered by BDDs is that they provide a *canonical representation* for boolean formulas. This property means that two boolean formulas are logically equivalent if and only if they have isomorphic representations. It greatly simplifies the execution of operations that are performed frequently like checking equivalence of two formulas or deciding if a given formula is satisfiable or not. Because of these characteristics,

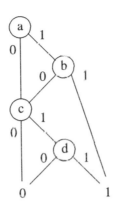

Figure 9.1   BDD for formula $(a \wedge b) \vee (c \wedge d)$

BDDs have found application in the implementation of many computer aided design and verification tools.

Boolean formulas can be represented by binary decision trees. The nodes in the decision tree correspond to the variables of the formula. Descendants of a node are labelled with *true* or *false*. The value of the formula for a given assignment of values to the variables can be found by traversing the tree from root to leaf. At each node the descendant labelled with the value of that variable is chosen. Each leaf corresponds to a particular assignment to the variables, and contains the truth value of the formula for that assignment.

This representation is not particularly compact, because it may store the same information repeatedly in different places. BDDs are derived from binary decision trees but their structure is a directed acyclic graph instead of a tree. Redundant information in the structure is avoided by eliminating common subtrees. As in decision trees, nodes are visited in sequence, from root to leaf. However, BDDs impose a total ordering in which the variables occur in this sequence. For example, the BDD in figure 9.1 represents the formula $f = (a \wedge b) \vee (c \wedge d)$ using the ordering $a < b < c < d$ for the variables.

Given an assignment for the variables in f we can decide if this assignment satisfies the formula by traversing the BDD from root to leaf. At each node we follow the path that corresponds to the value assigned to the variable in the node. The leaf indicates if the formula is satisfied or not for that particular assignment. Notice that redundancy is eliminated in two ways. Common subtrees are not replicated, as can be seen from the paths when a is false and when b is false. Also, when all the leaves of a subtree lead to the same value, the subtree is eliminated, and a leaf of that value is inserted at its place. Notice in the figure that when a and b are both true a subtree containing the variables c and d is eliminated because all of its leaves would have the value 1.

For any boolean formula and with a fixed variable ordering there exists a unique BDD [Bry86]. The size of the BDD is critically dependent on the variable ordering. It is exponential in the number of variables in the worst case. Given a good variable ordering, however, the size is linear in most practical cases. Using a good variable ordering is very important. But finding the optimal order is in itself a NP-complete problem. Nevertheless, there are many heuristics that work quite well in practice.

Efficient algorithms exist to handle boolean formulas represented by BDDs. Given BDD representations for f and g, algorithms for computing $\neg f$ and $f \vee g$ are given in [Bry86].

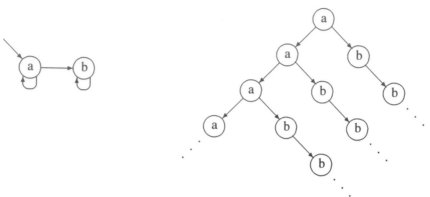

Figure 9.2 State transition graph and corresponding computation tree

Algorithms for quantification over boolean variables and substitution of variable names are also required by the model checker. It is simple to compute the restriction of a formula f with a variable v set to 0 or 1. We will denote the restriction of f with v set to 0 by $f|_{v=0}$, and the restriction of f with v set to 1 by $f|_{v=1}$. The formula $\exists v[f]$ is defined as $f|_{v=0} \vee f|_{v=1}$, and $\forall v[f]$ is defined as $\neg \exists v[\neg f]$. Substitution of variable names can be accomplished using the quantification algorithm. $f<v \leftarrow w>$ denotes the substitution of variable w for variable v in formula f. It is computed as $f<v \leftarrow w>= \exists v[(v \Leftrightarrow w) \wedge f]$. These operations are performed very frequently in the model checker, and more efficient algorithms are used in the actual system. Describing these algorithms is out of the scope of this paper, but they can be found in [BCL90].

9.4 COMPUTATION TREE LOGIC

Computation tree logic, CTL, is the logic used by SMV to express properties that will be verified. *Computation trees* are derived from state transition graphs. The graph structure is unwound into an infinite tree rooted at the initial state, as seen in figure 9.2. Paths in this tree represent all possible computations of the program being modelled. Formulas in CTL refer to the computation tree derived from the model. CTL is classified as a *branching time* logic, because it has operators that describe the branching structure of this tree.

Formulas in CTL are built from atomic propositions, where each proposition corresponds to a variable in the model, boolean connectives $\neg$ and $\wedge$, and *temporal operators*. Each operator consists of two parts: a path quantifier followed by a temporal operator. Path quantifiers indicate that the property should be true of *all* paths from a given state (**A**), or *some* path from a given state (**E**). The temporal quantifier describes how events should be ordered with respect to time for a path specified by the path quantifier. They have the following informal meanings:

- **F** φ (φ holds sometime in the future) is true of a path if there exists a state in the path that satisfies φ.
- **G** φ (φ holds globally) is true for a path if φ is satisfied by all states in the path.
- **X** φ (φ holds in the next state) means that φ is true in the next state of the path.
- φ **U** ψ (φ holds until ψ holds) is satisfied by a path if ψ is true in some state in the path, and in all preceding states, φ holds.

Formally, the syntax for CTL can be defined by:

- Every atomic proposition p is a CTL formula.
- If f and g are CTL formulas, then so are $\neg f$, $f \wedge g$, $\mathbf{EX}\ f$, $\mathbf{EG}\ f$ and $\mathbf{E}[f\ \mathbf{U}\ g]$.

The semantics of CTL formulas are defined with respect to a labeled state-transition graph, which is a 5-tuple $\mathcal{M} = (P, S, L, N, S_0)$, where P is a set of atomic propositions, S is a finite set of states, L is a function labeling each state with a set of atomic propositions, $N \subseteq S \times S$ is a transition relation, and S_0 is the set of initial states. A path is an infinite sequence of states $s_0 s_1 s_2...$, such that $N(s_i, s_{i+1})$ is true for every i.

If f is true in a state s of structure $\mathcal{M}$, we write $\mathcal{M}, s \models f$. We write $\mathcal{M} \models f$ if $\mathcal{M}, s \models f$ for all states s in S_0. The satisfaction relation is defined inductively as follows (Given the model $\mathcal{M}$, we abbreviate $\mathcal{M}, s \models \varphi$ by $s \models \varphi$):

1. If φ is the atomic proposition $v \in P$, then $s \models \varphi$ if and only if $v \in L(s)$.
2. $s \models \neg\varphi$ iff it is not the case that $s \models \varphi$.
3. $s \models \varphi \wedge \psi$ iff $s \models \varphi$ and $s \models \psi$.
4. $s \models \mathbf{EX}\ \varphi$ iff there exists a path $\pi = s_0 s_1 s_2...$ starting at $s = s_0$, such that $s_1 \models \varphi$.
5. $s \models \mathbf{EG}\ \varphi$ iff there exists a path π starting at s such that for every state s' on π, $s' \models \varphi$.
6. $s \models \mathbf{E}[\varphi\ \mathbf{U}\ \psi]$ iff there exists a path $\pi = s_0 s_1 s_2...$ starting at $s = s_0$ and some $i \geq 0$ such that $s_i \models \psi$ and for all $j < i$, $s_j \models \varphi$.

The following abbreviations are used in CTL formulas:

$$\mathbf{AX}\ f \equiv \neg\mathbf{EX}\ \neg f.$$
$$\mathbf{EF}\ f \equiv \mathbf{E}[\text{true}\mathbf{U}f]$$
$$\mathbf{AF}\ f \equiv \neg\mathbf{EG}\ \neg f$$
$$\mathbf{AG}\ f \equiv \neg\mathbf{EF}\ \neg f$$
$$\mathbf{A}[f\mathbf{U}g] \equiv \neg\mathbf{E}[\neg g\mathbf{U}\neg f \wedge \neg g] \wedge \neg\mathbf{EG}\neg g.$$

Some examples of CTL formulas are given below to illustrate the expressiveness of the logic.

- $\mathbf{AG}(req \rightarrow \mathbf{AF}\ ack)$: It is always the case that if the signal req is high, then eventually ack will also be high.
- $\mathbf{EF}(started \wedge \neg ready)$: It is possible to get to a state where $started$ holds but $ready$ does not hold.
- $\mathbf{AG}\ \mathbf{EF}\ restart$: From any state it is possible to get to the $restart$ state.
- $\mathbf{AG}(send \rightarrow \mathbf{A}[send\ \mathbf{U}\ recv])$: It is always the case that if $send$ occurs, then eventually $recv$ is true, and until that time, $send$ must remain true.

9.5 SYMBOLIC MODEL CHECKING

Early model checking algorithms represented the transition graph through adjacency lists. All existing states were explicitly enumerated. Since the model can have an exponential number of states in the worst case, this frequently caused state explosion problems. The size of systems that could be verified was severely limited. Symbolic model checking represents states and transitions using boolean formulas. This usually generates smaller representations, because it can automatically eliminate redundancy in the graph. Implementing these boolean formulas as BDDs leads to very efficient algorithms for model checking that are able to verify much larger systems than previous ones. This section will explain the symbolic model checking approach.

9.5.1 Representing the Model

A model of the system in our algorithm is a labeled state-transition graph $\mathcal{M}$, and assertions about the system are expressed as CTL formulas. The key to the efficiency of the algorithm is to use BDDs to represent the labeled state-transition graph and to verify if the formula is true or not. The following method will be used to represent the transition relation as a BDD. Assume that system behavior is determined by the boolean variables $V = \{v_0, ..., v_{n-1}\}$. Let $V' = \{v'_0, ..., v'_{n-1}\}$ be a second copy of these variables. We will use the variables in V to represent the value of the variables in the current state, and the variables in V' to represent the value in the next state. The relationship between values of variables in the current and the next states is written as a boolean formula using V and V'. This will generate the boolean formula N representing the transition relation. This formula will then be converted to a BDD.

$$N(v_0, ..., v_{n-1}, v'_0, ..., v'_{n-1})$$

By definition, time passes by one time unit at each transition. This does not restrict the models that can be verified by the method, because non-unit transitions can be constructed from a sequence of unit transitions. Non deterministic transition times can also be implemented in the same way, by using stuttering [Cam93].

A model can also be described by its parallel components. Given a set of processes and a state-transition graph for each, we can construct a global transition system using parallel composition. Both synchronous and asynchronous composition are implemented using BDDs. In synchronous composition, all processes transition at the same time, while in asynchronous composition only one transitions. The choice of which process executes is non-deterministic. Fairness is implemented to avoid starvation [McM92].

The composition algorithm is extremely expensive, it generates an exponential number of states in the composed graph. However, the efficiency of symbolic model checking and the fact that our method uses discrete time allows the use of composition in several practical problems without state explosion problems. For example, the aircraft controller described later is defined by 15 parallel processes.

Finally, we represent states by the values of the atomic propositions in those states. In order to guarantee that we can identify states uniquely, we must make the assumption that different states have different labeling of propositions. More formally, we assume that for any two states s_1 and s_2 in S, if $L(s_1) = L(s_2)$ then $s_1 = s_2$. This assumption does not, however, impose any restrictions on the model, since extra atomic propositions can be added in order to make $L(s_1) \neq L(s_2)$ for distinct states s_1 and s_2 [BCMD90].

9.5.2 The Model Checking Algorithm

Given a CTL formula φ and a model $\mathcal{M}$ represented as described above, we want to verify if φ is satisfied in the initial states of $\mathcal{M}$. The model checking algorithm is defined inductively over the structure of CTL formulas. It accepts the formula as an argument (and $\mathcal{M}$ as an implicit argument), recurses over the structure of φ and returns a BDD that has one boolean variable for every atomic proposition in V. The resulting BDD is true in a state if and only if φ is true in that state. The algorithm is:

- If φ is an atomic proposition p, return the BDD that is true if and only if p is true. This is simply the BDD for p.
- If φ is $\neg f$ or $f \wedge g$, use the standard BDD algorithms for computing boolean connectives.
- If φ is **EX** f, then we must verify if f is true in a successor state of the current state. **EX** f is true in a state t if and only if there exists a state s such that f is true in state s, and there exists a transition from t to s:

$$t \models \mathbf{EX} \, f \quad \text{iff} \quad \exists s [f \langle s \rangle \wedge N(t, s)]$$

where $f\langle s \rangle$ means the value of formula f in state s. This value can be computed using the existential quantification algorithms described previously. $f\langle s \rangle$ is true if and only if $s \models f$. However, this operation occurs frequently, and it is important to compute it in an efficient manner; efficient algorithms for this purpose are discussed in [BCL90].

- If φ is $\mathbf{E}[f\mathbf{U}g]$, the BDD that represents the states where $\mathbf{E}[f\mathbf{U}g]$ is true can be computed by iterating:

$$\mathbf{E}[f\mathbf{U}g] = g \vee (f \wedge \mathbf{EX} \, \mathbf{E}[f\mathbf{U}g])$$

- If φ is $\mathbf{EG}f$, the algorithm is defined in a similar way. It searches for the greatest fixpoint $\mathbf{EG}f$ instead, and uses the following formula:

$$\mathbf{EG}f = f \wedge \mathbf{EX} \, \mathbf{EG}f$$

- All other CTL operators are written in terms of the ones presented.

9.6 REAL-TIME LOGICS

The logic CTL can be used to specify many properties of finite state systems. However, there is an important class of properties that cannot be adequately handled using this logic. This class consists of the properties that involve *quantitative* constraints, that is, the class of properties which place bounds on response time. In CTL it is possible to state that some event will happen in the future. However, the property that some event will happen at most x time units in the future cannot be expressed directly, only by nesting **EX** or **AX** operators. In this section we will discuss one way of augmenting CTL to permit a more efficient representation of such properties.

In order to represent bounded properties, we add time intervals to the existing temporal operators, as described in [EMSS90]. The basic temporal operator that we use in our real-time logic is the *bounded until* operator which has the form: $\mathbf{U}_{[a,b]}$, where $[a, b]$ defines the time interval in which our property must be true. We say that $f\mathbf{U}_{[a,b]}g$ is true of some path if g holds in some future state s on the path, f is true in all states between the beginning of the path and s, and the distance from this state to s is within the interval $[a, b]$. The bounded **EG** operator can be defined similarly. Other temporal operators are defined in terms of these.

More formally, we extend our CTL semantics to include the *bounded until* by adding the following clauses to the formal semantics given in section 9.4:

6. $s \models E[\varphi U_{[a,b]}\psi]$ iff there exists a path $\pi = s_0 s_1 s_2 ...$ starting at $s = s_0$ and some i such that $a \leq i \leq b$ and $s_i \models \psi$ and for all $j < i$, $s_j \models \varphi$.

7. $s \models EG_{[a,b]}\varphi$ iff there exists a path $\pi = s_0 s_1 s_2 ...$ starting at $s = s_0$ and for all i such that $a \leq i \leq b$, $s_i \models \varphi$.

As an example of the use of the *bounded until* consider the property "It is always true that p may be followed by q within 3 time units". this property can be expressed as $AG(p \rightarrow EF_{[0,3]}q)$. The bounded **F** operator is derived from the *bounded until* just as in the unbounded case, i.e. $EF_{[a,b]}f \equiv E[\text{true}U_{[a,b]}f]$.

In order to implement this operator, we will use a fixpoint computation that is similar to the one implemented in CTL. It is easy to see that the formula $E[fU_{[a,b]}g]$ can be expressed in the form:

if $a > 0$ and $b > 0$: $E[fU_{[a,b]}g] = f \wedge EXE[fU_{[a-1,b-1]}g]$
if $b > 0$: $E[fU_{[0,b]}g] = g \vee (f \wedge EXE[fU_{[0,b-1]}g])$
and $E[fU_{[0,0]}g] = g$

Other operators are defined similarly.

Consider the first of these cases. We compute the sets of states where f is true for a steps. During this computation, a fixpoint may be reached before a iterations have passed. When this happens, we can skip to the second case. By using this optimization, the number of required iterations may be reduced when the time interval is large, but a fixpoint is reached quickly. The same optimization can also applied in the second case. If a fixpoint is reached before $b - a$ iterations, with b and a being respectively the upper and lower bounds of the operator, we can immediately proceed to the third case.

9.7 QUANTITATIVE ALGORITHMS

This section presents algorithms that compute quantitative timing information about a system, such as minimum and maximum time delays between specified events. We also present algorithms that compute the minimum and maximum number of occurrences of a condition on any path between two given events. These algorithms provide detailed information about the behavior of the system, and can be used to verify its temporal correctness, and well as its performance.

Our algorithms work on boolean formulas representing the sets of states in which the given events hold. They explore the state space starting in the set of states satisfying one of the events, traverse all possible execution sequences and stop when the second event is reached. The fact that all operations consider sets of states instead of individual states is one of the main reasons for the efficiency of our method.

We consider the minimum delay algorithm first (figure 9.3). The algorithm takes two sets of states as input, *start* and *final*. It returns the length of (i.e. number of edges in) a shortest path from a state in *start* to a state in *final*. If no such path exists, the algorithm returns infinity. The formula $T(S) = \{s' \mid N(s, s')$ holds for some $s \in S\}$ represents the set of all successors of states in a state set S. It can be easily constructed from the formula for S and the formula for the transition relation in one step, regardless of the number of states in S and $T(S)$. The function T, the state sets R and R', and the operations of intersection and union can all be easily implemented using BDDs.

proc *minimum (start, final)*
$i = 0$;
$R = start$;
$R' = T(R) \cup R$;
while $(R' \neq R \wedge R \cap final = \emptyset)$ **do**
      $i = i + 1$;
      $R = R'$;
      $R' = T(R') \cup R'$;
if $(R \cap final \neq \emptyset)$
      then return i;
      else return ∞;

proc *maximum (start, final)*
$i = 0$;
$R = TRUE$;
$R' = not\text{-}final$;
while $(R' \neq R \wedge R' \cap start \neq \emptyset)$ **do**
      $i = i + 1$;
      $R = R'$;
      $R' = T'^{-1}(R') \cap not\text{-}final$;
if $(R = R')$
      then return ∞;
      else return i;

Figure 9.3   Minimum and Maximum Delay Algorithms

The first algorithm is relatively straightforward. Intuitively, the loop in the algorithm computes the set of states that are reachable from *start*. If at any point, we encounter a state satisfying *final*, we return the number of steps taken to reach that state.

Next, we consider the maximum delay algorithm. This algorithm also takes *start* and *final* as input. It returns the length of a longest path from a state in *start* to a state in *final*. If there exists an infinite path beginning in a state in *start* that never reaches a state in *final*, the algorithm returns infinity. The function $T^{-1}(S')$ gives the set of states that are predecessors of some state in S' (i.e. $T^{-1}(S') = \{s \mid N(s, s')$ holds for some $s' \in S'\}$). We also denote by *not-final* the set of all states that are not in *final*. As before, the algorithm is implemented using BDDs, however, a backward search is required in this case.

We now present variations of these algorithms that determine the minimum and maximum number of times a given condition holds on any path from starting to final states. Both algorithms in this section take as input three sets of states: *start*, *cond* and *final*. Technically, the algorithms compute the minimum and the maximum number of states that belong to *cond*, over all finite paths that begin with a state in *start* and terminate upon reaching *final*.

To guarantee that the minimum (maximum) is well-defined, we assume that any path beginning in *start* must reach a state in *final* in a finite number of steps. This can be checked using the maximum delay algorithm described in the previous section. Finally, we ensure that all computations involve only reachable states, by intersecting *start* with the set of reachable states computed *a priori*.

To keep track at each step of the number of states in *cond* that have been traversed, we define a new state-transition system, in which the states are pairs consisting of a state in the original system and a positive integer. Thus, if the original state-transition graph has state set S, then the augmented state set will be $S_a = S \times \mathbb{N}$.

If $N \subseteq S \times S$ is the transition relation for the original state-transition graph, we define the augmented transition relation $N_a \subseteq S_a \times S_a$ as

$$N_a(\langle s, k \rangle, \langle s', k' \rangle) = N(s, s') \land (s' \in cond \land k' = k + 1 \lor s' \notin cond \land k' = k)$$

In other words, there will be a transition from $\langle s, k \rangle$ to $\langle s', k' \rangle$ in the augmented transition relation N_a iff there is a transition from s to s' in the original transition relation N and either $s' \in cond$ and $k' = k + 1$ or $s' \notin cond$ and $k' = k$. We also define T to be the function that for a given set $U \subseteq S_a$ returns the set of successors of all states in U. More formally, $T(U) = \{u' \mid N_a(u, u') \text{ holds for some } u \in U\}$. In the actual BDD-based implementation, an initial bound k_{max} can be selected to achieve a finite representation for k, and new BDD variables can be added dynamically if this bound is exceeded. The system is still finite-state because all paths we consider are finite and k is bounded by their maximum length.

> **proc** *mincount* (*start, cond, final*)
> *current_min* = ∞;
> $R = \{\langle s, 1 \rangle \mid s \in start \cap cond\} \cup \{\langle s, 0 \rangle \mid s \in start \cap \overline{cond}\}$;
> **loop**
>   *Reached_final* = $R \cap Final$;
>   **if** *Reached_final* $\neq \emptyset$ **then**
> $m = \min\{k \mid \langle s, k \rangle \in Reached\_final\}$;
>   **if** $m < current\_min$ **then** *current_min* = m;
> $R' = R \cap Not\_final$;
>   **if** $R' = \emptyset$ **then return** *current_min*;
> $R = T(R')$;
> **endloop**;

Figure 9.4 Minimum Condition Count Algorithm

The algorithm for computing the minimum count is given in figure 9.4. In the algorithm text, *Final* and *Not_final* denote the sets of states in *final* and $S - final$, paired with all possible values of k. More formally:

$$Final = \{\langle s, k \rangle \mid s \in final, k \in \mathbb{N}\} \quad \text{and} \quad Not\_final = \{\langle s, k \rangle \mid s \notin final, k \in \mathbb{N}\}$$

The algorithm uses R to represent the state set in S_a reached at the current iteration, while *Reached_final* and R' are its intersections with *Final* and *Not_final* respectively. Variable *current_min* denotes the minimum count for all previous iterations. The computation of the minimum value of k in a set of pairs $\langle s, k \rangle$ can be done by existentially quantifying the state variables (computing $K = \{k \mid \exists \langle s, k \rangle \in S\}$) and following the leftmost nonzero branch in the resulting BDD, provided an appropriate variable ordering is used.

At iteration i, the algorithm considers the endpoints of paths with i states. The reached states that belong to *final* are terminal states on paths that we need to consider. The minimum count for these paths is computed, using the counter component of the path endpoints, and the current value of the minimum is updated if necessary. For the reached states that do not belong to *final*, we continue the loop after computing their successors. If all reached states are in *final*, there are no further paths to consider and the algorithm returns the computed minimum.

Finally, we note that the algorithm for the maximum count has the same structure and can be obtained by replacing *min* with *max* and reversing the inequalities. Variants of both algorithms can be used to compute other measures that are a function of the number of states on a path that satisfy a given condition. For example, we can determine the minimum and the maximum number of states belonging to a given set *cond* over all paths of a certain length l in the state space.

9.8 EXAMPLES

One of the most critical applications of real-time systems is in aircraft control. It is extremely important that time bounds are not violated in such systems. Because of the risks involved in the failure of an aircraft, only conservative approaches to design and implementation are routinely used. Many modern techniques for software design such as formal methods are not commonly employed. We believe that formal verification can be very useful in increasing the reliability of these systems by assisting in the validation of schedulability and response times of the various components.

This section briefly describes an aircraft control system used in military airplanes. Such a control system can be characterized by a set of sensors and actuators connected to a central processor. This processor executes the software to analyze sensor data and control the actuators. Our model describes this control program and determines whether its timing constraints are met. The requirements used are similar to those of existing military aircraft, and the model is derived from the one described in [LVM91].

The aircraft controller is divided into systems and subsystems, each of which performs a specific task in controlling the airplane:

- Navigation: Computes aircraft position.
- Radar Control: Receives and processes data from radars. It also identifies targets and target position.
- Radar Warning Receiver: This system identifies possible threats to the aircraft.
- Weapon Control: Aims and activates aircraft weapons.
- Display: Updates information on the pilot's screen.
- Tracking: Updates target position. Data from this system is used to aim the weapons.
- Data Bus: Provides communication between processor and external devices.

Timing constraints for each subsystem are derived from factors such as required accuracy, human response characteristics and hardware requirements. The following table presents the subsystems being modelled, as well as their major timing requirements. In order to enforce the different timing constraints of the processes, priority scheduling is used. The priority assignment has been done according to the RMS theory [LSST91, LL73].

In this table the first two columns identify the process. The third column shows the period of the process in milliseconds. For example, the target update subsystem executes once every 100ms. The deadline is defined to be the same as the period. In other words, a process has to finish executing before its next instantiation starts. The next column presents the execution time of each instantiation of that process. The cpu utilization is then shown. The utilization is

System	Subsystem	Per.	Exec	%cpu	Pri
Display	status update	200	3	1.50	12
	keyset	200	1	0.50	16
	hook update	80	2	2.50	36
	graph. displ.	80	9	11.25	40
	store update	200	1	0.50	20
RWR	contact mgmt	25	5	20.00	72
Radar	target update	50	5	10.00	60
	track filter	25	2	8.00	84
NAV	nav update	50	8	16.00	56
	steer cmds.	200	3	1.50	24
Track	target update	100	5	5.00	32
Weapon	weapon prot.	200*	1	0.50	28
	weapon aim	50	3	6.00	64
	weapon rel.	200*	3	1.50	98
Dat Bus	poll device	40	1	2.50	68

* Weapon protocol is an aperiodic process with a deadline of 200ms.

** Weapon release has a period of 200ms, but its deadline is 5ms.

defined to be the percentage of the time this process is executing. It is computed by dividing the execution time by the period. The priority assigned to that process is the last column.

Concurrent processes are used to implement each subsystem. With the exception of the weapon system, all other systems contain only periodic processes. The weapon system contains a mixture of periodic and aperiodic processes. It is activated when the display keyset subsystem identifies that the pilot has pressed the firing button. This event causes the weapon protocol subsystem to be activated. It then signals the weapon aim subsystem that has been previously blocked. Weapon aim is then scheduled to be executed every 50ms. It aims the aircraft weapons based on the current position of the target. It also decides when to fire and then starts the weapon release subsystem. The firing sequence can be aborted until weapon release is scheduled, but not after this point. Weapon release then executes periodically and fires the weapons 5 times, once per second.

We have implemented this control system in the SMV language [McM92]. Boolean variables have been used to implement conditions such as request for execution, end of execution, and time-outs. The scheduler has also been implemented using boolean variables that indicate when each process could execute, or when it was blocked. Counters were used to keep track of the time elapsed at each point.

The SMV model checker has been used to verify its functional correctness, while its timing correctness has been checked using the quantitative algorithms described in this paper. In order to optimize response time, we have implemented a preemptive scheduler. However, preemptability is a feature that may not always be available. Non-preemptive schedulers are easier to implement, and allow for simpler programs but usually increase response time for higher priority processes. To assess the effect of preemption in our system we have also implemented a non-preemptive scheduler.

Using the model described above, we were able to compute the schedulability of the system. This is one of the most important properties of a real-time system. It states that no process will miss its deadline. In this example the deadlines are the same as the periods (except for the weapon release subsystem). We determine schedulability by computing the minimum and

Subsystem	dead line	Execution Times			
		preempt		no preempt	
		min	max	min	max
Weapon release	5	3	3	3	9
Radar track filter	25	2	5	2	10
Contact mgmt.	25	7	10	7	15
Data bus poll	40	1	11	1	14
Weapon aim	50	10	14	2	18
Radar target upd	50	12	19	12	19
NAV update	50	20	34	20	27
Display graphic	80	10	44	10	43
Display hook upd	80	14	46	14	47
Track target upd	100	26	51	26	51
Weapon protocol	200	1	21	3	46
NAV steer cmds.	200	35	85	36	74
Display store upd	200	36	95	37	97
Display keyset	200	37	96	38	98
Display status upd	200	40	99	41	101

maximum execution times for each process and checking if they always finish before their deadline. The RMS theory checks for schedulability by computing the CPU utilization of the process set. It may not provide any schedulability information if the utilization exceeds a certain threshold. Our method however, is always able to determine schedulability. Moreover, it only requires that processes be modelled as state graphs, while RMS imposes restrictions on their behavior.

The following table summarizes the execution times computed by our algorithms for both the preemptive and non-preemptive schedulers. Processes are shown in decreasing order of priority. We can see from this table that the process set is schedulable using preemptive scheduling. An analysis of a similar process set using RMS showed that only the first eight processes were guaranteed to meet their deadlines [LVM91]. From our results we can also identify many important parameters of the system. For example, the response time is usually very low for best-case computations, but it is also good for the worst case. Most processes finish in less than half the time they have to execute (they must finish before the deadline). This indicates that the system is still not close to saturation, although the total CPU utilization is high.

Notice also that preemption does not have a big impact on response times. Except for the most critical process, all others maintain their schedulability if a non-preemptive scheduler is used. Moreover, we can see that non-preemption causes weapon release to miss its deadline, but by a relatively small amount. If a preemptive scheduler were expensive, reducing the CPU utilization slightly might make the complete system schedulable without changing the scheduler. By having such information, the designer can easily assess the impact of various alternatives to improve the performance, without having to change the implementation. It should be noted that an analysis of this type can't be done using methods like the RMS utilization test, reachability computation or pure model checking.

The algorithms described can be used to analyze the system in many different ways. For example, the effect of preemption on execution time can be assessed as follows. We have computed the maximum and minimum execution times for processes *after* they have been granted the CPU. If minimum and maximum are not the same, the process can be preempted after starting execution. For example, the display graphic subsystem can finish in as little as 10ms and in as much as 44ms after it starts execution. In other words, preemption overhead can be as high as 34ms for this subsystem. The NAV steering subsystem has a minimum of 35ms and a maximum of 85ms. This means that other processes can delay it for 50ms. It is clear that NAV steering can be preempted for a longer time than display graphic, since it has lower priority. Our results, however, allow us to determine how much longer it can be preempted. In a similar fashion, we can compute the priority inversion time for high priority processes. This can aid in identifying the reasons why a system is not predictable, and help correct its behavior.

We examine one more property of this particular model. The weapon system is critical to the aircraft. It is very important that it responds quickly to the pilot's command. However, when a pilot presses the firing button, many subsystems are involved in identifying and responding to this event. By computing the minimum and maximum times between pressing the fire button and the execution of the weapon release process we are able to determine if the weapon system responds quickly enough to satisfy the aircraft requirements. In our example, the minimum time is 120ms and the maximum time is 167ms, not accounting for the possibility that the firing sequence may be aborted. Again, this type of analysis may be difficult to do with other tools. The RMS schedulability test cannot give tight bounds on specific response times for such properties, since its only parameter is CPU utilization. Algorithms that use reachability analysis are also inappropriate for such analysis. Specific exceptions, with previously defined time bounds, would have to be added to the model to observe these characteristics.

The finite-state model was implemented in about 600 lines of SMV code. The final model has about 10^{15} states, and the transition relation uses approximately 4600 BDD nodes. To compute each property described above took between 5 and 15 seconds using an i486 based workstation.

Another example that we have analyzed is a robotics system used in nuclear plants to measure the shape of pipes by moving around them with a distance sensor [HKL94]. The robot architecture has three subsystems: motor, measurement and command. The motor subsystem controls the robot movements and position. The function of the measurement subsystem is to activate and control the distance sensors. Finally, the command subsystem is responsible for receiving commands from the communication link and sending those commands to the appropriate subsystems. Each subsystem consists of a set of tasks. All tasks are periodic, and their timing requirements reflect the characteristics of the environment in which the robot works and the robot's expected response time. Each task consists of a sequence of blocks, each with a different timing requirement.

We have determined the schedulability of this task set. Moreover, we have also been able to discover inefficiencies in the design. In this example data dependencies are being affected by the priority structure of the task set. Data produced by a task A is used by a task B, but due to priority or periodicity constraints, task B is executing before task A. In this case, task B is using data generated by task A in the previous instantiation. In order to avoid using possibly old data, the design has been changed so task B is activated by task A, instead of periodically. The modified design is be analyzed by the same algorithms. It has a lighter load and data is consumed faster than in the original design.

A medical system used to monitor the condition of a patient has also been analyzed using our tools [Dro93]. Sensors are connected to the patient and continuously measure various parameters of his or her condition. The system records this data for analysis by physicians and also issues an alarm when abnormal conditions occur. Priority driven concurrent processes are used to control the various components of the monitor. The analysis of the system consists of verifying if the performance of the controller satisfied its expected response time. The results produced by the algorithms also allowed us to identify inefficiencies in a similar way as in the previous example. Again, an optimization has been implemented, and the modified model analyzed. In this example the information generated by the algorithms made it possible not only to analyze the original design, but to improve it. The analysis of this example can be found in [CCMM95].

We have also used our methods to do a performance analysis of the PCI local bus. PCI is a high performance bus architecture designed to become an industry standard for current and future computer systems [Int93]. It is used primarily in systems based on the Intel Pentium or the DEC Alpha processors. We have modelled the PCI bus, concentrating on its temporal characteristics, and analyzed its performance. We have computed transaction response time in various configurations of the system. We have been able to bound the response time of a PCI transaction as well as to produce detailed information about each phase of the communications protocol. In addition, we have computed the overhead imposed by arbitration, bus acquisition, and other phases of the protocol. This type of information allows the designers to understand the behavior of the system more accurately than the information generated by traditional verification methods. Our results also uncovered subtleties in the behavior of the system that could have been difficult to find otherwise. The complete description of this example can be found in [Int93].

9.9   CONCLUSIONS

We have described how symbolic model checking can be applied to the verification of real-time systems. Model checking algorithms are able to verify properties of extremely large systems efficiently. The procedure is completely automatic and provides a counterexample trace whenever a property is violated. We have extended an existing symbolic model checker to handle time bounded properties. The *bounded until* operator has been implemented to allow the expression of such properties.

As an important extension to this technique, we have introduced quantitative reasoning into the verification process. This allows us to evaluate the performance of a system in addition to determining its correctness. Our algorithms generate more detailed information about the behavior of a system than previous methods and can be used in several different ways to analyze a real-time system.

We have applied this method to several actual systems, and, in each case, we have been able to produce useful information that can allow designers to understand system behavior and improve its performance. To demonstrate how our technique works, we have discussed in detail the analysis of one such example, and briefly presented some of the others.

REFERENCES

[ACD90]   R. Alur, C. Courcourbetis, and D. Dill. Model-checking for real-time systems. In *Proceedings of the 5th Symp. on Logic in Computer Science*, pages 414–425, 1990.

[AD90]   R. Alur and D. Dill. Automata for modeling real-time systems. In *Lecture Notes in Computer Science, 17th ICALP*. Springer-Verlag, 1990.

[BCL90]   J. R. Burch, E. M. Clarke, and D. E. Long. Symbolic model checking with partitioned transition relations. In *VLSI 91*, Edinburgh, Scotland, 1990.

[BCM+90]   J. R. Burch, E. M. Clarke, K. L. McMillan, D. L. Dill, and J. Hwang. Symbolic model checking: 10^{20} states and beyond. In *LICS*, 1990.

[BCMD90]   J. R. Burch, E. M. Clarke, K. L. McMillan, and D. L. Dill. Sequential circuit verification using symbolic model checking. In *27th ACM/IEEE Design Automation Conference*, 1990.

[Bry86]   R. E. Bryant. Graph-based algorithms for boolean function manipulation. *IEEE Transactions on Computers*, C-35(8), 1986.

[Cam93]   S. V. Campos. The priority inversion problem and real-time symbolic model checking. Technical Report CMU-CS-93-125, Carnegie Mellon University, School of Computer Science, 1993.

[CCMM95]   S. V. Campos, E. M. Clarke, W. Marrero, and M. Minea. Timing analysis of industrial real-time systems. In *Workshop on Industrial-strength Formal specification Techniques*, 1995.

[CE81]   E. M. Clarke and E. A. Emerson. Synthesis of synchronization skeletons for branching time temporal logic. In *Logic of Programs: Workshop, Yorktown Heights, NY, May 1981*. Springer-Verlag, 1981. volume 131 of *Lecture Notes in Computer Science*.

[CES86]   E. M. Clarke, E. A. Emerson, and A. P. Sistla. Automatic verification of finite-state concurrent systems using temporal logic specifications. *ACM Transactions on Programming Languages and Systems*, 8(2):244–263, 1986.

[CGH+93]   E. M. Clarke, O. Grumberg, H. Hiraishi, S. Jha, D. E. Long, K. L. McMillan, and L. A. Ness. Verification of the Futurebus+ cache coherence protocol. In L. Claesen, editor, *International Symposium on Computer Hardware Description Languages an d their Applications*. North-Holland, April 1993.

[CHLR93]   P. C. Clements, C. L. Heitmeyer, B. G. Labaw, and A. T. Rose. MT: a toolset for specifying and analyzing real-time systems. In *IEEE Real-Time Systems Symposium*, 1993.

[Dro93]   P. Drongowski. Software architecture in real-time systems. In *IEEE Workshop on Real-Time Applications*, 1993.

[EMSS90]   E. A. Emerson, A. K. Mok, A. P. Sistla, and J. Srinivasan. Quantitative temporal reasoning. In *Lecture Notes in Computer Science*. Springer–Verlag, 1990.

[FC93]   A. N. Fredette and R. Cleaveland. RTSL: a language for real-time schedulability analysis. In *IEEE Real-Time Systems Symposium*, 1993.

[GL90]   R. Gerber and I. Lee. A proof system for communicating shared resources. In *IEEE Real-Time Systems Symposium*, 1990.

[HHWT95]   T. A. Henzinger, P. H. Ho, and H. Wong-Toi. HyTech: the next generation. In *IEEE Real-Time Systems Symposium*, 1995.

[HKL94]   M. G. Harbour, M. H. Klein, and J. P. Lehoczky. Timing analysis for fixed-priority scheduling of hard real-time systems. *IEEE Transactions on Software Engineering*, 20(1), 1994.

[HNSY92]   T. Henzinger, X. Nicollin, J. Sifakis, and S. Yovine. Symbolic model checking for real-time systems. In *Proceedings of the 7th Symp. on Logic in Computer Science*, 1992.

[Int93]   Intel Corporation. *PCI Local Bus Specification*, 1993.

[Lew90]   H. Lewis. A logic of concrete time intervals. In *Proceedings of the 5th Symp. on Logic in Computer Science*, pages 380–389, 1990.

[LL73]   C. L. Liu and J. W. Layland. Scheduling algorithms for multiprogramming in a hard real-time environment. *Journal of the ACM*, 20(1), 1973.

[LSST91]   J. P. Lehoczky, L. Sha, J. K. Strosnider, and H. Tokuda. Fixed priority scheduling theory for hard real-time systems. In *Foundations of Real-Time Computing — Scheduling and Resource Management*. Kluwer Academic Publishers, 1991.

[LVM91]   C. D. Locke, D. R. Vogel, and T. J. Mesler. Building a predictable avionics platform in Ada: a case study. In *IEEE Real-Time Systems Symposium*, 1991.

[McM92]   K. L. McMillan. *Symbolic model checking — an approach to the state explosion problem*. PhD thesis, SCS, Carnegie Mellon University, 1992.

[NSY92]   X. Nicollin, J. Sifakis, and S. Yovine. From atp to timed graphs and hybrid systems. In *Lecture Notes in Computer Science, Real-Time: Theory in Practice*. Springer-Verlag, 1992.

[SKG91]   L. Sha, M. H. Klein, and J. B. Goodenough. Rate monotonic analysis for real-time systems.

In *Foundations of Real-Time Computing — Scheduling and Resource Management*. Kluwer Academic Publishers, 1991.

[YMW93] J. Yang, A. Mok, and F. Wang. Symbolic model checking for event-driven real-time systems. In *IEEE Real-Time Systems Symposium*, 1993.

10

End-to-End Design of Real-Time Systems

RICHARD GERBER and DONG-IN KANG
University of Maryland College Park

SEONGSOO HONG
Seoul National University

MANAS SAKSENA
Concordia University

ABSTRACT

This chapter presents a comprehensive design methodology for guaranteeing end-to-end requirements of real-time systems. Applications are structured as a set of process components, connected by asynchronous channels, in which the endpoints are the system's external inputs and outputs. Timing constraints are then postulated between these inputs and outputs; they express properties such as end-to-end propagation delay, temporal input-sampling correlation, and allowable separation times between updated output values.

The automated design method works as follows: First new tasks are created to correlate related inputs. An optimization algorithm, whose objective is to minimize CPU utilization, transforms the end-to-end requirements into a set of intermediate rate constraints on the tasks. If the algorithm fails to find a solution to the constraints, a restructuring tool attempts to eliminate bottlenecks by transforming the application. Then it is re-submitted to the assignment algorithm. The final result is a schedulable set of fully periodic tasks that collaboratively maintain the end-to-end constraints.

10.1 INTRODUCTION

Most real-time systems possess only a small handful of *inherent* timing constraints that will "make or break" their correctness. These are called *end-to-end* constraints, and they are established on the systems' external inputs and outputs. Two examples are:

Formal Methods For Real-Time Computing, Edited by Heitmeyer and Mandrioli
© 1996 John Wiley & Sons Ltd

(1) *Temperature updates rely on pressure and temperature readings correlated within 10μs.*

(2) *Navigation coordinates are updated at a minimum rate of 40ms, and a maximum rate 80ms.*

But while such end-to-end timing parameters may indeed be few in number, maintaining *functionally correct* end-to-end values may involve a large set of interacting components. Thus, to ensure that the end-to-end constraints are satisfied, each of these components will, in turn, be subject to their own *intermediate* timing constraints. In this manner a small handful of end-to-end constraints may – in even a modest system – yield a great many intermediate constraints.

The task of imposing timing parameters on the functional components is a complex one, and it mandates some careful engineering. Consider the second example above. In an avionics system, a "navigation update" may require such inputs as "current heading," airspeed, pitch, roll, etc; each sampled within varying degrees of accuracy. Moreover, these attributes are used by other subsystems, each of which imposes its own tolerance to delay, and possesses its own output rate. Further, the navigation unit may itself have other outputs, which may have to be delivered at rates faster than 40ms, or perhaps slower than 80ms. And, to top it off, subsystems may share limited computer resources. A good engineer balances such factors, performs extensive trade-off analysis, simulations and sensitivity analysis, and proceeds to assign the constraints.

These intermediate constraints are inevitably on the conservative side, and moreover, they are conveyed to the programmers in terms of constant values. Thus a scenario like the following is often played out: The design engineers mandate that functional units A, B and C execute with periods 65ms, 22ms and 27ms, respectively. The programmers code up the system, and find that C grossly over-utilizes its CPU; further, they discover that most of C's outputs are not being read by the other subsystems. The programmers go back to the engineers and "negotiate" for new periods – for example 60ms, 10ms and 32ms. This process may continue for many iterations, until the system finally gets fabricated.

This scenario is due to a simple fact: the end-to-end requirements allow many possibilities for the intermediate constraints, and engineers make what they consider to be a rational selection. However, the basis for this selection can only include rough notions of software structuring and scheduling policies – after all, many times the hardware is not even fabricated at this point!

Our Approach. In this chapter we present an alternative strategy; One that maintains the timing constraints in their end-to-end form for as long as possible. Our design method iteratively instantiates the intermediate constraints while taking advantage of the leeway inherent in the end-to-end constraints. If the assignment algorithm fails to produce a full set of intermediate constraints, potential bottlenecks are identified. At this point, an application analysis tool takes over, determines potential solutions to the bottleneck, and if possible, restructures the application to avoid it. The result is then re-submitted into the assignment algorithm.

We have implemented a significant portion of our approach as part of integrated design tool development effort at the University of Maryland. The tool, named TimeWare/DesignAssistant, graphically and textually captures both a system design and its end-to-end requirements, and then produces intermediate constraints. Throughout the chapter, we use examples taken from the tool's graphical interface.

Working Assumptions. Due to the complexity of the general problem, we confine our discussion to systems possessing the following characteristics.

1: We assume our applications possess three classes of timing constraints which we call *freshness*, *correlation* and *separation*.

- A *freshness constraint* (sometimes called propagation delay) bounds the time it takes for data to flow through the system. For example, assume that an external output Y is a function of some system input X. Then a freshness relationship between X and Y might be: "If Y is delivered at time t, then the X-value used to compute Y is sampled no earlier than $t - 10ms$." We use the following notation to denote this constraint: "$F(Y|X) = 10$."

- A *correlation constraint* limits the maximum time-skew between several inputs used to produce an output. For example, if X_1 and X_2 are used to produce Y, then a correlation relationship may be "if Y is delivered at time t, then the X_1 and X_2 values used to compute Y are sampled no more than within 2ms of each other." We denote this constraint as "$C(Y|X_1, X_2) = 2$."

- A *separation constraint* constrains the jitter between consecutive values on a single output channel, say Y. For example, "Y is delivered at a minimum rate of 3ms, and a maximum rate of 13ms," denoted as $l(Y) = 3$ and $u(Y) = 13$, respectively.

While this constraint classification is not complete, it is sufficiently powerful to represent many timing properties one finds in a requirements document. (Our initial examples (1) and (2) are correlation and separation constraints, respectively.) Note that a single output Y_1 may – either directly or indirectly – be subject to several interdependent constraints. For example, Y_1 might require tightly correlated inputs, but may abide with relatively lax freshness constraints. However, perhaps Y_1 also requires data from an intermediate subsystem which is, in turn, shared with a very high-rate output Y_2.

2: Subsystems execute on a single CPU. Our approach can be extended for use in distributed systems; a topic we revisit in Section 10.8. For the sake of presenting the intermediate constraint-assignment technique, we limit ourselves to uniprocessor systems in this chapter.

3: The entities and relationships within a subsystem are already specified. For example, if a high-rate video stream passes through a monolithic, compute-intensive filter task, this situation may easily cause a bottleneck. If our algorithm fails to find a proper intermediate timing constraint for the filter, the tool will attempt to restructure it to optimize it as much as possible. In the end, however, it cannot redesign the system.

Finally, we stress that we are not offering a *completely automatic* solution. Even with a fully periodic task model, assigning periods to the intermediate components is a complex, nonlinear optimization problem which – at worst – can become combinatorially expensive. As for software restructuring, the specific tactics used to remove bottlenecks will often require user interaction.

Problem and Solution Strategy. We note the above restrictions, and tackle the intermediate constraint-assignment problem, as rendered by the following ingredients:

- A set of external inputs $\{X_1, \ldots, X_n\}$, outputs $\{Y_1, \ldots, Y_m\}$, and the end-to-end constraints between them.

- A set of intermediate component tasks $\{P_1, \ldots, P_l\}$.

- A task graph, denoting the communication paths from the inputs, through the tasks, and to outputs.

Solving the problem requires setting timing constraints for the intermediate components, so that all end-to-end constraints are met. Moreover, during any interval of time utilization may never exceed 100%.

Our solution employs the following ingredients: (1) A periodic, preemptive tasking model (where it is the our algorithm's duty to assign the rates); (2) a buffered, asynchronous communication scheme, allowing us to keep down IPC(Inter Process Communication) times; (3) the period-assignment, optimization algorithm, which forms the heart of the approach; and (4) the software-restructuring tool, which takes over when period-assignment fails.

Related Work. This research was, in large part, inspired by the real-time transaction model proposed by Burns *et al.* in [Aud93]. While the model was formulated to express database applications, it can easily incorporate variants of our *freshness* and *correlation* constraints. In the analogue to freshness, a persistent object has "absolute consistency within t" when it corresponds to real-world samples taken within maximum drift of t. In the analogue to correlation, a set of data objects possesses "relative consistency within t" when all of the set's elements are sampled within an interval of time t.

We believe that in output-driven applications of the variety we address, separation constraints are also necessary. Without postulating a minimum rate requirement, the freshness and correlation constraints can be vacuously satisfied – by never outputting any values! Thus the separation constraints enforce the system's progress over time.

Burns *et. al.* also propose a method for deriving the intermediate constraints; as in the data model, this approach was our departure point. Here the high-level requirements are re-written as a set of constraints on task periods and deadlines, and the transformed constraints can hopefully be solved. There is a big drawback, however: the correlation and freshness constraints can inordinately tighten deadlines. E.g., if a task's inputs must be correlated within a very tight degree of accuracy – say, several nanoseconds – the task's deadline has to be tightened accordingly. Similar problems accrue for freshness constraints. The net result may be an over-constrained system, and a potentially unschedulable one.

Our approach is different. With respect to tightly correlated samples, we put the emphasis on simply getting the data into the system, and then passing through in due time. However, since this in turn causes many different samples flowing through the system at varying rates, we perform "traffic control" via a novel use of "virtual sequence numbering." This results in significantly looser periods, constrained mainly by the freshness and separation requirements. We also present a period assignment problem which is optimal – though quite expensive in the worst case.

This work was also influenced by Jeffay's "real-time producer/consumer model" [Jef83], which possesses a task-graph structure similar to ours. In this model rates are chosen so that all messages "produced" are eventually "consumed." This semantics leads to a tight coupling between the execution of a consumer to that of its producers; thus it seems difficult to accommodate relative constraints such as those based on freshness.

Klein *et. al.* surveys the current engineering practice used in developing industrial real-time systems [Kle94]. As is stressed, the intermediate constraints should be primarily a function of the end-to-end constraints, but should, if possible, take into account sound real-time scheduling techniques. At this point, however, the "state-of-the-practice" is trial and error, as guided by engineering experience. This is exactly the problem we address in this chapter.

Organization of this Chapter.   The remainder of the chapter is organized as follows. In Section 10.2 we introduce the application model and formally define our problem. In Section 10.3 we show our method of transforming the end-to-end constraints into intermediate constraints on the tasks. In Section 10.4 we describe the constraint-solver in detail, and push through a small example. In Section 10.5 we describe the application transformer, and in Section 10.6 we show how the executable application is finally built. In Section 10.7 we discuss the prototype implementation of our tool.

10.2   PROBLEM DESCRIPTION AND OVERVIEW OF SOLUTION

We re-state our problem as follows:

- Given a task graph with end-to-end timing constraints on its inputs and outputs,
- Derive periods, offsets and deadlines for every task,
- Such that the end-to-end requirements are met.

In this section we define these terms, and present the techniques behind our solution strategy. We also provide an overview of our tool, named the TimeWare/DesignAssistant, which is based on the on the solutions described in this chapter. The tool consists of several components (see Figure 10.1), including an interactive, graphical interface for structuring the system components, and a set of toolbox functions that help automate the assignment of the intermediate process constraints. In Figure 10.1, the dotted rectangle represents the scope of the DesignAssistant's functionality. The tool's inputs are drawn as ovals and the outputs are drawn as dotted ovals.

10.2.1   The Asynchronous Task Graph

An application is rendered in an asynchronous task graph (ATG) format. Figure 10.2(A) shows an example ATG, drawn using the TimeWare/DesignAssistant interface. In general, an ATG $G(V, E)$ possesses the following attributes.

- $V = \mathcal{P} \cup \mathcal{D}$, where $\mathcal{P} = \{P_1, \ldots, P_n\}$, i.e., the set of tasks; and $\mathcal{D} = \{d_1, \ldots, d_m\}$, a set of asynchronous, buffered channels. In Figure 10.2(A) tasks are drawn as a circles around their associated names. The buffered channels are drawn as small rectangles, the inputs as white bold rectangles and the outputs as gray bold rectangles. We note that the external outputs and inputs are simply typed nodes in $\mathcal{D}$.
- $E \subseteq (\mathcal{P} \times \mathcal{D}) \cup (\mathcal{D} \times \mathcal{P})$ is a set of directed edges, such that if $P_i \to d_j$ and $P_l \to d_j$ are both in E, then $P_i = P_l$. That is, each channel has a single-writer/multi-reader restriction.
- All $P_i \in \mathcal{P}$ have the following attributes: a period T_i, an offset $O_i \geq 0$ (denoting the earliest start-time from the start-of-period), a deadline $D_i \leq T_i$ (denoting the latest finish-time relative to the start-of-period), and a maximum execution time e_i. The interval $[O_i, D_i]$ constrains the window W_i of execution, where $W_i = D_i - O_i$.

Note that initially the T_i's, O_i's and D_i's are open variables, and they get instantiated by the constraint-solver.

The semantics of an ATG are as follows. Whenever a task P_i executes, it reads data from all incoming channels d_j corresponding to the edges $d_j \to P_i$, and writes to all channels d_l

Figure 10.1 The structure of the TimeWare/DesignAssistant

corresponding to the edges $P_i \rightarrow d_l$. The actual ordering imposed on the reads and writes is inferred by the task P_i's structure.

The tool binds these abstract task and channel names to real code. Consider the ATG in Figure 10.2(A), whose node P_4 is "blown up" in Figure 10.2(B). As the Figure 10.2(B,Top) shows, the function "foo" in the file "code.c" is bound to the node "P4." The programmer must also bind the abstract channel names to the corresponding identifiers in the module. The lower window of the Figure 10.2(B) shows the C code within code.c, and the stylistic conventions used for channel binding.

As far as the programmer is concerned the task P_4 has a (yet-to-be-determined) period T_4, and a set of asynchronous channels, accessible via generic operations such as "**Read**" and "**Write**." All reads and writes on channels are asynchronous and non-blocking. While a writer always inserts a value onto the end of the channel, a reader can (and many times will) read data from any location. For example, perhaps a writer runs at a period of 20ms, with two readers running at 120ms and 40ms, respectively. The first reader may use every sixth value (and neglect the others), whereas the second reader may use every other value.

But this scheme raises a "chicken and egg" issue, one of many that we faced in this work. One of our objectives is to support software reuse, in which functional components may be deployed in different systems – and have their timing parameters automatically calibrated to the physical limitations of each. But this objective would be hindered if a designer had to employ the following tedious method: (1) to *first* run the constraint-solver, which would find the T_i's, and *then*, based on the results; (2) to hand-patch all of the modules with specialized IPC code, ensuring that the intermediate tasks correctly correlate their input samples.

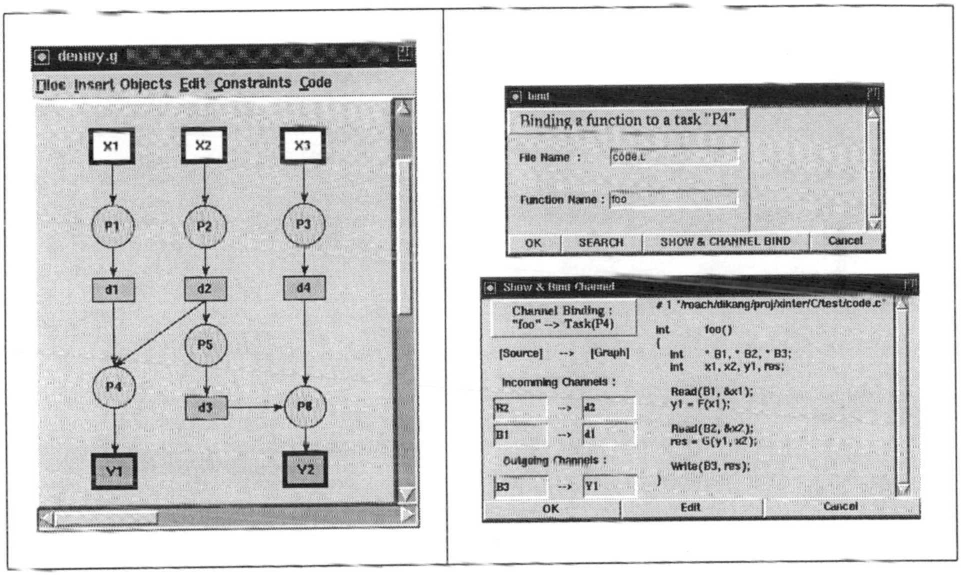

Figure 10.2   (A) A task graph and (B) code for Γ_4

We solve this problem as follows: after the constraint-assignment algorithm determines the task rates, a post-processing phase determines the actual space required for each channel. They are then automatically implemented as circular, slotted buffers. With the channel size information, the tool's Code Transformer automatically generates code to allocate and initialize each channel. It then patches the user's C code, instantiating each **"Read"** and **"Write"** operation to select the correct input value.

This type of scheme allows us to minimize the overhead incurred when blocking communication is used, and to concentrate exclusively on the assignment problem. In fact – as we show in the sequel – communication can be *completely unconditional*, in that we do not even require short locking for consistency. However, we pay a price for avoiding this overhead; namely, that the period assignments must ensure that no writer can overtake a reader currently accessing its slot.

Moreover, we note that our timing constraints define a system driven by time and *output requirements*. This is in contrast to reactive paradigms such as ESTEREL [Ber83], which are input-driven. Analogous to the "conceptually infinite buffering" assumptions, the rate assignment algorithm assumes that the external inputs are always fresh and available. The *derived* input-sampling rates then determine the *true* requirements on input-availability. And since an input X can be connected to another ATG's output Y, these requirements would be imposed on Y's timing constraints.

10.2.2   A Small Example

As a simple illustration, consider again the system whose ATG is shown in Figure 10.2(A).
It is composed of six interacting tasks with three external inputs and two external outputs.
Figure 10.3 shows the application's end-to-end constraints, which the DesignAssistant treats
as attributes of the ATG at hand.

```
  emacs: Emacs @ dizzy.cs.umd.edu

  /* ----- Constraints of the Sample Task Graph ----- */

  /* Freshness */
              F( Y1 | X1 ) = 30 ;      F( Y1 | X2 ) = 30 ;
              F( Y2 | X2 ) = 20 ;      F( Y2 | X3 ) = 15 ;

  /* Correlation */
              C( Y1 | X1, X2 ) = 3 ;
              C( Y2 | X2, X3 ) = 4 ;

  /* Separation */
              L( Y1 ) = 21 ;           U( Y1 ) = 31 ;
              L( Y2 ) = 29 ;           U( Y2 ) = 47 ;

  /* Max Execution Times */
              E( P1 ) = 6 ;   E( P2 ) = 3 ;   E( P3 ) = 3 ;
              E( P4 ) = 2 ;   E( P5 ) = 3 ;   E( P6 ) = 2 ;


--**-Emacs: demo3.9.const          (Text Fill)----All--------------------
```

Figure 10.3   Constraints description file of the sample task graph

While the system is small, it serves to illustrate several facets of the problem: (1) There
may be many possible choices of rates for each task; (2) correlation constraints may be tight
compared to the allowable end-to-end delay; (3) data streams may be shared by several outputs
(in this case that originating at X_2); and (4) outputs with the tightest separation constraints
may incur the highest execution-time costs (in this case Y_1, which exclusively requires P_1).

10.2.3   Problem Components

Guaranteeing the end-to-end constraints actually poses three sub-problems, which we define
as follows.

Correctness: Let C be the set of derived, intermediate constraints and $\mathcal{E}$ be the set of end-to-end
   constraints. Then all system behaviors that satisfy C also satisfy $\mathcal{E}$.

Feasibility: The task executions inferred by C never demand an interval of time during which
   utilization exceeds 100%.

Schedulability: There is a scheduling algorithm which can efficiently maintain the intermediate constraints C, and preserve feasibility.

In the problem we address, the three issues cannot be decoupled. Correctness, for example,
is often treated as verification problem using a logic such as RTL [Jah86]. Certainly, given
the ATG we could formulate $\mathcal{E}$ in RTL and query whether the constraint set is satisfiable.
However, a "yes" answer would give us little insight into finding a good choice for C – which
must, after all, be simple enough to schedule. Or, in the case of methods like model-checking
([Alu90], etc.), we could determine whether $C \Rightarrow \mathcal{E}$ is invariant with respect to the system. But
again, this would be an *a posteriori* solution, and assume that we already possess C. On the
other hand, a system that is feasible may still not be schedulable under a *known* algorithm;
i.e., one that can be efficiently managed by a realistic kernel.

In this chapter we put our emphasis on the first two issues. However, we have also imposed a
task model for which the greatest number of efficient scheduling algorithms are known: simple,
periodic dispatching with offsets and deadlines. In essence, by restricting C's free variables
to the T_i's, O_i's and D_i's, we ensure that feasible solutions to C can be easily checked for
schedulability.

The problem of scheduling a set of periodic real-time tasks on a single CPU has been studied
for many years. Such a task set can be dispatched by a calendar-based, non-preemptive schedule
(e.g., [Xu90, Yua94, Zha87]), or by a preemptive, static-priority scheme (e.g., [Bur94, Liu73,
Sha90, Tin94]). For the most part our results are independent of any particular scheduling
strategy, and can be used in concert with either non-preemptive or preemptive dispatching.

However, in the sequel we frequently assume an underlying static-priority architecture.
This is for two reasons. First, a straightforward priority assignment can often capture most
of the ATG's precedence relationships, which obviates the need for offset and deadline variables. Thus the space of feasible solutions can be simplified reducing the constraint-solver's
work. Second, priority-based scheduling has recently been shown to support all of the ATG's
inherent timing requirements: pre-period deadlines [Aud91], precedence constrained sub-
tasks [Har91], and offsets [Tin92]. A good overview to static priority scheduling may be
found in [Bur94].

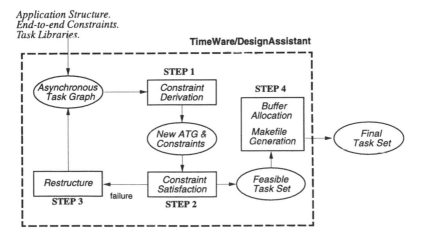

Figure 10.4   Overview of the approach

10.2.4   Overview of the Solution

Our solution is carried out in a four-step process, as shown in Figure 10.4. In **Step 1**, the intermediate constraints C are derived, which postulates the periods, deadlines and offsets as free variables. The challenge here is to balance several factors – correctness, feasibility and simplicity. That is, we require that any solution to C will enforce the end-to-end constraints $\mathcal{E}$, and that any solution must also be feasible. At the same time, we want to keep C as simple as possible, and to ensure that finding a solution is a relatively straightforward venture. This is particularly important since the feasibility criterion – defined by CPU utilization – introduces non-linearities into the constraint set. In balancing our goals we impose additional structure on the application; e.g., by creating new sampler tasks to get more tightly correlated inputs into the system.

In **Step 2** the constraint-solver finds a solution to C, which is done in several steps. First C is solved for the period variables, the T_i's, and then the resulting system is solved for the offsets and deadlines. Throughout this process we use several heuristics that exploit the ATG's structure.

If a solution to C cannot be found, the problem often lies in the original design itself. For example, perhaps a single, stateless server handles inputs from multiple clients, all of which run at wildly different rates. **Step 3**'s restructuring tool helps the programmer eliminate such bottlenecks, by automatically replicating strategic parts of the ATG.

In **Step 4**, the derived rates are used to reserve memory for the channels, and to instantiate the "**Read**" and "**Write**" operations. For example, consider P_4 in Figure 10.2(A) that reads from channels d_1 and d_2.

Now, assume that the constraint-solver assigns P_4 and P_2 periods of 30ms and 10ms, respectively. Then P_4's **Read** operation on d_2 would be replaced by a macro, which would read every third data item in the buffer – and would skip over the other two.

Harmonicity.   The above scheme works only if a producer can always ensure that it is not overtaking its consumers, and if the consumers can always determine which data item is the correct one to read. For example, P_4's job in managing d_2 is easy – since $T_2 = 10$ms and $T_4 = 30$ms, P_4 will read every third item out of the channel.

But P_4 has another input channel, d_1; moreover, temporally correlated samples from the two channels have to be used to produce a result. What would happen if the solver assigned P_1 a period of 30ms, but gave P_2 a period of 7ms?

If the tasks are scheduled in rate-monotonic order, then d_2 is filled five times during P_4's first frame, four times during the second frame, etc. In fact since 30 and 7 are relatively prime, P_4's selection logic to correlate inputs would be rather complicated. One solution would be to time-stamp each input X_1 and X_2, and then pass these stamps along with all intermediate results. But this would assume access to a precise hardware timer; moreover, time-stamps for multiple inputs would have to be composed in some manner. Worst of all, each small data value (e.g., an integer) would carry a large amount of reference information.

The obvious solution is the one that we adopt: to ensure that every "chain" possesses a common base clock-rate that is exactly the rate of the task at the head of the chain. In other words, we impose a harmonicity constraint between (producer, consumer) pairs; (i.e., pairs (P_p, P_c) where there are edges $P_p \rightarrow d$ and $d \rightarrow P_c$.)

Definition 10.2.1 (Harmonicity) *A task P_2 is harmonic with respect to a task P_1 if T_2 is exactly divisible by T_1 (represented as $T_2|T_1{}^1$).*

Consider Figure 10.2(A), in which there are three chains imposing harmonic relationships. In this tightly coupled system we have that $T_4|T_1$, $T_4|T_2$, $T_5|T_2$, $T_6|T_5$ and $T_6|T_3$.

10.3 STEP 1: DERIVING THE CONSTRAINTS

In this section we show the derivation process of intermediate constraints, and how they (conservatively) guarantee the end-to-end requirements. We start the process by synthesizing the intermediate correlation constraints, and then proceed to treat freshness and separation.

10.3.1 Synthesizing Correlation Constraints

Let's revisit our example task graph (now in Figure 10.5(A)), where the three inputs X_1, X_2 and X_3 are sampled by three separate tasks. If we wish to guarantee that P_1's sampling of X_1 is correctly correlated to P_2's sampling of X_2, we must pick short periods for both P_1 and P_2. Indeed, in many practical real-time systems, the correlation requirements may very well be tight, and way out of proportion with the freshness constraints. This typically results in periods that get tightened exclusively to accommodate correlation, which can easily lead to gross over-utilization. Engineers often call this problem "over-sampling," which is somewhat of a misnomer, since sampling rates may be tuned expressly for coordinating inputs. Instead, the problem arises from poor coupling of the sampling and computational activities.

Thus our approach is to decouple these components as much as possible, and to create specialized samplers for related inputs. For a given ATG, the sampler derivation is performed in the following manner.

> **foreach** Correlation constraint $C_l(Y_k|X_{l_1}, \ldots, X_{l_m})$
> > Create the set of all input-output pairs associated with C_l, i.e.,
> > $T_l := \{(X_{l_i}, Y_k)| X_{l_i} \in \{X_{l_1}, \ldots, X_{l_m}\}\}$
> **foreach** T_l, **foreach** T_k
> > If there's a common input X such that there exist outputs Y_i, Y_j
> > > with $(X, Y_i) \in T_l$, $(X, Y_j) \in T_k$, and
> > if chains from X to Y_l and X to Y_k share a common task, then
> > > Set $T_l := T_l \cup T_k$; $T_k := \emptyset$
> **foreach** T_l, identify all associated sampling tasks, i.e.,
> > $S_l := \{P|(X,Y) \in T_l \wedge X \rightarrow P\}$
> > If $|S_l| > 1$, create a periodic sampler P_{s_l} to take samples for inputs in T_l

Thus the incoming channels from inputs T_l to tasks in S_l are "intercepted" by the new sampler task P_{s_l}.

We return to our original example, which we repeat in Figure 10.5(A). Since both correlated inputs share the center stream, the result is a single group of correlated inputs $\{(X_1, X_2, X_3)\}$. This, in turn, results in the formation of the single sampler P_s. We assume P_s has a low execution cost of 1. The new, transformed graph is shown at the right column of Figure 10.5(B).

---

[1] $x|y$ iff $\exists \alpha :: \alpha y = x$ and $\alpha \geq 1$, where α is an integer.

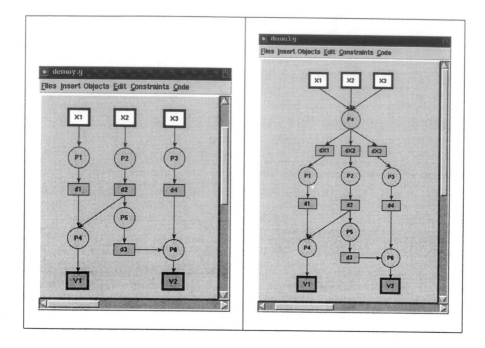

Figure 10.5   (A) Original task graph and (B) transformed task graph

As for the deadline-offset requirements, a sampler P_{s_l} is constrained by the following trivial relationship

$$D_{s_l} - O_{s_l} \leq t_{cor}$$

where t_{cor} is the maximum allowable time-drift on all correlated inputs read by P_{s_l}.

The sampler tasks ensure that correlated inputs are read into the system within their appropriate time bounds. This allows us to solve for process rates as a function of both the freshness and separation constraints, which vastly reduces the search space.

However we cannot ignore correlation altogether, since merely sampling the inputs at the same time does not guarantee that they will *remain* correlated as they pass through the system. The input samples may be processed by different streams (running at different rates), and thus they may still reach their join points at different absolute times.

For example, refer back to Figure 10.5, in which $F(Y_2|X_2) > F(Y_2|X_3)$. This disparity is the result of an under-specified system, and may have to be tightened. The reason is simple: if P_6's period is derived by using correlation as a dominant metric, the resulting solution may violate the tighter freshness constraints. On the other hand, if freshness is the dominant metric, then the correlation constraints may not be achieved.

We solve this problem by eliminating the "noise" that exists between the different set of requirements. Thus, whenever a fresh output is required, we ensure that there are correlated data sets to produce it. In our example this leads to tightening the original freshness requirement $F(Y_2|X_2)$ to $F(Y_2|X_3)$.

Thus we invoke this technique as a general principle. For an output Y with correlated input

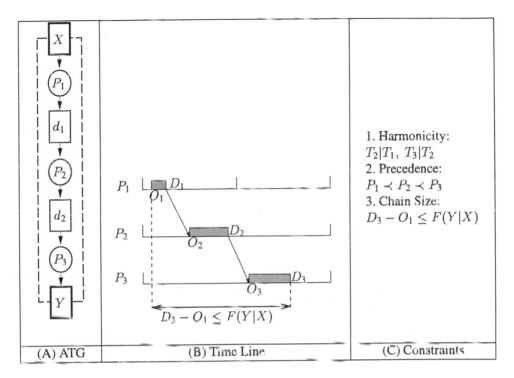

Figure 10.6   Freshness constraints with coupled tasks

sets $X_1, \ldots, X_m$, the associated freshness constraints are adjusted accordingly:

$$F(Y|X_1), \ldots, F(Y|X_m) := min\{F(Y|X_1), \ldots, F(Y|X_m)\}$$

10.3.2   Synthesizing Freshness Constraints

Consider a freshness constraint $F(Y|X) = t_f$, and recall its definition:

> *For every output of Y at some time t, the value of X used to compute Y must have been read no earlier that time $t - t_f$.*

As data flows through a task chain from X to Y, each task P adds two types of delay overhead to the data's end-to-end response time. One type is *execution time*, i.e., the time required for P to process the data, produce outputs, etc. In this chapter we assume that P's maximum execution time is fixed, and has already been optimized as much as possible by a good compiler.

The other type of delay is *transmission latency*, which is imposed while P waits for its correlated inputs to arrive for processing. Transmission time is not fixed; rather, it is largely dependent on our derived process-based constraints. Thus minimizing transmission time is our goal in achieving tight freshness constraints.

Fortunately, the harmonicity relationship between producers and consumers allows us to accomplish this goal. Consider a chain $P_1, P_2, \ldots, P_n$, where P_n is the output task, and P_1 is the input task. From the harmonicity constraints we get $T_{i+1}|T_i$, for $1 \le i < n$. Assuming that all tasks are started at time 0, whenever there is an invocation of the output task P_n, there are simultaneous invocations of every task in the freshness chain.

Consider Figure 10.6 in which there are three tasks P_1, P_2 and P_3 in a freshness chain. From the harmonicity assumption we have $T_3|T_2$ and $T_2|T_1$.

The other constraints are derived for the entire chain, under the scenario that within each task's minor frame, input data gets read in, it gets processed, and output data is produced. Under these constraints, the worst case end-to-end delay is given by $D_n - O_1$, and the freshness requirement is guaranteed if the following holds:

$$D_n - O_1 \leq t_f$$

Note that we also require a precedence between each producer/consumer task pair. As we show in Figure 10.6, this can be accomplished via the offset and deadline variables – i.e., by mandating that $D_i \leq O_{i+1}$, for $1 \leq i < n$.

But this approach has the following obvious drawback: *The end-to-end freshness t_f must be divided into fixed portions of slack at each node.* On a global system-wide level, this type of rigid flow control is not the best solution. It is not clear how to distribute the slack between intermediate tasks, without over-constraining the system. More importantly, with a rigid slack distribution, a consumer task would not be allowed to execute before its offset, *even if its input data is available.*[2]

Rather, we make a straightforward priority assignment for the tasks in each chain, and let the scheduler enforce the precedence between them. In this manner, we can do away with the intermediate offset variables. This leads to the following rule of thumb:

> *If the consumer task is not the head or tail of a chain, then its precedence requirement is deferred to the scheduler. Otherwise, the precedence requirement is satisfied through assignment of offsets.*

Example. Consider the freshness constraints for our example in Figure 10.5(A), $F(Y_1|X_1) = 30$, $F(Y_1|X_2) = 30$, $F(Y_2|X_2) = 15$, and $F(Y_2|X_3) = 15$. The requirement $F(Y_1|X_1) = 30$ specifies a chain window size of $D_4 - O_s \leq 30$. Since P_1 is an intermediate task we now have the precedence $P_s \prec P_1$, which will be handled by the scheduler. However, according to our "rule of thumb," we use the offset for P_4 to handle the precedence $P_1 \prec P_4$. This leads to the constraints $D_1 \leq O_4$ and $D_s \leq D_1 - e_1$. Similar inequalities are derived for the remaining freshness constraints, the result of which is shown in Table 10.1.

Table 10.1   Constraints due to freshness requirements

$F(Y_1|X_1)$	$F(Y_1|X_2)$	$F(Y_2|X_2)$	$F(Y_2|X_3)$
$D_4 - O_s \leq 30$	$D_4 - O_s \leq 30$	$D_6 - O_s \leq 15$	$D_6 - O_s \leq 15$
$O_s + e_s + e_1 \leq D_1$	$O_s + e_s + e_2 \leq D_2$	$O_s + e_s + e_2 + e_5 \leq D_5$	$O_s + e_s + e_3 \leq D_3$
$D_1 \leq O_4$	$D_2 \leq O_4$	$D_5 \leq O_6$	$D_3 \leq O_6$
$T_4|T_1, \quad T_1|T_s$	$T_4|T_2, \quad T_2|T_1$	$T_6|T_5, \quad T_5|T_2, \quad T_2|T_s$	$T_6|T_3, \quad T_3|T_s$

---

[2] Note that corresponding issues arise in real-time rate-control in high-speed networks.

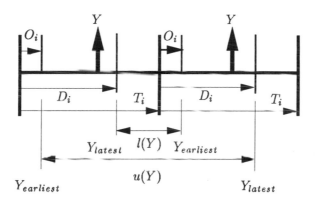

Figure 10.7   Separation constraints for two frames

10.3.3   Output Separation Constraints

Consider the separation constraints for an output Y, generated by some task P_i. As shown in Figure 10.7, the window of execution defined by O_i and D_i constrains the time variability within a period. Consider two frames of P_i's execution. The widest separation for two successive Y's can occur when the first frame starts as early as possible, and the second starts as late as possible. Conversely, the opposite situation leads to the smallest separation.

Thus, the separation constraints will be satisfied if the following holds true:

$$(T_i + D_i) - O_i \leq u(Y) \quad \text{and} \quad (T_i - D_i) + O_i \geq l(Y)$$

Example.   Consider the constraints that arise from output separation requirements, which are induced on the output tasks P_4 and P_6. The derived constraints are presented below:

$$(T_4 + D_4) - O_4 \leq u(Y_1) \qquad (T_4 - D_4) + O_4 \geq l(Y_1)$$
$$(T_6 + D_6) - O_6 \leq u(Y_2) \qquad (T_6 - D_6) + O_6 \geq l(Y_2)$$

10.3.4   Execution Constraints:

Clearly, each task needs sufficient time to execute. This simple fact imposes additional constraints, that ensure that each task's maximum execution time can fit into its window. Recall that (1) we use offset, deadline and period variables for tasks handling external input and output; and (2) we use period variables and precedence constraints for the intermediate constraints.

We can easily preserve these restrictions when dealing with execution time. For each external task P_i, the following inequalities ensure that window-size is sufficiently large for the CPU demand:

$$O_i + e_i \leq D_i, \quad O_i \geq 0 \quad D_i \leq T_i$$

On the other hand, the intermediate tasks can be handled by imposing restrictions on their constituent chains. For a single chain, let E denote the chain's execution time from the head to the last intermediate task (i.e., excluding the outputting task, if any). Then the chain-wise execution constraints are:

$$O_h + E \leq D_m, \quad D_m \leq T_m$$

where O_h is the head's offset, and where D_m and T_m are the last intermediate task's deadline and period, respectively.

Example.   Revisiting the example, we have the following execution-time constraints.

$$
\begin{array}{lll}
O_s + e_s \leq D_s, & O_s \geq 0, \quad D_s \leq T_s, & \text{sampler task} \\
O_i + e_i \leq D_i, & O_i \geq 0, \quad D_i \leq T_i, & i = \{4,6\} \\
O_s + e_s + e_i \leq D_i, & D_i \leq T_i & i = \{1,2,3\} \\
O_s + e_s + e_2 + e_5 \leq D_5, & D_5 \leq T_5 &
\end{array}
$$

This completes the set of task-wise constraints C imposed on our ATG. Thus far we have shown only one part of the problem – how C can derived from the end-to-end constraints. The end-to-end requirements will be maintained during runtime (1) if a solution to C is found, and (2) if the scheduler dispatches the tasks according to the solution's periods, offsets and deadlines. Since there are many existing schedulers that can handle problem (2), we now turn our attention to problem (1).

10.4   Step 2: CONSTRAINT SOLVER

The constraint solver generates instantiations for the periods, deadlines and offsets. In doing so, it addresses the notion of feasibility by using objective functions which (1) minimize the overall system utilization; and (2) maximize the window of execution for each task. Unfortunately, the non-linearities in the optimization criteria – as well as the harmonicity assumptions – lead to a very complex search problem.

We present a solution which decomposes the problem into relatively tractable parts. Our decomposition is motivated by the fact that the non-linear constraints are confined to the period variables, and do not involve deadlines or offsets. This suggests a straightforward approach, which is presented in Figure 10.8.

- The entire constraint set C is projected onto its subspace $\hat{C}$, constraining only the T_i's.
- The constraint set $\hat{C}$ is solved for feasible utilization.
- Since we now have values for the T_i's, we can instantiate them in the original constraint set C. This forms a new, reduced set of constraints $\bar{C}$, all of whose functions are affine in the O_i's and D_i's. Hence solutions can be found via linear optimization.

The back-edge in Figure 10.8 refers to the case where the nonlinear optimizer finds values for the T_i's, but no corresponding solution exists for the O_i's and D_i's. Hence, a new instantiation for the periods must be obtained – a process that continues until either a solution is found, or all possible values for the T_i's are exhausted.

10.4.1   Elimination of Offset and Deadline Variables

We use an extension of Fourier variable elimination [Dan73] to simplify our system of constraints. Intuitively, this step may be viewed as the projection of an n dimensional polytope (described by the constraints) onto its lower-dimensional shadow.

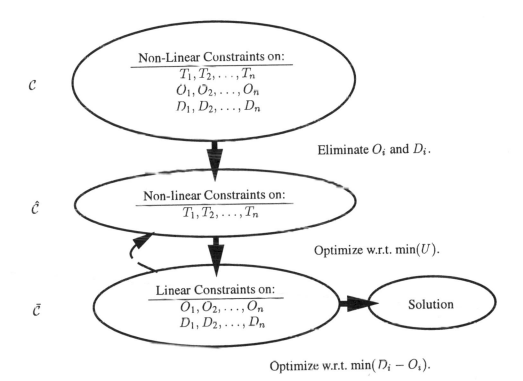

Figure 10.8 Top level algorithm to obtain task characteristics

In our case, the n-dimensional polytope is the object described by the initial constraint set $\mathcal{C}$, and the shadow is the subspace $\hat{\mathcal{C}}$, in which only the T_i's are free. The shadow is derived by eliminating one offset (or deadline) variable at a time, until only period variables remain. At each stage the new set of constraints is checked for inconsistencies. As an example, consider the two inequalities $x \le 4$ and $x \ge 7$. Such a situation means that the original system was over-specified – and the method terminates with failure.

Variable elimination can best be illustrated by a small example. Consider the following two inequalities on $W_4 = D_4 - O_4$:

$$W_4 \ge T_4 + 18 \qquad W_4 \le 31 - T_4$$

Each constraint defines a line; when W_4 and T_4 are restricted to nonzero solutions, the result is a 2-dimensional polygon. Eliminating the variable W_4 is simple, and is carried out as follows:

$$
\begin{aligned}
&T_4 + 18 \le W_4, \quad W_4 \le 31 - T_4 \\
\Rightarrow \quad &T_4 + 18 \le 31 - T_4 \\
\Rightarrow \quad &2T_4 \le 31 - 18 \\
\Rightarrow \quad &T_4 \le 6.5
\end{aligned}
$$

Since we are searching for integral, nonzero solutions to T_4, any integer in $[0 \ldots 6]$ can be considered a candidate.

When there are multiple constraints on W_4 – perhaps involving many other variables – the same process is used. Every constraint "$W_4 \leq \ldots$" is combined with every other constraint "$W_4 \geq \ldots$," until W_4 has been eliminated. The correctness of the method follows simply from the polytope's convexity, i.e., if the original set of constraints has a solution, then the solution is preserved in the shadow.

Unfortunately, the opposite is not true; hence the the requirement for the back-edge in Figure 10.8. As we have stated, the refined constraint set $\hat{C}$ may possess a solution for the T_i's that do not correspond to any integral-valued O_i's and D_i's. This situation occasionally arises from our quest for integer solutions to the T_i's – which is essential in preserving our harmonicity assumptions.

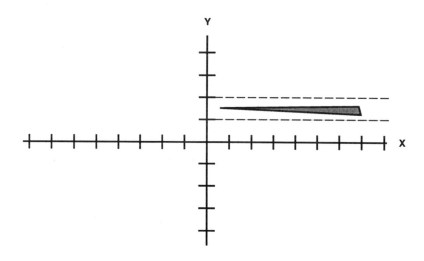

Figure 10.9   Variable elimination for integer solutions – A deviant case

For example, consider the triangle in Figure 10.9. The X-axis projection of the triangle has seven integer-solutions. On the other hand, none exist for Y, since all of the corresponding real-valued solutions are "trapped" between 1 and 2.

If, after obtaining a full set of T_i's, we are left without integer values for the O_i's and D_i's, we can resort to two possible alternatives:

1. Search for rational solutions to the offsets and deadlines, and reduce the clock-granularity accordingly, or
2. Try to find new values for the T_i's, which will hopefully lead to a full integer solution.

The Example Application – From C to $\hat{C}$.   We illustrate the effect of variable elimination on the example application presented earlier. The derived constraints impose lower and upper bounds on task periods, and are shown below. Also remaining are the original harmonicity constraints.

Linear	P_s	P_1	P_2	P_3	P_4	P_5	P_6
Constraints	$1 \leq T_s$	$7 \leq T_1$	$4 \leq T_2$	$4 \leq T_3$	$23 \leq T_4 \leq 29$	$7 \leq T_5$	$31 \leq T_6 \leq 45$
Harmonicity Constraints	$T_4\|T_1$,	$T_1\|T_s$,	$T_4\|T_2$,	$T_2\|T_1$,	$T_6\|T_5$,	$T_5\|T_2$,	$T_2\|T_s$,	$T_6\|T_3$,	$T_3\|T_s$

Here the constraints on the output tasks (P_4 and P_6) stem from the separation constraints, which impose upper and lower bounds on the periods.

10.4.2 From $\hat{C}$ to $\bar{C}$: Deriving the Periods

Once the deadlines and offsets have been eliminated, we have a set of constraints involving only the task periods. The objective at this point is to obtain a feasible period assignment which (1) satisfies the derived linear equations; (2) is subject to a realizable utilization, i.e., $U = \sum \frac{e_i}{T_i} \leq 1$; and (3) satisfies the harmonicity assumptions. That is, if a task P_i produces data for another task P_j, P_i's period T_i divides that of the consumer, T_j.

As in the example above, the maximum separation constraints will typically mandate that the solution-space for each T_i be bounded from above. Thus we are faced with a decidable problem – albeit a complex one. In fact there are cases which will defeat all known algorithms. In such cases there is no alternative to traversing the entire Cartesian-space

$$[l_1, u_1] \times [l_2, u_2] \times \ldots [l_n, u_n]$$

where there are n tasks, and where each T_i may range within $[l_i, u_i]$. Fortunately the harmonicity assumptions give rise to a heuristic which can prune the search space. We call it *harmonic chain merging*.

Let $Pred(i)$ ($Succ(i)$) denote the set of tasks which are predecessors (successors) of task P_i, i.e., those tasks from (to) which there is a directed path to (from) P_i. Since the harmonicity relationship is transitive, we have that if $P_j \in Succ(P_i)$, it follows that $T_j|T_i$. This simple fact leads to the following observation: we do not have to solve for each T_i as if it is an arbitrary variable in an arbitrary function. Rather, we can combine chains of processes, and then solve for their base periods. This dramatically reduces the number of free variables.

For our purposes, this translates into the following rule:

If a task P_i executes with period T_i, and if some $P_j \in Pred(P_i)$ has the property that $Succ(P_j) = \{P_i\}$, then P_j should also execute with period T_i.

In other words, we will never run a task faster than it needs to be run. In designs where the periods are ad-hoc artifacts, tuned to achieve the end-to-end constraints, such an approach would be highly unsafe. Here the rate constraints are *analytically derived* directly from the end-to-end requirements. *We know "how fast" a task needs to be run, and it makes no sense to run it faster.*

This allows us to simplify the ATG by merging nodes, and to limit the number of free variables in the problem. The method is summed up in the following steps:

(1) If $P_i \in Pred(P_j)$, then $T_j|T_i$ and consequently, $T_i \leq T_j$. The first pruning takes place by propagating this information to tighten the period bounds. Thus, for each task P_i, the

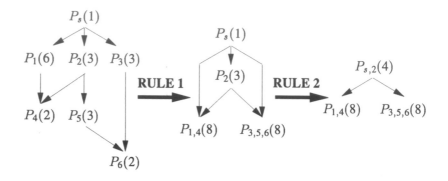

Figure 10.10   Task graph for harmonicity and its simplification

bounds are tightened as follows:

$$l_i = \max\{l_k \mid P_k \in Pred(P_i)\}$$
$$u_i = \min\{u_k \mid P_k \in Succ(P_i)\}$$

(2) The second step in the algorithm is to simplify the task graph. Consider a task P_i, which has an outgoing edge $P_i \rightarrow P_j$. Suppose $u_i \geq u_j$. Then the maximum value of T_i is constrained only by harmonicity restrictions. The simplification is done by merging P_i and P_j, whenever it is safe to set $T_i = T_j$, i.e., the restricted solution space contains the optimal solution. The following two rules give the condition when it safe to perform this simplification.

>   **Rule 1:** If a vertex P_i has a single outgoing edge $P_i \rightarrow P_j$, then P_i is merged with P_j.
>   **Rule 2:** If $Succ(P_i) \subseteq (Succ(P_j) \cup \{P_j\})$ for some edge $P_i \rightarrow P_j$, then P_i is merged with P_j.

Consider the graph in Figure 10.10. The parenthesized numbers denote the costs of corresponding nodes. In the graph, the nodes P_3, P_5, and P_1 have a single outgoing edge. Using **Rule 1**, we merge P_3 and P_5 with P_6, and P_1 with P_4. In the simplified graph, $Succ(P_s) = \{P_4, P_6, P_2\}$ and $Succ(P_2) = \{P_4, P_6\}$. Thus, we can invoke **Rule 2** to merge P_s with P_2. Also, our three merged tasks have the following allowable ranges:

$$
\begin{aligned}
P_{s,2} &\quad : \quad \{T_{s,2} \mid 4 \leq T_{s,2} \leq 29\} \\
P_{1,4} &\quad : \quad \{T_{1,4} \mid 23 \leq T_{1,4} \leq 29\} \\
P_{3,5,6} &\quad : \quad \{T_{3,5,6} \mid 31 \leq T_{3,5,6} \leq 45\}
\end{aligned}
$$

This scheme manages to reduce our original seven tasks to three sets of tasks, where each set can be represented as a pseudo-task with its own period, and an execution time equal to the sum of its constituent tasks.

At this point we have reduced the structure of the ATG as much as possible, and we turn to examining the search process. But the size of the search space can still be enormous, even for a modest ATG. For example, 10 free period variables, each of which contains 10 possible values constitute a space of 10^{10} solutions. Fortunately, harmonicity requirements play a significant role to reduce the search effort, since we need to look at only those period values that are integral multiples of certain base periods. In [Ger94] we presented a graph-theoretic algorithm which is capable of finding a feasible solution relying on backward and forward traversal of a task graph. Here we sketch the idea behind the algorithm; interested readers should consult [Ger94] for the technical details.

To sum up, the algorithm has the following properties.

(1) Period assignment is done in topological order. For a chain of tasks "$P_1 \rightarrow P_2 \rightarrow \cdots \rightarrow P_k$," each T_i must be an integral multiple of T_1, and thus T_i can be written as $a_i T_1$ for some $a_i \geq 1$. Whenever such a solution for T_i cannot be found, new periods for the immediate predecessors are determined.

(2) Whenever the system utilization approaches 100%, the current solution is rejected.

The algorithm can best be illustrated by our task graph in Figure 10.10: The T_i's are rewritten as below:

$$
\begin{array}{lll}
P_{s,2} & : \quad T_{s,2} & \\
P_{1,4} & : \quad T_{1,4} & = \quad a_1 T_{s,2} \\
P_{3,5,6} & : \quad T_{3,5,6} & = \quad a_2 T_{s,2}
\end{array}
$$

Now, feasible values are investigated for $T_{s,2}$, a_1 and a_2. First, $T_{s,2}$ is assigned its maximum allowable value 29, with leads to setting $a_1 = 1$. But with this assignment, no feasible value can be found for a_2. So a smaller value is tried for $T_{s,2}$, and so on. This process repeats until the algorithm terminates with a valuation of $T_{s,2} = 14$, $a_1 = 2$ and $a_2 = 3$ – which forms a feasible solution.

10.4.3   Deriving Offsets and Deadlines

Once the task periods are determined, we need to revisit the constraints to find a solution to the deadlines and offsets of the tasks. Here, the residue of variable elimination allows us to select values in the reverse order in which they are eliminated. Suppose we performed elimination on the following variables, in order: $x_1, x_2, \ldots, x_n$. When x_i is eliminated, the remaining free variables are $[x_{i+1}, \ldots, x_n]$. Since $[x_{i+1}, \ldots, x_n]$ are already bound to values, the constraints immediately give a lower and an upper bound on x_i.

We use this fact in assigning offsets and deadlines to the tasks. As the variables are assigned values, each variable can be individually optimized. Recall that the feasibility of a task set requires that the task set never demand a utilization greater than 1 in any time interval. We use a greedy heuristic, which attempts to maximize the window of execution for each task. For tasks which do not have an offset, this is straightforward, and can be achieved by maximizing the deadline. For input/output tasks which have offsets, we also need to fix the position of the window on the time-line. We do this by minimizing the offset for input tasks, and maximizing the deadline for output tasks.

The order in which the variables are assigned is given by the following strategy: First, we assign the windows for each input task, followed by the windows for each output task. Then, we assign the offsets for each task followed by deadline for each output task. Finally, the deadlines for the remaining tasks are assigned in a reverse topological order of the task graph. Thus, an assignment ordering for the example application is given as $\{W_s, W_4, W_6, O_s, D_4, D_6, D_5, D_3, D_1, D_2\}$. The final parameters, derived as a result of this ordering, are shown below.

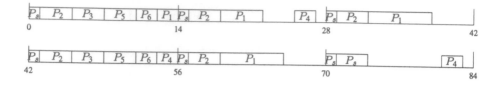

Figure 10.11   Feasible schedule for example application

	P_s	P_1	P_2	P_3	P_4	P_5	P_6
Period	14	28	14	42	28	42	42
Offset	0	0	0	0	25	0	10
Deadline	3	25	14	10	28	10	15
Exec. Time	1	6	3	3	2	3	2

A feasible schedule for the task set is shown in Figure 10.11. We note that the feasible schedule can be generated using the fixed priority ordering $P_s, P_2, P_3, P_5, P_6, P_1, P_4$.

10.5   Step 3: GRAPH TRANSFORMATION

When the constraint-solver fails, replicating part of a task graph may often prove useful in reducing the system's utilization. This benefit is realized by eliminating some of the tight harmonicity requirements, mainly by decoupling the tasks that possess common producers. As a result, the constraint derivation algorithm has more freedom in choosing looser periods for those tasks.

Recall the example application from Figure 10.5(B), and the constraints derived in Section 10.4. In the resulting system, the producer/consumer pair (P_2, P_5) has the largest period difference ($T_2 = 14$ and $T_5 = 42$). Note that the constraint solver mandated a tight period for P_2, due to the coupled harmonicity requirements $T_4|T_2$ and $T_5|T_2$. Thus, we choose to replicate the chain including P_2 from the sampler (P_s) to data object d_2. This decouples the data flow to Y_1 from that to Y_2. Figure 10.12 shows the result of the replication.

Running the constraint derivation algorithm again with the transformed graph in Figure 10.12, we obtain the following result. The transformed system has a utilization of 0.6805, which is significantly lower than that of the original task graph (0.7619).

	P_{s1}	P_1	P_2	P_4	P_{s2}	P'_2	P_3	P_5	P_6
Periods	29	29	29	29	45	45	45	45	45
Exec. Time	1	6	3	2	1	3	3	3	2

The subgraph replication technique begins with selecting a producer/consumer pair which requires replication. There exist two criteria in selecting a pair, depending on the desired goal. If the goal is reducing expected utilization, a producer/consumer pair with the maximum

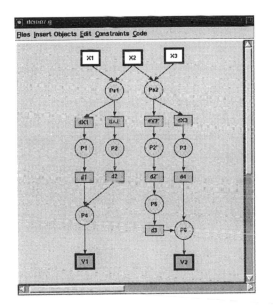

Figure 10.12   The replicated task graph

period difference is chosen first. On the other hand, if the goal is achieving feasibility, then we rely on the feedback from the constraint solver in determining the point of infeasibility.

After a producer/consumer pair is selected, the algorithm constructs a subgraph using a backward traversal of the task graph from the consumer. In order to avoid excessive replication, the traversal is terminated at the first confluence point. The resulting subgraph is then replicated and attached to the original graph.

The producer task in a replication may, in turn, be further specialized for the output it serves. For example, consider a task graph with two consumers P_{c1} and P_{c2} and a common producer P_p. If we replicate the producer, we have two independent producer/consumer pairs, namely (P_p, P_{c1}) and (P'_p, P_{c2}). Since P'_p only serves P_{c2}, we can eliminate all operations that only contribute to the output for P_{c1}. This is done by *dead code elimination*, a common compiler optimization. The same specialization is done for P_p.

10.6   Step 4: BUFFER ALLOCATION

Buffer allocation is the final step of our approach, and hence applied to the feasible task graph whose timing characteristics are completely derived. During this step, the compiler tool determines the buffer space required by each data object, and replaces its associated reads and writes with simple macros. The macros ensure that each consumer reads temporally correlated data from several data objects – even when *these* objects are produced at vastly different rates. The reads and writes are nonblocking and asynchronous, and hence we consider each buffer to have a "virtual sequence number."

Combining a set of correlated data at a given confluence point appears to be a nontrivial venture. After all, (1) producers and the consumers may be running at different rates; and

(2) the flow delays from a common sampler to the distinct producers may also be different. However, due to the harmonicity assumption the solution strategy is quite simple. Given that there are sufficient buffers for a data object, the following rule is used:

> "Whenever a consumer reads from a channel, it uses the *first* item that was generated within *its* current period."

For example, let P_p be a producer of a data object d, let $P_{c_1}, \ldots, P_{c_n}$ be the consumers that read d. Then the communication mechanism is realized by the following techniques (where $L = LCM_{1 \le i \le n}(T_{c_i})$ is the least common multiple of the periods):

(1) The data object d is implemented with $s = L/T_p$ buffers.

(2) The producer P_p circularly writes into each buffer, one at a time.

(3) The consumer P_{c_i} reads circularly from slots $(0, T_{c_i}/T_p, \ldots, m \cdot T_{c_i}/T_p)$ where $m = L/T_{c_i} - 1$.

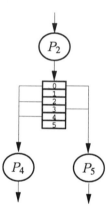

Figure 10.13   A task graph with buffers

Consider three tasks P_2, P_4 and P_5 in our example, before we performed graph replication. The two consumer tasks P_4 and P_5 run with periods 28 and 42, respectively, while the producer P_2 runs with period 14. Thus, the data object requires a 6 place buffer ($6 = LCM(28, 42)/14$), and P_4 reads from slots (0, 2, 4) while P_5 reads from slots (0, 3). Figure 10.13 shows the relevant part of the task graph after the buffer allocation.

After the buffer allocation, the compiler tool expands each data object into a multiple place buffer, and replaces each read and write operations with macros that perform proper pointer updates. Figure 10.14 shows the results of the macro-expansion, after it is applied to P_4's code from Figure 10.2(B). Note that P_1, P_2 and P_4 run at periods of 28, 14 and 28, respectively.

10.7   The Prototype Implementation

The objectives of the DesignAssistant are as follows.

(1) To provide a rapid prototyping tool for real-time system designers, so they can quickly build a running system for various analyses and optimizations.

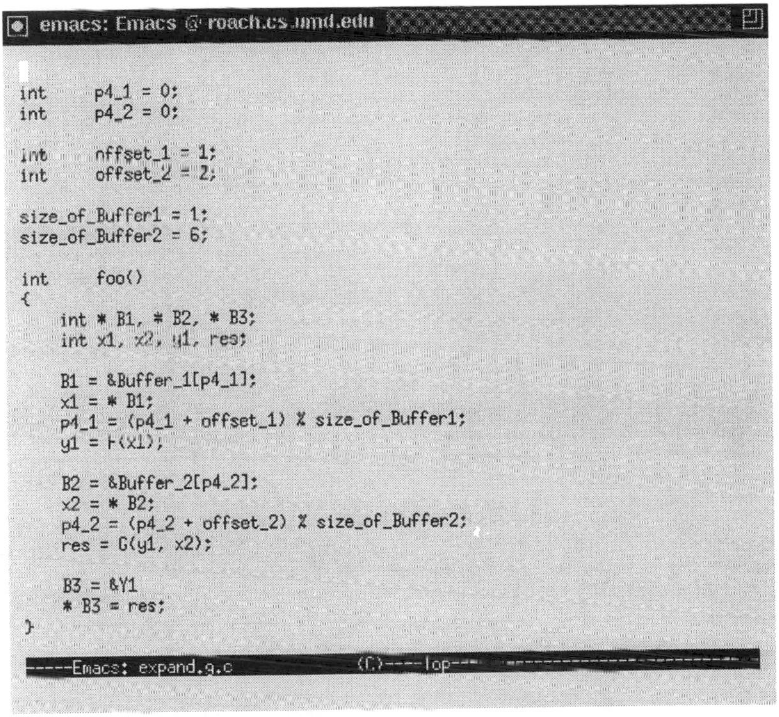

261

```
 emacs: Emacs @ roach.cs.umd.edu

int     p4_1 = 0;
int     p4_2 = 0;

int     nffset_1 = 1;
int     offset_2 = 2;

size_of_Buffer1 = 1;
size_of_Buffer2 = 6;

int     foo()
{
    int * B1, * B2, * B3;
    int x1, x2, y1, res;

    B1 = &Buffer_1[p4_1];
    x1 = * B1;
    p4_1 = (p4_1 + offset_1) % size_of_Buffer1;
    y1 = F(x1);

    B2 = &Buffer_2[p4_2];
    x2 = * B2;
    p4_2 = (p4_2 + offset_2) % size_of_Buffer2;
    res = G(y1, x2);

    B3 = &Y1
    * B3 = res;
}

-----Emacs: expand.g.c          (C)----Top--
```

Figure 10.14 Instantiated code with copy-in/copy-out channels and memory-mapped IO

(2) To let developers easily pin-point bottlenecks in the system.

(3) To help developers transform faulty components in their systems.

(4) To provide traceability between the entity-relationships in the high-level system design, and their manifestation in the low-level module code.

To achieve the the fourth goal, the DesignAssistant runs all tests from the same user interface in which the system topology is designed. The result is toolkit driver, whose operations allow drawing the system structure, binding code modules to task nodes, solving the constraints, and producing a Makefile to generate the application.

10.7.1 Graphical User Interface

Figure 10.15 shows three of tool screens, all of which were implemented using Tcl/Tk toolkits [Ous94]. The interactive graph editor (Figure 10.15(Left)) supports drawing and structuring the ATGs, and it allows hierarchical decomposition of ATGs based on black-box abstraction. That is, a sub-module node in an ATG can then be expanded into another ATG, with its inner structure drawn on a separate window. Figure 10.16 shows a hierarchical design equivalent to the "flat ATG" in Figure 10.15(Left). The sub-module's interfaces are drawn as small eclipses tagged by the connecting channels' names. For example, Figure 10.16(Right) shows that the buffer "dX1" is an external connection to the submodule "Sub_M1".

Each task node in an ATG must be associated with a piece of code which actually carries its computation. Since a single code module may be used for multiple task nodes in a number of distinct ATGs, it is necessary to support binding the abstract names in the ATG to associated

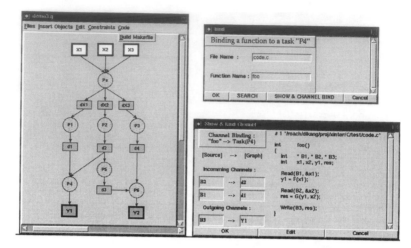

Figure 10.15 TimeWare/DesignAssistant Tool Screen

names within the code modules. Task and channel binding are shown in the top and bottom right windows of Figure 10.15, respectively. In Figure 10.15, node "P4" is bound to the function "foo" in the file "code.c," and channels B1, B2, and B3 are bound to d1, d2, and Y1 respectively.

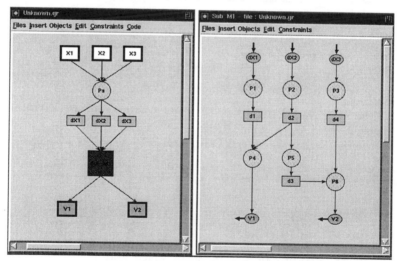

Figure 10.16 TimeWare/DesignAssistant Hierarchical Design Support

10.7.2 Constraint Solving

After accepting an ATG and associated attributes, our tool is ready to compute the task-specific parameters, using the algorithms we presented above. Computing the parameters consists of two parts: parsing and solving. Constraints accepted by the DesignAssistant are stored in a text file, as shown in Figure 10.3. Clicking the Solve button invokes parsing the constraints file, and generating an intermediate form for the solver to use. The solver's job is then to derive the periods, offsets, and deadlines, and to determine the size of each channel. If no such solution exists, an error is reported, and restructuring of the ATG is required.

10.7.3 Code Generation

When the analysis ensures that the design is consistent, the tool will produce compilable code via a Makefile. Clicking `Build Makefile` in within the `Code` menu (Figure 10.15(Left)) results in the the following three actions.

(1) An initialization module for the application is created, and buffer allocation code is inserted within it.
(2) Buffer pointers are instantiated for each producer-consumer relationship, and the"**Read**" and "**Write**" operations are replaced by specialized access code.
(3) A Makefile is produced to compile executable applications.

10.7.4 Current Limitations and Future Extensions

Even within the scope of single-CPU applications, the implementation still possesses several limitations. First, nodes in an ATG can only be instantiated by source code and not, for example, a binary application which uses standard-input and output to communicate. The reason is obvious: our buffer allocation and instantiation is realized by source code translation.

Another limitation is that the Makefile, when executed, generates a monolithic compiled kernel which implements the given ATG.

But these two problems are induced by the properties of most existing runtime system, and are not inherent to our design methodology. The problem is simple: there exist many different kernel models, each of which possesses its own native input-output mechanisms. Nonetheless, we are currently investigating specific real-time operating systems, and associated threads packages, which should allow us to relax these limitations.

10.8 CONCLUSION

We have presented a four-step design methodology to help synthesize end-to-end requirements into full-blown real-time systems. Our framework can be used as long as the following ingredients are provided: (1) the entity-relationships, as specified by an asynchronous task graph abstraction; and (2) end-to-end constraints imposed on freshness, input correlation and allowable output separation. This model is sufficiently expressive to capture the temporal requirements – as well as the modular structure – of many interesting systems from the domains of avionics, robotics, control and multimedia computing.

However, the asynchronous, fully periodic model does have its limitations; for example, we cannot support high-level blocking primitives such as RPCs. On the other hand, this deficit yields significant gains; e.g., handling streamed, tightly correlated data solely via the "virtual sequence numbers" afforded by the rate-assignments.

There is much work to be carried out. First, the constraint derivation algorithm can be extended to take full advantage of a wider spectrum of timing constraints, such as those encountered in input-driven, reactive systems. Also, we can harness finer-grained compiler transformations such as *program slicing* to help transform tasks into read-compute-write-compute phases, which will even further enhance schedulability. We have used this approach in a real-time compiler tool [Ger93], and there is reason to believe that its use would be even more effective here.

We are also streamlining our search algorithm, by incorporating scheduling-specific decisions into the constraint solver. We believe that when used properly, such policy-specific strategies will help significantly in pruning the search space.

But the greatest challenge lies in extending the technique to distributed systems. The output and its inputs do not necessarily reside in the same processor in distributed systems, and there may be arbitrary numbers of network links from an input to the output. The characteristics of the network should be considered in conjunction with those constraints presented earlier on. Accordingly, constraints solving strategy should be changed to reflect the network characteristic as another constraints. Certainly a global optimization is impractical, since the search-space is much too large. Rather, we are taking a compositional approach – finding approximate solutions for each node, and then refining each node's solution-space to accommodate the system's bound on network utilization.

ACKNOWLEDGEMENT

The authors gratefully acknowledge Bill Pugh, Jeff Fischer, Ladan Gharai and Tefvik Bultan, whose valuable suggestions greatly enhanced the quality of this work.

This research is supported in part by ONR grant N00014-94-10228, NSF grant CCR-9209333, and NSF Young Investigator Award CCR-9357850.

REFERENCES

[Alu90]   R. Alur and C. Courcoubetis and D. Dill. Model-Checking for Real-Time Systems. *Proc. of IEEE Symposium on Logic in Computer Science*, 1990
[Aud91]   N. Audsley and A. Burns and M. Richardson and A. Wellings. Hard Real-Time Scheduling: The Deadline-Monotonic Approach. *Proceedings of IEEE Workshop on Real-Time Operating Systems an d Software*, pages 133–137, May 1991.
[Aud93]   N. Audsley and A. Burns and M. Richardson and A. Wellings. Data Consistency in Hard Real-Time Systems. YCS 203, Department of Computer Science, University of York, England, June 1993.
[Ber83]   G. Berry and S. Moisan and J. Rigault. ESTEREL: Towards a Synchronous and Semantically Sound High Level Language for Real Time Applications. *Proceedings of IEEE Real-Time Systems Symposium*, pages 30–37, December 1983. IEEE Computer Society Press.
[Bur94]   A. Burns. Preemptive Priority Based Scheduling: An Appropriate Engineering Approach. *Principles of Real-Time Systems*, 1994.
[Dan73]   G. Dantzig and B. Eaves. Fourier-Motzkin Elimination and its Dual. *Journal of Combinatorial Theory (A)*, 14:288–297, 1973.
[Ger93]   R. Gerber and S. Hong. Semantics-Based Compiler Transformations for Enhanced Schedulability. *Proceedings of IEEE Real-Time Systems Symposium*, pages 232–242, December 1993. IEEE Computer Society Press.
[Ger94]   R. Gerber and S. Hong and M. Saksena. Guaranteeing End-to-End Timing Constraints by Calibrating Intermediate Processes. *Proceedings of IEEE Real-Time Systems Symposium*, pages 192–203, December 1994. IEEE Computer Society Press. Also to appear in *IEEE Transactions on Software Engineering*.
[Har91]   M. Harbour and M. Klein and J. Lehoczky. Fixed Priority Scheduling of Periodic Tasks with Varying Execution Priority. *Proceedings, IEEE Real-Time Systems Symposium*, pages 116–128, December 1991.

[Jah86]   F. Jahanian and A. Mok. Safety analysis of timing properties in Real-Time Systems. *IEEE Transactions on Software Engineering*, 12(9):890–904, 1986.

[Jef83]   K. Jeffay. The Real-Time Producer/Consumer Paradigm: A Paradigm for the Construction of Efficient, Predictable Real-Time Systems. *ACM/SIGAPP Symposium on Applied Computing*, pages 796–804, Feburary 1983. ACM Press.

[Kle94]   M. Klein and J. Lehoczky and R. Rajkumar. Rate-Monotonic Analysis for Real-Time Industrial Computing. *IEEE Computer*, pages 24–33, January 1994. IEEE Computer Society Press.

[Liu73]   C. Liu and J. Layland. Scheduling Algorithm for Multiprogramming in a Hard Real-Time Environment. *Journal of the ACM*, 20(1):46–61, January 1973.

[Ous94]   J. Ousterhout. *Tcl and the Tk Toolkit*. Addison Wesley, 1994.

[Sha90]   L. Sha and R. Rajkumar and J. Lehoczky. Priority Inheritance Protocols: An Approach to Real-Time Synchronization. *IEEE Transactions on Software Engineering*, 16(9):1175-1185, September 1990. IEEE Computer Society Press.

[Tin92]   K. Tindell. Using Offset Information to Analyse Static Priority Pre-emptively Scheduled Task Sets. YCS 182, Department of Computer Science, University of York, England, August 1992.

[Tin94]   K. Tindell and A. Burns and A. Wellings. An Extendible Approach For Analysing Fixed Priority Hard Real-Time Tasks. *The Journal of Real-Time Systems*, 6(2):133-152, March 1994.

[Xu90]   J. Xu and D. Parnas. Scheduling Processes with Release Times, Deadlines, Precedence and Exclusion Relations. *IEEE Transactions on Software Engineering*, 16(3):360-369, March 1990.

[Yua94]   X. Yuan and M. Saksena and A. Agrawala. A Decomposition Approach to Real-Time Scheduling. *The Journal of Real-Time Systems*, 6(1), January 1994.

[Zha87]   W. Zhao and K. Ramamritham and J. Stankovic. Scheduling Tasks with Resource Requirements in a Hard Real-Time System. *IEEE Transactions on Software Engineering*, 13(5):564-577, May 1987.

Index

Index compiled by Geoffrey Jones